Computer Supported Cooperative Work

Springer

London
Berlin
Heidelberg
New York
Barcelona
Hong Kong
Milan
Paris
Singapore
Tokyo

Also in this series

Peter Lloyd and Roger Whitehead (eds)
Transforming Organisations Through Groupware: Lotus Notes in Action
3-540-19961-6

Gerold Riempp
Wide Area Workflow Management: Creating Partnerships for the 21st
Century
3-540-76243-4

Reza Hazemi, Stephen Hailes and Steve Wilbur (eds)
The Digital University: Reinventing the Academy
1-85233-003-1

Celia T. Romm and Fay Sudweeks (eds)
Doing Business Electronically: A Global Perspective of Electronic
Commerce
3-540-76159-4

Fay Sudweeks and Celia T. Romm (eds)
Doing Business on the Internet: Opportunities and Pitfalls
1-85233-030-9

Alan J. Munro, Kristina Höök and David Benyon (eds)
Social Navigation of Information Space
1-85233-090-2

Mary Lou Maher, Simeon J. Simoff and Anna Cicognani
Understanding Virtual Design Studios
1-85233-154-2

Elayne Coakes, Dianne Willis and Raymond Lloyd-Jones (eds)
The New SocioTech: Graffiti on the Long Wall
1-85233-040-6

Elizabeth F. Churchill, David N. Snowdon and Alan J. Munro (eds)
Collaborative Virtual Environments: Digital Places and Spaces for
Interaction
1-85233-244-1

Barry Brown, Nicola Green and Richard Harper (eds)
Wireless World: Social and Interactional Aspects of the Mobile Age
1-85233-477-0

A list of out of print titles is available at the end of the book

Christine Steeples and Chris Jones (Eds)

Networked Learning: Perspectives and Issues

With 17 Figures

 Springer

Christine Steeples
Chris Jones
Centre for Studies in Advances Learning Technology (CSALT), Department
of Educational Research, Lancaster University, Lancaster, LA1 4YL

Series Editors
Dan Diaper, PhD, MBCS
Head, Department of Computing, School of Design, Engineering and Computing,
Bournemouth University, Talbot Campus, Fern Barrow, Poole, Dorset BH12 5BB, UK
Colston Sanger
Shottersley Research Limited, Little Shottersley, Farnham Lane
Haslemere, Surrey GU27 1HA, UK

British Library Cataloguing in Publication Data
A Catalogue record for this book is available from the British Library

Library of Congress Cataloging-in-Publication Data
Networked learning: perspectives and issues/Christine Steeples and Christopher Jones, eds.
    p. cm – (Computer supported cooperative work)
  Includes bibliographical references and indexes.
  ISBN 1-85233-471-1 (alk. paper)
    1. Education, Higher–Computer network resources. 2. Computer-assisted instruction.
    3. Distance education. I. Steeples, Christine, 1954– II. Jones, Christopher, 1951– III. Series.
  LB2395.7.N48 2001
  378.1'734–DC21   2001042936

ISBN 1-85233-471-1 Springer-Verlag London Berlin Heidelberg
a member of BertelsmannSpringer Science+Business Media GmbH
http://www.springer.co.uk

Typesetting: Camera ready by authors
Printed and bound at the Athenæum Press Ltd., Gateshead, Tyne & Wear
34/3830-543210 Printed on acid-free paper SPIN 10831217

For Mick and for my family
For Maggy, Rhia and Bron and in memory of Edna and Bert

Acknowledgements

This book originated in a workshop held at Higham Hall in Cumbria that was part-funded by a grant from the Committee on Awareness, Liaison and Training of JISC (the Joint Information Systems Committee of the UK Higher Education Funding Councils). The views expressed here are not necessarily those of JISC or CALT. Further information about the project can be obtained from the project's website (http://csalt.lancs.ac.uk/jisc/). We would like to acknowledge the contributions of all the members of the project team: Peter Goodyear, Vivien Hodgson, Mireia Asensio, Susan Armitage, Mark Bryson, Michael O'Donoghue and David Hutchison.

The book contains several chapters that were the product of other research conducted with the support of JISC and we would like to express our sincere thanks to everyone at JISC who assisted in all these projects but especially to Rachel Corrie, Jonathan Darby and Maria Lee.

We would also like to thank Alice Jesmont for her tireless help in all aspects of the administration of the project and the book. The final camera-ready copy was in large part the result of the sterling efforts of Debra Smith for which we are eternally grateful.

Contents

List of Contributors ix

Foreword xiii
J. Michael Spector

1 Perspectives and Issues in Networked Learning 1
Chris Jones and Christine Steeples

SECTION 1 The Context for Networked Learning 15

2 Networked Learning in Higher Education: The Mule in the Barn 17
Jonathan Darby

3 The Costs of Networked Learning 27
Charlotte Ash and Paul Bacsich

4 Psychological Foundations for Networked Learning 49
Peter Goodyear

5 Studying Networked Learning: Some Implications from Socially
Situated Learning Theory and Actor Network Theory 77
Steve Fox

6 The Changing Nature of Instructional Design for Networked
Learning 93
Radha Ganesan, Gerald S. Edmonds and J. Michael Spector

7 Views on Staff Development for Networked Learning 111
Carmel McNaught

8 Managing Institutional Change for Networked Learning:
A Multi-Stakeholder Approach 125
Jonathan Foster, Nicholas Bowskill, Vic Lally and David McConnell

9 Information Specialists and Networked Learner Support 143
Philippa Levy

10 Evaluating Networked Learning: Developing a Multi-Disciplinary,
Multi-Method Approach 169
*Charles Anderson, Kate Day, Denise Haywood, Jeff Haywood,
Ray Land and Hamish Macleod*

SECTION 2 Studies of Networked Learning **193**

11 Approaches to Researching Teaching and Learning Online 195
    Gilly Salmon

12 Learning from Watching Others Learn 213
    Terry Mayes, Finbar Dineen, Jean McKendree and John Lee

13 Issues for Democracy and Social Identity in Computer Mediated
    Communication and Networked Learning 229
    Vivien Hodgson

14 Small Group Teaching Across the Disciplines: Setting the Context
    for Networked Learning 243
    Nick Hammond, Annie Trapp and Catherine Bennett

15 Designs for Networked Learning in Higher Education:
    A Phenomenographic Investigation of Practitioners'
    Accounts of Design 253
    Chris Jones and Mireia Asensio

16 Online Collaborative Assessment: Power Relations and 'Critical
    Learning' 279
    Kiran Trehan and Michael Reynolds

17 The Campus Experience of Networked Learning 293
    Charles Crook

18 Learning Networks and the Issue of Communication Skills 309
    *Erica McAteer, Andrew Tolmie, Charles Crook,
    Hamish Macleod and Kerry Musselbrook*

19 Beyond E-Learning: A Future for Networked Learning 323
    Christine Steeples, Chris Jones and Peter Goodyear

Subject Index 343

List of Contributors

Dr. Charles Anderson, Department of Higher and Community Education, University of Edinburgh, Paterson's Land, Holyrood Road, Edinburgh EH8 8AQ, Scotland UK

Mireia Asensio, Department of Management Learning, Lancaster University, Lancaster LA1 4YL, UK

Charlotte Ash, School of Computing and Management Sciences, Sheffield Hallam University, Stoddart Building, Howard Street, Sheffield S1 1WB, UK

Professor Paul Bacsich, School of Computing and Management Sciences, Sheffield Hallam University, Stoddart Building, Howard Street, Sheffield S1 1WB, UK

Dr. Catherine Bennett, Department of Psychology, University of York, York YO10 5DD, UK

Nicholas Bowskill, Staff Development Unit, Level 6, University House, University of Sheffield, Western Bank, Sheffield S10 2TN, UK

Professor Charles Crook, Department of Human Sciences, Loughborough University, Loughborough, Leicestershire LE11 3TU, UK

Jonathan Darby, Technology-Assisted Lifelong Learning, Department for Continuing Education, Suite 6 Littlegate House, University of Oxford, 16/17 St Ebbes Street, Oxford OX1 1PT, UK

Dr. Kate Day, Department of Higher and Community Education, University of Edinburgh, Paterson's Land, Holyrood Road, Edinburgh EH8 8AQ, Scotland UK

Finbar Dineen, Centre for Research in Lifelong Learning, Glasgow Caledonian University, St. Andrew House, 141 West Nile Street, Glasgow G1 2RN, UK

Dr. Gerald S. Edmonds, Associate Director, Research and Evaluation, Project Advance, Syracuse University, 400 Ostrom Avenue, Syracuse, NY 13244, USA

Jonathan Foster, Department of Information Studies, University of Sheffield, Western Bank, Sheffield S10 2TN, UK

Dr. Steve Fox, Department of Management Learning, Lancaster University, Lancaster LA1 4YL, UK

Radha Ganesan, Department of Instructional Design, Development and Evaluation, Syracuse University, 330 Huntington Hall, Syracuse, NY 13244, USA

Professor Peter Goodyear, Centre for Studies in Advanced Learning Technology, Department of, Educational Research, Lancaster University, Lancaster LA1 4YL, UK

Dr. Nick Hammond, Department of Psychology, University of York, York YO10 5DD, UK

Denise Haywood, Department of Higher and Community Education, University of Edinburgh, Paterson's Land, Holyrood Road, Edinburgh EH8 8AQ, Scotland UK

Dr. Jeff Haywood, Department of Higher and Community Education, University of Edinburgh, Paterson's Land, Holyrood Road, Edinburgh EH8 8AQ, Scotland UK

Dr. Vivien Hodgson, Department of Management Learning, Lancaster University, Lancaster LA1 4YL, UK

Dr. Chris Jones, Centre for Studies in Advanced Learning Technology, Department of Educational Research, Lancaster University, Lancaster LA1 4YL, UK

Vic Lally, School of Education, University of Sheffield, 388 Glossop Road, Sheffield S10 2JA, UK

Dr. Ray Land, Department of Higher and Community Education, University of Edinburgh, Paterson's Land, Holyrood Road, Edinburgh EH8 8AQ, Scotland UK

Dr. John Lee, Human Communication Research Centre, University of Edinburgh, 2 Buccleuch Place, Edinburgh EH8 9LW, Scotland UK

Philippa Levy, Lecturer, Department of Information Studies, University of Sheffield, Western Bank, Sheffield S10 2TN, UK

Dr. Hamish Macleod, Department of Higher and Community Education, University of Edinburgh, Paterson's Land, Holyrood Road, Edinburgh EH8 8AQ, Scotland UK

Professor Terry Mayes, Centre for Research in Lifelong Learning, Glasgow Caledonian University, St. Andrew House, 141 West Nile Street, Glasgow G1 2RN, Scotland UK

Dr. Erica McAteer, Teaching and Learning Service, University of Glasgow, 69 Oakfield Avenue, Glasgow G12 8LW, Scotland UK

Professor David McConnell, School of Education, University of Sheffield, 388 Glossop Road, Sheffield S10 2JA, UK

Dr. Jean McKendree, Human Communication and Research Centre, University of Edinburgh, 2 Buccleuch Place, Edinburgh EH8 9LW, Scotland UK

Assoc. Professor Carmel McNaught, Professional Development, Learning Technology Services, RMIT University, GPO Box 2476V, Melbourne 3001, Australia

Kerry Musselbrook, University of Paisley, Paisley PA1 2BE, Scotland UK

Professor Michael Reynolds, Department of Management Learning, Management School, Lancaster University, Lancaster LA1 4YL, UK

Dr. Gilly Salmon, Centre for Information and Innovation, Open University Business School, Walton Hall, Milton Keynes MK7 6AA, UK

Professor J. Michael Spector, Department of Instructional Design, Development and Evaluation, Syracuse University, 330 Huntington Hall, Syracuse, NY 13244, USA

Christine Steeples, Centre for Studies in Advanced Learning Technology, Department of Educational Research, Lancaster University, Lancaster LA1 4YL, UK

Dr. Andrew Tolmie, Senior Lecturer in Psychology, Centre for Research into Interactive Learning, Department of Psychology, University of Strathclyde, 40 George Street, Glasgow G1 1QE, Scotland UK

Annie Trapp, Department of Psychology, University of York, York YO10 5DD, UK

Kiran Trehan, Management Department, University of Central England, Galton Building, Perry Barr, Birmingham B32 2SU, UK

Foreword

It is not uncommon to read reports of increased teacher and student interest in and use of the Internet. These reports often contain promises of improved education. However, such reports often include disturbing indicators of problems and pitfalls. For example, in a recent nationwide survey conducted by NetDay in the USA (see http://www.netday.org/), 87% of responding teachers reported that they were comfortable using the Internet, 84% reported that the Internet could improve the quality of education, but 67% said that the Internet was not effectively integrated into their teaching and 78% said that they did not have sufficient time to integrate Internet resources into their teaching (Heller, 2001). Networked learning in higher education has much to promise, but there are problems to overcome and pitfalls to avoid.

Promises, Promises, Promises

If one carefully examines the history of educational technology in the previous century, one is likely to find a history filled with broken promises. One can arbitrarily date the history of modern educational technology as beginning with the use of radio to deliver instruction in the early part of the 20th century. There have certainly been some successful uses of radio-based instruction in Australia, Canada, the USA and elsewhere (Beagles-Roos & Gat, 1983). Using radio for teaching in most instances was driven by the remoteness of learners and the ease with which radio could reach those learners. As with subsequent technologies, when radio-based instruction was introduced, there was much enthusiasm about its potential to improve learning on a global basis (Tyack & Cuban, 1995).

Such promises of dramatic improvements in learning coupled with the ability to reach learners neglected due to remoteness or resource constraints were repeated with the advent of television and then again with regard to the introduction of personal computers (Tyack & Cuban, 1995). In the 1980s it was predicted that intelligent tutoring systems would produce dramatically significant improvements in learning, similar to the two-sigma effects that Bloom (1984) had documented for some one-to-one human tutoring situations (see, for example, Burns & Capps, 1988). Such improvements did not materialize. What did materialize were less significant improvements in some very well-defined learning situations along with the realization that it is extremely difficult to create a dynamic computer model of what a learner understands about a particular domain at any given moment in time.

In the 1990s it was suggested that distributed learning and tele-collaboration would make traditional classroom teachers obsolete (see, for example, Koschmann, 1996). This has not happened. What has happened is that learners, teachers, designers and researchers have realized that collaboration at a distance is often quite difficult and challenging (see, for example, Feldman *et al.*, 2000). The role of the teacher is not likely to be eliminated by technology, although technology will surely affect the roles of both teachers and learners. The role of teaching in technology-intensive settings is more difficult and more crucial than ever before. Only a rare few master the skills required to effectively integrate technology into learning and instruction, and teachers themselves admit this (Heller, 2001).

Yet vast resources continue to be invested in technology-enhanced learning and instruction. Many have implicit faith that technology will make education better. Such faith is ill-founded. One lesson from the previous century with regard to the effective integration of technology into teaching and learning is that instructional planning is more complicated than ever before (see, for example, Spector & Anderson, 2000). The big lesson about technology and learning from the 20th century is that less is known about how people learn than many educational researchers are inclined to admit. It follows that promises of improved learning, on a global basis across significant differences in subject matter, learning objectives and learner populations, ought to be accompanied with the promise of providing credible evidence. The contributors to this volume are committed to this second promise. Thankfully, such a commitment is becoming more commonplace (see also Feldman *et al.*, 2000; Hanna & Associates, 2000; Spector & Anderson, 2000).

Problems, Pitfalls, and Perils

The problems that can occur when introducing network-based resources into teaching and learning are significant (see, for example, Feldman et al., 2000). There are problems concerning the proper preparation of both teachers and learners. These are more or less well documented, although the known pitfalls due to lack of teacher training and student preparation are often overlooked in the haste associated with acquiring and implementing the latest technologies. Institutional pressures are many and complex in nature. There are different groups lobbying for buying and controlling specific technologies. Overly restrictive institutional practices and short-sighted policy planning can result in wasteful investments and in the alienation of crucial constituencies (Rosenberg, 2001).

At a higher level, the social and global implications of the digital divide are much discussed but not especially well understood. Many who are conducting research in the area of networked learning are very optimistic with regard to the potential to confront the digital divide. Whether this occurs remains to be seen. It would appear that in the area of e-commerce, the divide is widening. Investments of the European Commission, the United Nations, the World Bank, and many national research foundations in spreading e-learning to developing countries may help in this regard.

It's All About Understanding

In the midst of the many promises and problems associated with using networked-based resources in teaching and learning, there are conceptual issues to confront. One such issue concerns the nature of learning. Some suggest that a new learning paradigm is emerging on account of new technologies (see, for example, Koschmann, 1996; Spector & Anderson, 2000). While it is true that technology has been a centerpiece in many instructional systems and learning environments, technology is not what learning is all about. Learning is essentially about change. Learning involves changes in attitudes, beliefs, capabilities, knowledge structures, and skills. When these changes have been observed and can be believed to be relatively stable and persist for some time, it is reasonable to conclude that learning has occurred. In short, the definition of learning is not changing. Rather, what is changing is how we facilitate and support effective learning, especially with regard to complex subject matter.

As a consequence, it is fair to conclude that the conceptualization of learning activities has undergone dramatic change in the last twenty years or so. Part of this conceptualization is renewed interest in how peers contribute to learning, especially with regard to subjects that are complex from the learner's perspective. Once interest is broadened from an individual learner to a learning community, the need to introduce new methods for assessment arises. Action research and activity theory provide new perspectives and methods (see, for example, Koschmann, 1996). However, their use is not yet so rigorous nor so widespread as to provide a solid basis for an improved understanding of the conditions that facilitate learning in various circumstances. This situation is likely to improve with time.

A large part of the so-called new learning paradigm involves a shift from what has been characterized as an atomistic perspective to a more holistic perspective (Spector & Anderson, 2000; Spector & Davidsen, 1999; Spector *et al.*, in press). The atomistic perspective emphasizes individual units of learning (specific and discrete conditions, methods, and outcomes) and tends to treat learners in a similarly isolated manner (focusing assessment on individual learners and evaluation on aggregates of individual assessments). This atomistic perspective can be contrasted with what Spector (1994, 1995) called the integrated perspective, and with what is here called the holistic perspective. The holistic perspective views a person as a member of a society and as a member of various language communities and communities of practice. The overall goal of a society or language community typically involves a strong survival element, although this is quite often not made explicit. Living consists of working and learning, which are viewed as essentially collaborative efforts to achieve commonly held goals. This social perspective, and the realization that learning is most often aimed at integrated collections of human activities (Gagné & Merrill, 1990) comprise a holistic perspective of learning. From the holistic perspective, learning is ultimately aimed at improving the understanding of various phenomena and situations and not merely about recalling specific facts or solving specific problems.

One change due to network technologies involves the blurring of the traditional distinction between learning and working. Individuals may shift seamlessly from performing a work activity into a system-initiated help environment. Workers may put one complex task on hold while taking time out for a focused tutorial. Individuals may initiate background agents to gather information on selected topics which are then pushed into windows that appear in the user's desktop work environment. Workers may shift from working alone on one isolated task to seeking guidance and advice from a networked community involved in similar activities. Other changes include the interaction of learners in a variety of ways around a variety of activities and tasks. Such changes require a more holistic perspective in order to understand what is occurring in these complex and dynamic contexts.

In Conclusion

The editors of this volume have put together a wonderful collection of thoughtful papers that address the promises as well as the problems associated with effective integration of network-based resources into learning and instruction. Contributing authors address issues at nearly every level. Social and institutional perspectives are included. Implications for designers and developers are discussed. There are chapters that examine various technologies and how they have or can be integrated into teaching and learning. Both teachers and learners are taken into account. New perspectives on assessment are examined.

Considered as a whole, this volume blends theory and research with practice and application while maintaining an orientation to the future. As the editors remark in the introduction, the rapid pace of technology development is driving us towards a somewhat uncertain future with regard to the effective use of networked technologies in learning. Work such as that represented in this volume will help clear the fog of breathtaking progress and pave the way for improved education on a global level. That, at least, is our hope.

While one ought to be skeptical about dramatic improvements in learning due to new technologies, one cannot ignore what is happening in education due to the advent of the Internet. Networked learning certainly has the potential to improve learning on a global basis and will surely influence the future in many of the ways suggested in this volume.

J. Michael Spector

References

Beagles-Roos, J., & Gat, I. (1983). Specific impact of radio and television on children's story comprehension. *Journal of Educational Psychology 75*, 128-137

Bloom, B.S. (1984). The 2 sigma problem: The search for methods of group instruction as effective as one-to-one tutoring. *Educational Researcher 13*, 3-16

Burns, H. L., & Capps, C.G. (Eds.) (1988). *Foundations of intelligent tutoring systems.* Hillsdale, NJ: Erlbaum

Feldman, A., Konold, C., Coutler, B. (2000). *Network science: A decade later.* Mahwah, NJ: Erlbaum

Gagné, R.M., & Merrill, M.D. (1990). Integrative goals for instructional design. *Educational Technology Research and Development*, 38(1), 23-30

Hanna, D.E., & Associates (Ed.) (2000). *Higher education in an era of digital competition: Choices and challenges.* Madison, WI: Atwood

Heller, N.B. (2001, April). *The Heller report.* Skokie, IL: Nelson B. Heller & Associates. Available at http://www.netday.org/pdfs/HELLER_040601.pdf

Koschmann, T. (Ed.) (1996). *CSCL: Theory and practice.* Hillsdale, NJ: Erlbaum

Rosenberg, M.J. (2001). *E-Learning: Strategies for delivering knowledge in the digital age.* New York: McGraw Hill

Spector, J.M. (1994). Integrating instructional science, learning theory, and technology. In R. D. Tennyson (Ed.), *Automating instructional design, development, and delivery* pp. 243-259. Berlin: Springer-Verlag

Spector, J.M. (1995). Integrating and humanizing the process of automating instructional design. In R. D. Tennyson & A. E. Barron (Eds.), *Automating instructional design: computer-based development and delivery tools* pp. 523-546. Berlin: Springer-Verlag.

Spector, J.M., & Anderson, T.M. (Eds.) (2000). *Integrated and holistic perspectives on learning and instruction: Understanding complexity.* Dordrecht: Kluwer

Spector, J.M., & Davidsen, P.I. (1999, April). *Transparency and interaction in system dynamics based learning environments.* Paper presented at the Annual Meeting of the American Educational Research Association, Montréal, Canada, April, 1999

Spector, J.M., Christensen, D.L., Sioutine, A.V., & McCormack, D. (in press). Models and simulations for learning in complex domains: Using causal loop diagrams for assessment and evaluation. *Computers in Human Behavior.*

Tyack, D. & Cuban, L. (1995). *Tinkering toward utopia: A century of public school reform.* Cambridge, Massachusetts: Harvard University Press.

1. Perspectives and Issues in Networked Learning

Chris Jones and Christine Steeples

1.1 Introduction

Computer networks are still a recent phenomena and research into the uses of such networks for communication and group work is less than 30 years old. In the 1970s the Institute of the Future began to explore issues that remain relevant today and they also began to explore methods of research that continue to have their place in networked learning research (Vallee *et al.*, 1974; 1974a; 1975). The continuity of research cannot blind us to the rapid changes and sudden shifts in the field. In particular the emergence and growth of the Web in the 1990s has had a profound impact, making networks the center and focus of developments in the way in which computers themselves had provided a focus previously. As this book was being written another wave of technological innovation is developing but we cannot yet know the degree to which the promise of this new technology will be realized (Chabot, 1999). Mobile and ubiquitous computing might be the next big thing with fixed networks built on wires and cables being replaced by cellular radio networks that allow for 'always on' broadband communication. Networked learning is a term that describes the new focus for attention, the network, but it does so in suitably ambiguous terms, as the focus of networked learning is both learning and the network.

Networks have been the subject of research well beyond the impact of the technology alone. The Networked Society is one of the suggested descriptions of the type of social system that is emerging in the late 1990s (Castells, 1996).

"Networks constitute the new social morphology of our societies, and the diffusion of networking logic substantially modifies the operation and outcomes in processes of production, experience, power, and culture. While the networking form of social organization has existed in other times and spaces, the new information technology paradigm provides the material basis for its expansion through the entire social structure" (Castells, 1996:468).

The term Networked Society competes with Information Society, Knowledge Society, Post-Modern and Post-Industrial Society in trying to grasp the central shifts that social systems are experiencing. Networks have been the focus for analyses of social settings without any specific reference to technology and have been applied to organizational forms in particular (Knoke & Kuklinski, 1982). It is claimed that networks are a different form of organization neither bureaucratic hierarchies nor simply the anarchy of the market (Thompson *et al.*, 1991). Networks have a latent political promise in that they appear to offer a Third Way between the excesses of previous systems. It is not our intention to explore this wider use of the idea of networks just to alert readers to the synergy that exists between our educational use of the term and much wider debates about the relationship between technology and social forms. Our use of networked learning is related to this wider debate in so far as we claim that networked learning is an available outcome of the deployment of networked technologies. Networked learning has a politics in that it involves conscious choices between alternatives.

Many of the chapters contained in this volume originated in papers delivered at a workshop held at Higham Hall in the Lake District in November 1999. The workshop was part of a funded project designed to study student experiences of networked learning. For the purposes of the project we defined networked learning as:

> Networked learning is learning in which information and communication technology (C&IT) is used to promote connections: between one learner and other learners, between learners and tutors; between a learning community and its learning resources.

The focus for our definition was learning, the network being the way in which different aspects of the process were linked together. The definition of networked learning we have provided points towards a social understanding of learning rather than an individualistic or information processing model (see Goodyear, Chapter 4 this volume). Networked learning in our view is a contingent outcome of the use of networks. There is no necessary connection between the increasing use of computer networks and learning. It is our contention that we need a detailed understanding of how social theories of learning are related to current practice. A thorough understanding of practice will rely on research into the actual use of computer networks to develop an understanding of the relationships that are possible between networks and learners.

In this chapter we wish to explore some of the perspectives and issues in the emerging field of networked learning. Our fundamental aim is to develop a research based practice of networked learning. The tone of our exploration is intentionally one that tries to bridge the many gaps between theoretical and practical approaches. The chapters in this book illustrate some of the concerns that are current in the field and they are largely research based. It is our contention that theory developed without concern for integration with practice is both irrelevant and likely to be poor quality theory. Equally our contention is that practice uninformed by a clear grasp of theory is blind, forever doomed to repeat old mistakes.

1.2 Convergence

Networked learning can be considered the outcome of convergence. Convergence both in the sense of the coming together of telecommunications and computer technologies in a digital form and the coming together of distance and place based learning into a new hybrid form (Mason & Kaye, 1990). Convergence in a technical sense is a term used to describe the development of digital technologies in both the telecommunications and computing industries and their coming together in new information technologies (Zorkoczy & Heap, 1995; Baldwin *et al.*, 1996). Information technologies are not simply the addition of telecommunications and computing technologies, they open up a new range of options and possibilities. For networked learning the new possibilities include the spread of the Internet at home and work, increasing bandwidth enabling greater interactivity and multimedia content and the prospect of wireless mobility. Convergence in the second educational sense points towards the breaking down of barriers between distance and place-based learning. The use of networked information technologies has blurred the boundaries between the methods used in both forms of education and the clienteles that they address. The process of convergence has been associated with the increasing use of communication and information technologies, in particular Computer-Mediated Communication (CMC). The idea of convergence points toward opportunities for multiple interactions and the breaking down of barriers of time and space but it also contains an often unconscious sense that it is the technology that is driving the educational changes.

The Internet emerged from its military beginnings and a period of academic development into a general social and commercial resource in the 1990s. The explosive growth of the Web since its emergence in the early 1990s has been the socio-technical motor for this change. The network society impacts on education in a number of discrete ways. For example, the debate about the skills required for social development has taken the form of debate around a skills deficit. Higher education has become the focus of intense pressure to expand and to provide students with the skills that are presumed to be required for the development of a networked society and a knowledge based economy (Trilling & Hood, 2001). At another level the networked society is described as a society of flows (Castells, 1999). The basis of research and the generation of new knowledge is said to be related to the flow of knowledge in such societies. Knowledge ceases to be the province of singular and privileged sources and becomes the property of a flow. It is also claimed that the forms that knowledge takes have altered. The text based Gutenberg galaxy lives on but is constantly threatened and undermined by the encroachment of images and sounds as new media reshape patterns of

representation and communication. Networked learning in this sense is one aspect
of an emergent networked society.

1.3   Perspectives – Ways of Seeing Networked Learning

The relationship between technology and social change has been much discussed in
recent years (MacKenzie & Wajcman, 1999). A variety of perspectives have
argued against the idea that technology somehow determines the effects that its
application will have. The variety of perspectives that argue for the social shaping
of technology not only point to the social formation of technologies but also to
ways in which users take up and make use of available technologies selectively.
Technological determinism, the idea that technology is an independent force, is
theoretically a much-derided approach.   In networked learning however
technological determinism still has a strong influence at a variety of levels. In
introducing the impacts that the technology might have upon organization and
management Bates writes:

> "If universities and colleges are successfully to adopt the use of
> technologies for teaching and learning, much more than minor
> adjustments in current practice will be required. Indeed the effective use
> of technology requires a revolution in thinking about teaching and
> learning." (Bates, 1999:xiii)

At the overall level of the social role and position of education the feminist
author Dale Spender delivered a keynote address at a recent conference to discuss
networked learning:

> "One point which needs to be emphasized is that the pressures that are
> building up in relation to universities, are not driven by any particular
> ideology (as yet); they are not the agendas of any specific individuals…
>
> The process is technology driven. Just as steam and electricity changed
> the way we organized society, … we are now caught up in the digital
> revolution." (Spender, 2000)

The first of these two examples is illustrative of a soft technological
determinism. The revolution is required in order to adopt technology successfully.
The second example is illustrative of a full blown hard technological determinism.
The technology simply changes society. Both examples are focused on the
university but there is a similar trend at the level of more detailed practice.
Networked technologies are said to require, or at least perform at their best when
accompanied by particular social or pedagogical arrangements.

This volume takes the view that the effects of networked learning cannot be 'read off' the technologies deployed and that to understand networked learning we need to observe the practice of networked learning. For this reason we advocate a research approach that has a strong empirical base. Detailed description practice is required to develop an understanding of the ways in which particular approaches are embodied in the mundane practical activities of networked learning. Secondly we do not believe that a largely unreflective practice can by itself optimize our use of networked technologies. A theoretically informed approach can allow for generalization and comparison between varieties of practice. It can also help prevent description from slipping into simple anecdote. Our aim is to develop a perspective on networked learning that tries to articulate the overall relationship between technology and the policies and pedagogies applied in the name of networked learning. That perspective needs to emphasize choice and the ways in which human intervention mobilizes technologies in a variety of ways rather than being the simple outcome of the technology itself.

It is over a decade ago that Robin Mason and Tony Kaye developed the idea of convergence particular to education (Mason & Kaye, 1990). It is worth reflecting, upon how far we have come along the route they outlined. The convergence hypothesis could be taken to imply that place-based education would need an institutional revision to bring the educational process towards that found in large distance learning institutions such as the Open University UK. Robin Mason who characterizes the University as a relic of pre-industrial society has likened the Open University's methods to an 'Industrial Model'. The craft working practices of the university, in which the individual lecturer designs and presents materials whilst also providing the social support necessary for learning, are contrasted with industrialized production methods. After ten years the craft production of learning remains the dominant form despite the rise of a variety of alternative models.

One alternative approach to the introduction of networked technologies into traditional universities was proposed by academics based at Lancaster University in the United Kingdom (Steeples, Goodyear & Mellar, 1994). This alternative to the industrial model explicitly situates itself in the changing pattern of pressures on higher education:

"• growth and diversification of the "client group" for HE and
• the demand for more open or more student-centered forms of education.

Growth in student numbers, without a corresponding increase in resources, is now the principal force for change acting on teaching in the UK university sector." (Steeples, Goodyear & Mellar, 1994:83)

Emphasizing responsive and flexible provision in dealing with increased numbers of students this approach contrasts itself with mass distance education by emphasizing small numbers of enrolled students and a frequently updated curriculum. The convergence of distance and place-based education in Just-in-time IT-based Open Learning (JITOL) is conceived of in terms that are quite distinct from the 'Industrial Model'. Both the approach taken at Lancaster University and the industrial model find their analogues in discussions about economic forms in a networked society. The industrial model is paralleled in forms of Neo-Taylorism and the Lancaster approach in the flexible specialization of new industries (Warhurst & Thompson, 1998). The significant feature for our purposes is to note the potential for quite different educational forms to be projected from similar technological bases.

1.4   Issues

A key aspect of the new paradigm outlined by Mason and Kaye was the use of cooperative and collaborative methods. This inevitably implied new roles for the tutor and a more active role for the student. The idea of a new paradigm has been widely used though it has been couched in a variety of terms. Computer conferencing and Computer-Mediated Communication (CMC) described the technology used and only implied the type of pedagogy that might be applicable for their use. Other terms such as Computer Supported Collaborative (or Cooperative) Learning (CSCL) were more explicit about their pedagogic aim (Koschmann, 1996; McConnell, 2000). In the literature concerning networked and online approaches to learning the idea of a new paradigm is commonplace and it is now sufficiently dated to question the use of the term 'new'. There is evidence that the use of collaborative methods and the ideas of a new paradigm have been taken up and absorbed into the outlook of experienced practitioners of networked learning (Jones *et al.*, 2000; Jones & Asensio, Chapter 15 this volume). Whilst this may be true of practitioners already involved in networked learning there is contrary evidence about the way pedagogy may be informing the wider use of C&IT in teaching (Hammond, Trapp & Bennett, Chapter 14 this volume). It appears that the take up of networked technologies in higher education is largely pragmatic rather than informed by any particular pedagogy.

At the same time there is evidence emerging of both student and tutor frustration with collaboration online (Hara & Kling, 1999). Hara and Kling summarized these frustrations as originating in technological problems: minimal and not timely feedback from the instructor; and ambiguous instructions on web sites as well as via e-mail. The ambiguity that can arise in even detailed and well designed instructions has been a feature found elsewhere and one that might be related to the medium itself and the way in which it reduces the ability to repair misunderstandings easily and promptly (Jones, 2000). Trehan and Reynolds (Chapter 16 this volume), examining students' experiences of collaborative assessment, report frustration and anxiety as common experiences amongst the participants. Crook (Chapter 17 this volume) reports that the introduction of networked technology may not be comfortable for students or willingly appropriated by them. Overall the idea that the technology either requires collaboration or is especially fitted to collaborative activity appears to be an unwarranted determinist assertion (see also Jones & Asensio, Chapter 15 this volume).

During the last decade there have been a significant number of centrally funded initiatives aimed at promoting the development of learning technology in the United Kingdom and Australian higher education and a variety of state and private interventions in the United States (Darby, Chapter 2 this volume). The Dearing Report argued that the United Kingdom was a world leader in this field (NCIHE 1997) and there has been a continued political pressure to use technology in response to globalization and international competition (Blunkett, 2000). On the other hand there are continuing concerns about the failure to embed the outcomes of development projects into mainstream learning and teaching practice (Andersen et al., Chapter 10 this volume). Andersen et al. approach an increasingly important question for networked learning when they examine evaluation methods that might be used to assess the impact of initiatives. This concern is not confined to the United Kingdom as similar concerns have been reported in two of the most recent Campus Computing Surveys from the United States (Green, 1999; Green, 2000). Networked learning can also have unpredictable consequences for costs and it is essential that decisions about initiatives are made with a firm grasp of the possible financial consequences. Ash and Bacsich (Chapter 3 this volume) review the current rudimentary position with regard to the assessment of costs in networked learning.

Networked learning has now moved to the point where it has in some sense come of age. Linda Harasim when delivering a keynote address at the CAL conference (Warwick UK) in April 2001 talked about the 'war' being over. What she was referring to was the move from being outsiders to being a part of the mainstream in education. The disciplinary expert has been the mainstay of university education. The drive to mass education and the pressure to move from a research-based to a teaching-based logic has begun to put teaching and learning at the center of higher education (Biggs, 1999). This book contains several chapters that examine in some detail the sort of changes this requires in higher education organizations and the idea of institutional readiness (McNaught and Foster et al., Chapters 7 and 8 this volume). The United Kingdom has embarked on the development, with government support, of an Institute for Learning and Teaching (ILT: http://www.ilt.ac.uk). This is a government-sponsored approach to building a professional organization for teachers in higher education and it has many dangers, not least its quasi-corporate status. This professional body has been accompanied by the development of a Learning and Teaching Support Network (LTSN: http://www.ltsn.ac.uk). The LTSN subject based centers, and a single generic center serving the entire sector, aim to develop high quality teaching and learning through the dissemination of good practice. There is no doubt that these two initiatives will serve as a major step towards the development of the idea of the professional teacher in higher education.

This political and social change is being worked through alongside the development of networked technologies. Networked learning is at a point of contestation between different views of education and learning. The trend towards globalization inherent in modern corporate capital is being played out through visions of networked learning that envisage corporate universities, with a global reach, disseminating learning as a commodity. Globalization provides another determinism that profoundly affects policy makers and educational practitioners by removing the possibility of choice (for example, Blunkett, 2000). A further example of the link between technological determinism and the globalization agenda can be found in Bird and Nicholson (1998). Consumerism and globalization in this view is at least partly driven by the changes in technology. Against the corporate agenda of neo-liberal capital stands an image of educational reform enabled by the same new technologies. In the place of learning as a commodity stands the idea of learning in a community of practice, learning as participation in civic life. The global reach of technology can be seen as opening up new ways for different cultures to retain their diversity in a common dialog. For informed choices to be made by policy makers, at all levels, good research evidence is required. It is a significant challenge to networked learning research that it should begin to provide the analysis that can inform the choices necessary in the process of change.

The idea of communities and practice has become a main point of reference in networked learning (Brown & Duguid, 2000). In the most elaborated statement of this outlook explicit links are drawn to network theory (Wenger, 1998:14, 283). Communities of practice can be viewed as nodes in a network, or as subsets of people that are part of wider networks of practice (Brown & Duguid, 2000:141-3). The perspective that is associated with the term community of practice has become widespread and has been used to inform a variety of approaches to networked learning. McAteer *et al.* (Chapter 18 this volume) develop the idea of context sensitive guidance for practitioners of networked learning. In attempting to devise a resource for practitioners they confront difficult issues of what materials and forms of representation might be useful in developing collaborative practices.

One central focus of this book is on developing a dialog between the needs of higher education staff (faculty), who are under pressure to apply networked learning techniques, and the research community who have been exploring networked learning for many years. Research currently provides much needed information and guidance to practitioners. However a great deal of research is not well connected to the needs of the practitioner and there is only a slow development of a mature research program that can provide materials that are both useful and well grounded. On the other hand, the practitioner community in higher education is only now beginning to develop a professional sense and structure that might allow for the proper development of a discussion about the pedagogy and technology of networked learning.

A central issue for networked learning is one of how it can best be investigated. If choices are to be made about the kinds of organizations and the kinds of pedagogies that networked learning affords then robust research evidence will be required. A variety of research methods have been proposed and this volume takes the view that methods of research for networked learning should be fit for the purposes set out for them. There is no one method of research advocated in the following chapters, indeed we are proud of the methodological diversity of the approaches adopted. Research methods themselves have begun to be scrutinized in relation to the changed conditions afforded by networks. Networks have changed the conditions within which research takes place. There is a growing literature that addresses the particular ways research is shaped by networked environments (Hine, 2000; Mann & Stewart, 2000; Wittel, 2000; Jones, S., 1999). In the chapters that follow action research, experimental approaches, actor network theory and phenomenography are applied for specific purposes.

The introduction of networked learning has been accompanied by a change in tutor role that has been summarized in the phrase: 'from the sage on the stage to the guide on the side'. This phrase links together two processes, both of which are addressed in the following chapters. Firstly the shift suggests a change in power relations with the tutor's role being one that is more equalized with that of the student. The position of the tutor, it suggests, moves from the stage to the students' side. Issues of power and equality take on practical importance to networked learning through the issue of assessment and accreditation. Recently Brown and Duguid (2000) have discussed the role of the university in warranting students learning and they argue that in some senses universities can be thought of as degree granting bodies. The impact of providing assessments of students and their activities, to provide credentials that the university can endorse, lies at the heart of higher education whether networked or not. The requirements of assessment affect the detailed educational interactions in a networked environment and ensure that power relations between staff (faculty) and students remain unequal (Jones, 2000). Secondly the move from sage to guide implies a significant change in role. These changes in role are explored in this volume from the perspective of the tutor/facilitator (Salmon, Chapter 11) and the perspective of the information specialist (Levy, Chapter 9). Elsewhere, Gilly Salmon has written a guide to the practice of e-moderating and her work is an example of a central theme of this book, the need to develop a practice based on principled research (Salmon, 2000). We hope that the chapters that follow will contribute to the further development of this theme.

1.5   Outline

The book is divided into two sections to reflect two main themes. Networked learning has grown up and out of its initial experimental and local phase. The research presented here makes use of particular examples to address common themes. The growing institutionalization and normalization of networked learning is approached in Section 1 through the lens of general issues, the policy context at the level of state and national governments, the costs of networked learning, learning itself and how staff development and design can take place across an institution or several institutions. The second section focuses on the methods used for research and the results that research can provide by examining local and national settings. Overall this book tries to provide practice-oriented research and hopes by doing this to help in the development of a research-based practice in networked learning.

The first section of the book brings together chapters that provide an essential perspective to some of the more detailed work reported later in the book. Following this introductory chapter, in **Chapter 2** Jonathan Darby presents a review of the initiatives that have been supported by the governments of a variety of states. He begins with a review of the United Kingdom and then compares that review with initiatives in Canada, Australia and the United States. The comparison brings out significant similarities and important differences and allows the reader to explore both the current state of development of national and state policies and to place in context the particular initiatives explored in greater depth elsewhere in this volume (for example in Chapter 10). In **Chapter 3,** Charlotte Ash and Paul Bacsich examine the costs of networked learning. This important review draws on the United States and United Kingdom experience in particular but addresses a key issue for the development of networked learning more generally. In many cases the assessment of costs is still at a most rudimentary level. In **Chapter 4,** Peter Goodyear examines the psychological foundations of networked learning and in particular the different ways of understanding learning in a networked environment. Networked learning has disrupted traditional and often taken for granted practices and has encouraged an examination of learning itself. Networked learning research and research in all aspects of computers in education implies that the new technologies entail new types of learning. Set firmly in the context of design for networked learning, this chapter provides a timely review of the theory and practice of learning. In **Chapter 5,** Steve Fox examines the use of both situated learning and actor-network theories in relation to networked learning. He argues that researchers need to take care to include the non-institutional settings in which networked learning takes place. In particular he makes the case for the application of actor-network theory for researching non-institutional networked learning. His point is that situated learning and actor-network theory both allow for the generation of adequate descriptions of the actual and novel uses to which networked learning is being put by its users.

In **Chapter 6,** Rhada Ganesan, Gerald Edmonds and Mike Spector explore the issue of collaborative design. They point to the development, under the auspices of Computer Supported Cooperative Work (CSCW), of systems allowing for distributed working. They go on to explore the potential that two software packages have for the distributed collaborative design of networked learning. The chapter is an example of networked learning coming of age, of the transition to a mainstream activity, suggesting that networks could be employed not only for learning but also for the design of that learning itself. In **Chapter 7,** Carmel McNaught offers an Australian example of an institution wide approach to staff development for networked learning. This example of an institution wide policy is complemented by the report by Jonathan Foster *et al.* in **Chapter 8** of the approach adopted in a similar United Kingdom university. Together these chapters offer a rich picture of the types of difficulties and opportunities that are faced when networked learning moves beyond the stage of experiments and use by small groups of enthusiasts to everyday use and implementation across an institution. In **Chapter 9,** Phillipa Levy reports on the place of information specialists in networked learning support. The introduction of networked learning on an institutional scale entails a new role for services that support the learner and educator. This chapter brings together the experiences of the United Kingdom in an international context to explore the new roles required of the information specialist as requirements move beyond the traditional structures of libraries and technical support. In **Chapter 10,** Charles Anderson *et al.* examine the evaluation approaches that can be taken to assess national or state wide initiatives in C&IT based learning. This work develops the insights offered in Chapter 2 by exploring in greater depth the ways of assessing the impacts of these initiatives.

The second section of the book is concerned with the detailed examination of various aspects of networked learning. The different chapters take up methodological perspectives and continue to present empirical evidence related to practical issues in networked learning. In **Chapter 11,** Gilly Salmon examines an action research approach to the design and development of networked learning. Drawing on extensive work in the training of e-moderators Salmon provides an example of principled design and research. Her approach can be contrasted with the different approaches taken in the following chapters. In **Chapter 12,** Terry Mayes *et al.* describe the use of an experimental method to examine the use that can be made of vicarious learning. In the history of networked learning the role of relatively passive learners has been stigmatized by the term 'lurking', this chapter explores the positive use that can be made of relatively passive participation in networked learning. In **Chapter 13,** Vivien Hodgson examines some of the fundamental claims made for networked learning in terms of the provision of more democratic and participative environments. Her examination of identity and gender is strongly linked to and complemented by the chapter by Trehan and Reynolds (Chapter 16), which examines the power relations involved in collaborative assessment.

Nick Hammond, Annie Trapp and Catherine Bennett in **Chapter 14** explore the use of small group teaching across three disciplines. This chapter is a further example of a close examination of the actual uses to which networked learning is being put. Avoiding theoretical presumptions the chapter points to the pragmatic take-up of networked learning by higher education staff (faculty). They note that even when pressed there is a reluctance to support their actions by reference to the learning process or an underlying pedagogy. In **Chapter 15,** Chris Jones and Mireia Asensio report a complementary finding. They note that experienced practitioners of networked learning do deploy a pedagogic reasoning in terms of design but worry that this philosophic and theoretical understanding is not widespread. They also note that while these experienced practitioners have a common underlying approach they have not developed a secure capacity to predict outcomes or derive rules of thumb to guide their practice. This theme is further developed by Christine Steeples and Chris Jones (Chapter 19). In **Chapter 16,** Kiran Trehan and Mike Reynolds explore one aspect of networked learning practice, collaborative assessment. Using a phenomenographic approach, similar to that used by Jones and Asensio, they provide further evidence of the impact of factors beyond the technology in a networked learning environment. Touching upon issues raised by Vivien Hodgson (Chapter 13), they note that the role of the tutor is embedded in a wider system of accountability and that the rhetoric of empowerment can disguise a practice that internalizes old disciplines.

In **Chapter 17** Charles Crook examines the place of the campus based student in a networked learning environment. This work is of considerable interest in the way that it examines the students' private networked environment, their 'learning nest' and begins to ask questions that will become ever more pressing with the advent of mobile or ubiquitous computing. The chapter points to a fundamental point of contestation between networks as delivery systems and networks as arenas for community development. The chapter suggests that students may be resistant to or uncomfortable with the uses to which networked learning may be put. The preceding chapters have pointed towards a number of problems that arise if one wants to generate guidelines. In **Chapter 18,** Erica McAteer *et al.* explicitly address this issue. This chapter explains the use of a web site with multiple points of entry rather than a linear text to present guidance that the user can tailor for themselves. This innovative use of networked media to inform the design of resources supports the chapter by Ganesan, Edmonds and Spector (Chapter 6) who advocate the use of network systems in design. It reinforces the point that networked learning can be a revision of the system of learning, its design, management and use and not simply a revision of the learner-teacher relationship. It also reinforces the institutional approach and counsels against the simple derivation of good practice, let alone 'best' practice.

Finally, in **Chapter 19,** Christine Steeples and Chris Jones examine the future of networked learning in the context of a discussion around e-learning. Looking beyond the hype that often surrounds e-learning, the chapter advocates networked learning as a suitable framework for both the development of research and the development of a new practice. This chapter asserts the central place of design for networked learning. It also looks at potential future developments for networked learning, including research into multimedia-based networked learning.

1.6   Acknowledgements

The workshop from which this book has developed was part-funded by a grant from the Committee on Awareness, Liaison and Training of JISC (the Joint Information Systems Committee of the UK higher education funding councils). The views expressed here are not necessarily those of JISC or CALT. Further information about the project can be obtained from the project's website (http://csalt.lancs.ac.uk/jisc/). We would like to acknowledge the contributions of other members of the project team: Susan Armitage, Mireia Asensio, Mark Bryson Peter Goodyear, Vivien Hodgson and Michael O'Donoghue.

1.7 References

Baldwin, T.F., Stevens McVoy, D. & Steinfield, C. (1996) *Convergence: Integrating Media, Information and Communication.* Thousand Oaks, CA: Sage

Bates, A.W. (1999) *Managing Technological Change: Strategies for Colleges and University Leaders.* San Fransisco: Jossey-Bass Publishers

Biggs, J. (1999) *Teaching for Quality Learning at University.* Buckingham: SRHE and the Open University Press

Bird, D. & Nicholson, B. (1998) A Critique of the Drive Towards the Globalization of Higher Education. *Association for Learning Technology Journal. 6* (1) pp6–12

Blunkett, D. (2000) Greenwich Speech. Department for Education and Employment. Available at: http://cms1.gre.ac.uk/dfee/#speech

Brown, J. S. & Duguid, P. (2000) *The Social Life of Information.* Boston MA: Harvard Business School Press

Castells, M. (1996) *The Information Age: Economy, Society and Culture Volume 1. The Rise of the Network Society.* Oxford: Blackwell

Castells, M. (1999) Flows, Networks and Identities: A Critical Theory of the Information Society. In Castells, M., Flecha, R., Freire, P., Giroux, H.A., Macedo, D. & Paul Willis (Eds.) *Critical Education in the New Information Age.* Lanham, Maryland: Rowman and Littlefield

Chabot, A.A. (1999) Student Portable Computing: Network Support for Itinerant and Mobile Computers. http://www.jtap.ac.uk/reports/word/jtap-052.doc

Green (1999) *Campus Computing 1999: The tenth national survey of desktop computing and information technology in higher education.* Encino CA: Campus Computing Project

Green (2000) *Campus Computing 2000: The eleventh national survey of desktop computing and information technology in higher education.* Encino CA: Campus Computing Project

Hara, N. & Kling, R. (1999) Students' Frustrations with a Web-Based Distance Education Course. *First Monday, 4*(12). http://firstmonday.org/issues/issue4_12/hara/index.html

Hine, C. (2000) *Virtual Ethnography.* London: Sage Publications

Jones, C. (1999) From the Sage on the Stage to What Exactly? Description and The Place of the Moderator in Co-operative and Collaborative Learning. *Association for Learning Technology Journal. 7*(3), pp27–36

Jones, C.R. (2000) Understanding Students' Experiences of Collaborative Networked Learning. In Asensio, M., Foster. J., Hodgson, V. & McConnell, D. (Eds.) *Networked Learning 2000: innovative approaches to lifelong learning and higher education through the internet. Proceedings of the Second International Conference.* Sheffield: Sheffield University http://collaborate.shef.ac.uk/nlpapers/C.R.Jones1.htm

Jones, C., Asensio, M. & Goodyear, P. (2000) Networked Learning in Higher Education: Practitioners' Perspectives. *Association for Learning Technology Journal. 8*(2) pp18-28

Jones, S. (Ed.) (1999) *Doing Internet Research: Critical Issues and Methods for Examining the Net.* Thousand Oaks CA: Sage Publications

Knoke, D. & Kuklinski, J.H. (1982) *Network Analysis.* Beverley Hills: Sage Publications

Koschmann, T. (Ed.) (1996) *CSCL: Theory and Practice of an Emerging Paradigm.* Mahwah, NJ. Lawrence Erlbaum Associates

McConnell, D. (2000) *Implementing Computer Supported Cooperative Learning* (2nd edition). London: Kogan Page

MacKenzie, D. & Wajcman, J. (Eds.) (1999) *The Social Shaping of Technology* (2nd edition). Buckingham: The Open University Press

Mann, C. & Stewart, F. (2000) *Internet Communication and Qualitative Research.*London: Sage Publications

Mason, R. & Kaye, A. (1990) Towards a New Paradigm for Distance Education. In L. Harasim (Ed.), *Online Education: Perspectives on a New Environment.* New York: Praeger

NCIHE (National Committee of Inquiry into Higher Education) (1997) *Higher Education in the Learning Society.* (The Dearing Report) Norwich: HMSO.

Salmon, G. (2000) *E-moderating: The Key to Teaching and Learning Online.* London: Kogan Page

Spender, D. (2000) The Role of a University in a Dot Com Society: What is it? http://collaborate.shef.ac.uk/nl2000.html

Steeples, C., Goodyear, P. & Mellar, H. (1994) Flexible Learning in Higher Education: The Use of Computer Mediated Communications, *Computers and Education* (22) pp83–90

Thompson, G., Frances, J., Levacic, R. & Mitchell, J. (Eds.) (1991) *Markets Hierarchies and Networks: The Coordination of Social Life.* London: Sage Publications

Trilling, B. & Hood, P. (2001) Learning, Technology and Education Reform in the Knowledge Age or 'We're wired, webbed and windowed, now what?' In Paechter, C., Edwards, R., Harrison, R. and Twining, P. *Learning Space and Identity.* London : Paul Chapman Publishing

Vallee, J., Lipinski, H. & Miller, R.H. (1974) *Group Communication Through Computers; Design and Use of the FORUM System.* Menlo Park, CA.: Institute for the Future.

Vallee, J., Johansen, R., Randolph, R.H. & Hastings, R.C. (1974a) *Group Communication Through Computers: A Study of Social Effects.* Menlo Park, CA.: Institute for the Future

Vallee, J., Johansen, R., Lipinski, H., Spangler, K., Wilson, T. & Hardy, A. (1975) *Group Communication Through Computers: Pragmatics and Dynamics.* Menlo Park, CA.: Institute for the Future

Warhurst, C. & Thompson, P. (1998). Hands, Hearts and Minds: Changing Work and Workers at the End of the Century. In Thompson, P. and Warhurst, C. (Eds.) *Workplaces of the Future.* London: Macmillan Business

Wenger, E. (1998). *Communities of Practice: Learning, Meaning, and Identity.* Cambridge: Cambridge University Press

Wittel, A. (2000, January) Ethnography on the move: From field to net to Internet [23 paragraphs]. *Forum Qualitative Sozialforschung/Forum: Qualitative Social Research [Online journal],* *1*(1). http://qualitative-research.net/fqs

Zorkoczy, P. & Heap, N. (1995) *Information Technology: An Introduction,* (4th edition). London: Pitman Publishing

Section 1

The Context for Networked Learning

2. Networked Learning in Higher Education: The Mule in the Barn

Jonathan Darby

2.1 Introduction

Higher education is driven by curiosity. It is not only a fundamental driver for research but it also provides the justification for much of what is taught in our universities. It is therefore not surprising that higher education should have a fascination with technology, going back at least as far as the invention of the printing press.

Technology in education has until recently been applied mainly to the representation and transmission of knowledge. The printing press transformed the nature of higher education by allowing one scholar's ideas to be shared among all of his or her peers as well as students of the subject, but it only had an indirect influence on the nature of interpersonal discourse in education. Television too, much heralded in the 1960s as the technology that would transform education, was a vehicle for the transmission of knowledge and not a medium that leant itself to social interaction. Only with the advent of videoconferencing has television started to support interaction around transmitted knowledge.

Computers too were initially used to transmit knowledge, though even the earliest mainframe-based computer-based learning packages sought to be interactive. Take for example the MacMan[1] series of medical simulations developed at the McMaster University Medical School in Canada in the early 1970s (Dickinson *et al.*, 1971). Students were able to try various treatments on a simulated patient and observe the results. However the interaction was strictly with the computer model and not with other students or with teaching staff.

Networked learning has become a reality primarily through the merging of computer-based communication (principally e-mail) and the information transmission capabilities of the World Wide Web (WWW). Initially WWW was another format for knowledge transmission with no facilities to support interpersonal communication. With the advent of Java and Web scripting languages it became possible to build communication elements into Websites so

---

[1]   MacMan software (free download): atuin.chime.ucl.ac.uk/Models/macman.htm

creating the potential for the Internet to become truly interactive. Networked learning has become a reality but the implications offered by the technology convergence that has enabled it are only just becoming apparent.

The application of technology is determined at least as much by the social context in which it operates as by the capabilities of the relevant technology available to it. A banker from the nineteenth century entering a modern bank would find little to relate to. However an academic from the nineteenth century could enter a library or lecture theatre today and immediately feel at home. This lack of impact by technology on such a significant sector has been noted by many national, international and independent agencies who have attempted to edge forward the uptake of technology in education through targeted funding. Most have identified one or two apparent blockages and devised programs intended to overcome them. In some cases they have been unsuccessful as the blockage proved less easy to shift than anticipated. Even where a program was successful in addressing the identified problems the benefits were generally less than had been anticipated as frequently the removal of one blockage revealed another that had not previously been apparent. The experience of learning technology practitioners over the last twenty-five years has been rather like climbing a mountain. A peak appears in sight but when it is reached it turns out to have been just a foothill and a higher peak becomes visible. When this is reached however the new vista reveals a further higher peak, and this process appears to continue almost indefinitely.

Government action aimed at unlocking the potential that Communication and Information Technology (C&IT) offers began in the United Kingdom in the early 1980s. The Computer Board for Universities and Research Councils (a predecessor of the Joint Information Systems Committee[2]) commissioned a study of computer facilities for teaching in 1983 (Nelson, 1983) which identified fourteen ways that C&IT could be used in support of teaching and learning ranging from use of standard application packages through electronic mail and 'telesoftware' to simulations and modelling.

The significance of the report was that it marked the first occasion that a government agency gave recognition to the need for action to influence educational practice in higher education through the use of technology. The report had two main consequences. It raised awareness in universities of the need to make provision for networked computers to be used by students to support their studies. Universities throughout the UK sought to achieve the target given in the report of one workstation per ten students. An even more significant response to the report however was the establishment of the Computers in Teaching Initiative (CTI). This program, launched in 1984, for the first time placed resources in the hands of academics to enable them to apply technology in ways that made sense to them from the perspective of their discipline. The 139 projects funded by the initiative over the course of six years were not in general very technically sophisticated but they did demonstrate convincingly that C&IT had a significant role to play across the complete spectrum of higher education teaching. One unanticipated outcome

---

[2]   Joint Information Systems Committee: www.jisc.ac.uk

of the CTI was the extent to which it altered the teaching practices of those that participated in it. Gershuny and Slater, in their report on the first phase of the CTI, noted as a major consequence of the CTI projects a "shift of the teaching pattern from a lecture towards a tutorial basis" (Gershuny & Slater, 1989). This applied not only to courses for which computer-based learning applications had been developed but also to others that the CTI project team members had responsibility for.

The CTI had been set up as a 'pump-priming' exercize. It was anticipated that by funding projects across the sector (there were projects in practically every university as well as every discipline) new approaches to teaching and learning, informed by the project outcomes, would spread without further intervention. This proved not to be the case. There was very little uptake of CTI products outside the originating departments, and universities did not on the whole rush to establish learning technology services and programs of their own. Having scaled the peak of developing educationally relevant computer-based learning materials the challenge then revealed was that of dissemination and staff education. This was tackled through a reinvented 'Phase 2' Computers in Teaching Initiative. Through it 24 centers were established, each with the remit to identify and disseminate good practice in a specific discipline. This program appeared to strike a chord as what was initially conceived of as a three-year initiative ended up running for ten years.

Each CTI center researched and evaluated the tools, techniques and packages that were relevant to their discipline, and then the staff of the centers used the discipline networks that they were already part of to communicate their findings to their peers (Heller et al., 1992). When evaluated by the Higher Education Funding Council for England[3] in 1998 the CTI was found to have had a significant impact on thinking and practice within departments but only relatively little impact on institutional policy (HEFCE, 1998). As a consequence much of the educational gains made by the CTI at departmental level were not translated into practice because of a lack of institutional support for new approaches to teaching and learning. The CTI, while remarkably successful in achieving its objectives, did not achieve the breakthrough it sought. Rather its work helped to reveal other unaddressed blockages such as the need to address economic, organizational and strategic issues at institutional and system-wide levels.

Overlapping with the CTI from 1992 was the much larger Teaching and Learning Technology Program (TLTP)[4]. It was based on the assumption that what was now needed to unlock the potential of technology in teaching and learning was a critical mass of learning materials that met common national needs. In pursuit of this the program proceeded to fund relatively large multi-institution projects that had been able to convince the selectors that they were representative of the discipline they served. While there were a few notable successes, the bulk of TLTP products failed to achieve widespread acceptance. This was perhaps due to shortcomings of an educational nature (few products at the design stage were

---

[3]   HEFCE review of the Computers in Teaching Initiative: www.hefce.ac.uk/Initiat/CTI
[4]   Teaching and Learning Technology Program: www.ncteam.ac.uk/tltp

assessed against pedagogic criteria) and a failure to recognize the diversity of need that the products needed to serve (with implications for adaptability and modifiability). The response from TLTP was to launch a new round of projects in 1998 centering on implementation. As these reach completion during 2001 it will be possible to assess whether this approach has succeeded in changing practice more effectively than past efforts but early indications are that impact has been slight. It is perhaps a further indicator that single issue programs such as CTI and TLTP are unlikely to have a lasting impact, even if they achieve all of their objectives. This is because they are forced to ignore related issues which, unless addressed with equal vigour, will prevent significant organizational change. An example of this would be the failure to plan for and resource the ongoing support and development of TLTP software with the consequence that many initially successful products have subsequently fallen out of use.

One initiative that aims to overcome the limitations of a narrow focus by addressing a broad spread of issues affecting innovation in teaching and learning is the Learning and Teaching Support Network (LTSN)[5]. This was defined after careful analysis of the CTI and TLTP experiences and extensive consultation with UK higher education. It aims to place C&IT in the broader context of teaching and learning and combine the discipline focus of the CTI (LTSN also works through 24 discipline-based centers), with technical expertize provided through a Technology Center, and a Generic Center for non-disciplinary aspects of teaching and learning.

The most significant UK government initiative to date with respect to networked learning is the e-University Project[6] which was announced by the Secretary of State for Education David Blunkett in February 2000. The remit of the e-University development team is to create an organization that is inclusive of the whole of UK higher education, delivers internationally (as well as nationally) the best of what the UK has to offer and involves the private sector as an equal partner. To create a viable e-University from scratch is a difficult undertaking, but to create one that is attractive to students and commercially viable while at the same time reflecting the desires and wishes of the existing higher education institutions, is a powerful challenge. There will be a strong tension between what is in the interests of the e-University as an organization in its own right and the perceived interests of individual established universities.

This tension is perhaps most apparent in the area of accreditation. When the Open University[7] (OU) 'opened its doors' to its first students in 1971, the courses the students took gave them credit towards a degree awarded by the Open University. The OU rapidly gained a reputation for the quality of its courses and the cachet of an OU degree rose accordingly. The e-University on the other hand dropped its plans to accredit its courses directly in the face of concerns from established universities that this would allow the e-University to become a competing institution. Instead students who study an e-University-badged course

5   Learning and Teaching Support Network: www.ltsn.ac.uk
6   The e-University Project: www.hefce.ac.uk/Partners/euniv
7   The Open University: www.open.ac.uk

will be offered accreditation via the institution that developed it. For students who wish to take courses from several different participating institutions it is planning to appoint an 'accreditor of last resort', which will be an existing higher education institution, who will become the students' degree awarding body. Compromises such as this put at risk the coherence of vision and clarity of purpose that are essential for the success of a venture as innovative as the e-University.

Experiences in the UK have been paralleled in other countries but with significant differences which reflect each country's education traditions and government structures. Closest to the UK in many respects has been Australia. The Committee for the Advancement of University Teaching[8], established by the Australian government in 1992, made several hundred awards to university departments to support innovative uses of technology in teaching. While these were on a smaller scale than either CTI Phase 1 or TLTP they nevertheless served to stimulate a lot of thinking and experimentation. In 1974 the Committee established the UniServe program with five discipline-based support centers, partially modeled on the CTI. Government funding was not sustained and the program folded, however UniServe Science[9] at the University of Sydney remains very active through the support of its host university.

As a vast country with a scattered population, distance learning has always played a central role in educational policymaking in Australia. A study commissioned by the Department of Education, Training and Youth Affairs resulted in a seminal report "The Business of Borderless Education"[10] (Cunningham et al. 2000), which analyzed the factors influencing networked learning and the implications for a higher education system such as Australia's. There was no direct Government response to the report but in January 2001 the opposition Australian Labour Party unveiled plans for a 'University of Australia Online' that would create 100,000 new undergraduate places by 2010. If these plans are acted upon it will create a direct and comparably sized competitor to Britain's e-University.

Canada shares with Australia the characteristic of a very large territory and a dispersed population. Like Australia it has a tradition of distance learning. The premier distance learning institution is Athabasca University[11] which was established in 1970, shortly after the British Open University. Athabasca has taken the lead in networked learning in Canada offering a growing number of courses via their own *e-Class* learning environment. It has also combined with six other Canadian universities to create the Canadian Virtual University (CVU)[12].

---

[8]   Australian Universities Teaching Committee (successor to the Committee for the Advancement of University Teaching): www.autc.gov.au
[9]   UniServe Science: www.usyd.edu.au/su/SCH
[10] The Business of Borderless Education (free download): www.detya.gov.au/highered/eippubs.htm
[11] Athabasca University: www.athabascau.ca
[12] Canadian Virtual University: www.cvu-uvc.ca

Recent developments in Canada have paid particular attention to the possibilities offered by broadband networking. Canarie[13] is a not-for-profit corporation supported by its members, project partners and the Federal Government whose mission is to accelerate Canada's advanced Internet development and use. It launched a $26m funding program for Learning in 1999 'to encourage the development and use of broadband networks in education and training'[14].

In the USA networked learning has developed in a rather different manner. Government funding, with just a few exceptions, has been applied at state rather than federal level[15]. Some State Governments have chosen to concentrate support for networked learning in a single institution. One of the most successful examples of this approach is the University of Maryland University College[16]. It offers several hundred courses online. Most students studying these courses are working in mixed mode – that is to say they are taking a combination of conventionally-delivered and online courses. A smaller proportion are studying wholly online.

Other states have concentrated on producing virtual universities in which some or all State-funded institutions participate. Illustrative of this approach is the Kentucky Virtual University[17] which was established specifically to address Kentucky's ranking near the bottom of US league tables for educational achievement. It offers a portal for almost 100 universities and colleges in the State and a support and delivery infrastructure that significantly lowers the entry cost to universities and colleges adopting networked learning.

The Western Governors University[18] is an example of a regional initiative having been established in 1996 by ten Western states (Arizona, Colorado, Idaho, Nebraska, New Mexico, North Dakota, Oregon, Utah, Washington and Wyoming). While still small (500 students enrolled as of February 2001) the University has attracted several new member states and has also signed collaboration agreements with some non-US universities.

One non-governmental program that has had a significant impact on the development of networked learning in the USA has been the Asynchronous Learning Networks[19] initiative of the Alfred P Sloan Foundation. Under the slogan "Learning Anytime – Anywhere" it has been funding for the last seven years projects that can demonstrate the value and relevance of networked learning at all levels in higher education. It has been a major goal of the initiative to demonstrate affordability. Projects have been favoured that promise large numbers of students

---

[13]   Canarie Inc: www.canarie.ca

[14]   Fund for the Improvement of Post-Secondary Education:
       www.ed.gov/offices/OPE/FIPSE

[15]   The most significant US Federal Government initiative for higher education networked
       learning has been the Learning Anywhere Anytime Partnerships initiative of the Fund
       for the Improvement of Post-Secondary Education.

[16]   University of Maryland University College Online Programs:
       www.umuc.edu/gen/virtuniv.html

[17]   Kentucky Virtual University: www.kcvu.org

[18]   Western Governors University: www.wgu.edu

[19]   Asynchronous Learning Networks: www.aln.org

rather than experimental and radical uses of technology to support new modes of learning.   As a consequence the ALN program has been successful in demonstrating that networked learning can be incorporated into otherwise conventionally delivered courses with advantage, but it has not proved particularly effective in stimulating innovation.

Despite these significant US State Government and foundation-driven initiatives the most challenging developments have occurred from the corporate sector. The University of Phoenix[20], founded in 1976, has become the largest for-profit university in the US.   While the majority of its education is still delivered conventionally through its 90 campuses, most of its courses can also be taken online and the percentage of students studying this way is growing. In 2000 it had more than 75,000 enrolled on degree courses. What sets it apart from other online educators is that it is already making a profit ($1 m in the six months to 28 February 2001) and is experiencing growth in overall student numbers that few of its public sector competitors can match.

Of the newer for-profit companies seeking to exploit networked learning perhaps the most interesting is UNext.com[21]. The company, founded by University of Chicago Professor Andrew Rosenfield in 1999, is aiming to set the gold standard for corporate education by signing up top tier universities to partner with the company in defining and developing courses in management and the professions. Unlike its rivals, it invested heavily in pedagogic research and pilot testing to inform its approach to course definition, production and delivery. As a consequence its courses, based in the main on a problem-based approach to learning, do not look like direct analogues of conventionally delivered courses but start to take on the characteristics of a new learning system that uses technology to integrate delivery of knowledge with interaction, communication and application.

Networked learning is still in its infancy. For a potential student of an online course the picture is a confusing one. What appear to be similar offerings may in practice offer the student very different learning experiences. Most online courses are direct analogues of conventionally delivered courses copying directly their structure, modes of assessment, timetable, *etc.* Worse, many course implementors have paid little attention to what additional resources might be required for remote delivery. These courses consist of little more than the documents that already exist to support the conventionally delivered version (lecture notes, reading lists, article offprints, *etc.*) placed into a generic virtual learning environment and do not provide any alternatives to the face-to-face elements that the student is missing. The time required to create such courses is usually estimated in hours rather than person months or years. Such 'online courses' may well facilitate learning by students who are attending the classes as well, but they are a wholly inadequate basis for the education of remote students.

---

20   University of Phoenix: www.phoenix.edu
21   UNext.com: www.unext.com

The announcement in April 2001 by the Massachusetts Institute of Technology (MIT)[22] that it was to make nearly all its course materials available free online sent a frisson through the higher education online learning community as it signalled an end to this passing off of supporting resources as complete online courses. MIT had recognized that it did not accord with its educational standards to follow the quick and dirty route to getting together a portfolio of online courses that so many others had pursued. What was particularly smart about its decision to make its on-campus course supporting materials available outside MIT was the calculation that it had more to gain from doing so than from the more obvious policy of restricting access to its students and staff. It seems highly probable that the wider exposure of its courses will indeed increase the attractiveness of the Institute to students, staff, benefactors and funders and so help it maintain and enhance its position in relation to its peer institutions.

Even the online courses of today that have been produced with realistic levels of investment and close attention to quality are almost all first generation products. They seek to replicate as closely as they can the form and format of traditional courses. The next generation of online courses will need to be designed from first principles.   Following careful definition of required learning outcomes an educationally-driven selection from a set of interconnectable course elements will lead to structures and communication systems that provide support for student learning that matches remote students needs and circumstances.

Only a few teams are currently working on second generation networked learning approaches.   One is UNext.com.   Another is the Technology-Assisted Lifelong Learning program at the University of Oxford[23].   It has defined a course definition and production methodology that combines very small scale learning objects[24] into a structured learning environment implemented using spinal documents to contextualize both content and activity elements. The use of learning objects allows mixed media to be used without incurring the very high costs usually associated with multimedia and the spinal documents help the student remain orientated to broader concepts when working on detail. This approach has proved particularly effective with students who are coming to higher education long after the completion of their formal school education.

"For 50-year-old postman Jim Moffat from Chesterton, near Bicester, the Internet computing course helped him to gain new skills at a time which

---

[22]   Massachusetts   Institute   of   Technology   OpenCourseWare   announcement: web.mit.edu/newsoffice/nr/2001/ocw.html
[23]   Oxford University Technology-Assisted Lifelong Learning: www.tall.ox.ac.uk
[24]   Oxford's learning object model differs significantly from that being developed under the auspices of the Advanced Digital Learning Network (ADL).   Their Sharable Content Object Reference Model (SCORM) treats learning objects as complete mini-courses that are potentially free-standing.   Oxford's approach is to treat learning objects as basic building blocks that define a learning activity.   While each is designed to achieve a specified learning outcome, and they can be combined in many permutations, they may not have any learning value except in combination with other learning objects.

best suited him. As someone who left school at 15 and hasn't studied regularly since, Jim felt somewhat daunted at the thought of setting foot in a classroom again. However he now ranks the course ... as one of the 'highlights' of his life." (Oxford University, 2001)

2.2   Conclusion

Networked learning impacts on almost all aspects of established educational practice. Piecemeal approaches, while they may be interesting and illuminating, do not contribute to lasting change. The key to realizing the transforming potential of networked learning will be to find a way to connect all the disparate elements. A particularly significant division of elements is that between the public and private sectors. Educational institutions evolve over time through small incremental steps. Small and medium enterprizes are usually better placed to adopt genuinely radical approaches.   Each views networked learning from diametrically opposed viewpoints.

The assiduous editor of this book very reasonably asked me to explain my subtitle. A two-part title has become standard, helping as it does to differentiate between a plethora of writings with identical before-the-colon titles, and I included my 'mule in the barn' partly in the hopes of imbuing my 'networked learning in higher education' with an element of mystery. However now that my bluff has been called I offer the following explanation. The mule is a hybrid creature that can only be produced through the union of two different species, but from this union comes a vigour that exceeds that of either parent. Networked learning requires a similar union between the traditional strengths of higher education institutions and the entrepreneurship of the business sector. This union is starting to occur but as yet the product is still being treated as an exotic manifestation. The mule has yet to leave the barn and show what it is capable of. There is a warning in the analogy however.   The mule is infertile and cannot reproduce itself. Networked learning needs to be constantly refreshed from other sources. It is a dynamic form of education that will need constant reinvention over the decades ahead.   Networked learning is neither a pedagogy nor a technology – it is an attitude of mind – it is being open to new ideas and insights. The future of networked learning is unpredictable but it can be predicted with confidence that it will look very different from today's mule in the barn.

2.3   References

Cunningham, S. *et al.* (2000) *The Business of Borderless Education.* Canberra: DETYA

Dickinson, C.J., Ingram, D. & Shephard, P. (1971) *J. Physiol (Lond) 1,* (9) 216

Gershuny, J.I. & Slater, J.B (1989) *Computers in Teaching Initiative: Report.* Oxford: CTISS

Heller, S.R., Kibby, M.R. & Darby, J. (1992) (Eds) UK Computers in Teaching Initiative Special Issue, *Computers and Education 19* (1/2)

Higher Education Funding Council for England (1998) *An evaluation of the Computers in Teaching Initiative and Teaching and Learning Technology Support Network, Report 98/47.* Bristol: HEFCE

Nelson, D.A (1983) *Report of a Working Party on Computer Facilities for Teaching in Universities.* London: Computer Board for Universities and Research Councils

Oxford University (2001) *Oxford Blueprint 1*, (3) 8

3. The Costs of Networked Learning

Charlotte Ash and Paul Bacsich

3.1 Introduction

Many people doubt whether costing should appear on the educational agenda, and we expect that many readers of this book will skip this chapter in favour of the more academic, pedagogic ones. Unfortunately for these readers, costing is playing an increasingly important role in education, at all levels. In higher education, the need to meet the increasing demand for places from students on ever-reducing, and already over-allocated, budgets, whilst maintaining quality, is stretching institutions sometimes beyond the limit. While the majority of top and middle managers are keen to assess the costs of providing different courses, most academics see the subject as an unnecessary intrusion on their 'turf'.

In this chapter we hope to give an overview of costing, why costing is important, and the work that has been done in this area previously and on a number of current studies. The chapter will conclude with a comparative discussion of these studies and a list of ten principles of good costing.

Although there is a long tradition of costing distance education (see in particular Rumble, 1997), the issue has taken some time to permeate to more traditional providers. Today costing is near the forefront of the educational agenda and mainly for the same reasons: the need to increase student numbers on decreasing budgets, whilst maintaining quality. The deployment of new technologies, such as the internet, over the last decade has resulted in new learning paradigms. Learning at a distance is no longer restricted to paper-based materials and conventional lecture-based university courses are becoming more varied in delivery format. Technology is allowing a much larger and more diversified group of learners to gain access to higher education. Managed or virtual learning environments (MLEs, VLEs), electronic or virtual campuses, online learning and technology-enhanced education are all familiar terms, and the latest phrase, e-learning, has rapidly entered common vocabulary.

Collaboration between internal faculties and departments, and between different institutions, even on a multinational basis, is becoming increasingly common for teaching as well as research. At present in any such collaboration each partner is likely to have different management, planning and financial accounting approaches, leading to difficulties in collaboration. Thus there is a great need for a uniform planning and costing methodology so that such collaborations can thrive and that organizations can negotiate with each other using a common vocabulary. Only in that way can misunderstandings be avoided. In summary, a universal approach is needed in all multi-institution, multi-faculty, and multi-national research and teaching ventures.

While universities primarily still deliver higher education, other providers are becoming a threat to this dominance, especially with the use of technology. Universities are facing ever-increasing competition from virtual universities, the non-educational sector (corporate universities) and institutions abroad. This in turn is forcing the UK higher education sector to look more closely than it is used to at the costs of providing its courses – since students, especially at post-graduate level, are attracted by good quality education at an attractive price.

An increasing number of externally funded research projects are taking place, mainly with European funding. These projects usually have a highly rigid reporting procedure, including the provision of an excruciating level of detail on expenditure. In addition, the UK Research Funding Councils are driving for greater transparency of costing in institutions: universities are having to account for all funding received for research and prove that it has been spent on research. It is hoped that this will alleviate the bleed from research to teaching, or the opposite. We are sure that it is only a matter of time before the same methodology is applied to teaching, whether it is suitable or not.

Thus, there are a number of reasons compelling universities to look more closely at their costing structures. There is also a comprehensive drive towards networked learning (Bacsich *et al.*, 1999). Where established, networked learning is generally instigated and delivered by a small number of enthusiastic academic staff in an institution, eager to explore new methods of developing materials and teaching students. Although some institutions have a clear strategic path and in a few there is some degree of centralized management of innovation, on the whole, work in this area is limited to small pockets of innovation – through rapidly growing and coalescing.

Even so, institutions feel that this is an uncharted area; they are unsure about the structure and status of such activities. There is not an accepted uniform methodology to explain how a move towards networked learning could benefit institutions in both the long and short term. Some of the more prominent driving and restraining forces are shown in the table below:

Table 3.1 Driving and restraining forces

Driving Forces	Restraining Forces
Individual members of academic staff	Lack of training in using the technology
Dynamism from top management	Lack of time for development
Project champions (where established)	Lack of pedagogical evidence to support a move towards networked learning
Increasing student numbers with ever-decreasing budgets	Concerns about the quality of materials and the lack of standards for measuring quality

Students are also a driving force for networked learning – our research shows that although students believe that networked learning is increasing the cost of their education, they also believe that this is offset by a general view that it is also enhancing their experiences, making learning more enjoyable and profitable.

Despite a growing body of work about costing networked learning, from Rawlings *et al.* (1993) onwards through Bates (1995), Rumble (1999) and our own work (Bacsich *et al.*, 1999), people are still debating about the presumed efficiency, effectiveness and additional benefits of such activities. Without this information, costing is cold and worthless. There is a genuine need to develop a methodology to measure effectiveness. A recent US report notes that "while the debate [about effectiveness] will continue, it is too late to turn back. Recent history suggests that both the variety of offerings and the number of individuals availing themselves of these alternative forms of learning will not only increase but will increase dramatically. The alternatives are entering and in some circumstances, becoming the mainstream." (NCHEMS, 2001)

Thus it seems inevitable that we are moving towards enhancing conventional learning paradigms with technology, and costing all forms of education, in order to maintain market competitiveness. The need is to provide the best experience we can offer to the students that wish to participate, whilst retaining high quality and keeping within budgets.

3.2   Costing of Education – Previous Work

The literature on costing most relevant to the new area of networked learning comes from the field of distance education. As Jef Moonen from the University of Twente, Netherlands, states, "There are very few studies in the literature which contain detailed information about the costs involved in flexible delivery. Because of the nature of things, there is more reliable information on the cost of distance learning than on traditional on-campus teaching" (Moonen, 1998). Educationalists have seen the development of distance education delivery methods grow from audio and video tape, through to satellite broadcast, computer mediated conferencing and networked learning (Rawlings *et al.,* 1993). Technology has made distance largely immaterial.

When we reviewed previous work on costing innovative learning systems we concluded that no one body of work encompassed all of the issues or travelled sufficiently far towards reaching operational conclusions, especially in a manner convincing to finance departments. But there were many useful contributions, starting with the one below. Moonen (1997) identified four reasons why costs are difficult to quantify:

- There is disagreement about which costs should be taken into account.
- Reliable data is unavailable because it is not collected in a systematic manner.
- Recorded costs are unstable and evolving.

- Some data is perceived as confidential and may not be made publicly available.

To develop a costing model for UK higher education, these barriers have to be surmounted. In addition, we identified a larger barrier intrinsic to this sector:

- Each previous costings approach used a different vocabulary, and these have to be 'standardized' before they can be understood.

3.2.1 Costs to Stakeholders

An Australian study, funded by the Committee for University Teaching and Staff Development (CUTSD), looked at the costs and benefits of information technologies in learning and teaching. The authors (Alexander *et al.,* 1998) identified multiple stakeholders who, "...are affected by the development and use of information technologies: students, staff, departments, institutions and society itself". Further, the authors argued, "Each of these can be said to incur a cost, as well as potentially receiving benefits".

Using this approach the literature is reviewed here under three sections: costs to the institution, to staff and to students; we consider these three to be the main stakeholders in networked learning.

Institutional Costs

The 1997 Information Technology Assisted Teaching and Learning (ITATL) report concluded that there were no robust mechanisms for determining the costs of developing courses and related delivery costs (HEFCE, 1997). This lack of data is due to the difficulty institutions have in identifying the total cost for Communications and Information Technology (C&IT) and distinguishing the cost of C&IT-enhanced teaching and learning in a networked environment (HEFCE, 2000). Moreover, in the UK higher education sector, budgets are devolved directly to academic departments. Therefore without a centrally imposed recording methodology, and one operating at a highly granular level, the center will never be able to ascertain what is being spent on networked learning.

In particular in the UK, the annual statistics published by UCISA make it difficult to identify expenditure on C&IT (HEFCE, 2000). Institutions tend to confine themselves to the top-sliced amount for educational technology or 'IT spend'. The paucity of data is due to the difficulty that institutions have of identifying the total cost for C&IT and separating it among the users and applications in a networked environment. Moreover where budgets are devolved to academic departments the center cannot always ascertain what is being spent for what. (For example, is a PC projector a C&IT or an audio-visual item?) Conversely, a department might consider only the direct costs of C&IT and not central costs or staff time, *i.e.,* the institutional costs (HEFCE, 2000).

One of the main expenses for institutions embarking upon Web-based or other means of electronic delivery of courses is that of investment in infrastructure, such as IT-equipped lecture theatres and computer laboratories (Alexander *et al.*, 1998), and course set-up development. These start-up costs can amount to five years of a lecturer's salary (Arizona Learning Systems, 1998). These costs have to be amortized over a long period of time or over significant numbers of students reached to provide a shrewd investment.

Massy and Zemsky (1995) claim that IT leads to economies of scale. After (sometimes large) initial investment, the incremental cost of usage per additional student is low. There is also access to huge amounts of information at a low incremental cost. Rawlings *et al.* (1993) state: "...factors tending towards cost-effectiveness include scale of use (students and hours) and use of equipment and services on a marginal-cost basis".

The ITATL study noted, "...many development costs are hidden, or are excluded from direct calculation, and thus their true extent may not be traceable, under-budgeted, or honoured only in the breach" (HEFCE, 1997). Development is a huge hidden cost in institutional terms: both the time of staff to develop resources and the additional technical support and related training costs are generally not accounted for and so are absorbed into existing budgets for staff development and academic planning. In addition, the study concluded that there were no robust mechanisms for determining the costs of developing courses and related delivery costs (HEFCE, 1997).

Another study highlighted the need for increased technical support with regard to online learning programs (CRE, 1998). This is not only for academic staff during the development stages but continuous assistance for both staff and students during the delivery of the program.

Institutions will save in terms of space requirements if networked learning is offered to students wishing to remain at home, but this reduction in the requirement for buildings must be supported by significant financial investment in secure and reliable networks. A study by the Association of European Universities noted, "Another hidden cost overlooked until now... is that of down-time or the time when the computer network is failing and all computer activity is interrupted" (CRE, 1998). This leaves the institution with unproductive staff and students.

An additional and often overlooked cost to any institution encouraging networked learning was identified by the ITATL study (HEFCE, 1997). Staff and students perceive internet charges via the institutional server as a zero cost. Whether 'surfing' is for work or pleasure, institutions pay these charges. Given present institutional accounting procedures, it is difficult to devolve these costs to individual programs and they therefore constitute a large hidden cost absorbed by the institution.

Staff Own Costs

Rumble (1997) points out the difficulty of assessing academic staff costs in an environment where staff pay is not directly related to the time they spend working on activities, and where their time can not be attributed to different activities. He notes the dangers of assuming that staff will always put in long, unpaid-for hours –

both in terms of stress if they do and because of political changes in the acceptability of such practices.

The long, unpaid hours of academic staff are not just prevalent in the UK. Kirkpatrick and Jakupec report that, "Most teaching staff [in Australia] are prepared to go 'beyond the call of duty' but this can only be sustained up to a point. The current educational environment where staff are facing heavier teaching loads, larger classes and increased pressure to attract external funding and to publish challenges the commitment of most professionals." (Kirkpatrick & Jakupec, 1999)

Further to this, Dolton (1994) studied the use of computing on academic courses in Higher Education. He repeated a conclusion from a review by the Computers in Teaching Initiative, "... the amount of human resources to mount software, write it, service courses, give courses and teach computing to staff and students is huge and should not be underestimated".

Increased student-to-tutor communication in online learning programs is extensively documented. Arizona Learning Systems (1998) report that faculty spend more time communicating with students (from 30 minutes to 4 hours per student per week) than they would have done for a traditional classroom lecture with associated follow-up time.

In addition, Rumble (1999) feels that the biggest and the least costed aspect of online learning is the cost of learner support. Tutors at the UK Open University consistently suggest that they are spending more time supporting learners online than was the case when they supported them through correspondence and telephone contact. Like academic staff in other higher education institutions, they are not being paid, or recognized, for this increased workload.

Tonks and Long (1989), in their study of the hidden costs of simulation software concluded that "timetable hours for staff and for students become a poor measure of effort and of contact when using simulations". This illustrates that even ten years ago it was being noted that teaching hours were not an accurate measure of academic workload when teaching material and communication with tutors was in an electronic format.

In 1997, a study by management accountants KPMG and the Higher Education Funding Councils noted the lack of a consistent, detailed and acceptable method of recording staff time and effort and assigning it to different activities. The study identified the 'cultural' difficulties in getting academic staff to accurately complete an activity-based time sheet. Two years earlier, Temple (1995) found that employers focused on the direct costs of the training programs and were "unaccustomed to identifying the indirect costs that the project was encouraging them to do".

Despite Tonks and Long's statement of 1989 and the KPMG study of 1997, a realistic and workable method of recording and then assigning staff time to activity has still not been found. In the 'Guide to Costing and Pricing in Higher Education' the Joint Costing and Pricing Steering Group states "... in estimating the time spent by academic staff on teaching, research and other direct activities, some HEIs use workload models for planning and monitoring academic activities; some use estimates of staff time prepared by program managers or by staff themselves; others conduct diary or time sheet exercizes on either a one-off or a recurring basis" (JCPSG, 1999).

Moonen (1997) says the "...major cost issues associated with flexible delivery are related to the preparation time required for the presentation of learning material, and the a-synchronous support extended to students". Further, staff asynchronous contact with students is difficult to regulate and difficult to measure. Several projects have claimed to illustrate increased preparation times for networked learning.

Draper and Faubister (1998) identified the unquantifiable aspect of 'thinking' or preparation time and time for the gestation of ideas. They also identified the concept that the value of time is not fixed – time lost or saved in a high-pressure situation can have a completely different effect to that in a low-pressure situation.

When experienced instructors were first interviewed, as reported in the Flashlight "Cost Analysis Handbook" (Ehrmann & Milam, 1999), they all remarked that teaching at a distance was more time-consuming than teaching on-campus. Then they were asked to break down their activities into different functional categories, both for courses taught on-campus and off-campus, and a dramatically different picture emerged. About one third of the faculty had indeed spent more time teaching their distance learning course. Another third had the opposite experience: it was actually their on-campus courses that were more time-consuming. The remaining third found that they were spending equal time for on- and off-campus courses. Perhaps first impressions by academic staff of their own use of time can be deceiving.

Meanwhile the ITATL study stated, "The significant quantities of time allocated by academic and technical staff to ITATL development within institutions were ... allocated a zero or minute cost value" by the institution (HEFCE, 1997). Institutions are encouraging academic staff to develop electronic learning materials to enhance and extend the reach of their courses but are unwilling to relieve them of additional teaching and departmental responsibilities, thus resulting in the ever-lengthening academic working day. In an Australian study of university IT projects (Alexander et al., 1998), nearly three-quarters of the projects reported that time for project development was greater than expected.

The Australian report also noted that staff incurred a high personal cost "in terms of time, resulting in a loss of research and personal time" (Alexander et al., 1998). This can also be extended to include loss of tenure and promotion as well as increased work-related stress and is often categorized as an opportunity cost (HEFCE, 1997). Networked learning is seen as carrying a price in terms of opportunities foregone in other areas of activity, for both institutions and for individual academic staff.

Student Own Costs

A number of references are made in the literature about the transference of costs to students with the development of electronic learning environments. According to the report of the latest (US) Campus Computing study, significant numbers of students in the USA are being charged separately for computing facilities, at an average cost of $120 per year (Green, 1999).

Moonen states in Collis (1996) that to reduce costs in the long run some costs must be shifted to students, who must also take more responsibility for their own study and expect less personal contact with instructors. Similarly, O'Rourke, examining the Canadian experience, comments, " … shifts in responsibility for obtaining and paying for access may not just be the outcome of a particular technology, but may represent a fundamental shift in perspective" of who is responsible for the cost of education (O'Rourke, 1999).

Rumble (1997) declares that a successful online learning community must eventually rely on student ownership of computers. The 1997 Dearing Report proposed 100% student ownership of personal computers by the year 2005/06 (NICHE, 1997) but as a recent HEFCE report points out, this transfers the costs – not only of purchase, but also of maintenance, insurance and running – to the student and does not (seem to) substantially reduce the cost of IT provision to the institution (HEFCE, 2000).

The reasons for this are not clear, but our view is that use of student-owned computers increases overall demand for computing, leading to more plug-in points and larger servers, and also that additional support staff are needed to cope with the wider variety of systems deployed.

The National Union of Students conducted a survey of hidden course costs in 1996. Three years later this data was used in a consultation document about top-up fees. It was found that students were being charged for: printing, photocopying, art materials, year-abroad costs, IT costs, laboratory equipment, studio levies, compulsory field trips, photocopied hand-outs, equipment hire and study packs (NUS, 1999). In over 80% of cases, those students who were being charged extra course costs had not been informed of such costs before entry to the institution, despite Dearing stating that "students will need information about the adequacy of an institution's provision of equipment for their use and must know in advance of study what expectations there are of students providing their own access" and therefore, implicitly, the associated costs (NICHE, 1997). The average student had to pay around $800 per year on hidden course costs. Travel costs proved the most expensive hidden course cost. The average student paid out $250 per year on travel. Buying books and written materials also proved expensive at $250 per year for the average student. With students fearing that marks will be reduced (or assignments rejected) if assignments are not typewritten, the average student spent an average of $100 on hardware, but only $20 on software (NUS, 1999).

Notably, when Crabb (1990) developed a methodology for costing open learning, he included a cost to the learner of fees, materials, incidental expenses (travel) and equipment. The Australian study considered it important to value student time, the cost to students of the time they spend on education-related activities, i.e., time spent learning, travelling, seeking resources, etc. (Alexander, McKenzie & Geissinger, 1998).

The other major area of hidden costs concerns the growing price students are paying for education in a previously free system. The cost of technology is being passed on to students, directly in the USA and (so far), less so, in the UK (Harvey *et al.,* 1998, in Ehrmann & Milam, 1999). Students however appear unaware of the potential savings and possible increased benefits of learning with technology, such as reduced travel expenses and more productive use of their time (Ehrmann & Milam, 1999).

Peebles (1997) regarded the most significant decision at Indiana University to institute a form of Activity-Based Costing (ABC). This allows the derivation of a notion of 'unit costs' for the delivery of services. Rumble (1997) also advocates ABC. With no ABC mechanism in place, there is ignorance of the unit of costs for various transactions, ignorance of the value-added of each transaction, ignorance of the impact of cost reduction efforts, and ignorance of how to respond to fall/growth in student numbers – moreover, transaction costs cannot be attached to individuals or different groups of students.

3.3   Current Costings Studies

At present there are four costings studies that are either ongoing or recently completed. Although each is individual in remit all are surprisingly similar in outcomes and conclusions.

- In the US, the National Center for Higher Education Management Systems (NCHEMS) and the Western Co-operative for Educational Telecommunications (WCET), a unit of the Western Interstate Commission for Higher Education (WICHE), are collaborating on a project funded by FIPSE (Fund for the Improvement of Post-secondary Education).
- In addition, the Flashlight costing methodology is becoming widely accepted in the US.
- In Australia, a project was directly funded by the Department for Education, Training and Youth Affairs, and completed with assistance from Ernst and Young in late 1998.
- Finally in the UK, the 'Costs of Networked Learning' project started in 1999 at Sheffield Hallam University, largely funded by the Joint Information Systems Committee (JISC), and is ongoing.

Each of these will be outlined below; however it is recommended that, for full information, the original sources are consulted.

3.3.1   Technology Costing Methodology, United States of America

The 'Technology Costing Methodology' (TCM) project, funded by the Fund for the Improvement of Post-secondary Education (FIPSE), began at the end of 1998. It aims to develop an authoritative costing methodology for calculating the costs within institutions, in order to establish whether technology led activities do contain costs, and across institutions, thus allowing for the comparison of costing information.

The project is a joint venture between the Western Co-operative for Educational Telecommunications, a unit of the Western Interstate Commission for Higher Education (WICHE), and the National Center for Higher Education Management Systems (NCHEMS). The project team is using the 'Cost Finding Principles' developed by NCHEMS in 1974 as a basis for this new work.

The study has identified that due to the increase in the use of educational technology decision-makers are asking questions that had not previously been considered important. These include:

- What are the per-student costs of alternative forms of networked learning?
- How do costs of alternative methods compare to more traditional methods?
- Under what conditions, if any, do alternative mechanisms become cost-effective?
- Are the learning results as good as those achieved through classroom-based models?

The project team hopes to put decision-makers in a position where these queries can be answered, with the outcomes of the TCM project.

The project has two main aims:

1. To provide decision-makers with the data that allows the costs of alternative modes of delivery to be compared; and
2. To propose a set of procedures allowing multiple institutions to compare costs by placing the separate data in a common framework.

The preliminary handbook states that there is no need for institutions to change the way they currently record costs but rather the project hopes to provide a set of procedures to set common ground to allow these comparisons to be made.

The preliminary handbook notes the importance of separating course-related costs, the costs of offering the course regardless of student costs, and student-related costs, those which vary depending on the number of students enrolled. The methodology is notionally based on ABC, but leaves the division of activities to the discretion of the institution. The report suggests the recording of time is based on average rather than actual salary costs. The 'Technology Costing Methodology' has developed an eight stage process for determining course costs. These stages are outlined below:

1. Identify courses for which cost calculations are to be made.
2. Write a description of the delivery mechanism and resources being used.
3. Establish the activity structure that describes the course.
4. Assign costs of various objects of expenditure to the activity structure.
5. Sum the component costs to find the total costs of delivering the course.
6. Note the number of students on the course and associated credit hours.

7. Calculate costs per student and per credit hour by dividing Step 5 by Step 6.
8. Calculate the costs of underutilized capacity.

The methodology is currently being trialed in a number of institutions. These case studies will be used to identify problem areas in the preliminary handbook and to illustrate particular points in the final report.

3.3.2   Flashlight, United States of America

Flashlight is a program of the Teaching, Learning, and Technology (TLT) Group, an affiliate of the American Association for Higher Education (AAHE). The program was initially established as an Annenberg/CPB project in 1993. The program provides training, consulting and evaluation tool kits – the latest of these is a 'Cost Analysis Handbook'.

The Handbook claims that "educational technology introduced over the past 50 years has supplemented and often enhanced – but not supplanted – traditional classroom instruction, thus adding to its cost, not reducing it" (Ehrmann & Milam, 1999). This implies that they expect no direct savings for universities and colleges using Computer Assisted Learning and Information and Communications Technology, a rather conservative view.

The Handbook states that it has been created to help users understand the cost issues involved in incorporating new technologies into teaching and learning. The report notes that the analysis of costs in technology enhanced teaching and learning is only part of a larger enquiry – it concentrates on how resources are used and "how they might be better used in more effective and efficient ways".

The Economic Model developed by Flashlight explores the use of resources by units to create specific products or services (outputs); this is expressed by a simple three-stage linear diagram. The model explores the relationship between the resources, units and outputs in terms of ABC. The Handbook describes ABC thus:

> "Traditional accounting breaks costs down by organizational units and usually attends only to expenditures and revenues. Activity-Based Costing breaks down costs by basic types of activities. These costs may cut across organizational boundaries..." (Ehrmann & Milam, 1999)

The Handbook provides the process for building an Economic Model which should help readers to focus on the crucial, and "sometimes hidden", uses of resources by describing patterns between the use of resources such as time, money and space. Users follow these seven steps to build a model that is individual and targeted to their particular institution or problem.

The Economic Model is completed in seven steps:

1. Identify your resource concerns and the specific questions you want answered.
2. Identify your outputs.

3. Identify the activities that are required to produce your outputs.
4. Identify the academic and support units that participate in these activities.
5. Identify the resources these units consume in their activities.
6. Calculate the costs for these activities.
7. Add all the costs of all activities to arrive at your output costs.

The Handbook addresses each step in turn using the pilot projects to illustrate difficulties or specific examples of usage, "to breathe life into the myriad of decisions that must be made in implementing and evaluating an innovation".

The Flashlight 'Cost Analysis Handbook' proposes a breakdown of staff time into six categories: teaching, research/scholarship, professional growth, administration, consulting/freelance work and 'other', thus allowing academic time to be costed directly to activities. Surprisingly, the Handbook makes no reference to how time should be recorded.

The Handbook notes that there are many difficulties in accessing costs in higher education including: the various pricing and accounting methods used by different institutions at different stages, and the issues of hidden subsidies such as external funding. It goes on to mention that the framework offered appears simple to achieve but that the hardest task is often gathering the actual costs to begin with.

Part three of the Handbook constructs a sample model using examples from the pilot projects. It states quite clearly that "one of the most critical steps in cost analysis involves the process of defining activities and breaking these up into tasks". The report encourages the developer to think of the Economic Model as "a pyramid of linked spreadsheets, the first spreadsheet contains data on total costs while those cells are linked to totals and sub totals on lower levels which break the total and sub total costs down to individual cost categories for selected activities and tasks". This is a nice theory and a good analogy, but, we suspect, 'mind-blowing' in practical application.

3.3.3   Department for Education, Training and Youth Affairs, Australia

In 1998, the Australian Department for Education, Training and Youth Affairs (DETYA) funded a project, which analyzed the need for, and then developed, a costing methodology for use within Australian Higher Education. Recent policy changes had led to a more competitive environment and in order to take advantage of this, Australian universities needed to be able to measure the full costs of their activities in a more robust manner. The deficiency of costing information was noted to have been of little concern in the previously non-competitive market, but now universities had to be able to assimilate accurate and timely costing information.

The DETYA report, which was undertaken with the assistance of Ernst and Young, noted that while costing systems appear simple in concept, they are often complicated and costly to implement successfully, resulting in animosity. Cultural resistance, considered to be one of the largest problems, was suggested to be easier to overcome by establishing effective communication channels and appropriate staff training.

The study was split into two sections; the first, an issues report, conducted interviews at eleven 'interested' institutions and administered a sector-wide survey on costings issues. The high number of returns and detailed comments of the survey participants indicated the need for detailed costing information. The interviews centered on topics such as: what cost information already existed; what cost information was desirable; and how this information should be collected. The second section of the report trialed the ideas in the participating institutions.

The project team decided that their research pointed them towards an Activity-Based Management (ABM) approach. This is based upon two guiding principles: activities consume resources; and then services, customers or other cost objectives consume activities. In an increasingly commercial environment the reports states that it is helpful to link the costs of provision, such as a course, or research project, with the revenue received from its participants. While ABC provides accurate product and service costs, ABM offers a clearer insight into what causes costs to exist and what drives costs, and then uses these details to inform strategic planning. In simple terms, ABM occurs when ABC information is acted upon – in other words, understanding what activities are undertaken, for what purpose and what resources they consume allows managers to make considered beneficial changes to the way institutions are run to improve overall performance. This is neatly summed up in this quote taken from the report: "It is considered that ABM can provide at least three important benefits to a university, namely: more accurate cost information, closer insights into the costs of production and better information concerning the strategic consequences of business decisions" (DETYA, 1998a).

ABM has two phases of model building, activities and cost objects, and four major steps in each:

1. Project scoping and start-up.
2. Costing activities.
3. Costing cost objects.
4. Reporting.

The DETYA report also provides a comprehensive 15-stage lifecycle costing model to express the chain of income and expenditure. Among others, they judge that the following activities take place:

- Development of a new course.
- Marketing.
- Processing of enrolments.
- Provision of direct teaching, course support, library/computing facilities and student support.
- Graduation of students.
- Provision of various types of infrastructure (building, administrative and academic).

The whole methodology has been trialed in differing departments and faculties of three institutions – the results of these case studies are still awaited. Although encouraging the universities in Australia to participate, DETYA seems clear that it will not be moving on to a more directive phase where institutions are told to adopt such principles.

3.3.4   The Costs of Networked Learning, United Kingdom

The 'Costs of Networked Learning' (CNL) project, upon which much of this chapter is based, was undertaken by Sheffield Hallam University between January and June 1999. The final report was published in October of the same year. The main aims of the project were to identify the unrecorded or hidden costs involved in networked learning and to produce a planning document and financial schema that together would accurately record the costs of networked learning for the benefit of policy makers, course providers and students. The initial remit of the project was to produce the planning document and financial schema as mentioned above; the project team have been successful in securing further funding to take the theoretical framework arrived at in phase one and to develop it into a practical handbook. This section will look only at the outcomes of phase one of the project; for more detailed information please refer directly to our project report (Bacsich et al., 1999).

The Financial Schema
Our research showed that the 'traditional' financial model used in the UK, which underpins university, department, and course planning, is defective in at least four ways:

- It takes no account of the costs incurred (or saved) by the additional stakeholders in the learning process other than the institution – in other words, it treats the institution as a *closed system*.
- It assumes a crude allocation of overheads (e.g. by simple cost drivers such as staff numbers or space occupied) rather than an approach based on usage (e.g. number of online student hours per year).
- It takes little account of the division of academic time into research, teaching and administration.
- It takes no account of the activities *within* the course development process.
- One of the main problems leading to the above deficiencies is the lack of a concise, usable financial *proforma* which is flexible enough to apply to a number of different learning situations.

During the study we analyzed around ten different schemas. These include the KPMG Costing Guidelines (1997) for university financial planning, the US Flashlight Cost Analysis Handbook (Ehrmann & Milam, 1999) which is rapidly gaining popularity in US HE (discussed above), and a number of more traditional schemas including some from the training sector. The financial schema adopts

Activity-Based costing at its heart, and also the stakeholder approach, as discovered early in the project, of the institution, staff and students. With these two criteria the project expected that the hidden costs could be uncovered.

The KPMG Guidelines were completed in 1997 as a venture between the joint Funding Councils and KPMG Management Consultants. Two main conclusions were reached, based on a survey administered by the Funding Council and a review of costing practices at ten volunteer institutions. These conclusions were:

- The UK HE sector places a high importance on accurate costing information.
- An acceptable method of recording staff costs against activities is needed.

The Report proposes a five-step process for recording costs:

1. Determine the cost objective.
2. Identify activities which contribute to the cost objective.
3. Assign resource costs to activities.
4. Link activities to the cost objective.
5. Analyze and report results.

The authors identified the cost objective as the purpose of costing; this will influence the process used and accuracy required. It identified three methods of assigning costs to objectives: direct attribution; estimation; and apportionment based on prior knowledge and experience.

The report states that a typical UK university expenditure account will contain four categories: staff costs, including wages, salaries, social security and pension costs; depreciation; other operating expenses; and interest payable. To ensure that the schema works on a number of levels, we have excluded interest payable and included overheads, as this category is so easily misunderstood. If we link the stakeholder categories (agreed upon earlier in the project), Institution, Staff and Students, to the expenditure categories, we get the matrix in the table below.

Table 3.2 Example of the financial schema

Expenditure dimension	Stakeholder dimension			Total
	Institution	Staff	Student	
Staff costs	Salaries, wages, pensions *etc.*	Opportunity cost of not doing a better job	Opportunity cost of learning not earning	
Depreciation	Buildings, computing provision	Own home computer and accessories	Own home computer and accessories	
Expenses	Subsistence, registration	Expenses incurred on business travel	IT consumables, connection charges	
Overhead	Software licences	Additional energy requirements	Additional insurance	
Total				

The KPMG work also reported that for the majority of academic staff the following breakdown of time would be suitable:

- Teaching, including main course undergraduate and postgraduate.
- Research, including grants, contracts and general research.
- Other service activities including short courses and consultancy.
- Department administration and other professional activities (e.g. chair of a professional body).
- Faculty and university administration.

Regarding finding out the amount of time that staff spent on the various activities, the following sources of activity information were considered:

- Use information from the department's workload planning systems.
- Ask program managers to estimate staff time spent on each activity.
- Conduct a survey of academic staff to estimate the proportion of time they spend on each activity.
- Conduct a diary or timesheet exercize, as a one-off or ongoing project.

The Development of a Course Lifecycle Model

The provisional course lifecycle model was developed as a result of the literature review. Cost items mentioned by other authors were listed and a short report compiled to analyze the currently available models used for costing educational practice. The study team had already discussed at length the inappropriateness of traditional financial management accounting procedures, which are not suited to exposing the hidden costs of networked learning.

After many discussions a three-phase model was proposed. The following table illustrates how some course-related activities fit into the above model.

Table 3.3 Breakdown of three-phase model

Planning and Development	Brainstorming initial concept Writing the business plan Purchasing and evaluating existing materials or developing your own
Production and Delivery	Curriculum delivery Progress monitoring Marking and feedback
Evaluation and Maintenance	Quality assurance exercizes Replacement and updating of materials Evaluation against course aims outlined in business plan

However, this model did not arrive overnight. First, the team held a series of short consultative meetings with a number of academics at Sheffield Hallam University about the lifecycle of course development and delivery. A three-unit human resource model of academic staff, support staff and students and a five-phase cyclic model which encompassed providing both the learning experience and the learning environment was proposed. The model aimed to show the relationship between people and activities and therefore expose possible areas of hidden costs.

This model was tested at two stages in the course of the project; with interviewees during the institutional visits and at a one-day workshop held to progress the thoughts of the study team.

Subsequently, it was decided by the study team that the five-phase model was too complex and that a four-phase Business-Process-Re-engineering (BPR) model, as proposed by the workshop attendees, would not resonate with the UK Higher Education sector, or make apparent the hidden costs.

The three-phase model was then rechecked against the literature including additional training-focused literature (analyzed later on in the project, due to its bias towards ABC). The table below contains a summary showing how the most significant models compare.

Table 3.4 Analysis of three phase model against leading experts

Standard	Bates (1995)	Rumble (1997)	Stahmer (1995)	Moonen (1997)
Planning & Development	Production	Production including Development	Research & Planning Development	Development
Production & Delivery	Delivery	Transmission & Distribution Reception	Delivery	Production, Delivery, Operation...
Maintenance & Evaluation	(omitted)	(omitted)	(omitted)	... and Maintenance

It is worth noting that evaluation is not covered when costs are considered, even though the authors involved are well aware of evaluation issues.

The Planning Document

Any proposed planning framework needs to resonate with financial managers, planners, and administrative and academic staff. It therefore needs to be understandable and usable with the minimum amount of guidance. It also needs to be based on tried and accepted methods. The framework is expected to be relevant to different approaches to networked learning and make apparent which costs should be recorded and where, thus eliminating hidden costs.

A planning document was proposed with similar features to our financial schema, such as the levels of operability and focus on ABC.

The Study Team surveyed the research literature produced by major academic authorities that is relevant to the area of planning and decision-making in the use of C&IT for teaching in higher education. There is, in our view, relatively little in the literature of value to planners and finance staff, with the exception of Tony Bates' ACTIONS methodology (1995).

In his book 'Technology, Open Learning and Distance Education', Bates (1995) devotes a great deal of attention to the planning process, or as he calls it, "building a framework for decision-making".

This requires a framework to work in a variety of contexts, and a number of levels, including institution-wide and at the course level. In addition, it should give equal attention to instructional and operational issues, identify differences between technologies and accommodate new developments in technology. However, Bates does not state explicitly (though we believe it to be implicit in his work) that the framework should accommodate conventional teaching and learning solutions.

Bates' framework has received a great deal of attention worldwide. It is entitled **ACTIONS**.

Table 3.5 Our representation of the ACTIONS model

Access	How accessible is a particular technology for learners?
	How flexible is it for a particular target group?
Costs	What is the cost structure of each technology?
	What is the unit cost per learner?
Teaching and Learning	What kinds of learning are needed?
	What instructional approaches will best meet this need?
	What are the best technologies for supporting this teaching and learning?
Organizational issues	What are the organizational requirements and the barriers to be removed, before this technology can be used successfully?
	What changes in organization can be made?
Novelty	How new is this technology?
Speed	How quickly can courses be mounted with this technology?
	How quickly can materials be changed?

The Higher Education Funding Council for England (HEFCE) has recently looked at the planning process, in 'Appraising Investment Decisions' (1999). Annex C to this document outlines how the proposed methodology can be used to decide on a teaching and learning issue. The CNL study team rewrote the HEFCE document to reposition it fully to the development of courses, and we believe the result is surprisingly convincing.

Thus, instead of trying (as several have done) to transform educators' attempts at course planning into planners' language, we propose to transform planners' attempts at planning into educators' language. This has the additional advantage in that as decisions about networked learning begin to impact on the estate's strategy (e.g. by substituting home-based learning for lecturing or by providing video lecturing to remote sites), at least both sides of the debate will speak the same language.

What the HEFCE document lacks is the educational framework. We recommend that this is added from the authoritative work of Bates (1995).

3.4   Conclusions

While each of the four costing projects outlined above is individual in remit and outcomes, they all display a number of similarities, including the main aims of the projects and the context within which each has been funded. Each methodology aimed to produce a comprehensive costing framework to allow users to assess the costs of using networked learning, and the consequent impact on the institution. Two of the methodologies put forward the view that costings information should be particular to the institution to which it refers, indeed the US Flashlight Cost Analysis Handbook (CAH) methodology only offers guidance and the building blocks for the individual institution to construct its own costing framework. In contrast, the US Technology Costing Methodology (TCM) and the UK Costs of Networked Learning (CNL) Program both stress the importance of being able to compare costing information both within and between institutions.

All four of the costings studies are addressing the same need, namely to determine the costs of using networked learning either to support more conventional teaching methods or to reach completely new markets by using fully online courses. The Cost Analysis Handbook produced by the US Flashlight team notes that much of the educational technology that has been adopted is in addition to traditional methods rather than substituting for at least part of the provision, thus greatly increasing the cost. Other related issues such as the effectiveness of networked learning and how the costs of networked learning compare to those of conventional teaching are present explicitly in only one of the above projects, the US-based TCM. Work in these areas is being undertaken as separate studies by the other two projects.

All of the projects have adopted ABC at the core of their frameworks for recording the costs of networked learning. This method of accounting which allocates the costs directly to activities, rather than to vague, overarching categories, is essential for breaking down institutional costs in more detail than the accepted norm. Only with ABC can we hope to accurately record the costs of networked learning, and other types of learning on a number of levels.

The Australian report, compiled with the help of Ernst and Young, takes this one step further and proposes the use of ABM, a set of strategic principles based on institutional activities. With the adoption of ABC, issues such as the recording of staff time by activity and the breakdown of the academic working day will have to be resolved. At this stage only Flashlight indicates within the study a suitable breakdown of the activities academic staff are involved in. None of the methodologies have explicitly approached the issue how exactly to record staff time but all have acknowledged its importance. Hopefully as the projects move forward into further phases, as all are doing, this problem will be resolved.

The UK-based 'Costs of Networked Learning' project appears to be alone in realizing the importance of addressing costing issues from a multi-stakeholder viewpoint. We believe that it is crucial to understand that both staff and students personally incur, and save, costs as a result of networked learning. Indeed the CNL project notes that as far as costing is concerned the University can no longer be treated as a closed institution. The CNL project is also alone with regard to its proposed course lifecycle model; although the DETYA work does propose a lifecycle model of institutional activities within which the course lifecycle sits.

Above all, each project presents an individual framework for costing networked learning. The Flashlight team propose a seven-stage process for building your own model, the 'Technology Costing Methodology' and the DETYA work both propose a number of steps to follow in order to cost networked learning and the UK-based CNL work presents a financial schema upon which costs can be recorded.

Next Steps

Hopefully, this short canter through some of the main issues of, and projects concentrating on, the costs of networked learning has been a valuable use of your time. We aimed to present a reasoned discussion as to why costing networked learning has become important and then communicate to you an outline of the most recent, and in some cases current, costings studies.

Taking our own work in this area, and that of our colleagues involved in other costings studies, we have compiled the following 'Principles of Good Costing':

- Must be based on Activity-Based Costing.
- Must utilize a stakeholder approach.
- Must go hand-in-hand with planning and evaluation.
- Must be universal, or at least cross-sectoral.
- Must have well-rooted pedagogic basis.
- Must be free-standing, so that use does not rely on extensive training.
- Must allow comparisons both internally and externally.
- Must be ongoing, not just end of year.
- Must be based on real "consumption" figures not guesstimates.
- Must function on a number of levels – from the whole institution to a single course.

3.5   Acknowledgements

The authors would like to acknowledge the support of the Joint Information Systems Committee and Sheffield Hallam University for funding the 'Costs of Networked Learning' project. In addition the authors would like to thank the Flashlight team, the WICHE and NCHEMS project group, and DETYA, not only for allowing their work to be discussed here but also for their open approach to collaboration on a worldwide basis.

3.6   References

Alexander, S., Mckenzie, J., & Geissinger, H. (1998) *An Evaluation of Information Technology Projects for University Learning*. Australia: Committee for University Teaching and Staff Development

Arizona Learning Systems (1998*) Preliminary Cost Methodology for Distance Learning*, Report dated 21 August 1998, Arizona Learning Systems and the State Board of Directors for Community Colleges of Arizona

Bacsich, P., Ash, C., Boniwell, K., Kaplan, L., Mardell, J., & Caven-Atack, A. (1999*) The Costs of Networked Learning*. Sheffield Hallam University, Sheffield

Bates, A.W. (1995) *Technology, Open Learning and Distance Education*. London: Routledge

Collis, B. (1996) *Tele-Learning in a Digital World: The future of distance learning*. London: International Thompson Computer Press

Crabb, G. (Ed.) (1990) *Costing Open and Flexible Learning*. Coventry: NCET

CRE (1998*) Restructuring the University: New Technologies for Teaching and Learning: Guidance to universities on strategy. (CRE Guide No. 1)* Geneva: Association of European Universities

DETYA (1998a) *Costing Methodology For Use Within Australian Higher Education Institutions* Australia: DETYA

DETYA (1998b) *Issues Report On Costing Within Australian Higher Education Institutions.* Australia: DETYA

Dolton, P., Douglass Klein, J. & Weir, I. (1994) The economic evaluation of peer counselling in facilitating computer use in Higher Education. *Education Economics 2*, 313-326

Draper, S.W. & Foubister, S.P. (1998) Cost benefit analysis of remote collaborative tutorial teaching. In Oliver, M. (Ed.*) Innovation in the Evaluation of Learning Technology*. London: University of North London

Ehrmann, S.C. & Milam, J.H. (1999) *Flashlight Cost Analysis Handbook Version 1.0: Modeling Resource Use in Teaching and Learning with Technology*. Washington DC: The TLT Group

Green, K.C. (1999) *Campus Computing 1998: The ninth national survey of desktop computing and information technology in higher education*. California: The Campus Computing Project

Harvey, J., Kirshstein, R.J. & Wellman, J.V. (1998*) Straight Talk About College Costs And Prices: The report of the National Commission on the Cost of Higher education*. Washington DC: American Institute of Research

HEFCE (1997) *Information Assisted Teaching and Learning in Higher Education*, HEFCE Research Series. Bristol: HEFCE

HEFCE (1999) *Appraising Investment Decisions. (HEFCE Guide 99/21)* Bristol: HEFCE

HEFCE (2000) *Communications and Information Technology Audit: Delivering Enhanced Learning - A study of the use of C&IT materials in teaching and learning in Higher and Further Education in the UK*. Bristol: HEFCE

JCPSG (1999) *Costing and Pricing for Decision Makers in Higher Education: User Guide.* Bristol: HEFCE

Kirkpatrick, D. & Jakupec, V. (1999) Becoming flexible: what does it mean? In Tait, A. & Mills, R. (Eds.) *The Convergence of Distance and Conventional Education: Patterns of flexibility for the individual learner.* New York: Routledge

KPMG Management Consulting and Joint Funding Councils (1997) *Management Information for Decision Making: Costing Guidelines for Higher Education Institutions.* Bristol: HEFCE

Massy, W.F. & Zemsky, R. (1995) *Using Information Technology to Enhance Academic Productivity, Report from an Educom Roundtable.* http://www.educause.edu/nlii/keydocs/massy.html

Moonen, J. (1997) The efficiency of telelearning. *Journal of Asynchronous Learning Networks 1* (2) http://www.aln.org/alnweb/journal/issue2/moonen.htm

Moonen, J. (1998) The cost-effectiveness of flexible delivery. In Van der Wende, M. (ed) *Virtual Mobility: New technologies and the internationalization of higher education. (Nuffic Papers, no 9)* The Hague: Organization for International Cooperation in Higher Education

NCHEMS (2001) *Procedures For Calculating The Costs Of Alternative Modes Of Instructional Delivery,* in print.

NICHE (1997) *Higher Education in the Learning Society.* London: HMSO

NUS (1999) *Consultation on Section 28 of the Teaching and Higher Education Act, Submission to the DfEE* London: National Union of Students

O'Rourke, J. (1999) Canaries in the mine? Women's experience and new learning technologies. In Tait, A. & Mills, R. (Eds) *The Convergence of Distance and Conventional Education: Patterns of flexibility for the individual learner.* London: Routledge

Peebles, C.S. (1997) *Cost, Quality and Value: Assessing the networked information value chain at Indiana University.* http://www.cni.org/regconfs/1997/ukoln-content/repor~24.html

Rawlings, A., Fox, S., Hobb, V., Fox, N., Bacsich, P. & Curran C. (1993) *Telematic Networks for Open and Distance Learning in the Tertiary Sector. Scenarios, Costings and Survey. Final Report. (Volume 1-2)* Heerlen: EADTU

Rumble, G. (1997) *The Costs and Economics of Open and Distance Learning.* London: Kogan Page

Rumble, G. (1999) *The Costs of Networked Learning: What have we learnt?* Paper presented at the FLISH99 Conference. http://www.shu.ac.uk/flish/rumblep.htm

Stahmer, A. (1995) *Assessing Costs, Benefits and Return on Investment for Technology-based Training: Tools for decision makers,* Paper presented at Online Educa Berlin, 1st. International Conference on Technology Supported Learning

Temple, H. (1995) *Cost-effectiveness of Open Learning for Small Firms: A study of First Experiences of Open Learning.* Sheffield: DfEE

Tonks, D. & Long, G. (1989) The hidden costs of marketing simulations. *Simulation/Games for Learning 19,* 24-34

4. Psychological Foundations for Networked Learning

Peter Goodyear

4.1 Introduction

This chapter is intended to provide an account of the psychology of networked learning for the practical purpose of informing educational design decisions in this rapidly changing area. Because of the relative rapidity of change in the technological platforms being used, the account is necessarily at a somewhat abstract level. It is meant to underpin the formation of some practical pedagogical knowledge that can outlast some of the more detailed operational changes in networked learning environments.

A multiplicity of accounts of learning can be found in the educational and psychological literature. For university staff who have no formal background in the learning sciences, this apparent richness can be a source of great confusion. It is commonly said that no two educational theories agree, that no two 'educational experts' will give the same advice, and that it is almost impossible to derive specific practical implications from the abstractions of educational theory. Add to this the fact that some of what comes to the hand of the university teacher, in the 'learning theory' literature, has a dubious conceptual, theoretical or empirical basis, and the situation becomes deeply frustrating.

In this chapter, I will offer (a) a single, simple, coherent account of learning which articulates the best knowledge available to us from the learning sciences, (b) an extension of parts of this account, suited to the specific needs of those planning to teach through the use of networked learning methods, and (c) some implications for educational design decisions. Since this is a book about networked learning in higher education, I will focus on what we know about adult learning (as distinct from the bulk of the learning literature which relates to the education of children) and about academic learning (which is different, in some important ways, from learning through everyday experience).[1]

It is important to be realistic about what an account of learning can and cannot be expected to do. It cannot be expected to provide rules or algorithms for optimizing learning. Interpretive work must be done to draw out specific implications for practice and there will usually be rival interpretations. At some point, a personal pedagogical commitment needs to be made – not a pure act of faith, but one that allows principled action to be taken. It is also important to recognize that there is a legitimate gap between the tasks we set for learners (based on the best of what we know from the learning sciences) and the activities in which they actually engage. In higher education, particularly, we cannot expect our learners to be totally compliant – pedagogy and educational design will only take us so far (Goodyear, 2000). I will try to sketch the scope and limits of what is on offer in this chapter. After that, I will offer a brief analysis of some relevant characteristics of both higher education and networked learning, to reduce the size of the problem we would be tackling if confronted with all kinds of learning at all levels of education. Then I will sketch a model of learning as a process of *guided knowledge construction*, before moving to a consideration of some special aspects of *collaborative networked learning*. This is interspersed with some suggestions about implications for practice of the account of learning on offer. However, the chapter concludes with a section on how we can use educational design as a way of embodying and sharing some implications of the theoretical accounts of 'good learning'.

4.2   Scope and Limits

Part of my argument in this chapter is that Psychology has some useful conceptual resources on which we should draw in understanding, planning and managing what goes on in networked learning situations. Psychology does not offer a definitive or comprehensive account of learning. Indeed, much of the most innovative work on human learning in the last 10-15 years represents a reaction to some of the positions adopted by Psychology. For example, during the 1970s and 80s,

---

[1]   Tom Shuell and Diana Laurillard have separately advanced the case that much of what Psychology calls 'learning' is different in kind from the learning that is fostered in educational organizations like schools and universities. The learning (in people but also in rats, pigeons *et al.*) that most psychologists have studied over the last 100 years or so is a natural process which depends on cognitive capabilities we have developed in order to survive in our various ecological niches. Shuell distinguishes this natural learning from 'learning from instruction' (Shuell, 1992). Laurillard draws our attention to a peculiar characteristic of academic knowledge: that it is 'articulated' knowledge, consisting of other peoples' descriptions of the world. This 'second order' quality distinguishes it from much of the 'first order' knowledge which we acquire through direct experience of the world. 'Natural' learning is mainly concerned with percepts, while academic learning is more concerned with precepts (Laurillard, 1987).

Cognitive Psychology made great strides in developing explanations of learning, based on information processing models of human cognition. These were capable of modeling, with impressive detail and accuracy, some important aspects of human problem-solving and knowledge-acquisition – particularly in areas such as the acquisition of cognitive skills (Anderson, 1983; Klahr *et al.*, 1987; Chipman & Meyrowitz, 1993; Ohlsson, 1995; Anderson & Lebiere, 1998). As is often the case in science, some of the most impressive results were achieved by simplifying the phenomena under consideration and by adopting a narrow interpretive focus in modelling empirical results. (As Diana Laurillard pointed out, what psychologists tend to mean when they talk about 'learning' is different from what educators and educational researchers mean (Laurillard, 1987). Much of what teachers mean when they talk about 'learning' is still missing from the models of information-processing in cognitive science.)

The accounts produced by Cognitive Psychology came under fire for neglecting the socially situated nature of human thought and action and for placing disembodied, symbolic representations of thought above the messy improvizations and contingencies of real-world action (see the critiques of e.g. Lave, 1988; Suchman, 1987; Brown *et al.* 1989; Greeno, 1997 and the rejoinders of e.g. Anderson *et al.*, 1996, 1997). The learning sciences are now beginning to achieve a greater range in their representation of the phenomena of human learning and to regain some of the methodological rigour of the work in information-processing Cognitive Psychology. In this chapter, I will be drawing particularly on work emerging from the Cognitive Psychology tradition, but will also be drawing on aspects of work which have more to say about social aspects of learning. Networked learning is inherently social – part of the point of encouraging online communications within a learning group (or 'learning community') is to capitalize on some of the social aspects of learning. Consequently I will be paying particular attention to some of the work on collaborative learning, on epistemic tasks/games and on the co-construction of working knowledge. Some writers in the field of networked learning advocate, but find difficulty in explaining, networked collaborative learning. I will draw on some work by Pierre Dillenbourg and colleagues (e.g. Dillenbourg, 1999) to try to add some plausible psychological detail to some of the existing sketches of what empowers good networked collaborative learning. Online discussion *can* be a fruitful source of insights into academic ideas, but it can also appear to be directionless, trivial and self-indulgent. There is still only a partial account available of how language and understanding connect. I will introduce some ideas about discourse and understanding – clarifying the nature of, and claiming some importance for, epistemic tasks (or epistemic games) as ways of conceptualizing and improving students' understanding. Finally, I will draw on some of the implications of our own research on the co-construction of working knowledge. I will introduce the idea of 'working knowledge' as a useful though imprecise organizing construct within higher education and will show how networked learning can help with continuing professional development programs, conceived as the collaborative creation of working knowledge.

4.3   Conceptions of Learning in Higher Education

Given the contested nature of higher education and its fundamental purposes, it is difficult to talk about effective learning without establishing some common ground about valued kinds of learning outcome. I will focus on three conceptions of the nature and purposes of higher education in order to sketch the main kinds of learning outcomes they imply. The three can be called academic, generic competence and reflexive (Goodyear, 1999). The academic conception is relatively traditional; the generic competence and reflexive conceptions appear less so. I will sketch each in turn, before attempting a synthesis.

4.3.1   Academic

As the primary form of traditional university education, this asks students to become competent in academic discourse, with its heavy reliance on declarative conceptual knowledge, contemplative forms of analysis and use of textual (including mathematical) representations (Barnett, 1997). Implicitly or explicitly, it acts as if the aim were to induct students into the work and world of the academic and their discipline. Though its position as the dominant model for higher education is now seriously contested, it nevertheless underpins much of what goes on in educational technology. Diana Laurillard's influential book on *Rethinking University Teaching* (1993), for example, pays no sustained attention to other conceptions of what university education might be for. The main kind of learning outcome associated with this conception is the ability to recall declarative conceptual knowledge and deploy it in the construction of arguments, or in the solution of problems more generally.

4.3.2   Generic Competence

Through a variety of organizations and methods, employers have been pressing higher education to pay more attention to the qualities they claim they need in the new graduates they wish to recruit. These demands *may* include the kinds of specialized technical knowledge acquired by some students on some courses but increasingly they refer to generic competencies (otherwise known as core skills or transferable skills). Frequently mentioned generic competencies include literacy, numeracy, communication, foreign language, leadership, teamworking and IT skills (e.g. Harvey & Mason, 1996; Assiter, 1995; NCIHE, 1997).

Lee Harvey's 'Quality in Higher Education' survey data provide some useful evidence about what U.K. employers feel they need, and are getting, from recent graduates (see e.g. Harvey & Mason, 1996:17-23). In summary, employers:

- Rarely rate specialized knowledge as a key factor determining whether they will hire a recent graduate, since this knowledge is unlikely to add enough to the organization's expertize to affect its competitive edge, is liable to rapid obsolescence and is rarely in a form which the graduate can apply in the solution of important work-related problems;

- Value graduates' intellectual flexibility, powers of logical analysis, ability to conceptualize issues rapidly and to deal with large amounts of information but believe that graduates are insufficiently innovative, in part because they are insufficiently sensitive to the organizational implications of innovation;

- Feel that graduates are generally better able to deal with some of the basic requirements of working in a modern organization (being dependable and highly motivated) than others (e.g. coping with pressure, managing time);

- Believe that graduates are usually naive about organizational politics, industrial relations, knowing how to deal with people of different seniorities, and at recognizing other peoples' motivations;

- Believe that graduates lack tact and are arrogant, especially in their relations with non-graduate working colleagues; though they are often excellent teamworkers;

- Comment very negatively about graduates' communication skills, especially about listening skills ('hearing what is meant as well as what is said'), oral presentation skills and the range of writing skills (especially the difficulties they have in writing persuasive cases). Employers did not value IT skills particularly highly (29th of 62) and were generally very satisfied with graduates' IT skills (4th of 62).

Reflecting on this data and the results of similar studies of employers' expressed needs, Harvey and Knight (1996) conclude that organizations which recruit graduates are looking, above all else, for *transformative potential*. That is, they want new graduates entering their employ to have the capacity to transform their organization, not merely to enhance its productivity and competitiveness along current lines. Elements of this transformative potential can be discerned in the six bullet points above and include willingness to learn; ability to deal with change and question assumptions; analytic, critical and problem-solving skills, as well as the knowledge and ideas (a 'fresh creative mind') brought to the organization (Harvey & Mason, 1996:14).

4.3.3   Critical Being and Reflexivity

This third conception is best articulated in the writing of Ronald Barnett (e.g. 1994, 1997a, 1997b, 2000; Barnett & Griffin, 1997). Rejecting 'academicist' and 'operational competence' conceptions, Barnett looks to a higher education "fit for the 21st century". He argues that individual reflexivity ("the capacity to go on interrogating one's taken-for-granted universe") is necessary for dealing with an essentially unknowable modern world. Higher education needs to respond by:

- Supporting the student in their acquisition of discursive competence: offering a deep understanding of some discursive realm and an insight into what it is

like to handle with confidence the concepts, theories and ideas of a field of
thought, to handle complex ideas in communication with others;
- Encouraging self-reflexiveness: by framing the student's initiation into a field
  of thought such that they see its essential openness and how they may be
  actors in it;
- Encouraging informed but critical action: understanding the power and
  limitations of the field as a resource for action (Barnett, 1997b:22-25).

A key part of Barnett's argument rests on a postmodernist conviction that we
can have no certain knowledge of the world, and that consequently knowledge and
skills become redundant or marginal (Barnett & Griffin, 1997:29).

4.3.4   Synthesis

There are some striking differences between these three conceptions.   The
'academic' conception values the acquisition and use of declarative 'second order'
knowledge. Barnett's conception sidelines knowledge and promotes the adoption
of a critical stance. The 'generic competence' conception values a range of key
skills and pre-dispositions, and an ability to acquire and use 'local' organizational
knowledge.

Considering these views, I have difficulty with the postmodern thesis that all
knowledge is socially constructed or highly volatile and hence fundamentally
arbitrary or marginal. This position does not stand examination if one is concerned
about the effectiveness of action in the world. This argument applies whether one
is considering the knowledge used by a surgeon in carrying out a routine operation,
the knowledge used by an apprentice academic in debating key ideas within her
discipline or the knowledge used by a project team member in a company. Insofar
as we feel a moral duty to help our students act effectively in the world then we
cannot subscribe to the 'end of knowledge' position.

Knowledge then becomes a common theme, but it is a special kind of
knowledge. This leads me towards two ideas that help articulate some core values
in higher education.

1. The idea that higher education is a site for the development and use of
   'working knowledge'.
2. The idea that the speed of change in modern knowledge-based economies,
   coupled with a need to be open to diverse views on what counts as
   worthwhile knowledge, requires students to develop a flexibility in their use
   of knowledge – something Alan Collins calls 'epistemic fluency' (Morrison
   & Collins, 1996).

Working Knowledge
I like the term 'working knowledge' because it sets up a number of appealing
resonances:

- The idea of knowledge which is relevant to one's work (when the work may be in academia or in what other people take to be the real world);
- The idea of knowledge and knowing as active and dynamic rather than passive and static. Having and using
-
-   is about much more than 'simple' recall of information from a static knowledge base tucked away in your memory. Remembering itself is reconstructive. 'Working knowledge' stands in sharp contrast to what Whitehead described as 'inert knowledge';
- The idea of knowledge being 'just sufficient' to support action. Having a 'working knowledge' of something implies a degree of improvization and a 'seat of the pants' approach: a willingness to take reasonable risks by acting at the edges of one's knowledge.

Learning in higher education should be imbued with a belief in the particular value of 'working knowledge'. Understanding and engaging with different 'ways of knowing' is key to effective action in academia *and* in the workplaces of today's knowledge economy.

Epistemic Fluency

Knowledge is constructed by the knower. People can help each other in the activities of knowledge construction. Thus, we can speak of collaborative knowledge construction or of the co-construction of knowledge. Morrison and Collins (1996) use the idea of epistemic forms and epistemic games to describe what might be involved in processes of collaborative knowledge construction. *Epistemic forms* are target knowledge building structures characteristic of, and made available by, a culture. They are guides to enquiry. Examples of epistemic forms are models (of various kinds, such as systems dynamics models, developmental sequence models), hierarchies, taxonomies, lists and axiom systems. *Epistemic games* are 'sets of moves, constraints, and strategies that guide the construction of knowledge around a particular epistemic form' (Morrison & Collins, 1996:109). An epistemic game is a way of constructing knowledge. In the complex societies of late modernity, there are many ways of knowing – many kinds of epistemic game. Morrison and Collins hold that epistemic game theory can bridge gaps between theories of conceptual change and sociolinguistic theories of language use. Since the co-construction of knowledge occurs through discourse, epistemic games offer a uniform way of analyzing knowledge building and social interaction. The development of *epistemic fluency* – the ability to recognize and practice a variety of epistemic games – occurs through *participation* in epistemic games, not just by watching them or being told about them. Epistemic fluency develops through interaction with other people who are already relatively more fluent (Morrison & Collins, 1996:114).

This suggests a particularly powerful way of thinking about networked learning, it is an opportunity to develop epistemic fluency through participation in epistemic games. The corresponding foci for educational design will be (a) identifying valued epistemic games and forms, (b) designing tasks which initiate appropriate epistemic games, (c) creating opportunities for more and less experienced players to play together and (d) making available, in the online space, tools and other artefacts appropriate for the collaborative manipulation of epistemic forms. I will give an example of what I mean later in the chapter.

4.4   Special Characteristics of Networked Learning

In this chapter, I follow the definition of 'networked learning' that we developed for our study of *Students' experiences of networked learning in Higher Education* (see Jones & Steeples, also Steeples & Jones, this volume).

Networked learning is learning in which communications and information technology (C&IT) is used to promote connections: between one learner and other learners, between learners and tutors; between a learning community and its learning resources.   Such communication can be synchronous and/or asynchronous. It can be text-only or multimedia. It may involve learners who are geographically distributed and/or learners who spend much of their time at a common location.

An important point flows from this definition, with respect to our focus on learning itself.   We need to understand learning as an individual cognitive accomplishment but we also need to understand some of the special characteristics of learning with others. It is important to move beyond merely acknowledging the importance of the social context of individual learning and beyond subscription to a hope that 'creating a learning community' (networked or otherwise) solves all one's educational design problems. The writings of people like John Seely Brown, Lucy Suchman, Jean Lave and Etienne Wenger have been enormously useful in countering the individualistic excesses of information-processing cognitive psychology. They have given us some evocative images and metaphors for what is coming to be called the 'New Learning' (Simons *et al.,* 2000).   Ideas about cognitive apprenticeship, situated learning and communities of practice have done much to revitalize thinking about learning in universities and elsewhere (Brown *et al*, 1989; Suchman, 1987; Lave & Wenger, 1991; Wenger, 1998). However, as Alan Schoenfeld has observed, much work remains to be done, at a detailed level, to flesh out our understanding of *how* (for example) peripheral participation in a community of practice engages with the acquisition of competence, understanding and status (Schoenfeld, 1999). In connecting the special, social, characteristics of networked learning to a psychological account of learning, I will draw on three lines of research that seem to me to offer aspects of a more detailed and useful interpretation. These are:

1. The work of Pierre Dillenbourg, and others, on the cognitive mechanisms, interactions and situations which underpin some important manifestations of

networked collaborative learning (Dillenbourg, 1999; Dillenbourg *et al.*, 1996)

2. The work of Allan Collins, Stellan Ohlsson and David Perkins on epistemic fluency, epistemic games and tasks and epistemic forms (Collins & Ferguson, 1993; Morrison & Collins, 1996; Ohlsson, 1995; Perkins & Blythe, 1994)

3. Some of our own research on the co-construction of working knowledge, which draws in turn on the thinking and design experiments of Carl Bereiter and Marlene Scardamalia (e.g. Goodyear, 1995; Steeples & Goodyear, 1999; Scardamalia & Bereiter, 1994).

4.5   Constructive Alignment

John Biggs' recent book on *Teaching for Quality Learning at University* (Biggs, 1999) acts as a strong reminder that teaching (and educational design more generally) needs to pay close attention to *what the learner is doing*. As we shall see in a moment, learning depends crucially on the activity of the learner, mental and physical. At the university level, we cannot control this activity at all closely. But we do need to recognize that some of the features of the educational setting which *are* under our control can be powerful influences on what the learner does. Biggs uses the phrase 'constructive alignment' to denote the aim of removing inconsistencies between the curriculum we teach, the teaching methods we use, our assessment procedures, the educational environment we create and the learning objectives we want our students to achieve (see, e.g. Biggs, 1999:25ff). In particular, 'constructive alignment' focuses attention on having clearly defined learning objectives, well-chosen learning tasks and appropriate forms of assessment. An important job for educational design is the articulation of educational purposes and the construction of tasks appropriate to those purposes (whether assessment tasks or otherwise). In short, educational design needs to focus on the constructive alignment of desired learning outcomes and appropriate learning activities. This needs some understanding of how different kinds of learning activity relate to different kinds of learning outcome.

4.6   Models of Learning

This section draws on the work of Tom Shuell (e.g. 1992) and offers a sketch of four 'models of learning'. The last of these encapsulates some core ideas from research in cognitive psychology and provides one of the best-supported accounts of learning in educational contexts. The first three – especially the first and second – are common, though often implicit, in contemporary higher education practice.

4.6.1   Shuell's Models of Learning

Learning as Passive Reception
This is so well-established as a model that we sometimes fail to recognize that we are using its assumptions in our decisions about teaching. Passive reception implies a view of knowledge as something that can be broken into discrete 'chunks' and passed intact from a teacher to a learner. It is usually accompanied by a view of the learner as inactive: an empty vessel to be filled. When teachers use a phrase such as 'getting something across', they are implicitly subscribing to this model.

Learning as Discovery
This is the mirror image of passive reception. It argues that knowledge cannot be pre-digested and passed from one mind to another. Rather, the learner must work hard at interpreting what they experience, building their own unique understandings through voyages of personal discovery. Since it is hard for a teacher (or any 'outsider') to know what will best fuel a learner's personal sense-making, the discovery approach tends to frown on intervention, leaving the learner free to plot their own course (see for example some of the positions adopted by radical constructivists – Cunningham, 1992a,b; Jonassen *et al.*, 1995).

Learning as Knowledge Deficit and Accrual
This model shares some features of 'passive reception' but is rarer in the teaching world. It is quite common, however, among builders of some kinds of computer-based learning software. It defines the goal of learning as the acquisition of knowledge in the form held by experts in the subject concerned. According to this model, learners move from novice to expert by accruing the expert's knowledge 'brick by brick'. Designers and researchers who use this model tend to place a lot of emphasis on accurate delineation of the expert's knowledge, paying less attention to the processes actually involved in acquiring expertize.

Learning as Guided Construction
This is the model which fits best with current scientific ideas about learning. 'Guided construction' gives the learner a very active part in their own learning – constructing their own knowledge in a way that resembles the discovery approach. However, the model also gives an important role to external guidance, whether from a teacher, a computer program, online resources or other learners. 'Guided construction' values the 'floundering' that is involved when one does not quite know how to solve a problem. It values subsequent reflection, through which one makes sense of the experience. It values the ability to stand back from one's learning and problem-solving, in order to take stock and switch to another strategy if appropriate. But in all this it gives a legitimate role to 'outside' sources of guidance and support.

There is a growing consensus around 'good learning', perhaps best summarized by thinking of learning as a guided process of knowledge-construction (see e.g. Shuell, 1992; Biggs, 1999; Simons *et al.*, 2000). We are likely to have greater success in improving networked learning outcomes if we design in accordance with a model that emphasizes the following five characteristics of learning: learning is active, cumulative, individual, self-regulated and goal-oriented (Shuell, 1992; Goodyear and NLinHE Project Team, 2000).

Learning is Active

The learner must carry out a variety of cognitive operations on new information, in order to make it personally meaningful. The type of cognitive processing in which the learner engages will be the major determinant of what (how effectively) they learn. One important contrast between the types of cognitive processes that a learner may carry out is between 'deep processing' and 'shallow processing'. In the former, the learner expends considerable mental effort in making personal sense of new information, with the result that they can be said to understand it. In the latter, they may (at best) add the information to memory in such a way that they can repeat it word-for-word, but without any semblance of real understanding (Marton *et al.*, 1997).

Learning is Cumulative

What a learner already knows will play a large part in determining what sense they can make of new information. The extent of relevant prior knowledge – particularly knowledge *activated* during the learning process – is a major factor in determining the efficacy of a particular learning event.

Learning is Individual

Every learner builds their own knowledge in an idiosyncratic way, using past experience and existing knowledge to make sense of new information. Since no two learners have the same knowledge and experience, all new information is dealt with in different ways by different learners. This does *not* mean that a teacher can have no insight into a learner's idiosyncratic ways of knowing.

Learning is Self-Regulated

Effective learning is characterized by both (a) the learner's awareness of their own learning activity (for example, they do not get bogged down in the details of a problem but can come up for air from time to time and reflect on what's happening), and (b) the learner's ability to take action based on this reflection. When a learner (metaphorically) stands back from their current task, or 'moves up' to look at it from a higher level, they are said to be engaging in metacognitive activity. Metacognitive skills include reflectiveness and self-regulation. Effective learners often have a good idea about how they learn, and are able to use that knowledge to monitor and adjust their approach to problems (Vermunt & Rijswijk, 1988; Vermunt, 1998).

Learning is Goal-Oriented

Teachers don't always have clear ideas about why they are asking learners to undertake certain tasks (for example, working through a set of exercizes in a text book). The model of learning we are advocating says that clear goals are needed if learning is to be effective, and that these goals need to be understood by the learner. These goals may be set by the learner, or the teacher, or through a process of negotiation involving both. The important thing is that the goals are explicit and remain explicit.

Basing the design of a networked learning system around a strong and coherent model of learning is the best we can currently do if we want to improve the chances of improving learning outcomes. We also need to think about other aspects of the learning process and especially we need to consider the learner's *experience* of networked learning. The more we think of learners as free consumers of learning opportunities in a global e-learning supermarket, the more we have to worry about the quality of their experience. Even if we reject such a consumerist image of learning, there are many good reasons to pay attention to the learner's subjective experience. A learner who is frustrated or demotivated by their networked learning experience is unlikely to do well and is unlikely to volunteer to try networked learning again (Hara & Kling, 1999).

4.7   Collaborative Learning – Cognitive Mechanisms

Dillenbourg (1999) offers an excellent account of collaboration in learning processes from a cognitive psychology perspective. He is especially interested in problem-based tasks and looks at both paired and group-based collaborations.

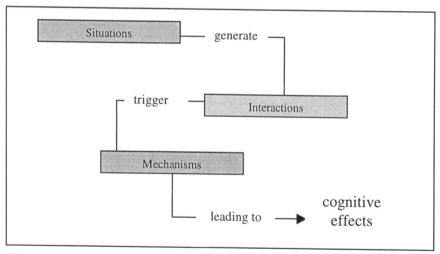

Figure 4.1 Indirect connections between learning situations and cognitive effects (learning outcomes)

Figure 4.1 is an interpretation of how he links learning situations, interactions, cognitive mechanisms and cognitive effects when groups engage in solving problems. This model is useful in that it emphasizes the indirect connection between a collaborative learning situation and its learning outcomes. There are important intervening variables: situations generate interaction patterns; interactions trigger cognitive mechanisms; mechanisms generate cognitive effects. What the learner *does* is important (interactions; cognitive processes and mechanisms). We cannot influence this directly, but we can try to create *situations* which are conducive to promoting helpful interactions.

The cognitive mechanisms Dillenbourg suggests include:

Conflict or disagreement referring to when diverging viewpoints lead to verbal interactions in order to resolve a conflict. Social factors can help force the group to find a solution. This can occur through diverging views rather than a need for a situation of intense conflict. It is the verbal interactions generated during the resolution that can help promote learning.

A slightly 'softer' take is where group members pose alternative propositions. Encouraging groups to offer alternative proposals can help reduce or even avoid a confirmatory bias that can occur in groups where members find it easier to agree with each other than to propose an alternative viewpoint.

(Self-) explanation is a mechanism that can be used e.g. in learning pairs where a more able learner explains to the other. In this process of giving an explanation there can be learning gains for both the person explaining and for the person hearing the explanation. However there is need to ensure that the person explaining gives an elaborated explanation, in order for there to be learning gain. Self-explanations can also be valuable.

Internalization happens when a conversation leads to a progressive integrating of ideas under discussion into one's own reasoning. For internalization to be triggered, the ideas must be within the neighbourhood of the person's current cognitive level. This mechanism therefore echoes Vygotsky's work on a 'zone of proximal development'.

Appropriation is an interesting notion in that Dillenbourg suggests that interpretations or playing-back of our ideas, by others to ourselves, can actually help us to gain a richer understanding of our original conceptions.

Shared cognitive load is a principle of economy, in that group-based work can allow members spontaneously to share out a task, to avoid redundancies and to optimize effort matched to the skills or knowledge within the group.

Mutual regulation occurs when group members justify their actions to each other. This can be quite a normal part of group work, where members report on their actions to each other for progress checking, *etc.*

Social grounding is the process by which a member of a group or pair can maintain belief that their partners have understood that their meaning. It is a process by which a shared understanding is formed and developed.

One will quickly realize, looking at these mechanisms, that they can be highly inter-related. For example, by explaining to others, mutual regulation can occur and appropriation can be used to help the process of social grounding.

4.7.1   Situations

One way to think about these mechanisms constructively is to examine the kinds of collaborative learning *situations* we can design for online activity, and identify how likely those situations are to generate *interactions*, among the group of students, which may in turn trigger or support appropriate cognitive *mechanisms*. One quickly realizes that some mechanisms are likely to be more easily enabled. For example, online discussions require learners to create explanations, that might involve the members posing alternative positions, wherein the process of social grounding can occur. Reporting back, in a group-based project task, by one of its members, can ensure mutual regulation. A group-based task may help share cognitive load especially if the mix of skills within the group is optimized. In which case, less able members (in specific skills areas) may gain by observing the performance of the more able in those specific skills areas (internalization).

One might also want to think about the types of situations that can provoke disagreement or generate conflicting ideas that need to be resolved. What situations might involve learners giving interpretations of each other's views? This might be encouraged through role-play for example.

4.8   Understanding, Discourse and Epistemic Games

The literature on learning in higher education is surprizingly quiet with respect to what both lay people and practitioners might expect to be a key construct – that of 'understanding'. (See Entwistle & Entwistle, 1997; Marton & Booth, 1997.) What does it mean to understand something? Stellan Ohlsson (1995) offers an interesting approach to this problem. He uses the idea of epistemic tasks to cast aspects of understanding into the language of discourse and action. He offers the definitions summarized in Table 4.1 as a complete taxonomy of epistemic tasks. Each of these connects understanding with the production of discourse.

What have these to do with the psychology of networked learning? At one level I think they are useful as guides to the assessment or evaluation of online discourse. Analyzing the content of networked learning discussions is a troublesome research area and several commentators have remarked on the difficulty of connecting online texts to discourse to learning (see e.g. Henri, 1991; Howell-Richardson & Mellar, 1996; Hara *et al.*, 2000). Part of the problem arises from the lack of a strong theoretical model that can claim to link language and learning. Ohlsson's account of epistemic tasks begins to do this. Secondly, one can argue that the tasks have design potential and that in the social or collaborative learning situations of networked learning they become candidates for epistemic games of the kind referred to by Allan Collins.

Table 4.1 Ohlsson's taxonomy of epistemic tasks

Describing	To fashion a discourse referring to an object/event such that a person who partakes of that discourse acquires an accurate conception of the object/event
Explaining	To fashion a discourse in relation to an event such that a person who partakes of that discourse understands why that event happened
Predicting	To fashion a discourse such that a person who partakes of that discourse becomes convinced that such and such an event will happen (under such and such circumstances)
Arguing	To state reasons for (or against) a particular position on some issue, thereby increasing (or decreasing) the recipient's confidence that the position is right
Critiquing (evaluating)	To fashion a discourse about something (especially a cultural product) such that a person who partakes of that discourse becomes aware of the good and bad points of that thing
Explicating	To explicate a concept is to fashion a discourse such that the person who partakes of that discourse acquires a clearer understanding of its meaning
Defining	To define a term is to propose a usage for it

4.9   Co-construction of Knowledge

An important context for thinking about epistemic games is in relation to knowledge-sharing activities in online programs of continuing professional development (CPD). The use of networked learning methods for CPD has a relatively long history at Lancaster University. Such programs have been running at Masters level since 1989 in Management Learning and in Educational Research (see e.g. Hardy *et al.* 1991; McConnell, 2000; Goodyear & Steeples, 1993). In research projects associated with these CPD programs, we have developed ideas about the facilitation of knowledge-sharing in geographically distributed (but electronically networked) professional communities. Combining our language with that of Allan Collins, Marlene Scardamalia and Carl Bereiter, this can be thought of as the co-construction of working knowledge (c.f. work in the CSILE project, during the early 1990s: Scardamalia & Bereiter, 1994). Combining it with the language of Jean Lave and Etienne Wenger, our concern is for the reification of working knowledge within distributed communities of practice (Wenger, 1998).

Figure 4.2 gives a simple view of what is meant here. It portrays a cycle of learning, working through phases of externalization, sharing, discussion, refinement and internalization. Seen at the level of the individual learner/worker:

- *externalization* is the process through which the tacit knowledge embedded in working practices is made articulate (e.g. through the creation of textual descriptions);
- *sharing* is the dissemination of those descriptions within a community;
- *discussion* is the process of public debate, comment, etc, focused on the shared descriptions;
- *refinement* is the process of suggesting improvements to the practices described, or elaborations (*etc.*) of the knowledge embedded in them;
- *internalization* is the process through which disembodied descriptions of (improved, elaborated) working knowledge and working practices are re-appropriated by the learner/worker, resulting in changes to their working practices (Goodyear, 1995; Sgouropoulou *et al.*, 2000).

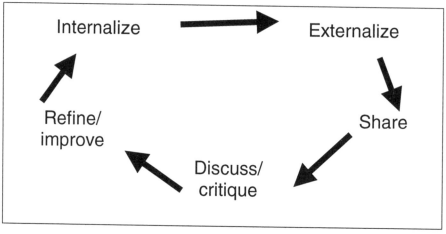

Figure 4.2 The JITOL/SHARP learning cycle

The learning cycle creates periods within which participants in a networked learning CPD program are engaged in epistemic games, but not quite as conceived by Collins. The differences arise from a number of sources. First, Collins was primarily concerned with articulated (academic or 'second-order') knowledge. Figure 4.2 is concerned with knowledge which is largely tacit. Collins was thinking of a hierarchical learning situation, whereas the learning cycle depicted above makes no assumptions about who is more or less experienced with respect to playing epistemic games. Indeed, I would now argue that one of its weaknesses is that it does not see as problematic the cognitive difficulties inherent in playing epistemic games with working knowledge. This has implications for three areas of educational design – the design of tasks, the design of physical resources and the composition of learning communities. I will address each of these in the remainder of this chapter. In the case of epistemic games with working knowledge, task design needs to focus on ways in which we encourage learners to work through the successive phases of the learning cycle. The design of physical resources needs to ensure that the shared spaces within which collaborative CPD takes place provide appropriate epistemic forms (and the tools for working upon them). In planning the composition of learning communities, we need to ensure that experienced players of the relevant epistemic games are available. Players of the traditional epistemic games of academia are not in short supply – most people can quickly learn to moderate an electronic seminar. Unfortunately this is not yet the case when the epistemic games are played with tacit knowledge.

4.10   Design Implications

How can we use some of this understanding of learning to improve and/or simplify the process of designing networked learning situations? Figure 4.3 provides a schema for the educational design problem-space.

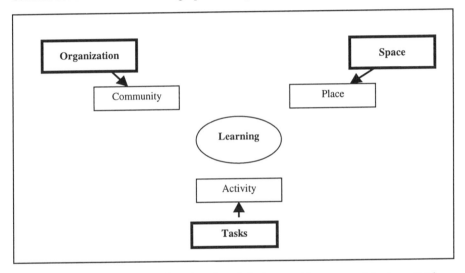

Figure 4.3 Three aspects to the educational design problem-space (Goodyear, 2000)

Two sets of remarks need to be made about this schema. The first concerns an implicit claim about the threefold nature of the educational design problem-space. The second is about indirection in design.

Learning and learning outcomes are central to educational design. Good learning is our target. Seeing learning as a process of guided construction of knowledge means that we have to pay close attention to the learner's activity – cognitive and otherwise. Without appropriate kinds of cognitive activity, there will be no useful learning. But Figure 4.3 also reminds us that learning is situated – both socially and physically. The learner's cognitive activity will be influenced by interaction with their peers and teachers. Moreover, their approach to learning, their experience of learning and their sense of self as a learner and as a competent person will be influenced strongly by their social and cultural setting. In this sense, learning is socially situated. Physical setting is also important, especially when we are thinking about learning that is aided by technologies of one kind or another. The tools and other resources available will influence learning. They will not *determine* the nature or success of that learning, but the affordances of the physical resources in the 'learnplace' are important in shaping learning activity and outcomes. Learning is physically as well as socially situated (Barnes, 2000).

The second point to be made in relation to the design schema in Figure 4.3 is that design should, and perhaps must, approach these aspects of learning *indirectly*. That is, we should recognize that we cannot influence directly the learner's cognitive activity. We can, however, design tasks as resources for the learner's action. We can ask the learner to critique Buggins's views on monetarism. How they do this will, to a great extent, depend on them. Similarly we cannot create or design communities – the best we can do is help set up some organizational forms or structures that are likely to be conducive to the formation and well-being of convivial learning relationships. Learning communities may then emerge. Thirdly, we must recognize that the learner has freedom to reconfigure or customize their learnplace. We can design what we hope will be useful physical resources – communications tools or shared virtual spaces, for example. But we cannot know, and should not try to intervene in, the detailed configuration of the learnplace.[2]

On this view, educational design for networked learning involves three connected sets of design considerations – design of tasks, design of supportive organizational forms/structures and design of supportive tools/physical environments which each learner can customize to meet their own needs. Educational design does not involve starting with a blank sheet of paper. The experienced designer will have to hand candidate design solutions or templates – for each of these three sets of design components. These solutions can be modified to meet the requirements of the new design problem on which they are working. Thus design solutions, design templates etc can act as 'carriers of good practice' and as reifications of beliefs about how learning can best be supported (Pirolli, 1991; Goodyear, 1997). In the next three sections I point to some relevant examples for each of the three design components.

4.10.1 Networked Learning Tasks

An important implication of a commitment to *active* learning is that it shifts emphasis away from teaching as the transmission of information towards teaching as the design of good learning tasks and supportive learning environments. It shifts us from content towards activity. This is potentially a controversial area, so I need to be clear – content (knowledge encapsulated in text, in discourse, *etc.*) is not sidelined, but it becomes more obviously a resource for activity. Whenever we

---

[2] Consider for example how a learner organizes their study notes on their personal computer or how they store messages from a networked learning discussion to which they wish to be able to refer while off line. We can give some tips about useful ways of organizing notes or messages, but control over these important local elements of the learner's physical environment must remain in their hands.

think about content, we should think about what the learner is meant to *do* with that content. I will turn to some other areas needing design attention before the end of this chapter, but for now I want to focus on the design of online learning tasks. This is necessary (a) because task design needs to be supportive of learners' *activity*, (b) because some of the literature about networked, online or e-learning implies that most of the educational decision-making is concerned with making *content* available online, and (c) neglect of task design tends to have two consequences – either students flounder around unproductively and unhappily, not knowing what is expected of them or tutors find themselves spending much more time than they can afford trying to animate online discussions (McConnell, 2000; Salmon, 2000)

Table 4.2 Paulsen's taxonomy of online techniques (after Paulsen, 1995)

One-alone Techniques

> Online databases
> Online journals
> Online applications
> Software libraries
> Online interest groups
> Interviews

One-to-one Techniques

> Learning contracts
> Apprenticeships
> Internships
> Correspondence studies

One-to-many Techniques

> Lectures
> Symposiums
> Skits

Many-to-many Techniques

> Discussion groups
> Debates
> Simulations or games
> Role plays
> Case studies
> Transcript based assignments
> Brainstorming
> Delphi techniques
> Nominal group techniques
> Forums
> Project groups

By an 'online task' I mean something that has been set as an assignment, challenge, specification for work to be done, *etc.*, in the networked learning environment – typically in a shared online discussion space or some other jointly owned and used space. Remember, a task is what gets set – an activity is what follows as the learners' response to the task specified. Task specifications can be very general (e.g. 'please use the online discussion space to share your thoughts about important issues arising in this course') but there are often real advantages to making the task specifications narrower and more precise (e.g. 'please read the articles by Buggins and Brown, write a 200 word summary of their key ideas, and pose two or three questions about points which you feel are unclear in their argument. In week two, when everyone has had chance to raise questions, please share any thoughts you may have about what appear to be the most problematic areas of their argument').

The nature of the tasks themselves will depend on the learning goals you have for the students and your beliefs about how best their activity in the online space can help them achieve these goals. A number of taxonomies of task types or genres exist in the literature, and these can be useful in working out what specific tasks to set, in light of the learning goals you have. For example, Paulsen (1995) has reviewed a wide range of networked learning and teaching techniques and has produced the taxonomy reproduced in Table 4.2 above. Such a taxonomy, if you have it to hand at the time you are working out specifications for online tasks, can be a useful tool insofar as it reminds you of a larger range of task types than you might otherwise consider. Customizing a task from Paulsen's taxonomy is easier than inventing one from scratch.

4.10.2 Networked Learning, Space and Place

The second aspect of educational design, according to the schema presented in Figure 4.3, is that of 'space' and 'place'. This means the physical environment in which the learner's activity is situated. The 'space:place' nomenclature draws on a distinction found in Geography (and sometimes in Architecture). Place is concrete, space abstract. Both consist of an interpenetration of the virtual and material (Mitchell, 1995). Some of the work of educational design leads to the creation or modification of spaces within which learning takes place. The detailed nature of a learner's actual 'learnplace' will vary from learner to learner. Learners configure their own learnplaces, using (in part) the resources we make available in the common spaces of the university and of cyberspace (see also Crook, this volume).

The psychological importance of the resources (*etc.*) to be found in the physical environment (material and virtual) should not be underestimated. For one thing, they have enormous scope. Consider that we are referring here to libraries and books, laboratories and equipment, computers and software, all the resources of the Web, all the printed and electronic texts produced by a course team (course handbooks, study guides, reading lists, assessment regulations, assessment specifications, handouts, feedback on essays, *etc.*) and the texts produced by learners (the learner's own sets of notes, drafts of essays *etc.* together with whatever they can access that is produced by other learners, such as through online essay banks). The affordances of what the learner has to hand will necessarily play an influential role in shaping the nature of their learning activities and of its outcomes.   Until recent times, little design attention has been paid to the integration of these seemingly diverse elements (Ford *et al.,* 1996), though the take-up in HE of 'managed' or 'virtual' learning environments (MLEs and VLEs) is causing many academics and academic service providers to engage in a radical rethink. Still in need of urgent attention is some systematic knowledge of how learners create their own learnplaces from the resources we (and others) provide for them.

4.10.3 Networked Learning Communities and the Design of Supportive Organizational Forms and Structures

This is the third aspect of the scheme presented in Figure 3. Imagine you are about to create a new networked learning course based on a course which you have previously taught by more conventional means – lectures, seminars and coursework essays, for example. Your university has adopted a standard virtual learning environment for all such courses – WebCT for example. You register all the students for your course as users of WebCT and give them access to the WebCT areas specific to your course. Have you created an online learning community? Of course not. Once the course begins, you write some encouraging words of welcome in the main discussion area and emphasize the importance of sharing knowledge and learning experiences. Have you created an online learning community? No. At the end of the course, you look back through the transcripts of online discussions (*etc.*) and you talk to the students. You ask them if they feel that they have been participating in an online learning community. Most or all of them say they have. The transcripts bear this out. Did you create the online learning community? No.

Successful online/networked learning communities emerge and shape themselves. You, as a member (even a powerful member) of the community can help influence the life and character of the community but you cannot *create* a community. What you *can* do is set up or modify existing organizational forms, structures, relationships, protocols *etc.* which it is reasonable to believe will be conducive to the emergence of a worthwhile learning community. Some literature exists from which we might identify some factors which are conducive to the emergence and reproduction of online communities in general (rather than to learning communities per se).   Our primary source here is the work of Peter Kollock (Kollock, 1997; Smith & Kollock, 1999).

Kollock derives his principles about design for online communities from the literature on co-operation and social dilemmas.

"At the root of the problem of co-operation is the fact that there is often a tension between individual and collective rationality. That is to say that in many situations, behaviour that is reasonable and justifiable for the individual leads to a poorer outcome for all. Such situations are termed social dilemmas..." (Kollock & Smith, 1996:109).

The analysis of social dilemmas – which has been widespread in sociology, psychology, political science and economics – leads to some simple conclusions about issues such as the likelihood of two people co-operating rather than acting selfishly. Three minimum conditions for co-operation emerge:

1. There must be some likelihood that the two people will meet again (therefore successful communities must promote on-going interaction).
2. Individuals must be able to identify one another.
3. Individuals must have information about how the other person has behaved in the past (the community needs to have an organizational memory).

Kollock also draws on research which has studied whole communities acting together. Communities that have been successful in managing collective resources and social dilemmas have had the following features:

1. A clearly defined group boundary, to help identify who is making use of group resources (few online communities have tools which facilitate this).
2. Local customization of norms and rules about the use of group resources (enabling people in the group who were knowledgeable and committed, to have a say in shaping the group's rules).
3. `A system for monitoring and sanctioning members' behaviour (without recourse to an external authority).
4. Access to low cost conflict-resolution mechanisms.

From these observations, Kollock (1997) assembles a set of design principles relevant to online communities. These are summarized in Table 4.3 below.

Not all of the principles are readily applicable to the design of organizational forms, protocols *etc.* for networked *learning* communities. However, many of them resonate with the concerns identified, and guidance offered by, experienced moderators of networked learning courses (see e.g. McConnell, 2000; Salmon, 2000). My closing point here would be to suggest that some of the most critical areas for educational design are concerned with *compatible combinations* of task design and the design of organizational processes, forms and protocols. Tasks designed with eyes too narrowly focused on well-specified learning outcomes may prove detrimental to the ongoing life and health of a networked learning community. Too heavy a preoccupation with the vivacity of a networked learning community may result in plenty of talk but all too little learning.

Table 4.3 Kollock's summary of design principles for online communities
(after Kollock, 1997)

Requirements for the possibility of co-operation:
    Arrange that individuals will meet each other again
    They must be able to recognize each other
    They must have information about how the other has behaved until now
Ostrom's design principles of successful communities:
    Group boundaries are clearly defined
    Rules governing the use of collective goods are well matched to local needs and conditions
    Most individuals affected by these rules can participate in modifying the rules
    The right of community members to devise their own rules is respected by external authorities
    A system for monitoring members' behavior exists; this monitoring is undertaken by the community members themselves
    A graduated system of sanctions is used
    Community members have access to low-cost conflict resolution mechanisms
Godwin's principles for making virtual communities work:
    Use software that promotes good discussion
    Don't impose a length limitation on postings
    Front-load your system with talkative, diverse people
    Let the users resolve their own disputes
    Provide institutional memory
    Promote continuity
    Be host to a particular interest group
    Provide places for children
Confront the users with a crisis

4.11   References

Anderson, J. (1983) *The architecture of cognition*. Cambridge Mass: Harvard University Press

Anderson, J. & Lebiere, C. (1998) *The atomic components of thought*. Mahwah NJ: Lawrence Erlbaum Associates

Anderson, J., Reder, L. & Simon, H. (1996) Situated learning and education. *Educational Reseacher*, 25(4), 5-11

Anderson, J., Reder, L. & Simon, H. (1997) Situative versus cognitive perspectives: form versus substance. *Educational Reseacher*, 26(1), 18-21

Assiter, A. (Ed) (1995) *Transferable skills in higher education*. London: Kogan Page

Barnes, S. (2000) What does electronic conferencing afford distance education? *Distance Education*, 21(2), pp236-247

Barnett, R. (1994) *The limits of competence: knowledge, higher education and society*. Buckingham: Open University Press

Barnett, R. (1997a) *Higher education: a critical business.* Buckingham: Open University Press

Barnett, R. (1997b) *Towards a higher education for a new century.* London: Institute of Education University of London

Barnett, R. (2000) *Realizing the university in an age of supercomplexity.* Buckingham: SRHE/Open University Press

Barnett, R. & Griffin, A. (Eds) (1997) *The end of knowledge in higher education.* London: Cassell

Biggs, J. (1999) *Teaching for quality learning at university: what the student does.* Buckingham: Open University Press

Brown, J., Collins, A. & Duguid, P. (1989) Situated cognition and the culture of learning. *Educational Researcher, 18,* 32-42

Chipman, S. & Meyrowitz, A. (Eds) (1993) *Foundations of knowledge acquisition: cognitive models of complex learning.* Boston MA: Kluwer

Collins, A. & Ferguson, W. (1993) Epistemic forms and epistemic games. *Educational Psychologist, 28*(1), 25-42

Cunningham, D. (1992a) Assessing constructions and constructing assessments: a dialog. In Duffy, T. & Jonassen, D. (Eds) *Constructivism and the technology of instruction* (pp.35-44). Hillsdale New Jersey: Lawrence Erlbaum Associates

Cunningham, D. (1992b) In defense of extremism. In Duffy, T. & Jonassen, D. (Eds) *Constructivism and the technology of instruction* (pp. 157-160). Hillsdale New Jersey: Lawrence Erlbaum Associates

Dillenbourg, P. (1999) Introduction: what do you mean by "collaborative learning"? In Dillenbourg, P. (Ed) *Collaborative learning: cognitive and computational approaches.* Amsterdam: Pergamon.

Dillenbourg, P., Baker, M., Blaye, A. & O'Malley, C. (1996) The evolution of research on collaborative learning In Reiman, P. & Spada, S. *Learning in humans and machines: towards an interdisciplinary learning science* Oxford: Elsevier Science

Entwistle, N. & Entwistle, A. (1997) Revision and the experience of understanding. In Marton, F., Hounsell, D. & Entwistle, N. (Eds) *The experience of learning* (2nd ed., pp. 145-55). Edinburgh: Scottish Academic Press

Ford, P., Goodyear, P., Heseltine, R., Lewis, R., Darby, J., Graves, J., Sartorius, P., Harwood, D. & King, T. (1996) *Managing change in higher education: a learning environment architecture.* Buckingham: Open University Press

Goodyear, P. (1995) Situated action and distributed knowledge: a JITOL perspective on electronic performance support systems. *Educational and Training Technology International, 32*(1), 45-55

Goodyear, P. (1997) Instructional design environments: methods and tools for the design of complex instructional systems. In Dijkstra, S. *et al* (Eds) *Instructional design: international perspectives.* Mahwah NJ: Lawrence Erlbaum Associates

Goodyear, P. (1999) New technology in higher education: understanding the innovation process. In Eurelings, A., Gastkemper, F., Komers, P., Lewis, R., van Meel, R. & Melief, B. (Eds) *Integrating Information and Communication Technology in Higher Education* (pp. 107-136) Deventer: Kluwer

Goodyear, P. (2000) Seeing learning as work: implications for understanding and improving analysis and design. *Journal of Courseware Engineering, 2,* 3-11

Goodyear, P. and NLinHE Project Team (2000) *Effective networked learning in higher education,* Lancaster: CSALT

Goodyear, P. & Steeples, C. (1993) Computer-mediated communication in the professional development of workers in the advanced learning technologies industry. In Eccleston, J., Barta, B. & Hambusch, R. (Eds) *The computer-mediated education of information technology professionals and advanced end-users* (pp239-247) Amsterdam: Elsevier

Greeno, J. (1997) On claims that answer the wrong question. *Educational Researcher, 26* (1), 5-17

Hara, N. & Kling, R. (1999) Students' frustrations with a web-based distance education course. *First Monday, 4*(12)

Hara, N., Bonk, C.J. & Angeli, C. (2000) Content analysis of online discussion in an applied educational psychology course. *Instructional Science, 28* (2), 115-152

Hardy, G., Hodgson, V., McConnell, D. & Reynolds, M. (1991) *Computer Mediated Communication for Management Training and Development: A research report* Lancaster: CSML, Lancaster University

Harvey, L. & Knight, P. (1996) *Transforming higher education.* Buckingham: Open University Press

Harvey, L. & Mason, S. (1996) A quality graduate. In Tait, J. & Knight, P. (Eds) *The management of independent learning* (pp13-28). London: Kogan Page

Henri, F. (1991) Computer conferencing and content analysis. In Kaye, A. (Ed) *Collaborative learning through computer conferencing: the Najaden papers* (pp115-136). Berlin: Springer Verlag

Howell-Richardson, C. & Mellar, H. (1996) A methodology for the analysis of patterns of participation within computer-mediated communication courses. *Instructional Science, 24,* 47-69

Jonassen, D., Davidson, M., Collins, M., Campbell, J. & Haag, B. (1995) Constructivism and computer-mediated communication in distance education. *American Journal of Distance Education, 9*(2), 7-26

Klahr, D., Langley, P. & Neches, R. (Eds) (1987) *Production system models of learning and development.* Cambridge MA: MIT Press

Kollock. P. (1997) Design principles for online communities. *The Internet and Society: Harvard Conference Proceedings,* Cambridge Mass: O'Reilly & Associates

Kollock, P. & Smith, M. (1996) Managing the virtual commons: cooperation and conflict in computer communities. In Herring, S. (Ed) *Computer mediated communication: linguistic, social, and cross cultural perspectives,* Amsterdam: John Benjamins, pp109-128

Laurillard, D. (1987) The different forms of learning in psychology and education. In Richardson, J., Eysenck, M. & Warren Piper, D. (Eds.) *Student Learning: Research in education and cognitive psychology.* Buckingham: Open University Press, pp198-207

Laurillard, D. (1993) *Rethinking university teaching: a framework for the effective use of educational technology.* London: Routledge

Lave, J. (1988) *Cognition in practice.* Cambridge: Cambridge University Press

Lave, J. & Wenger, E. (1991) *Situated learning: legitimate peripheral participation*. Cambridge: Cambridge University Press

Marton, F. & Booth, S. (1997) *Learning and awareness*. Mahwah New Jersey: Lawrence Erlbaum Associates

Marton, F., Hounsell, D. & Entwistle, N. (Eds) (1997) *The experience of learning* (2nd ed.). Edinburgh: Scottish Academic Press

McConnell, D. (2000) *Implementing computer supported cooperative learning*. (2nd ed.) London: Kogan Page

Mitchell, W.J. (1995) *City of bits: space, place, and the infobahn*. Cambridge Mass: MIT Press

Morrison, D. & Collins, A. (1996) Epistemic fluency and constructivist learning environments. In Wilson, B. (Ed) *Constructivist Learning Environments* (pp107-119) Englewood Cliffs, NJ: Educational Technology Publications.

National Committee of Inquiry into Higher Education (1997) *Higher education in the learning society*, London: HMSO (the Dearing Report)

Ohlsson, S. (1995) Learning to do and learning to understand: a lesson and a challenge for cognitive modelling. In Reimann, P. & Spada, H. (Eds) *Learning in humans and machines: towards an interdisciplinary learning science* (pp37-62). London: Pergamon

Paulsen, M. (1995) *The online report on pedagogical techniques for computer-mediated communication*. Available: http://www.nki.no/~morten.

Perkins, D. & Blythe, T. (1994) Putting understanding up front. *Educational Leadership, 51*, (5) 4-7

Pirolli, P. (1991) Computer-aided instructional design systems. In Burns, H., Parlett, J. & Redfield, C. (Eds) *Intelligent tutoring systems: evolution in design* (pp105-125). Hillsdale New Jersey: Lawrence Erlbaum Associates

Salmon, G. (2000) *E-moderating: the key to teaching and learning online*. London: Kogan Page

Scardamalia, M. & Bereiter, C. (1994) Computer support for knowledge building communities. *Journal of the Learning Sciences, 3*(3), 265-283

Schoenfeld, A. (1999) Looking toward the 21st century: challenges of educational theory and practice. *Educational Researcher, 28* (7), 4-14

Sgouropoulou, C., Koutoumanos, T., Goodyear, P. & Skordalakis, E. (2000) Acquiring working knowledge through asynchronous multimedia conferencing. *Educational Technology and Society, 3*(3)

Shuell, T. (1992) Designing instructional computing systems for meaningful learning. In Jones, M. & Winne, P. (Eds) *Adaptive Learning Environments*. New York: Springer Verlag

Simons, P., van der Linden, J. & Duffy, T., (Eds) (2000) *New Learning*, Dordrecht: Wolters/Kluwer

Smith, M. & Kollock, P. (Eds) (1999) *Communities in cyberspace*. London: Routledge

Steeples, C. & Goodyear, P. (1999) Enabling professional learning in distributed communities of practice: descriptors for multimedia objects. *Journal of Network and Computer Applications, 22*, 133-145

Suchman, L. (1987) *Plans and situated action*. Cambridge: Cambridge University Press

Vermunt, J. (1998) The regulation of constructive learning processes. *British Journal of Educational Psychology, 68* (2), 149

Vermunt, J. & Rijswijk, F. (1988) Analysis and development of students' skill in self-regulated learning. *Higher Education, 17,* 647-682

Wenger, E. (1998) *Communities of practice.* Cambridge: Cambridge University Press

5. Studying Networked Learning: Some Implications from Socially Situated Learning Theory and Actor Network Theory

Steve Fox

5.1 Introduction

In this paper, I want to discuss networked learning (NL) in the light of actor network theory (ANT) and related social theories of learning and knowing. For many, the term NL implies innovative, and therefore probably better, forms of educational learning process, as the subtitle to a recent conference makes clear: "Networked Learning 2000: Innovative Approaches to Lifelong Learning and Higher Education Through the Internet" (Asensio *et al.*, 2000). Through the discussion in this chapter, I wish to problematize the notion of networked learning, both in terms of what is meant by 'learning' and what is meant by 'networked.'

Firstly, looking at learning I will argue that by seeing NL as yet another form of 'educationalized learning'[1] we are privileging educationalized notions of the learning process over non-educationalized notions. I argue this would be regrettable because it serves to occlude all the many forms of 'networked' learning which might be studied if we took a wider view of the term. Several authors have drawn attention to what they variously call 'natural learning' (Burgoyne & Hodgson, 1983); 'informal and incidental learning' (Marsick & Watkins, 1990); 'socially situated learning' (Lave & Wenger, 1991) and 'non-canonical learning' (Brown & Duguid, 1991). Although these authors differ in how they theorize learning processes, what they have in common is that: (a) they see learning occurring outside of formal educational settings and (b) consider it worth researching learning outside of educationalized settings.

---

[1] The term 'educationalized learning' was recently used by Jean Lave at a seminar on Learning and Practice held by the Learning and Critique Network at Manchester, 8 November 2000. Through this term she drew attention to the way in which most academic conceptions of learning are uncritically rooted in presumptions that learning takes place primarily within educational relationships and institutions. Elsewhere, in discussing Lave's work, I have referred to a 'learning iceberg' to indicate that what we think of as education is simply the most visible tip of an otherwise invisible mass – learning in all its myriad forms (Fox, 1997a, 1997b).

If NL were simply to focus on educationalized learning processes through cyberspace, it would miss all the natural, informal and situated learning which occurs, through the internet as well as through other social networks and spaces, outside of deliberately designed educational activities. Elsewhere, I have argued that learning is a pervasive process in everyday life (Fox, 1994) and that it is worth studying it in everyday contexts as well as inside classrooms and other educational contexts.

The possibility exists that the study of learning, even networked learning, which occurs 'naturally', 'incidentally', 'situatedly' and 'pervasively' in everyday life and workplaces in particular, will repay educational designers, just as clothes designers frequently benefit from the close observation of street fashion. But arguably, there is surely justification enough in studying 'natural' learning simply for its own sake, with a view to enriching our understanding of learning. Lave and Wenger (1991), in particular, have argued strongly that learning research needs to look outside of schooled or educationalized settings if it is to fully understand the processes of learning.

Second, the notion of networked learning typically implies *networked* electronically *through* the internet. Again I find this notion limited as it seems to occlude a much wider conception of what networks may be. By seeing the internet as a medium through which learning takes place, we tend to see the medium as a transparent vehicle within which a meeting of minds and stored information is possible. However, one body of social theory which has done much to extend our understanding of networks is actor-network theory (Callon, 1986a, 1986b; Law, 1987, 1992) which looks at networks as heterogeneously spanning humans, non-human technical artefacts, as well as natural objects occurring in the world. This perspective could certainly embrace human networks through the internet but is not limited to this. It alerts our attention to the fact that social networks are nearly always mediated technically by some form of material medium, the electronic medium of cyberspace being only one form[2]. Further, it shows how the medium is itself part of wider networks and possesses its own active and reactive or resistive properties.

Once we look at networks as being beyond the internet and including other technologies, the built-environment at large and human social structures, whether hierarchies or looser networks, we raise questions about learning processes beyond

---

[2]   If Lave and Wenger (1991) provide a critique of an overly educationalized learning theory, then we might say that ANT provides a critique of overly socialized social theory, which may sound like a contradiction in terms. The point is that we cannot understand 'the social' as if it were somehow transcendent of, or abstracted from, the material world. For ANT the social and material worlds interpenetrate and social networks are inseparable from material networks just as for Lave and Wenger (1991) learning worth researching is inherent in situated concrete settings rather than a decontextualized, disembodied, sequestered world of abstract ideas or a purely cognitive realm. Thus both ANT and situated learning theory (SLT) or community of practice theory, strive to escape the mind-body dualism which in western thought goes back to Plato's distinction between transcendental ideas and reality, articulated in the story of the prisoner in the cave. How the two approaches, SLT and ANT, are similar and diverge, is discussed in Fox (2000).

how they can best be educationally designed. Once we head in this direction, I am not sure that the discussion need ever return to the pressing concerns of educational designers, since the anthropology and social theory of learning and networks (to put it differently) might be more interesting. There could be decades of things to discover before any kind of instrumental implications are drawn, but in the present paper I shall point to some issues which designers of educationalized NL might consider. These issues include: how to configure 'the learner'; how we see cyberspace in contrast to other socio-material spaces; how we understand the dualistic relations between concrete practice and abstract ideas; and what implications we might draw for radical or progressive education in contrast with more traditional and utilitarian education.

5.2   Ways of Looking at Networked Learning?

Compared to mainstream classroom based education NL is often presented as being better in some way: more efficient, democratic, participative, emancipatory, for example. NL can be seen as truer to the humanistic spirit of 'open learning' and not simply about distance learning. NL can be seen as offering idealized online 'learning communities' (Davis & Denning, 2000), perhaps within the spirit of what Hague and Loader call "digital democracy" (Hague & Loader, 1999). In these ways NL readily cites the influence of critical pedagogy such as Freire (1972) and Giroux (1983).

In what follows we will first look at NL in the light of the radical critiques levelled at its mainstream alternative, face-to-face classroom based teaching or education. Second we will examine how situated learning looks at mainstream education, whether traditional or based on critical pedagogy, and how it moves our attention away from educationalized learning towards social learning more widely. Third, within social learning, we will look at how ANT too looks at learning and knowledge and networks as it occurs outside of classrooms.

5.3   Networked Learning and Critical Pedagogy

Critical pedagogy has developed a critique of mass-education or schooling. It claims that the banking model of education has an alienating impact on students and teachers alike (Freire, 1972). This model of education sees pupils or students as depositories to be filled up by teachers who have already been filled up. The contents are pre-produced as an abstract body of knowledge, by researchers whose intellectual labour is already divided by subject area, and distributed through the curriculum by teachers in schools and other institutions which are factories for filling minds. Both teachers and students are alienated in this form of education.

It is against the potentially alienating effects of traditional education that the 'learning community' concept has been articulated. Learning community based pedagogy aims to maximize student and/or pupil participation in the framing of the topic of learning and the skill of critique. In contrast to the banking model, Freire refers to the idea of problem-posing education (1972), in which students participate in defining the problems they work to understand.

Increased participation implies that each student's individual presence is recognized by the critical educator and that their personal interests and motivations are engaged. The student is encouraged to identify problems with the content knowledge and to address these problems, in effect personalizing the process of knowledge transmission. Without this personal problematization of content, learning is simply a memory test; the content being a standardized body of knowledge and orthodox interpretations. For Freire, this 'banking model of education' is alienating to both teachers and students, whose latitude to create novel interpretations is constrained.

The concept of the learning community seeks to reverse the alienating effect of traditional authoritarian education. As bel hooks tells us:

"To begin, the professor must genuinely value everyone's presence. There must be an ongoing recognition that everyone influences the classroom dynamic that everyone contributes. These contributions are resources. Used constructively they enhance the capacity of any class to create an open learning community" (hooks, 1994:8).

The learning community concept involves increased levels of *participation:* each individual is recognized, their presence valued and their contributions produce resources which enhance the collective good. Further, the learning community concept involves "...some deconstruction of the traditional notion that only the professor is responsible for classroom dynamics" (ibid.). The professor cannot escape a higher level of responsibility for these dynamics, but ultimately "...excitement is generated by collective effort" (ibid.). Learning community based educational philosophy and practice requires a sharing of responsibility for learning methods, the curriculum followed, and assessment procedures adopted. And, while these participative practices take time, they allow participants to customize their own pursuit of learning helping to prevent the estrangement of the person from knowledge.

Critical pedagogy can be transformative of the institutions of schooling but depends upon teachers who are personally committed to its principles and who have secured positions of sufficient power within the hierarchy. These positions need to be strong enough to allow teachers a certain discretion in the management of classroom dynamics. However, more traditional, authoritarian educational policies seek to reduce the teacher's span of discretion by the top-down imposition of prescribed curricula and teaching methods, often in the name of quality control.

Seen against this background, NL opens a new educational space beyond the traditional classroom, a new public sphere to be fought over by proponents of different schools of educational theory and policy. NL can be seen as a progressive site of radical pedagogical experiments, emphasizing the anti-hierarchical structure of the web and the way in which social status differences become invisible in cyberspace, or it can be seen as an instrumentally superior form of knowledge transmission. It has been claimed that the internet and the web are a means to increase direct democratic participation and to strengthen political community (Arterton, 1987; Grossman, 1995), although this is a matter of some contention (Hale, Musso & Weare, 1999). Alternatively the emphasis may be placed on the potential functional efficiency of NL, and the fact that the curriculum can be centrally managed more tightly. In the employment context, vocational learning can be self-managed in the learner's own time minimizing costs to employers and tax-payer. Hodgson (2000) has argued that there are two broad orientations to open and distance learning; the dissemination model (similar to the banking theory of knowledge) and the development orientation which develops the 'whole person'.

Given these debates, NL can be seen as simply new turf for old battles to be fought upon. 'Progressive educators,' in the mould of Rousseau and Dewey, are pitted against 'authoritarian educators,' in the mould of Plato and Mill (Moore, 1974). However, an alternative way of looking at networked learning is socially situated learning theory. This is relevant because it draws our attention away from formal educationalized learning to what Brown and Duguid called "learning-in-working" (1991:41).

5.4   Networked Learning and Socially Situated Learning

The above kinds of debate, between radical/progressive and conventional/ authoritarian education theory, have tended to work within the presumption that schooling is necessary to learning. As such they are open to challenge from the viewpoint of 'situated learning' (Lave & Wenger, 1991). This theoretical stand-point argues that 'learning' and 'education' are not the same thing. Elsewhere, in discussing situated learning, I have described education as the tip of a learning iceberg (Fox, 1997a, 1997b) by which I mean that learning is going on pervasively in everyday life and formal education is just the visible tip. However, what is interesting about situated learning is that it draws our attention away from all formal educational attempts to manage learning towards the many social spaces where learning takes place 'naturally,' so to speak.

Lave and Wenger (1991) draw our attention to a number of situated practices, how, for example, Vai and Golan tailors learn their craft. How Mayan midwives learn the practice of midwifery outside of the formalized body of knowledge and techniques packaged as Western obstetrics. How US naval quartermasters learn the art of navigating a ship by doing it in the company of more experienced officers who frequently have to correct the bad habits their younger colleagues acquired at training school, and more. These studies suggest that learning does not necessarily require formal education nor the institutions of education which have pervasively shaped the notion of learning in western culture and that to understand learning, researchers should study it in communities of practice and develop a view of learning that can "stand on its own" (Lave & Wenger, 1991:39-40). As Lave and Wenger expand on this point:

"Such decoupling [of learning and education] does not deny that learning can take place where there is teaching, but does not take intentional instruction to be in itself the source or cause of learning" (40-1).

Lave and Wenger suggest that education has trammelled our notion of what learning can be. They point to the multitudinous communities of practice with which members identify, learning to practice numerous activities knowledgeably and skilfully. These learning processes take place 'in the wild', as it were (see Hutchins, 1993, for instance) outside of schools and formal educational environments and are to an extent romanticized by Lave and Wenger, in ways not un-reminiscent of Rousseau's call for a "return to nature" (Moore, 1974:33).

Given the distinction between learning and education emphasized by Lave and Wenger (1991) we might ask whether NL should refer to formal attempts to educate, or to the naturally occurring attempts to learn by socially situated interactants in cyberspace, or to both and the inter-relations between them. Looked at from a situated learning perspective, networked learning is what goes on in e-mail, intranets, chat-rooms, bulletin boards, MUDs and all the other cyber-spaces which educators have not yet got their hands on in an effort to construct cyber-classrooms (see Reid, 1999, for a study of MUDs for example). From a situated learning perspective, all forms of schooling, whether they are based in classrooms or on networked learning, authoritarian or participative, are a distraction from many varieties of learning that are not shaped by educationalized notions of learning at all but are intrinsic to activities. For "the organization of schooling as an educational form is predicated on claims that knowledge can be decontextualized" (Lave & Wenger, 1991:40), whereas the organization of activity cannot. As Lave and Wenger explain:

"... both theoretical analyzes and instructional prescriptions tend to be driven by reference to reified 'knowledge domains', and by constraints imposed by the general requirements of universal learning mechanisms understood in terms of acquisition and assimilation" (Lave & Wenger, 1991:52).

Situated learning theory seeks to understand learning in context, in situ, in practice, in activity. Not that schools are not very specific forms of context (Lave & Wenger, 1991:40) but the type of context they are is arguably not the same as we find in the study of activity or work systems.

Cyberspace presents a problematic social space to the researcher. Its textual similarity to written printed media and hence 'reified knowledge domains' give it the appearance of a more abstract and decontextualized environment than the face-to-face social world, and yet we can do things with words (Austin, 1962); we can act in cyberspace. Arguably, it is not simply an extension of everyday social space. Overridingly, the language of the web, and cyberspace is suggestive of a limitless universe, a universal abstract knowledge. Consequently NL is not simply an electronic version of normal face-to-face education, on the spectrum from authoritarian to progressive. A central feature of cyberspace in general, and hence of NL in particular, is that it is a sphere of human activity which is mediated technologically. A key difference between NL and social learning more widely, including formal face-to-face education, is the dependency upon electronic communications technology. It is possible that this technology is no different in principle from any technology, in that it provides a set of artefacts and symbols used in practice. How we understand this relationship between technology and human action is a matter which actor-network theory has done much to expand, as we will see in the next section. But the point is that, as forms of technology, networked learning and cyberspace more generally are a different form of medium, not like a static book or a pre-programed broadcast. Rather, MUDs, chat-rooms, e-mail all have the characteristic of live TV, and are interactive. The social and technological are inseparable (see Reid, 1999, for an analysis of this interplay).

Recent situated learning theory touches on the place of technical artefacts within communities of practice (Wenger, 1998) but places most of the analytical emphasis upon the social negotiation of meaning. Artefacts are there in the background and they embody human knowledge, but they do not act other than in the hands of humans. In contrast actor-network theory claims to place an equal analytical emphasis upon the technological artefacts and the social meanings, in this way it is of particular relevance to the study of networked learning, where the technological and social are so inseparable. In this alternative social theoretical perspective, natural things, made objects, technological artefacts, all *act* and all *participate* in networks with each other and this changes the terms of debate established by situated learning theorists. It is this approach we shall now introduce and discuss in relation to NL.

5.5   Actor Network Theory

To say that non-human entities 'act' may sound like anthropomorphism but it is not, in the sense ANT gives to the term. ANT does not ascribe human qualities to non-humans such as objects, animals or artefacts, such as 'volition,' 'emotion' or 'cunning;' although in some cases – animals perhaps – all these things may be ascribable. But ANT recognizes that things *act* upon each other and upon humans. Not all things act, however, at least in obvious ways. Traffic lights signal 'stop' by turning red, but they do not act to stop the driver; rather the driver acts in accordance with rules and customs upon seeing the signal. It is the network of roads, cars, signals, highway code, and humans that acts, each of these components, human and non-human, acting upon the others. A clear example of a non-human thing which does act upon humans directly is the 'door groom' discussed by Latour (1991). This device, which some doors are equipped with, closes the door shut after someone has left it open. Usually such devices work by some kind of spring mechanism, which shuts the door. Force is exerted by the device which accordingly 'acts'. Another example discussed by Latour is the heavy key weight which many hotels attach to their room keys to prevent guests forgetting to leave their key. Hotels could simply leave a notice on the back of guest room doors, saying 'please deposit your key at reception'. Again, this would signal the required action on the part of guests, just as red traffic lights do, but no force is exerted. The threat of force may be invoked but is not exerted directly, whereas the key weight is a heavy force which acts upon the guest and shapes their behaviour. Force is involved in action as ANT defines it, even if this is a form of force which is resistive, such as inertia.

Thus things, especially made objects or technical devices, act upon other things and upon humans. However, things do not act at random. They only act upon each other and upon humans when they participate in the same network however small or large. If hotel guests all lived in the same town as the hotel, a small and local network, then key weights may not be necessary. The fact that hotel guests are likely to never return is the reason key weights are needed in the network. Likewise natural objects such as rivers, seas, tornadoes, mountains, all act in the sense that they influence the course of action within some network or other. Mountains may be there for millennia and may participate in a succession of networks over time. They may be a natural defence between two warring states in one century, and a popular ski resort in the next and simultaneously may participate in a geological network of tectonic plates which are slowly moving together. Thus objects, like humans, can belong to numerous networks simultaneously and in succession. And not all of these networks are defined by or intended for use by humans, many of them exist on their own and all humans can do is to identify them, as with the tectonic plate example. Only some of these networks exist symbiotically with humans.

Humans are aware of some of the networks that shape aspects of their lives but how many are they not aware of? Actor-network theory recognizes that things, people, whatever, only ever 'act' *in* 'networks'. Action by one entity does not take place except within *a* network. Actors exist in networks without which their 'actions' are meaningless or rather inactive. To avoid the anthropomorphic connotations of the term 'actor,' ANT prefers the term 'actant' which suggests both an agent and an active (or even reactive) process, which could be chemical or electrical as much as human, such as the 'setting agent' in jelly.

If we take this general notion of actor-networks, in which actants of all kinds, human and non-human, promiscuously and heterogeneously act upon each other, then we have the basic idea of actor-network theory. And if we begin to apply this concept of the actor-network to notions of networked learning, we must begin to reconfigure several aspects of traditional learning theory.

One of the first ways in which traditional learning theory should be revised concerns the hallowed notion of "the learner" and the associated notion of "the learning process". In traditional cognitive theory, the learner is typically an individual and more often than not a child or young adult. The learning process is conceived as happening within the individual's mind which functions as a memory device and a knowledge organizing device. Educational theory assumes that the order in which knowledge is taught shapes the way it is organized by the mind and hence pays attention to matters like curriculum. It also assumes that some methods are better for some subjects than others. In both traditional cognitive and educational theory, knowledge is presumed to exist already within the mind of a teacher or other expert but also codified and stored in books, papers, diagrams, figures, formulae and other such representational devices, which are further organized by syllabus and teaching methods.   Hence in essence, knowledge is abstract.

   In socially situated learning theory, knowledge is embodied in practice which is socially reproduced, supervized and modified over time.   If it is anywhere the knowledge is socially distributed within a community of practitioners, rather than within an individual learner's mind.   The learning process is one of 'legitimate peripheral participation', through which newcomers learn socially approved activities and skills from old-timers with whom they identify, and learners are mostly adults or at least young adults.   In actor-network theory, we find some elements in common with traditional cognitive and educational theory and some from socially situated learning theory. Knowledge is embodied in a heterogeneous network comprising humans and non-humans which are, by design (both deliberate and emergent) programed or trained to act in prescribed ways.   These networks might include multiple communities of practice, but also include other social groups, concrete materials, artefacts, and representational devices.   The learner here is neither an individual nor a community of practice necessarily, but could be any component part of the network and/or the network as a whole.   Similarly, the learning process may occur at any point in this network.   Whereas Lave and Wenger's notion of communities of practice tend toward continuity through processes of social reproduction, actor-network theory stresses the friability of networks, that links can be broken as well as forged, although some sub-networks might hold together longer than the network as a whole.   The point is that learning at some point in a network can transform the network, extend its nodes, multiply relations between nodes, cut out nodes, and sever the connections between nodes. Learning is one of the processes which builds up and breaks down networks, although there may be other processes which achieve similar effects.

   ANT adopts a view of knowledge which is much influenced by Foucault; a view that sees knowledge and power as different yet inseparable sides of the same coin (see Latour, 1986; Law, 1991).   Thus the emphasis is upon the concrete power of knowledge when it is in use.   As Latour, discussing power, (1986:265) puts this:

> "...when you simply have power – *in potentia* – nothing happens and you are powerless; when you exert power – *in actu* – *others* are performing the action and not you... Power is not something you may possess and hoard... Power is, on the contrary, what has to be explained by the action of the others who obey the dictator..."

Accordingly, power and knowledge, are only of analytic interest to ANT when they are in use.   Saying that power cannot be hoarded or possessed is not to say that the conditions for the effective use of power cannot be put firmly in place in a network but the bottom-line is that power is manifest in its use, not its potential to be used; and we may say the same for knowledge.   Thus we can stockpile money, munitions, defensive barriers and all the other paraphernalia of strategy but this only gives the potential for power.   Actual power exists in the effective use of these networks of resources.   This discussion relates back to the banking model of education, where knowledge can be deposited in the memory for later use. ANT is not arguing that we are unable to memorize, possess or hoard information but is emphasizing that knowledge, like power, only exists when being used effectively.

To illustrate: books written within scientific and scholarly communities may be revised and thus embody more up to date information through the exertions of their writers. However, writers do not exist in a vacuum they participate in communities of practice and in actor-networks comprized of humans (some organized in communities of practice) technology, materials, popular discourses, practices of counting, rationalizing, theorizing, observing, *etc.* And it is instructive to consider how technology has come to play a crucial part in the way such revisions take place. Latour (1990) describes the revolution in learning and scholarship brought about by the printing press, looking at one field, astronomy, as a particular example.

Latour draws extensively upon Elizabeth Eisenstein's remarkable book *The Printing Press as an Agent of Change* (1979). The invention of print in the fifteenth century and its effect on science and technology is something of a cliché amongst historians but Eisenstein's book shows how the printing press is a device which makes both the *mobilization* and *immutability* of inscriptions of all kinds possible. By mobilization I mean that through printing, inscriptions can be produced and disseminated more easily. By immutabilty I mean that inscriptions are made invariant or standard through print across space and time. For Latour, these properties of the press are key to the development of knowledge after its invention. Prior to the press, books were hand-copied (in a *scriptorium*) and hence extremely rare, often inaccurate (after the third or fourth hand-transcribed copy) and remotely dispersed amongst the monasteries, university libraries and private collections of Europe. Scholars located at isolated sites had only a selection of Europe's books and these contained inaccuracies.

After print is invented there follows a period in which all the canonical texts from antiquity down through the renaissance are produced and distributed widely, the main perceived benefit being that ancient texts may now be preserved more easily. But once texts can be reproduced cheaply in large volume demand for them expands. Anyone, rather than a few monks, can now have access to the writings of Plato or Ovid. It is now possible for many scholars to study the same book and because printed books initially simply repeated the inaccuracies in the hand-written copies from which they are struck, by making the inaccuracies visible on a wide scale, it becomes possible for the learned people of Europe to detect the errors and correct them for future production runs, although this takes time. Eventually, there is a vastly larger body of standardized texts widely distributed (*i.e., mobile*) amongst the centers of learning and now they are all relatively correct (*i.e., immutable*) the same canonical books may now be found in each library collection – a standardization has occurred. The books include graphics, models, calculations, formulae and illustrations which were originally subject to the same inaccuracies as written texts but which are now systematically corrected and the possibility of exact representation has become possible.

But then after all the typographical errors have been eliminated, and the same collections of books can be found on the shelves of most learned astronomers in Europe, it is now possible for a single scholar, sitting in their study, to juxtapose ideas, facts and figures found in books in a new way and then talk to other astronomers about their insights, cross-referring to the texts each will reliably have on their shelves. An example is Tycho Brahe, the Danish astronomer, who was the last of the great naked eye observers of the night sky. He certainly was not the first astronomer to look at old books as much as at the sky, but:

> "...he did have at his disposal, as few had before him, two separate sets of computations based on two different theories, compiled several centuries apart which he could compare with each other." (Eisenstein, 1979:624, quoted by Latour, 1990:43)

Whereas conventional historians say that Brahe was the first to look at planetary motion with a free mind without the prejudices of the dark ages, Eisenstein says that the important thing is not the freedom of his mind but that he is the first to look at all the former predictions and his own written down in the same form:

> "...he was also the first careful observer who took full advantage of the new powers of the press – powers which enabled astronomers to detect anomalies in old records, to pinpoint more precisely and register in catalogues the location of each star, to enlist collaborators in many regions, fix fresh observations in permanent form and make necessary corrections in successive editions." (Eisenstein, 1979:625, quoted by Latour, 1990:43)

The example shows how actor-networks shift and change over time. The same planets seen by ancient, mediaeval and modern astronomers are linked through a succession of theories which are gradually unified through the exertions of an international community of scholars able to see the same charts and calculations and compare notes on how to interpret these thanks to the new technology of the printing press which gives everyone the same body of abstract and standardized knowledge to look at. Suddenly calculations made in different centuries under the auspices of totally different theories can be seen to fit together but not just because Tycho Brahe's mind was free of superstition or even of the influence of currently strong local theory, but because the new technology had contributed to the building up of standardized collections of astronomical classics, allowing him a panoramic view of theory and observations through the centuries. Further the technology of print allowed him to communicate almost simultaneously (*i.e.,* in a matter of years) with all his contemporaries around the world by publishing his own theory and observations.

Crucially for actor-network theory, the printing example shows us that it is through technology that lettering and inscriptions of all kinds become standardized or immutable and also readily mobile. This gives the impression that meanings are abstract but this is the effect of a technology which reduces the concrete particulars of hand-written text to standardized type-face. It is print, rather than Platonic idealism, which produces the widespread dualism of concrete and abstract knowledge. Abstraction is simply a by-product of a technology which is used on a mass scale.

In the case of astronomy, we see an emergent international research community (which shares something with the notion of a community of practice as described by Lave and Wenger (1991)) at a crucial point in its history. Its use of old books and charts and subsequently the telescope and new technologies will in time produce the theories and findings that will comprise the curriculum in university astronomy classes. What Latour's use of Eisenstein's work shows us, is the dependence of the community and its learning upon the mundane technology of printed media. The widespread dissemination of standardized texts in the same form as each other facilitate new ways of looking at facts which have been recorded for centuries and the collection of new facts. The abstraction of facts from old records, is not a purely cognitive process but a practical technologically facilitated one; that requires a community of practice, which is marked by competitive and collaborative claims on how to interpret old books and the night sky.

From an actor-network perspective, situated learning theory possibly overplays the abstract-concrete dualism. Abstraction is seen as a practically accomplished matter, one which relies more than anything upon new technology which brings standardization, immutability and mobility, to the contents of old and new books. It is easy to see that the internet, and the digitalization of all kinds of information, from text to visual images and sound, has made another steep step-change possible in the rate and clarity of communication amongst specialists. However, it is important to look at how this technology produces new communities and how their learning severs the ties which hold existing communities together as well as building new structures.

From an actor-network standpoint, networked learning that simply seeks to reproduce in cyberspace the characteristics of educational settings, misses the main event, namely the appearance and emergence of new networks and the collapse of old. Learning is an aspect of the process through which new networks are knitted together, but this is a competitive, even combative, as well as a collaborative process. A further point Latour draws from his discussion, is that "...the cost of disagreeing will increase" (Latour, 1990:34). For Tycho Brahe, as for subsequent generations of scientist, the visual transparency of their truth claims, led to disputes, disagreements and rival schools of thought. The effect of printing press technology was that scientific arguments were now settled by reference to figures, graphs, images, regression lines, supporting any truth claim with the customary: 'from figure 1 it can be shown that statement S is the case'. To disagree with any such claim, an opponent would have to marshal a similar body of data and represent it using the same or better technology. Thus the history of science is full of new inventions (electron microscopes, telescopes, satellites, ultra-scans, *etc.*) all designed to help us *see* and know better than before. As Latour puts it:

> "...the proof race is similar to the arms race because the feedback system
> is the same. Once one competitor starts building up harder facts, the
> others have to do the same or else submit." (Latour, 1990:35)

Who will win in an antagonistic encounter between two authors and between them and all the others they need to build up a statement S? Answer: the one able *to muster on the spot the largest number of well aligned and faithful allies.* This definition of victory is common to war, politics, law and ... now ... science and technology (Latour, 1990:23).

The identification of collaborative and competing networks and their characteristic learning patterns, through research, is arguably what networked learning should be about, rather than the design of new utopian cyber-classrooms. These networks are not only found in science but in corporate contexts too, where strategic decision making depends upon board room presentations marshalling facts and figures garnered from around the world. To study how such networks learn, NL would be accepting the critique of conventional education and educationaliżed cognitivist notions of learning, levelled by Lave and Wenger (1991), and would be accepting an actor-network account of 'the social' bit of socially situated learning theory. Some of the issues involved are suggested in a recent collection edited by Steve Jones (1999), such as Fernback's (1999) discussion of the definition of cyber-community. However, ANT's wider point is that actor-networks are not simply built from new media technologies, but by 'users' who do new things with new forms of communication. The new politics of anarchy and anti-capitalist social movements are cases in point.

In conclusion, the main point of this chapter is not to totally redirect the project of networked learning from creating new kinds of electronically mediated educational experience and institution. Rather it is to add to that project a further concern with researching the actual and novel uses to which the internet is being put by users - individuals, groups, communities, social movements - whose actions, facilitated by the new technology have consequences for existing social institutions from politics to education to the family and more. To follow Lave and Wenger (1991), it is as important to conduct research on what I have here called 'wild learning,' occurring naturally outside classrooms and schools, as it is to refine the learning processes going on within educational settings with the aid of the new technology.

If we were to follow Lave and Wenger in regard to electronically networked socially situated learning, occurring in the wild, then actor-network theory provides a way of looking at the issues from a standpoint which emphasizes the network as much as the learner or actor. Actors can only act or learn within networks, just as Tycho Brahe could only see the night sky from within a network produced by the mundane technology of the printing press. Rather than thinking of 'the learner' as being an individual mind, like a mental container, waiting to be filled up we must see the learner as an integral part of a network, an actant amongst heterogeneous actants, and the whole network exists as a learning/acting process. The learning process, in this account of social theory, is a concrete effect of a network and the learning process in turn transforms the network. To study how this takes place in actual case studies is what I recommend here as the study of networked learning. It may be possible that the findings of such research might facilitate the better design of electronically mediated learning spaces. However, the main benefit of this research would be to simply understand 'naturally' occurring networked learning.

5.6   References

Arterton, C. (1987) *Teledemocracy: Can Technology Protect Democracy?* Newbury Park, CA: Sage

Asensio, M., Foster, J., Hodgson, V. & McConnell, D. (Eds.) (2000) *Networked Learning 2000: Innovative Approaches to Lifelong Learning and Higher Education Through the Internet.* Proceedings of the 2nd International Conference, Lancaster University, 2000

Austin, J.L. (1962) *How to do things with words: the William James lectures delivered at Harvard University in 1955.* 2nd edn. In Urmson, J.O. & Sbisa, M. (eds.) Oxford: Oxford University Press

Brown, J. S. & Duguid. P. (1991) Organizational learning and communities of practice: toward a unified view of learning, working and innovation. *Organization Science, 2* (1) 40-57

Burgoyne, J.G. & Hodgson, V. (1983) Natural learning and managerial action: a phenomenological study in the field setting. *Journal of Management Studies, 20* (3) 387-99

Callon, M. (1986a) Some elements in a sociology of translation: domestication of the scallops and fishermen of St. Brieuc Bay. In Law, J. (Ed.) *Power, Action and Belief* (pp196-233). London: Routledge

Callon, M. (1986b) The sociology of an actor-network the case of the electric vehicle. In Law, J. & Rip, A. (Eds.) *Mapping the Dynamics of Science and Technology* (pp19-34). London: Macmillan

Davis, M. & Denning, K. (2000) 'Online Learning: Frontiers in the Creation of Learning Communities.' In Asensio, M., Foster, J., Hodgson, V. & McConnell, D. (Eds.) *Networked Learning 2000: Innovative Approaches to Lifelong Learning and Higher Education Through the Internet.* Proceedings of the 2nd International Conference, Lancaster University, 2000

Eisenstein, E. (1979) *The Printing Press as an Agent of Change.* Cambridge: Cambridge University Press

Fernback, J. (1999) There is a there there: notes toward a definition of cybercommunity. In Jones, S. (Ed.) *Doing Internet Research: Critical Issues and Methods for Examining the Net.* Thousand Oaks: Sage

Fox, S. (1994) Debating management learning 1. *Management Learning, 25* (1) 83-93

Fox, S. (1997a) Situated learning theory versus traditional cognitive learning theory: why management education should not ignore management learning.' *Systems Practice, 10* (6) 727-747

Fox, S. (1997b) From management education and development to the study of management learning. In Burgoyne, J. & Reynolds, M. (Eds.) *Management Learning: Integrating Perspectives in Theory and Practice.* London: Sage

Fox, S. (2000) Communities of practice: Foucault and Actor-Network theory. *Journal of Management Studies, 37* (6) 853-867

Freire, P. (1972) *Pedagogy of the Oppressed.* M. Bergman Ramos (trans.). Harmondsworth: Penguin

Giroux, H. A. (1983) *Theory and Resistance in Education: A Pedagogy for the Opposition.* London: Heinemann

Grossman, L.K. (1995) *The Electronic Republic: Reshaping Democracy in the Information Age.* New York: Viking

Hague, B.N. & Loader, B.D. (Eds.) (1999) *Digital Democracy: Discourse and Decision Making in the Information Age.* London: Routledge

Hale, M., Musso, J. & Weare, C. (1999) Developing digital democracy: evidence from Californian municipal web pages. In Hague, B.N. & Loader, B.D. (Eds.) *Digital Democracy: Discourse and Decision Making in the Information Age.* London: Routledge

Hodgson, V. (2000) Changing concepts of the boundaries within ODL. In Asensio, M., Foster, J., Hodgson, V. & McConnell, D. (Eds.) *Networked Learning 2000: Innovative Approaches to Lifelong Learning and Higher Education Through the Internet.* Proceedings of the 2nd International Conference, Lancaster University, 2000

hooks, b. (1994) *Teaching to Transgress: Education as the Practice of Freedom.* New York: Routledge

Hutchins, E. (1993) Learning to navigate. In Chaiklin, S. & Lave, J. (Eds.) *Understanding Practice: Perspectives on Activity and Context.* Cambridge: Cambridge University Press

Jones, S. (Ed.) (1999) *Doing Internet Research: Critical Issues and Methods for Examining the Net.* Thousand Oaks: Sage

Latour, B. (1986) The powers of association. In Law, J. (Ed.), *Power, Action and Belief* (pp264-80). London: Routledge

Latour, B. (1990) Drawing things together. In Lynch, M. & Woolgar, S. (Eds.) *Representations in Scientific Practice.* Cambridge, MA: MIT Press

Latour, B. (1991) Technology is society made durable. In Law, J. (Ed.) *A Sociology of Monsters* (pp103-31). London: Routledge

Lave, J. & Wenger, E. (1991) *Situated Learning: Legitimate Peripheral Participation.* Cambridge: Cambridge University Press

Law, J. (1987) Technology and heterogeneous engineering: the case of the Portuguese expansion'. In Bijker, W.E., Hughes, T.P. & Pinch, T. (Eds.), *Social Construction of Technological Systems* (pp111-34). Cambridge, MA: MIT Press

Law, J. (1991) Introduction: monsters, machines and sociotechnical relations. In Law, J. (Ed.) *A Sociology of Monsters* (pp1-23). London: Routledge

Law, J. (1992) Notes on the theory of the actor network: ordering, strategy and heterogeneity. *Systems Practice,* 5: 379-93

Lingis, A. (2000) *Dangerous Emotions.* Berkeley: University of California Press

Marsick, V.J. & Watkins, K. (1990) *Informal and Incidental Learning in the Workplace.* London: Routledge

Moore, T.W. (1974) *Educational Theory: An Introduction.* London: Routledge & Kegan Paul

Reid, E. (1999) Hierarchy and power: social control in cyberspace. In Smith, M.A. & Kollock, P. (Eds.) *Communities in Cyberspace.* London: Routledge

Wenger, E. (1998) *Communities of Practice: Learning, Meaning, and Identity.* Cambridge: Cambridge University Press

6. The Changing Nature of Instructional Design for Networked Learning

Radha Ganesan, Gerald S. Edmonds and J. Michael Spector

6.1 Introduction

Networked learning systems bring learning support and instructional materials directly to learners who can potentially access materials from anywhere at anytime. This may be accomplished by employing a number of tools and methods ranging from simple e-mail to computer supported collaborative work environments. It is possible to make use of networks to share web-based resources and deploy powerful electronic performance support systems (see Figure 6.1). We shall use the term 'networked learning' to refer to this broad range of tools and technologies. Networked learning is an established reality in many different kinds of learning settings, ranging from homes to schools to offices. The obvious conclusions are that networked learning must be meeting some learning needs and it must be reasonably effective and efficient; otherwise, the fad would have passed and interest would be waning. While developments and learning effects in networked and collaborative settings have received a great deal of attention in recent years, there is not nearly as much literature on the changing nature of instructional design due to networked learning.

This chapter addresses the instructional design issues with regard to networked and distributed learning environments. We are especially interested in how designing networked learning environments may be causing designers to reconceptualize the design process itself. Our objective is twofold: (1) we want to represent the challenges of designing distributed learning environments; and, (2) we want to provide insight into how some designers are meeting these challenges. Not surprisingly, one way to meet the challenges of designing for distributed environments is to make use of the very technology that makes the design process more complex – distributed computer networks.

As always, there are some design efforts for networked environments that are reasonably small and discrete and easily managed using existing design models and frameworks. However, networked learning environments have a tendency to grow in scale rather quickly. As the efforts become larger involving multiple institutions, cultures, languages or subject areas, the associated design tasks can become overwhelming. As with other complex and ill-structured tasks, collaboration can help in a number of ways, including representing and managing

complex problem areas and distributing and co-ordinating a variety of design tasks
and activities.

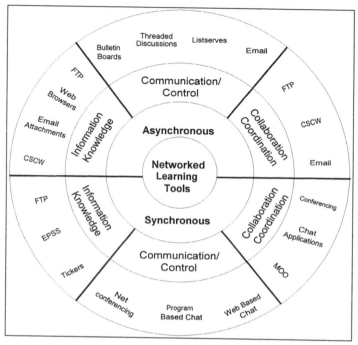

Figure 6.1 Networked learning tools

We begin by providing a historical context for networked learning. We next
focus on the complexity of instructional design, especially in light of new
technologies and paradigms. We then discuss collaborative distance learning and
the associated notion of computer-supported collaborative work (CSCW). We then
present a model for integrating communication, co-ordination and control into a
knowledge management system for the collaborative design of instruction.

6.2   Conceptual Background

Networked learning dates to the implementation of the mainframe PLATO®
system. As documented by Wooley (1994), the PLATO system was developed at
the University of Illinois by Don Bitzer and colleagues and became the foundation
for the Computer-based Education Research Laboratory (CERL). An underlying
authoring language called TUTOR was developed. In addition, a system for
creating and circulating notes was also developed. Originally these notes were
intended for personal use, but they quickly evolved into group notes, greatly
expanding the way that networked communications were used to support learning.
Control Data Corporation developed PLATO into a commercially successful

system outside academia. PLATO provided the foundation for many related products and systems, including AuthorWare, Lotus Notes, TENCORE, and VAX Notes. PLATO survives today at The Roach Organization, Inc. Wooley (1994) reports that the PLATO system logged 10 million hours of use between 1978 and 1985 at CERL.

This brief history of PLATO suggests several key dimensions upon which we shall build. The first is that communication among learners was successful far beyond all early expectations. Moreover, one of the communication features in PLATO was so generally successful that it has evolved into such group work support environments as LOTUS Notes. What happened that made this early online learning system so successful in so many ways? The most likely explanation is the Internet, of course, although much credit should be given to the innovation and foresight shown by the developers of PLATO and its progeny.

Once easy and facile communications among distance learners (and workers) became commonplace, the next issue to address became co-ordination. As more and more people are involved in either a learning activity or a work task, it becomes important not only to support communication among these people, but also to provide them with the means to co-ordinate and track their activities and progress toward the project's goals. There are many dimensions to co-ordination, ranging from structuring notes to scheduling activities to negotiating roles and responsibilities (Malone & Crowston, 1993). At the co-ordination level, it makes sense to think of specific course events and learning activities as opposed to thinking of simple communication support for entire courses. This, of course, allows us to think about distributed support for learning in a much richer way than the simpler two-dimensional distinction often drawn between online courses and classroom instruction. We shall return to this notion later, but it leads us to the final piece of our conceptual background, namely that of control.

The notion of control may be anathema to some who might argue that providing proper support for communication and co-ordination are sufficient and that trying to control what others do and think is not necessary and indeed impossible. Our view is that control follows quite naturally from the notions of communicating and co-ordinating. From a computer systems perspective, there are control functions associated with the operating system and the various events co-ordinated by the operating system. From a cognitive psychology perspective, there are executive control functions associated with individual reasoning, and these are essential for the development of higher order learning and metacognition. From a management perspective, the activities of multiple actors require oversight if they are to be properly supported. From an instructional design perspective, the issue of learner control versus system control remains a real and ongoing concern, as illustrated by the widespread adoption of the cognitive apprenticeship model (Collins, 1991; Collins *et al.*, 1989).

By focusing on communication, co-ordination and control we do not intend to diminish the role of information and knowledge in the design of a learning environment or instructional system. Indeed, information is basic to nearly everything that occurs in a networked system. Information is being passed, parsed, and processed in a wide variety of ways at many different levels. As computer and network systems have advanced, it became obvious that databases (structured collections of information) were vital. Even more useful were knowledge management systems that provide rules for accessing, browsing, interpreting, interrelating, modifying, reusing, and extending the information in a database.

We need information and the means to structure and manage that information in order to have an effective networked system (see Spector & Anderson, 2000). When learning tasks are complex and socially situated, as is the case more and more often (Jonassen *et al.*, 2000), we need to provide support for collaboration and co-operation on a variety of learning activities. Most often, the support is related to the co-ordination and communication functions of a networked environment. However, as tasks and activities are distributed, it becomes important to maintain some kind of control to insure that work is not redundant or lost, that appropriate information and knowledge is accessible and shared, and that project deficiencies are repaired.

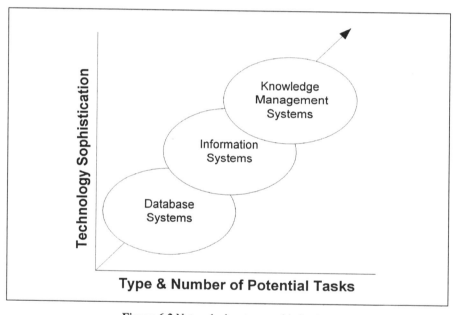

Figure 6.2 Networked system sophistication

In what follows, we discuss issues concerning communication, co-ordination and control as they pertain to designers. This allows us to examine how we can use networked computer systems as tools for supporting the design of large-scale, networked and distributed learning environments and instructional systems. We argue that a collaborative design model is a natural evolution of the way that we are planning and implementing learning and instructional systems. We do not argue that one ought to substitute computer-mediated communication, co-ordination and control for face-to-face methods. Our position is that there are good reasons why more and more designers will make use of distributed and collaborative models, just as there are good reasons why networked and distributed learning is growing. Those reasons include these realities: (1) design expertize for technology-based settings is relatively scarce and distributed; (2) technology-based solutions are expensive and the leverage of lessons learned by others is vital; and, (3) the complexities introduced by new technologies and paradigms requires a broad perspective. Our emphasis is not with specific technologies, although we shall mention two systems that are being used for the collaborative design of learning and instruction. We are more interested in the instructional design process once it is situated in the context of a distributed (computer-supported collaborative) work environment.

6.3   The Complexity of Instructional Design

There are numerous and different kinds of tasks involved in the analysis, planning, implementation and evaluation of large-scale projects involving learning environments and instructional systems. In this chapter we do not distinguish a learning environment from an instructional system, although we realize that there are reasons in other contexts for doing so.

Instructional design is a complex and ill-structured process (Goel & Pirolli, 1989). Apart from the complexities introduced by technology, there are a diverse set of problems and considerations that comprise instructional design (Rowland, 1992). One aspect of instructional design complexity concerns the variety of things that must be done. An instructional designer may interact with managers, with people performing tasks to be trained, with subject experts, with system specialists, and so on. A designer may have to propose solutions and defend project plans, manage a project, choose media, develop storyboards and other products, conduct evaluations, and so on. It is rare to find one individual who is good at all of these different activities or who would have the time to perform them all on a large-scale effort or for many different projects. As project complexity grows, so grows the need to collaborate with others and co-ordinate these various activities.

Another aspect of instructional design complexity concerns the ill-structured nature of goals and requirements. It is quite rare to find a client who has well-articulated goals and requirements for a learning environment or instructional system. It is much more common to encounter a goal such as this: put these courses on the web and make them better. The designer who confronts ill-structured goals confronts a negotiation task that is dynamic in the sense that goals and requirements are likely to evolve as the project proceeds; managing activities in the face of changing requirements is a complex task that often falls to the instructional designer. Effective management in this context requires effective communication, and control processes.

Associated with this particular challenge is the negotiation of how best to achieve goals and requirements. There are almost always alternative ways to implement a learning environment. Costs are usually a primary concern, although contexts, learning outcomes and organizational impact are of obvious importance. Again it is difficult to imagine any one person mastering such different areas of expertize.

Further, when we get to the details of a course or lesson design, we confront the issue of distributing specific course events and activities versus putting the entire course online. We noted this distinction earlier, and it represents one of the big lessons learned over the years with regard to educational technology. That lesson is that it is not likely to be effective or efficient to simply replace one delivery medium with another without consideration given to particular learning activities and situations. We have been tempted to think that we can replace a less experienced science teacher with a video series of a master science teacher, or that we could replace classroom instruction on geometry with a computer-based geometry tutor. The real complexity for designers arises when they try to match subject matter with learner characteristics and appropriate instructional methods. New technologies offer designers many options for combining instructional contexts. The traditional model of instructor-led workshops is giving way to hybrid course designs that include a combination of technology-mediated events and more traditional classroom events. Distributed forms of interaction, such as virtual communities and tele-mentoring, are now possible. These types of interactions allow for the community of learners to engage in information exchanges, communication and collaboration following the formal instructional period. Learning can be embedded in workplace systems. Distributed learning environments, then, encompass a wide array of scenarios, which can potentially involve the use of many different technologies and learning contexts. This most certainly adds significantly to the complexity of designing effective instruction.

6.3.1   New Technologies and Paradigms

We should first make clear a distinction between networked and distributed systems. We have used these terms interchangeably but there are differences. Networked systems imply a particular kind of technology infrastructure, namely a computer network. Distributed systems imply a particular kind of working environment or knowledge infrastructure, namely the fact that key actors may be involved in different locations and access and share information at different times. These two concepts do not divide the world up exactly the same way, but there are obvious relationships. When the working situation is distributed, as so many are (Salomon, 1993), it becomes quite natural to consider a network supported solution.

Many have argued that the dominant learning paradigm has changed. Jonassen and colleagues (1999, 2000) argue that the new learning paradigm is predominantly and fundamentally constructivist. Resnick and colleagues (1991) argued earlier that the new paradigm was socially shared cognition. These views are generally compatible and are espoused by many other prominent educational researchers (see, for example, Bruner, 1985; Lave, 1988; Lave & Wenger, 1990; Pea, 1993; Spector & Anderson, 2000). The reality that these changes represent for the designer is not revolutionary, but they do add to the complexity of design. It is not simple to decide to what extent an open-ended, exploratory environment is likely to be effective with a particular group of learners for a particular subject, or to compare that alternative with a guided discovery alternative. Deciding how to effectively implement and support socially situated learning activities is likewise complex. Balancing costs and expected outcomes of alternative solutions is no simple matter, especially since newer approaches have little effectiveness data on which to build realistic expectations.

Changes more revolutionary than constructivism are underway, however, and they most definitely make instructional design more challenging than ever before. These changes are occurring in the workplace and involve adult learners. One set of organizational changes involves an attitude with regard to workplace learning. It is partly a result of the growing support for lifelong learning and it is partly a result of emphasis on developing a genuine learning organization (Dean & Ripley, 1998; Senge, 1990; Wagner, 2000). The complexity that these changes produce for the designer include the requirement to take a much larger and longer perspective than the traditional focused perspective of designing a course.

Associated with these organizational changes is a change in the way we are coming to think about learning with regard to adults in the workplace. Goodyear (2000) argues that there is a growing shift for adult knowledge workers to become actively involved in their continuing education and to demand flexible and adaptable support to further their training and education. Not only do designers have to consider new learning paradigms, they now have to consider new working paradigms and organizational settings.

Finally, some of these new learning opportunities will be embedded in or associated with information systems already in place in work settings. A designer cannot simply produce a learning solution apart from some consideration of such systems. Indeed, the requirement may be to embed the training within an information or knowledge management system, as we shall soon see. Again, such a situation increases the complexity of instructional design decision-making.

6.4   Collaboration, CSCW and Group Support

Instructional Design is increasingly using computer-supported systems to facilitate its process. This phenomenon is most commonly referred to as Computer-Supported Collaborative Work (CSCW) and Group Decision Support Systems (GDSS). These new technologies allow for creating environments and processes that support instructional design activities in a distributed setting as an essential part of refining the routine.

The term Computer-Supported Collaborative Work (CSCW) originated with Greif and Cashman (Bannon, 1991). Computer scientists coined this term for a small invited workshop focusing on the development of computer systems that would support people in their work related activities (Bannon, 1991). Though computer-supported systems are being increasingly accepted in this field, a consensus has not yet emerged on a definition for the term that could be accepted by all (Bannon, 1991; Wilson, 1991). Some use the term to express the idea of collaboration among people using computers (Howard, 1988; Kling, 1991); while others regard it as a representation of a paradigm shift (Hughes, Randall & Shapiro, 1991; Suchman, 1989). Still others view CSCW as referring to software for groups of people or groupware.

CSCW systems are in general customized to support multiple people working at the same workstation or across networked systems. We believe that it is essential to match work activities and practice with appropriate technologies. In designing instructional systems and learning environments, a key element is collaboration. And in such an environment, CSCW has a natural role to play in instructional design. This is best illustrated by our two examples.

Our understanding of the term CSCW falls in line with Bannon and Schmidt's (1989:3-5) definition of CSCW. They define it as "an endeavour to understand the nature and characteristics of co-operative work with the objective of designing adequate computer-based technologies". This definition of CSCW combines the understanding of the way people work in groups; and how the computer networking technologies, and associated hardware, software, services and strategies can be designed to support their work-related activities. The intent here is to provide an environment that supports workplace collaboration. Earlier we have been using simple tools such as e-mail to support collaborative work. These systems are designed to support in exchanging ideas, accessing information, and providing feedback on problem-solving activities. Such tools while providing communication support for collaborative work lack explicit co-ordination and control functionalities. By offering an extensible centralized architecture and cross-platform browser and integrated with user environments, the Web may provide a means of introducing CSCW systems which offer much richer support for collaboration than e-mail and FTP, and thus serve as an `enabling technology' for CSCW (Eseryel & Ganesan, 2001). These experiences led to the notion of developing integrated platform for CSCW applications. New and more powerful CSCW application software is being developed which include functionalities that address key issues such as:

- group awareness;
- multi-user interfaces;
- synchronized control;
- communication and co-ordination among group members;
- shared information space; and
- support of a diverse environment, which integrates with the existing single-user applications.

Examples of such CSWC application software include Xerox's DocuShare and Seven Mountains' Enterprize (Integrate and Aspire).

An early example of online group support for complex tasks is group model building. The process of model construction requires the commitment and input of all stakeholders (Vennix 1996). In the field of systems dynamics tools and techniques were developed to foster the process of group-model building (Morecroft & Sterman, 1994; Richardson & Andersen, 1995). The model builders' tools and techniques supported decision-making, small-group communication and project management (Vennix 1996). The group model building process and techniques may likewise inform instructional planning and analysis. The added advantage is that participants in group planning processes fits well with the notion of participatory design. Moreover, the success of Vennix and others in the area of group model building demonstrates that group work on complex tasks in a distributed environment can be effective.

As mentioned above, several small and focused communities of professional practice make effective use of online collaborative support for complex tasks. But what we need is a community of practice for distributed design and development of learning environments and instructional systems. The CSCW technologies can offer new kinds of interactions and activities for designers working in a distributed environment.

6.5   Collaborative Design and Knowledge Management

As the educational field is becoming increasingly networked, more and more educational institutions are providing online training and education. Managing these large volumes of information and knowledge assets is one of the crucial issues covered by the technology called knowledge management. We assert that knowledge management technology could be successfully applied to the educational field. We focus on the use of shared workspaces and knowledge management cognitive tools to support the design process.

There are several systems being used to support the collaborative design of instruction, including Lotus Notes, an outgrowth of the early PLATO system. We are familiar with two such systems and report briefly here on their capabilities and usage: Xerox Corporations' *DocuShare & FlowPort* and SevenMountains' *7M Enterprize (Integrate & Aspire).*

6.5.1   Xerox DocuShare and FlowPort

DocuShare is a web-based document management system that requires users to have access to the Internet and familiarity with a web browser. DocuShare is a powerful yet extremely simple software tool that allows the sharing of users' documents with others via the web. Each user can add, post, change, search for and retrieve information in a secure, controlled environment. Users can exchange text, images, video (avi, quicktime, mpg), office documents, sound files – anything in digital format over the web – without FTP software, browser plug-ins, or HTML skills. Users have four methods of putting documents onto the web: (1) through their web browser by clicking 'Add File'; (2) by dragging and dropping files to a networked folder; (3) from with their word-processors or other ODMA software applications (just choose Save and DocuShare asks if you would like to store the file on the web); and (4) paper documents can be added directly to the web as a PDF using a scanner and additional software called FlowPort. In addition, DocuShare allows for the storing of URL's, shared calendars, and bulletin boards. Every document is indexed to allow for the capability to search for any piece of text contained in a document. DocuShare can also track from 1 to 999 different versions of a document complete with date, time and user stamp. For users that may be using different applications, for example MS Word and Corel's WordPerfect, DocuShare has an automatic HTML conversion feature that allows users of different programs the ability to view documents.

Design teams can use DocuShare to manage all the documents (digital or paper) associated with an instructional design project. A collection (a directory or folder) is created for the project and users are given a user-id and password to access the collection. As a project is divided into manageable pieces or team members assume different roles (e.g., project manager) sub-collections can be created, for example: (1) Project Management Plan; (2) Front-End Analysis; (3) Learner Analysis; (4) Goal Analysis; (5) Instructional or task analysis, etc. Team members can also create bulletin boards and start adding documents to the project's collections. Since all the documents and communication are stored on one central accessible server individual members do not have to manage or track documents on their individual computers. As team members checkout a document DocuShare 'locks' the original to prevent parallel changes while another team member is adding or editing material. Once the document is checked back into the collection the lock is removed and other team members can checkout the document. The training required to use DocuShare is minimal and the program itself contains a CBT lesson as well as a user job-aid of quick instructions and a longer user manual. DocuShare has been used to host online and hybrid courses at Syracuse University and is now being used as front-end planning and document sharing system for groups of instructors and designers working together on a variety of courses. Figure 6.3 depicts a screen from the Syracuse University DocuShare environment.

The first use of DocuShare to support collaborative design and development occurred in 1999 in Syracuse University's IDE 617 Instructional Product Development course. In this course, students work in teams to design and develop an instructional product for a real client who has submitted a project for consideration. One team used DocuShare to support their teams' efforts. Team 1 was working on a project for Syracuse University Project Advance to develop a software-training manual. The team had an opportunity to meet once a week to plan their activities and then to use the software to support their efforts. The team established collections that mirrored the sections described in the Dick and Carey instructional design model. Each team member could then upload material required in each section of the model as well as reacting to each other's documents. They also created a collection for their final product. The team would also indicate which folders and items were to be reviewed by the instructor who would download the document, make comments and upload the edited document. The team created a calendar to track events. The team reported that the use of the CSCW worked well for managing the design process. DocuShare has also been used to support online course design, development and implementation.

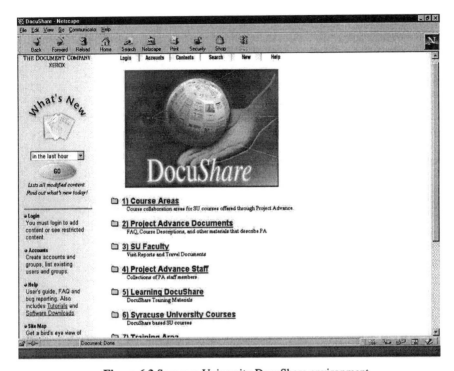

Figure 6.3 Syracuse University DocuShare environment

The use of the Docushare CSCW proved so successful, easy to use and maintain, it was expanded to include instructional support for geographically dispersed adjunct instructors of the university involved in a partnership program, campus based dissemination of course evaluations, office management of paper and an affiliated State college's graduate admissions process.

6.5.2   7M Integrate and Aspire

The Seven Mountains' Integrate and Aspire distributed document and project management system consists of an information management component that provides generic document management functions such as creating, storing, editing, viewing, searching, deleting, publishing, distributing, routing, and managing versions. This information management component is a building block for other applications that extend the capabilities and functionality into areas such as knowledge and project management. The particular way that 7M applications are structured is very much in line with the structure presented in our Figure 6.1 in the conceptual background section of this chapter. Information is basic to all aspects of a networked system. Communications might be considered the lifeblood. As soon as collaboration and co-ordination (typical project activities) are introduced, control becomes paramount.

This system is being used by the European consortium working on the Adapt-IT project to develop a set of integrated tools for the design of instruction for the aviation industry. This project team is also using 7M to collaborative design test pieces of instructional plans. Figure 6.4 depicts the 7M environment at the University of Bergen as used to support collaborative design of tools and materials for the Adapt-IT project. The word file can be opened from the 7M environment and viewed, checked out (locked for changes), downloaded or uploaded, and checked-in (released to others). The system automatically tracks and archives multiple versions, as does the Xerox system.

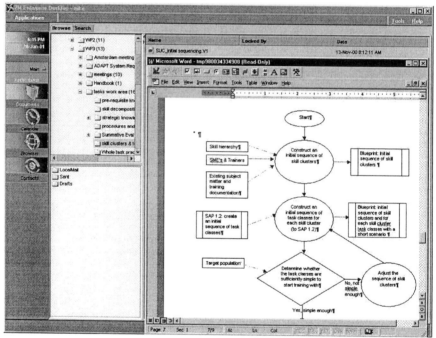

Figure 6.4 Adapt-IT 7M environment hosted at the University of Bergen

Thus far, the seven participating partners from five different countries involved in the Adapt-IT project have successfully collaborated in the design of an online tutorial. As well as several learning support modules for air traffic control and aircraft maintenance training project working meetings are regularly held in a virtual setting using 7M Integrate as the core technology. It is clear that this technology has significantly reduced travel costs and promoted frequent collaboration on complex tasks.

6.6 Discussion

Collaborative software that allows users to easily communicate, co-ordinate, collaborate and control teamwork was uncommon until recently. Previous developments such as Plato Notes, the growth of the web and the creation of virtual shared spaces lead to the development of new ways of computer-mediated work in the form of CSCW. Internet tools such as e-mail, listservs, and threaded discussions were useful for communicating among team members but using these media to distribute and collaborate on documents is burdensome. Using these media to edit documents can be confusing and time-consuming. For example, if the owner of a document e-mails it to ten other team members, ten versions of the document now exist all with the potential to contain edits, and rewrites. If an e-mail routing slip (as in Microsoft Outlook) is attached to a document and sent to users in a linear manner, as with paper documents, one user can stop the entire process. The creation of web pages to share information is also not a practical approach. The creation of web pages relies on a user's ability to use an HTML editor, FTP skills to upload the document or the reliance on a webmaster to complete those tasks. Tools such as DocuShare and 7M Integrate allow users to employ the software applications they already use. If a user can point and click or drag and drop they can use the software to share information with other team members. In addition, these software packages remove the burden of document control and co-ordination from a project manager as the software tracks different versions of a document and manages the checking out and checking in of documents. CSCW software allows for geographically separated team members to contribute to a project.

Whenever newer information and communications technologies have emerged, the trend has been for those technologies to find their way into the fields of learning and instructional delivery. For example, when the Internet exploded in the field of education, the concentration was on providing distance-learning using the Web. Not much thought was given to the design aspects of the instructional materials or the entire learning environment. We could use those new technologies to support instructional design as well, and recent work in the area of web-based learning reflect a much more mature use of the web to support learning and instruction. Our experiences with tools like Xerox's Docushare and 7M in the Adapt-It Project demonstrate that we can also use CSCW tools to support the design of instruction. These and similar tools provide a new dimension of distributed support for instructional design that is likely to have an impact on how instructional designers work. We do not yet know what that impact will be but we can hope that practice will be improved as a result.

6.7   Concluding Remarks

While networked learning systems are becoming more common, the use of such systems in supporting the design of instruction is still quite uncommon. Some of the same tools that are used to support learning and working are also useful to instructional design teams as support for managing, creating and implementing instructional design projects. For instance, software such as DocuShare and 7M Integrate represent a new stage of collaborative web-based software systems. They require no special tools and, more importantly, do not require the user to adjust their program and tool preferences to be able to benefit from such environments. In addition, the ease of moving documents and instructional design materials and artefacts onto the web makes it easy to quickly and efficiently share resources with remote team members.   Additionally, the software removes the control and tracking burden from a project manager and from team members. The software provides a central repository that tracks multiple versions of a document complete with date and time stamp, comments, and version history. DocuShare and 7M make the web transparent in that there is no need for users to know HTML or how to FTP. A user simply can drag and drop a file into a folder that then is instantaneously posted onto the web with set permission to share with a team. These software programs potentially open new avenues for collaborative instructional design. What patterns of interaction among instructional design team members will emerge around the integration of such collaborative work tools remains to be seen, however.

Group model building in system dynamics demonstrates that collaborative and distributed groups working on complex tasks can be effective. The use of CSCW and GDSS systems changes the nature of design into a collaborative endeavour not dependent on time or geographic location. These systems also remove much of the barrier on an instructional design team for tracking and managing documents that are produced. Networked learning makes information available and allows for collaboration across time and space; the same applies to networked working. The knowledge and skills of subject specialists, information specialists, computing specialists and others working collaboratively is crucial for using networked technologies and information effectively.

Networked communication and information technologies are creating a significantly new environment for higher education. A wide variety and kinds of information and computer technologies now under development will be essential to developing networked learning communities of the future and will determine both the course and the pace of ongoing developments. The Internet technologies will provide the essential medium/catalyst for creating such networked learning environments in the near future. What we now need are studies that begin to build towards a model of collaborative design. We now have a few isolated cases of where people are engaged in collaborative model building (a complex cognitive activity) and collaborative instructional design (also a complex cognitive activity). We have very little evidence on which to base broad conclusions or to form strong beliefs about causal relationships between forms of collaboration, forms of complex cognitive activities, and associated outcomes. What we have are great possibilities but very little evidence with regard to what forms of collaboration work best in various situations.

6.8   References

Bannon, L.J. (1991) From human factors to human actors: the role of psychology and human-computer interaction studies in system design. In Greenbaum, J. & Kyng, M. (Eds.) *Design at Work: Co-operative Design of Computer Systems*, 25-44. Hillsdale, NJ: Lawrence Erlbaum Associates. Reprinted in Baecker, R.M., Grudin, J., Buxton, W.A.S. & Greenberg, S. (1995) *Readings in Human-Computer Interaction: Toward the year 2000*, pp205-214 (2nd edition). San Francisco, CA: Morgan Kaufmann Publishers. http://www.ul.ie/~idc/library/papersreports/LiamBannon/6/HFHA.html

Bannon, L. & Schmidt, K. (1989) CSCW: Four Characters in Search of a Context. In *Proc. First European Conference on CSCW*, Gatwick, UK, September. (Reprinted in Bowers, J. & Benford, S. (Eds.) (1991*). Studies in Computer Supported Co-operative Work: Theory, Practice and Design*. Amsterdam: North-Holland pp3-16

Bruner, J.S. (1985) Models of the Learner. *Educational Researcher, 14*(6), 5-8

Clement, A. & van den Besselaar, P. (1993) Participatory Design Projects: A Retrospective Look. *Communications of the ACM, 36,* (6)

Collins, A., Brown, J.S., & Newman, S.E. (1989) Cognitive Apprenticeship: Teaching the Crafts of Reading, Writing, and Mathematics. In Resnick, L.B. (Ed.), *Knowing, Learning, and Instruction: Essays in Honour of Robert Glaser*. Mahwah, New Jersey: Lawrence Erlbaum Associates pp53-494

Collins, A. (1991) Cognitive Apprenticeship and Instructional Technology. In Idol, L. & Jones, B.F. (Eds.), *Educational Values and Cognitive Instruction: Implications for Reform*. Hillsdale, NJ: Lawrence Erlbaum Associates

Dean, P.J. & Ripley, D.E. (1998) *Performance Improvement Interventions: Instructional Design and Training International* Washington, DC: Society for Performance Improvement.

Goel, V. & Pirolli, P. (1989) Motivating the Notion of Generic Design Within Information Processing: The Design Space Problem. *AI Magazine, 10*(1) 18-36

Greif, I, (Ed.) (1988*) Computer-Supported Co-operative Work: A Book of Readings*. San Mateo, CA: Morgan Kaufmann

Goodyear, P. (2000) Environments for Lifelong Learning: Ergonomics, Architecture and Education Design. In Spector, J.M. & Anderson, T.M. (Eds.), *Integrated and Holistic Perspectives on Learning, Instruction and Technology: Understanding Complexity*. Dordrecht: Kluwer Academic.

Eseryel, D. & Ganesan, R. (2001) Distributed Group Design Process: A Framework *Proceedings of EdMedia 2001*, Tampere, Finland.

Howard, R. (1988) Panel Remarks: CSCW: What Does it Mean*? Proceedings of CSCW'88*, Portland, OR:

Hughes, J., Randall, D. & Shapiro, D. (1991) CSCW: Discipline or Paradigm? In Bannon, L., Robinson, M. & Schmidt, K. (Eds.) *Proceedings of the Second European Conference on CSCW - ECSCW'91.* Dordrecht: Kluwer

Jonassen, D.H., Hernandez-Serrano, J. & Choi, I. (2000) Integrating Constructivism and Learning Technologies. In Spector, J.M. & Anderson, T.M. (Eds.), *Integrated and Holistic Perspectives on Learning, Instruction and Technology: Understanding Complexity,* pp103-128. Dordrecht: Kluwer Academic

Jonassen, D.H., Peck, K.L. & Wilson, G.G. (1999) *Learning with Technology: A constructivist perspective.* Columbus, OH: Prentice Hall.

Kling, R. (1991) Co-operation, Co-ordination and Control in Computer-Supported Work. *Communications of the ACM, 34(12),* pp83-88

Lave, J. (1988) *Cognition in Practice: Mind, Mathematics, and Culture in Everyday Life.* Cambridge, UK: Cambridge University Press

Lave, J. & Wenger, E. (1990) *Situated Learning: Legitimate Peripheral Participation,* Cambridge University Press, Cambridge, UK

Malone, T. & Crowston, K. (1993) The Interdisciplinary Study of Co-ordination. *Computing Surveys, 26* (1), pp87-119

Morecroft, D.W. & Sterman, J.D. (Eds.) (1994) *Modelling for Learning Organizations.* Portland, OR: Productivity Press

Pea, R. (1993) Practices of Distributed Intelligence and Designs for Education. In Salomon, G. (Ed.) *Distributed Cognition: Psychological and Educational Considerations, 47-87.* Cambridge, UK: Cambridge University Press

Resnick, L., Levine, J. & Teasley, S. (1991) (Eds.) *Perspectives on Socially Shared Cognition.* Washington, DC: APA Press.

Richardson, G.P. & Andersen, D.F. (1995) Teamwork in Group Model-Building. *System Dynamics Review, 11* (2), pp113-137

Rowland, G. (1992) What Do Instructional Designers Actually Do? An Initial Investigation of Expert Practice. *Performance Improvement Quarterly 5(2),* pp65-86

Salomon, G. (1993) (Ed.). *Distributed Cognitions: Psychological and Educational Considerations.* Cambridge, UK: Cambridge University Press

Senge, P.M. (1990) *The Fifth Discipline: The Art and Practice of the Learning Organization.* New York: Doubleday

Spector, J.M. & Anderson, T.M. (Eds.) (2000*) Integrated and Holistic Perspectives on Learning, Instruction and Technology: Understanding Complex Domains.* Dordrecht: Kluwer Academic

Suchman, L. (1989) *Notes on Computer Support for Co-operative Work. Working Paper WP-12,* Dept. of Computer Science, University of Jyvaskyla, SF-40100, Jyvaskyla, Finland

Vennix, J.A.M. (1996) *Group Model Building: Facilitating Team Learning Using System Dynamics.* Chichester: John Wiley & Sons

Wagner, E. (2000) Leveraging Technology in the Service of Lifelong Learning. In Spector, J.M. & Anderson, T.M. (Eds.), *Integrated and Holistic Perspectives on Learning, Instruction and Technology: Understanding Complexity.* Dordrecht: Kluwer Academic

Wilson, P. (1991) *Computer Supported Co-operative Work: An Introduction.* Oxford: Intellect Books

Woolley, D.R. (1994, July) PLATO: The Emergence of Online Community. *Computer-Mediated Communication Magazine 1*(3), 5

7. Views on Staff Development for Networked Learning

Carmel McNaught

7.1 Introduction

Effective staff development is the weaving together of many strands. We need to support staff in their current work, while providing them with ideas, incentives and resources to look for new ways to design learning environments that will enhance student learning. When staff development is concerned with how to incorporate networked learning into university courses, an extra layer of complexity enters into the situation because the technology and its educational implications are still very new for many staff. It is particularly important that staff development be combined with specific projects where change is occurring so that staff can continually test out new skills and strategies and get feedback themselves on how effective using networked learning will be for them in their teaching. Ideas are not hard to find. Incentives and resources are another matter.

The chapter outlines some general principles for effective staff development. In order to get effective changes in academic work practices, there is a need for staff development at a local level with time release as an essential component, as exemplified by the Royal Melbourne Institute of Technology's (RMIT) Learning Technology Mentor Program. There is also a need to provide flexible staff development programs. Two ways of doing this are outlined below: the use of a suite of resources and the development of flexible ways to achieve credit towards qualifications for work done during staff development programs. Finally, some questions that have arisen from our work are offered for others to reflect on.

7.2 Universities as Organizations that Support or Hinder Innovation

Universities in Australia are currently in an environment of intense change. They are being required to educate more students, from an increasing variety of backgrounds, with decreasing government funding. Universities are required to compete vigorously for student enrolments and external sources of funding. In this environment, universities have had to reassess their fundamental business and the way they go about it. Information Technology (IT) is viewed as an important factor in streamlining their operations.

In a recent investigation into the factors supporting the adoption of computer-facilitated learning (CFL)[1] at Australian universities (McNaught *et al.*, 2000), three major themes emerged. These were *Policy*, *Culture* and *Support*. The considerable overlap between and within these themes is illustrated in Figure 7.1. There needs to be a congruence of policy, culture and support factors if significant adoption of CFL strategies is to occur.

The *Policy* theme looked at specific institutional policies, such as equity and intellectual property, the alignment of policy throughout the organization, the direction of policy change (bottom-up or top-down) and a number of strategic processes which flowed on from policies such as grant schemes.

Culture incorporated factors such as collaboration within institutions, and personal motivation of staff to use CFL, as well as particular aspects of funding, staff rewards and time, leadership, teaching and learning models, and attitudes such as 'not invented here'.

Support incorporated a whole gamut of institutional issues including IT, library and administrative infrastructure, professional development for staff, student support, educational and instructional design support for academic staff, funding and grant schemes, and IT literacy.

Several universal factors in relation to widespread use of CFL were identified:

- coherence of policy across all levels of institutional operations and specific policies which impact on CFL within each institution;
- intellectual property, particularly the role of copyright in emerging online environments;
- leadership and institutional culture;
- staff issues and attitudes: namely, professional development and training, staff recognition and rewards, and motivation for individuals to use CFL; and
- specific resourcing issues related to funding for maintenance or updating of CFL materials and approaches, staff time release and support staff.

The breadth of these factors can be quite daunting. What we have tried to do at RMIT University is to work on several of these fronts at once though developing policy and processes to support staff across the entire university. The focus of the rest of the chapter will be on how we have conceptualized and developed our staff development program as a strategy to build up staff capability across the entire university.

---

[1]   The term computer-facilitated learning is now commonly used in Australia. It is a reaction against the term computer-based learning. Learning is not based on computers, but computers can be used to facilitate the learning process.

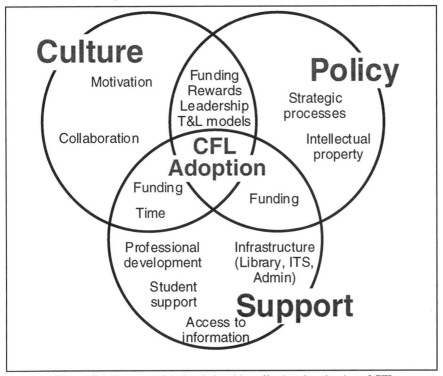

Figure 7.1 Themes and their relationships affecting the adoption of CFL

7.3   Staff Development and Training

We should not underestimate the difficulties involved in innovation and change. Marris (1986) parallels the sense of loss during bereavement to the resistance one can feel when letting go of known ways of doing things and embarking on new strategies. For many academics the increasing emphasis on the use of computer technology for administration, research and teaching is highly threatening. We need to recognize these fears and devise plans that build staff confidence and motivation, and provide adequate support and training opportunities.

Staff development can no longer be a pleasant 'cottage industry' on the fringes of academe or the enthusiastic enterprize of a few individuals supported by 'soft' money. Effective staff development is positioned at the center of university functioning and yet needs to retain connections with the needs and perceptions of teaching staff. This is a demanding challenge. Staff development programs that are successful in meeting the needs of complex modern Australian universities need to be supported strategically (and financially) by their own universities.

The number of players in the professional development area is large, including:

- more 'traditional' academic development units, concentrating on general teaching and learning support; these can be centrally located or faculties;
- units where the key focus is the use of communication and information technologies in teaching and learning; these can be centrally located or faculties; often they are called flexible learning units;
- units which focus on courseware production using technology; these can be centrally located or faculties; some of these are units which have evolved from print-based distance education units;
- centrally-based Information Technology Services units; and
- university libraries.

Hughes, Hewson and Nightingale (1997) in a study of 20 Australian universities describe three approaches to staff development for the use of information technology in teaching – integrated, parallel and distributed. Here is a brief description of these three approaches.

In the *integrated approach* (eggs in one basket!) there are strong structural links between units or section of the one unit which provide general teaching and learning (TandL) support, support for using IT in TandL, and production support for courseware. This is essentially a top-down approach with benefits that the policy framework is likely to be more coherent; and there may be more efficient planning of resources and avoidance of duplication. However, individual approaches are less likely to be recognized and ease of access by all staff may be limited. Further, an emphasis on one technological solution may emerge and overwhelm educational design.

In the *parallel approach* (never the twain shall meet?) separate units for general TandL support and for support for using IT in TandL exist. This can allow due recognition to be given to a wide range of TandL issues (e.g. internationalization) and not just educational design associated with the use of IT, as well allowing the development of expertize relating to the new technologies. However, co-operation between the various units may be difficult to achieve and there is a potential for confusion and competition to emerge. Also, this approach may result in a narrow range of educational issues being addressed in the IT in TandL units.

The *distributed approach* (organic sprouting) is more bottom-up than the other two approaches. A range of units, centrally located and in faculties, develop that are not tightly co-ordinated. Project management remains with local projects. This can be an 'organic' solution where unnecessary controls do not hamper innovation, and can be economical as skills are sought when they are needed. However, the potential exists for innovations to falter without visible institutional support, and can result in waste and duplication of effort and resources, including equipment, across the institution. Because these units are often small, the project management may be weak due to insufficient educational expertize.

In reality, universities use a combination of approaches, though with a trend in one direction. The model of these three approaches is useful as a tool for assessing the potential strengths and weaknesses of the combination of any particular set of support units in a given university.

In the national study cited earlier (McNaught *et al.*, 2000), six key issues in staff development were strongly voiced:

- The appropriate balance point between centrally provided and local staff development services needs to be determined in each university. Central services can be more clearly linked to university priorities; faculty or department services can be more in touch with local needs.
- As technology becomes more mainstream, support services need to be scaled up. This involves deciding on the level of support that can be afforded and the model of support that is most apposite. The educational design and evaluation, technical, and media production support services that universities currently have are under strain. It is unlikely that the existing examples of good practice in courseware at each university will be sufficient in themselves as models for other staff to use in developing new subjects or renewing their existing subjects. However, by modelling good practice themselves, mentors can assist colleagues to make optimal use of resources.
- A follow-on issue is determining the optimal relationship between staff development and production support services. Again, this needs to be decided in each university context.
- Even if an integrated model of professional development is adopted, there are still many professional development providers at most universities. Mapping the services of each provider and ensuring reasonable co-ordination is increasingly important as the need for support services scales up.
- Academic and general staff work load is a key issue. Careful work planning to ensure that staff have time to learn new skills and manage new processes is essential.
- We are in a time of rapid change. It is important that professional development support be flexible, appropriate and adaptable. It should make sense to staff, be linked to practice and be appropriately timed.

7.4   Applying these Ideas to the Context of RMIT University

RMIT University is an 'old' (in Australian terms; RMIT began in 1887) technological university. It is highly diverse – it is a cross-sectoral (includes vocational sector) university and has the largest number of international students of any Australian university. There are seven strong faculties that often resist central directions. In recent years there has not been a strong staff development program.

In the program, which is described below, RMIT wanted staff development which is linked to RMIT business and vision, promotes sound educational practice, ensures flexible learning is 'owned' in every department, organizes adequate support for all staff, and results in low increase in staff work loads.

There are two key policy documents which are currently guiding the direction RMIT adopts in the next three to five years. The first is the Teaching and Learning Strategy (TandLS).

7.4.1 RMIT Teaching and Learning Strategy

The RMIT Teaching and Learning Strategy aims to provide a student-centered learning environment where:

- subjects and the courses they comprise are designed to develop the following graduate attributes in students: knowledgeable, critical, responsible, creative and with a capacity for life-long learning, leadership and employment and an international outlook;
- the system is flexible enough to suit the particular learning needs of students in terms of their prior experience and current situation;
- courses are designed and implemented holistically with coherent connections between subjects comprising the core of a course;
- students and the community are seen as significant stakeholders;
- assessment is directly related to the explicitly stated objectives of subjects; and
- quality improvement and quality assurance based on reflective practice and customer-focused systems design are ubiquitous.

There are resources allocated to implement the TandLS both in human and financial terms. For example, each faculty has two senior positions (Director of Teaching Quality, DoTQ, and Director of Information Technology, DoIT) established by secondment of academic staff members from within the faculty. The DoTQs have responsibility for all course design and accreditation matters and for quality assurance processes. The DoITs have been engaged in upgrading the IT infrastructure across the whole university, as well as supporting the Learning Technology Mentor program (see below). Each faculty has a developing Faculty Education Services Group (FESG) where technical and educational support for staff is available.

The conceptualization of the Teaching and Learning Strategy involves a ripple effect from central policy through to specific student learning environments. In this process, the faculties act as important links between overarching university policy and practical changes in teaching programs. It is at faculty level that university policy is contextualized in a proactive way that is relevant to learning in specific discipline areas in the 21st century. At RMIT, faculties have developed IT strategy plans as drivers for the strategic re-development of IT infrastructure. They have also developed course and subject renewal guidelines as drivers for the strategic re-development of subjects and courses. It is also at faculty level that program implementation strategies can be enacted to provide opportunities and skills for staff to engage with new ideas and new technologies as a set of new opportunities, rather than a set of imposed demands. Hopefully, this can lead to the design of student learning environments which combine all we know about using technology as a set of cognitive tools (Jonassen & Reeves, 1996) in order to design active learning environments.

Monitoring staff workload is crucial. Staff are required to produce work plans to set out the achievements expected over a year, along with their professional development plans. Progress against the goals is then reviewed with their supervisors. We are aiming to more closely link the work plans to quality assurance processes, in order to promote the reflection, particularly with teaching practice, as Boyer (1990), Laurillard (1993) and Biggs (1999) have all urged.

7.4.2   RMIT IT Alignment Program

RMIT University established a project team in 1998 to develop an information technology strategy designed to facilitate the implementation of the objectives of the Teaching and Learning Strategy for electronically mediated flexible learning environments. The Information Technology Alignment Program (ITAP) report forms the basis for a $A50 million investment by RMIT over the four years 1999-2002. The report had 113 specific recommendations relating to these areas of work:

- IT infrastructure aligned with the needs of education to deliver the systems and hardware necessary to provide students with an electronically connected learning environment and access to computer-based learning resources;
- a Distributed Learning System (DLS) compliant with the emerging Educom/CAUSE Instructional Management System (IMS);
- an Academic Management System (AMS), fully integrated with the DLS to provide enrolment and subject and course progress records electronically accessible to academics and students;
- an extensive review of all academic processes within the university in a Business Process Re-engineering (BPR) project; and
- extensive staff development.

Learning Technology Services (LTS) is a centrally funded group to plan, develop, support, evaluate and report on the progress of the ITAP.

Prior to and since the ITAP Report, there has been substantial investment by RMIT to promote quality learning outcomes. The investment is quite considerable, with approximately 5% of each faculty budget being set aside, along with central money, to fund the course and subject renewal process. Also, major upgrading of the RMIT network, and student and staff computer facilities have occurred over the last two years. As stated above, we have tried to move on several fronts at once and many of the policies and processes that have been developed are still being refined. We have a sense of trying to juggle several balls at once; the art is keeping them all in the air and in relation to each other. The feedback and accountability loops do not function smoothly as yet, so there is often little direct evidence of the effectiveness of particular strategies. Within some faculties, feedback and evaluation occurs, but in others it is ad hoc and under-developed (Kenny & McNaught, 2000).

Through our Distributed Learning System (DLS) we offer staff a set of online tools to assist them in renewing their courses and subjects. An earlier report on RMIT's work (McNaught *et al.*, 1999) describes the toolset, early implementation experiences and early evaluations.

We are seeing that staff development and support for developing online learning materials and strategies must become distributed across the organization. Therefore the role of the faculty-based Faculty Education Services Groups (FESGs) is pivotal. Growth needs to occur in these units rather than at the center. We believe that technical support staff, educational designers and graphical designers are needed at faculty level and the courseware production that should exist at the center is some support for high-end media production and multimedia production. We are trying to combine the benefits of both the integrated and distributed approached mentioned earlier by Hughes *et al.* (1997).

7.5 Staff Development Through the Learning Technology Mentor Program

Learning Technology Mentors (LTMs) have been appointed in each department of the University. There are 145 Learning Technology Mentors (LTMs) – two in each department of the university and some in central areas such as the Library. These are mostly academic and teaching staff who have funded one day a week time release to develop online materials and support their colleagues in their departments to engage with online teaching and learning. Each LTM has 26 days time release. Some LTMs have been continued as Experienced LTMs with further time release to engage in more strategic roles in their faculties, such as quality assurance of online subjects, development and implementation of online publishing standards, *etc.*

The primary goals of Learning Technology Mentors (LTMs) relate to:

1. Carrying out subject renewal, including adoption of the Distributed Learning System (DLS). The LTMs may renew subjects that they co-ordinate, or mentor and support colleagues as collaborative subject renewal projects.
2. Co-ordinating and contributing to staff development with a view to enhancing departmental capacity to engage in subject renewal. This includes staff development in the DLS and associated tools, but in several cases (especially in vocational education departments where previous IT infrastructure has been weak) relates to foundation computer skills, e.g. Word and Internet.

While the majority of the Faculty mentors undertake at least one of these roles the mentor activities vary according to faculty, departmental and individual priorities.

Other roles include:

1. Leading or participating in special strategic projects for the department generally associated with renewal (e.g. co-ordinating or assisting the selection of subjects for priority renewal, setting up a department intranet facility).
2. Providing technical support in developing a DLS presence.

These LTMs undertook an extensive staff development program about a week long. Some of the key topics relate to RMIT's vision with respect to the university's position as a major international technological university. The Boyer (1990) Scholarship model has been used for some time as an integrating model for all RMIT work. Within this framework, the evolution of the Teaching and Learning Strategy over the last few years, and the structure and function of the IT Alignment Program are discussed. The course and subject renewal guidelines that exist in all faculties are discussed with a particular emphasis on the concept of graduate capabilities. The principles of course design are then enacted through training in the DLS toolset and consideration of how the use of the DLS tools relates to the renewal of subjects.

Additional staff development sessions were run each week. These sessions cover a range of practical 'hands-on' sessions, as well as workshops in areas such as assessment and evaluation strategies for online learning, student induction methods, managing digital resources, project management, *etc.*

Fifty-three of the 61 1999 LTMs produced reports on their work (Some LTMs left RMIT or for various health and other personal reasons were not able to complete their LTM duties). These reports were analyzed to see if the goals listed above had been achieved. LTMs also provided feedback about their work regularly through an online questionnaire and several case studies of online subjects were undertaken with staff who were LTMs. In 2000, a further 84 LTMs completed the program; reports are currently being analyzed.

All of this evidence has clearly indicated that the LTM initiative has been useful in:

- sharing awareness of the DLS and Faculty course renewal;
- skilling a range of staff with basic DLS capability in most departments; and
- identifying and developing a first set of active and highly skilled subject renewal 'champions' who could continue to support strategy implementation.

All of the above is fairly conventional staff development, albeit on a larger scale than is currently undertaken at other Australian universities. In what ways does the model relate to the principles of flexible learning that we are training staff to use?

7.6   Flexible Methods For Staff Development About Flexible Learning

We have approached the question of flexible staff development from two aspects. We do not believe in totally online staff development activities. Cultural change is a more complex situation, and the vibrancy of face-to-face workshop discussion and exploration is not likely to be achieved as regularly in online discussion forums. We have online staff development discussion areas but they are not heavily used. Instead we have tried two approaches:

7.6.1   The Use of a Suite of Resources

In the year and a half that the program has existed, we have built up a suite of practical resources, including the following:

- project planning checklists, to assist staff in scoping and costing online development;
- publishing standards checklists;
- quality assurance checklist for online learning. This has been opted as a standard procedure for all online subjects by the university;
- an LTM manual which is a collection of readings and checklists such as how to run an effective threaded discussion; how to incorporate principles of student-centeredness into renewing subjects;
- evaluation materials. We provide online questionnaires, and evaluation planning guides. Many of these were written for, or adapted from, Phillips, Bain, McNaught, Rice and Tripp (2000), a current national project on evaluation of computer-facilitated learning materials;
- many of these resources are available at a 'Renewal@rmit' website (http://www.lts.rmit.edu.au/renewal/), where links to other information exists, activities are provided, and a set of DLS exemplars are located.

7.6.2   The Development of Flexible Ways to Achieve Qualifications for Staff Development Programs

At RMIT we take the view that staff can obtain credit towards a formal university qualification for any substantial staff development activity they undertake. For example, all LTMs developed a work contract with the author who heads the Professional Development Team of Learning Technology Services. These contracts included specification of:

- the specific subject(s) being renewed, involving use of the DLS, the LTM will be working on in 2000/2001. These subjects need to relate to approved faculty plans for the production of quality assured material;

- the subjects that the LTM will be assisting colleagues in planning the renewal of for 2000/2001;
- staff development activities to be undertaken, such as presentation to the department, appropriate course teams, lunch-time seminars and demonstrations; and
- other activities relating to specific interests/ activities of the LTM such as online assessment strategies, development of a list of local and international examples within the department's discipline field.

If individual staff wish, their reports on this work can be formalized into accreditation for a unit in a Graduate Certificate of Flexible Delivery.

At RMIT we have a suite of Graduate Certificates that staff can undertake. These are:

- Graduate Certificate in Tertiary Teaching and Learning;
- Graduate Certificate in Flexible Delivery;
- Graduate Certificate in Industrial Education and Training (largely for staff in the vocational education and training sector);
- Graduate Certificate in Leadership (for staff in management positions, either senior administrative positions such as faculty executive officers, or academic heads of department);
- Graduate Certificate in Information Technology (specifically for technical staff).

Table 4.1 Examples of professional work that articulate into formal qualifications

Key evidence of professional work sought	Subject that staff can gain credit for	Course where partial credit is achieved
Report on work as a Learning Technology Mentor	Teaching and Learning Online	Graduate Certificate in Flexible Delivery
Reflective journal kept by sessional teachers	Teacher Training Program	Graduate Certificate in Tertiary Teaching and Learning
Development of a work plan which links work done in the workplace to key institutional priorities and strategies	Tertiary Institutions – Theory and Practice	Articulates to both Graduate Certificate in Leadership, and Graduate Certificate in Information Technology

All of these Graduate Certificates can be studied as formal courses. However, what we have been trying to do is give staff credit for their normal work when they can demonstrate by the production of a portfolio that they have achieved the learning outcomes listed in the subject guides. This enables staff to achieve credit for at least one out of four subjects in the Graduate Certificate courses through scholarly reflection on their own professional work. We do provide workshops and resources but the majority of the work is based on reflective professional practice. Three examples of work that is overseen by Learning Technology Services are given in Table 4.1 above

7.7   Next Steps and Conclusions

Providing effective staff development for a university involves work on several fronts. We have tried to provide a scheme at RMIT that tries to combine some clearly focused central support with local action in every department of the university. We have tried to ensure that staff are allocated time to learn new skills and apply them. And we have tried to ensure that staff who engage in innovative work (which always means a greater personal investment than the time allocated) can be rewarded in tangible ways with formal qualifications. Support, time and rewards – these three factors are essential to ensuring real growth and change. The trick is often to sustain the investment for a long enough time to ensure that new practices and processes are effectively embedded across the whole institution.

We are now nearly two years into this staff development approach and have begun to formulate our experience as a series of questions that need constant attention. These questions are offered here to assist others in their planning and evaluation of their own staff development schemes.

Have we got the *balance between central support and local action* correct? Is our work too driven by central policy and not sufficiently owned by faculties? We have tried to emphasize the pivotal role of faculties in our design, but the reality is that the ITAP is a central university initiative. Building relationships of trust and shared purpose is not easy, but is essential if productive work is to be achieved.

We are committed to time release but *how practical is time release* when there is a shortage of short-term, part-time staff who can come in to fill the replacement posts? Many staff have ended up doing their LTM work on top of their normal teaching and research activities because of the difficulty of finding suitable staff for short-term appointments. The dedication of these staff is wonderful but it is not a sustainable situation.

What is the *optimal number of Learning Technology Mentors*? We have two or three in each department and are now trying to consolidate their roles within departments. We are fairly happy with this number.

What *rewards are there for the LTMs* in terms of promotion? It certainly adds weight to a teaching portfolio but is this enough when the calls for research outputs remain constant?

Many staff comment that they *haven't time to get formal qualifications* and so have not yet taken advantage of the credits available into Graduate Certificate programs. When will they ever get this time?

How sustainable is the whole concept of building up staff capability across a whole institution? How patient is the modern large university about investing in the future when there are real immediate needs? We are currently facing pressures to increase the amount of 'quality' 'marketable' online courseware with the inevitable options of short-circuiting staff development and emphasizing courseware production instead. Can we get this *balance about short-term and long-term goals* right? This is a particularly difficult issue in many Australian universities at present where central government funding is dwindling and the opportunities of global markets are a strong incentive. 'Stuff' on the web is easier to achieve than reflective renewal of course and subjects.

I have no definitive answers to all these questions. What we continually seek to do is to reflect on all of them and see if we can get our balance point more finely tuned. That is the art of the game. What is our advice to others universities thinking of large-scale staff development programs relating to networked learning? I'm sure we were right to seek an integrated strategy for networked learning. Moving on several fronts relating to policy, infrastructure and support at once is absolutely essential. Working right across the university in all departments is also essential, so as to develop local ownership and build general staff capability within a reasonably short time frame. Without the substantial investment in time and money that large-scale staff development programs demand, there is unlikely to be significant changes in effective use of networked learning across the university.

We have a great deal of consolidation and development to do. We have been delighted by the enthusiasm of many Learning Technology Mentors and other staff in our programs. We have a sense of gathering momentum. Several faculties are showing real commitment, though a couple might still need a persuasive nudge. Have we reached critical mass yet, where the appropriate use of technology for networked learning will roll out across the University? Probably not, but we feel we are on the right track.

7.8   References

Biggs, J. (1999) What the student does: Teaching for enhanced learning. *Higher Education Research and Development, 18*(1), pp57-75

Boyer, E. L. (1990) *Scholarship reconsidered: priorities of the professoriate.* Princeton, New Jersey: The Carnegie Foundation for the Advancement of Teaching

Hughes, C., Hewson, L. & Nightingale, P. (1997) Developing new roles and skills. In Yetton, P. and associates *Managing the introduction of technology in the delivery and administration of higher education*, pp49-79, Evaluations and Investigations Program report 97/3, Canberra: Australian Government Publishing Service. http://www.detya.gov.au/highered/eippubs1997.htm

Jonassen, D. H., & Reeves, T. C. (1996) Learning with technology: Using computers as cognitive tools. In Jonassen, D.H. (Ed.) *Handbook of research for educational communications and technology*, pp693-719. New York: Simon and Schuster Macmillan

Kenny, J. & McNaught, C. (2000) Promoting quality outcomes in higher education using new learning technologies: Processes and plans at RMIT. In Sims, R., O'Reilly, M. & Sawkins, S. (Eds) *Learning to choose. Choosing to learn*, pp655-664. Proceedings of the

17th annual Australian Society for Computers in Learning in Tertiary Education 2000 conference, Southern Cross University, Coffs Harbour, 9-14 December

Laurillard, D. (1993) *Rethinking university teaching: A framework for the effective use of educational technology.* London: Routledge

Marris, P. (1986) *Loss and change* (revised edition), London: Routledge and Kegan Paul

McNaught, C. & Kennedy, P. (2000) Staff development at RMIT: bottom-up work serviced by top-down investment and policy. *Association of Learning Technology Journal, 8*(1) pp4-18

McNaught, C., Phillips, P., Rossiter, D. & Winn, J. (2000) *Developing a framework for a usable and useful inventory of computer-facilitated learning and support materials in Australian universities.* Evaluations and Investigations Program report 99/11. Canberra: Higher Education Division Department of Employment, Education, Training and Youth Affairs. http://www.detya.gov.au/highered/eippubs.htm#99_11

Phillips, R., Bain, J., McNaught, C., Rice M. & Tripp, D. (2000) *Handbook for learning-centered evaluation of computer facilitated learning projects in higher education.* Murdoch University http://cleo.murdoch.edu.au/projects/cutsd99/

8. Managing Institutional Change for Networked Learning: A Multi-Stakeholder Approach

Jonathan Foster, Nicholas Bowskill, Vic Lally and David McConnell

8.1 Introduction

This chapter describes a survey of the views held by university stakeholders as to the readiness of their university for implementing networked learning. Stakeholders included members of the university's Networked Learning Strategy Group and further representatives from academic, management and support staff. A number of factors relevant to a discussion as to the readiness of an institution for implementing networked learning are identified. These factors include stakeholders' understandings of networked learning, their opinions of the current situation at the university with regard to the implementation of networked learning, their visions for the development of networked learning, and enabling and constraining factors that affect the realizations of those visions. Stakeholders' individual views are presented along with an interpretation of the shared response by each group to each of the factors mentioned. An evaluation of the university's current readiness for implementing networked learning is presented. It is considered that the university's readiness to implement networked learning is at an early stage. Networked learning is practised within the university but conducted in the main by interested but isolated individuals with little central support. In conclusion it is suggested that if the university wishes to engage in the development of networked learning further emphasis needs to be placed on the internal infrastructure within the university that supports the delivery of networked learning and on collaboration with external agencies. Such external collaboration is considered to be not only national but also international.

8.2 The Computer Based Collaborative Group Work Project

The Computer Based Collaborative Group Work Project (CBCGW) (CBCGW, 1998) is one of thirty-two projects in the United Kingdom supported by the

Teaching & Learning Technology Program (TLTP) Phase 3 (TLTP, 1998). The project's work can be categorized into five strands. These are:

- a study of institutional readiness for networked, collaborative, learning;
- the development, research, evaluation and dissemination of a rich professional development environment for university staff;
- a full case study evaluation of generic online teaching and learning strategies in continuing professional development;
- an evaluation of groupware for networked collaborative learning;
- the establishment of a Web-based national professional development center for CBCGW in higher education.

This chapter deals with the first of these interdependent strands and adopts an institutional view of the process of managing change for the implementation of networked learning.

8.2.1   The British Educational Policy Context

In 1997 the results of a major review of the British higher education system, which has come to be known as the Dearing Report, were published (NCIHE, 1997). The vision of higher education that guides the Dearing Report is one of widening participation and of lifelong learning, leading to the development of a 'learning society'. Such a vision is supported by institutional structures that meet across what had previously been treated as largely distinct domains. Academic, commercial and industrial institutions are brought together as part of 'a new compact':

> "...at the heart of our vision of higher education is the free-standing institution, which offers teaching to the highest level in an environment of scholarship and independent enquiry. But, collectively and individually, these institutions are becoming ever more central to the economic wellbeing of the nation, localities and individuals. There is a growing bond of interdependence, in which each is looking for much from the other. That interdependence needs to be more clearly recognized by all participants [...] we think in terms of a compact between higher education and society which reflects their strong bond of mutual independence" (NCIHE, 1997:11, 12).

In order that higher education and its institutions are able to support the vision of a 'learning society' the Dearing report recommends, *inter alia*, that the higher education sector needs to:

> "... take full advantage of the advances in communications and information technology, which will radically alter the shape and delivery of learning throughout the world" (NCIHE, 1997:10)

The potential impact of communications and information technology (C&IT) on higher education is evident throughout the report in its discussion of different aspects of higher education provision: 'students and learning', 'supporting research and scholarship', 'staff in higher education' and the 'management and governance of higher education institutions'. The importance attached to the use of C&IT by the Dearing committee is further underlined by the allocation of a separate chapter to the topic in which the following assertion is made:

> "... while the effective adoption of C&IT in higher education requires appropriate technology, adequate resources and staff development, success depends on the effective management of change." (NCIHE, 1997:203)

Given current UK educational policy there is clearly justification for adopting an institutional view when considering the implementation of networked learning. This higher education policy background along with TLTP3's focus on embedding and evaluating implementations of teaching and learning technologies provided the rationale for the institutional strand of the project. Before addressing our methodology and methods and presenting an analysis of our results, we review literature on 'institutional change and C&IT' and the notion of 'institutional readiness'.

8.3   Institutional Change and C&IT

The main sources of change for adopting technology in UK universities at the current time have arguably been forces external to higher education. A number of UK government-funded initiatives have explicitly addressed the subject of institutional change. These include the Computers in Teaching Initiative, earlier phases of the TLTP, the Fund for the Development of Teaching and Learning, and the Teaching and Learning Technology Support Network. The Learning Technology Dissemination Initiative and the Teaching and Learning in Scottish Metropolitan Area Networks (TALISMAN) projects have also increased exposure to the question of integrating C&IT into UK learning and teaching. The Joint Information Systems Committee have reported "on examples of successful deployment of IT within UK HEIs" (JISC, 1998) and incorporates a section on 'networked learning'. The JISC Assist Program (JISC ASSIST, 1998a, 1998b) has also contributed to the managerial and strategic agenda arising from the innovative exploitation of C&IT. Each of these projects and programs has generated research data at the institutional level of educational technology development. The institutional dimension of learning and teaching is currently very much part of the UK's educational policy landscape and has received attention from the Higher Education Funding Council for England (HEFCE) in both learning and teaching (HEFCE, 1998, 1999a, 1999b) and research contexts (Gibbs, 1999). HEFCE has made the institutional level an explicit part of its three-level approach to recent funding for learning and teaching, while Gibbs' (1999) research describes the current situation in the UK with regard to institutional learning and teaching strategies. Through his observation of strategy formulation within UK universities Gibbs suggests that what is important is not so much *what* strategy but *how* this strategy is developed and proceeds to describe available options.

The Dearing Report mentions that the impact of external forces on universities will depend on the mission of a particular university. In this respect the impact of C&IT on research-led universities has received particular attention (Griffiths & Gatien, 1999; Young 1999; Tearle, Davis, Birbeck, 1998). Rather than create new activities Griffiths and Gatien have described how information technology may tend to support, enhance and extend traditional activities within research universities e.g. research collaboration and administration.   And Young has reported on a US initiative where fourteen North American research universities "plan to work together to market their distance-education efforts through a central Web directory listing all their online programs" (Young, 1999). Further verifiable impacts of C&IT on research-led institutions have occurred in a number of areas e.g. open learning resources, teaching and learning projects, new staff skills and institutional policy (TLTSN, 1998). Other themes that have arisen in the course of research (Luddecke, 1998) are:

- departmental and institutional strategies for increasing flexibility;
- implementing open/distance learning (including commitment, resourcing, collaboration and quality assurance);
- effective change practices.

This last theme is backed up by other research:

> "... consideration should be given to the management of change processes and the re-organization of teaching and learning. It was felt this was essential to ensure the effective and efficient deployment of...resources, without it results could include increased cost and decreased effectiveness." (Davis, 1997:67)

In sum although research-led universities may at first present an unpromising seedbed for change, a number of authors have described the change processes that are beginning to take place and the issues and problems faced by change agents within such contexts.

Strategies for the management of change are then clearly important. Possible strategies available to managers include: organizing a vision for teaching and learning, managing the technological, organizational and human resource infrastructure; and conducting research and evaluation (Bates, 1999). There also needs to be a focus on managing the change at at least the individual, departmental and institutional levels:

> "... as in any learning process there has to be a meta-level function that reflects on the process at the next level down in order to set up improvements to it. Therefore, in thinking about how development and

implementation should be organized, we must be aware that every level of operation presupposes a higher level that is monitoring and reflecting on the way the lower level carries out its tasks. The same people may be on both levels; the two levels define different aspects of their activity." (Laurillard, 1993:225-26)

The Dearing vision also states that developments internal to an institution need to be accompanied by a push towards external and inter-institutional collaboration[1] with other agencies. This push towards external collaboration is part of what we call 'institutional readiness', a topic to which we now turn.

8.4   Institutional Readiness

The process of managing change has been described as falling into three broad phases: initiation, implementation, continuation (Fullan, 1991). Hence ahead of any implementation process there needs to be a focus on an initiation phase:

"Phase 1 – variously labelled initiation, mobilization, or adoption – consists of the process that leads up to and includes a decision to adopt or proceed with a change" (p.47).

In his discussion of the development of another type of educational institution, schools, Fullan introduces the concept of 'institutional readiness' as a component of this first phase:

"...the best beginnings combine the three R's of relevance, readiness, and resources [...] readiness involves the school's practical and conceptual capacity to initiate, develop, or adopt a given innovation...readiness may be approached in terms of 'individual' and 'organizational' factors. For individuals: Does it address a perceived need? Is it a reasonable change? Do they possess the requisite knowledge and skills? Do they have the time? For organizations: Is the change compatible with the culture of the school? Are facilities, equipment, materials, and supplies available? Are there other crises or other change efforts in progress? The greater the number of "no's", the more reason to take another look at readiness" (pp63-64).

It has further been argued that the impact of any externally-driven change will be cushioned by an organization's capacity for development (Hopkins, Harris and Jackson, 1997).

Capacity building remains a cornerstone of Fullan's approach and has recently been coupled with a need to recognize 'external accountability'. Fullan calls this 'outside collaboration' (Fullan, 1999). The task facing change management then

---

[1]   See MECPOL (1998) for a European collaboration.

is to manage both internal capacity-building and external accountability, "two-way inside-outside reciprocity is the elusive key to large-scale reform" (Fullan, 1999:62).

Our review has highlighted some of the issues that are relevant at an institutional level to addressing the problems associated with the adoption and use of C&IT. In particular we have highlighted the need for the institution to strike a balance between developing its internal capacity for change and responding to external agencies. After a review of the methodology and methods employed for researching institutional readiness an analysis of our data is presented.

8.5   Methodology and Methods

The purpose of the institutional strand of the CBCGW project was to survey and evaluate the readiness of the university for implementing networked learning. The research followed a survey methodology with empirical data generated from interviews with key stakeholders and a review of institutional documents related to the development of networked learning.

The project first identified a number of different groups of stakeholders whom we considered to be influential in developing networked learning within the university. This included representatives from the following groups: academic, management, support services and members of the university's Networked Learning Strategy group, the latter group comprising members from all of the former three groups. The team then designed, piloted, revised and implemented an interview instrument highlighting the main areas considered to be relevant to a survey and evaluation of the university's readiness to implement networked, specifically networked collaborative, learning[2]. Stakeholders were asked about their understanding of networked learning, their views on the current situation in the university, their vision for its development, what the enabling and constraining factors might be and what it would mean to say that the university is ready to support networked learning. Each member of the project team was involved in the interviewing process and twenty-two interviews were conducted over a four-month period during January to April 1999.

8.6   Analysis

8.6.1   Introduction

Fullan (1991) identifies two main aspects of the meaning of change, the objective meaning of the change process and the subjective meaning of change for those involved in the change situation. These subjective meanings may be different not

---

[2]   See Asensio, M., Foster, J., Hodgson, V. & McConnell, D. (Eds.) (2000) for a recent cross-section of research and practice in networked learning.

only for individuals but also for groups of individuals (e.g. academics, managers, support staff). He suggests, importantly, that change depends on shared meaning. It is then a necessary but not a sufficient condition for change to provide a definition of 'institutional readiness'. One also needs to understand the meanings of readiness held by those who 'own' the problem situation. The following analysis examines the responses to the interview questions according to three groups of stakeholders: academics, support staff and managers. An attempt is made both to survey and grasp the subjective meanings of those involved in the problem situation and to provide an interpretation of the shared meaning for each peer group. Our analysis is focused on the following areas:

- Conceptions of online and networked learning.
- The current situation at the university
- Vision
- Enabling and constraining factors
- The university's readiness for implementing networked learning

8.6.2   Survey of Views

Conceptions of Online and Networked Learning
It has been argued that:

> "Face-to-face teaching and learning on campus is now…incorporating some forms of networked learning, freeing staff and learners to work at times which suit them and to use resources, and methods of working together, that were not possible a few years ago" (McConnell, 1999:178).

The first question interviewees were asked was what they understood by the term online learning (historically an older term) and whether they saw any distinction between 'online' learning and 'networked' learning.

Academic views emphasized 'interaction' and 'materials' in online learning, with a shift from the individual interacting with materials to the group interacting with materials and with each other in networked learning. Support staff emphasized 'materials' and 'access to materials' in online learning and suggested a 'community', a 'collaborative environment' and much more of the learning and teaching infrastructure e.g. support, examination and assessment available online in networked learning. There was no dominant view among management as to the nature of online learning. Raising the issue however as to whether interviewees perceived a distinction between online and networked learning provoked talk of a 'collaborative element' and a 'kind of community'. In sum, we found some evidence to suggest that people use words like 'group' and 'community' in order to distinguish networked learning from online learning (the latter being something that the student is able to do independently with learning materials).

The Current Situation

From an academic's point of view the current situation has been described as 'opaque'. Although informal networks of people interested in the development of networked learning exist, it is considered that there is also a lack of awareness and knowledge of what is generally occurring on a larger scale. The university support structure is considered to be fragmented, with expertize present but uncoordinated. There is some concern that networked learning methods need to be integrated into current teaching methods rather than be seen as a substitute for teaching. Furthermore there needs to be some demonstrable benefit. The university is also considered to be on a learning curve vis-a-vis structural (organizational) and infrastructural (technical) issues.

Support staff put forward the view that there exist informal pockets of expertize and practice within the university but that this is not accompanied by strategic thinking at the institutional level. Development is *ad hoc* with a need for strategic management. It is suggested that there is some difficulty with the terminology and that there is no great understanding of either networked or collaborative learning. The university is regarded as a hierarchical institution that would require a cultural shift in order to assimilate networked learning.

Management views highlighted some of the barriers that need to be overcome. These barriers included organizational structure and technological infrastructure. In addition:

> "...we are developing strategy but unless somebody sorts out the underlying structure and infrastructure we are not going to be able to deliver it [...] it is not putting the strategy in place; it's delivering it".

Other views on the current situation include the observation that there is a 'willingness to try and go for it' but that at the same time there exists a lack of an 'understanding of the investment required'; and, although 'there are a lot of staff at various levels keen to develop it', there are 'serious problems about reward mechanisms'. One manager put it this way:

> "...we have actually not yet put together a sufficiently impressive case to convince our colleagues of what we are trying to do is sensible because there is a majority out there who are (a) sceptical or (b) think online learning means world wide web and that is it and it's trivial and their view of that if it were correct, yes it would be trivial, but their perspective is actually naïve".

It would appear that, taken as a whole, most stakeholders are in agreement that there exist pockets of informal academic practice and corporate expertize but that the latter is as yet uncoordinated with investment in technical infrastructure also a major concern. There also appears to be a genuine lack of understanding among some stakeholders as to the best, indeed an effective, way forward. Such comments echo other commentators who suggest that an integrated approach to whole institutional development is needed for the successful implementation of information technology (Fullan, 1999; Davis, 1997; Somekh, Whitty & Coveney,

1997). One way to provide integration is through an organizing vision, a topic to which we now turn.

Vision

Interviewees were asked whether they had a vision as to how networked learning might develop within the university over the next five to ten years. Themes included a focus on how to handle an international learning base (its impact on face to face teaching and how this could be organized), the subject discipline itself, and how external collaboration with agencies outside of the university could be harnessed. The university was not regarded as a site for a complete change to 100% networked learning but more of a hybrid. There were a lot of things that the university already did well and a mix of face-to-face and networked learning would be more appropriate. Other themes included the need to address questions of access (not only the technical infrastructure but also the supporting cost structure for remote access of university services) and incentives.

Support staff views included a focus not only on a strong educational base that would support developments in networked learning but also a focus on staffing, staff development and strategy.

Management vision confirmed that it was not envisaged that a major shift will occur but that networked learning would be used to support activities that the university 'would otherwise engage in'. It would be expected that some form of networked learning would be occurring in all departments although a mixture of bottom-up and top-down approaches would be needed. The university's mission as a research-led university would mean that the implementation of a virtual university built on the distance learning model would be impossible to imagine under current conditions:

"...it would be consistent with this university's mission to say we are not actually interested in encouraging distance learning, we are not particularly interested in encouraging networked learning as part of our strategic mission but merely to support the activities we would otherwise engage in".

Consideration was also voiced as to external collaboration, both with other universities for the standardization of materials and some curricula for efficiency gains, and with commercial organizations in order to generate investment. Research into teaching was also mentioned as being relevant to the development of networked learning. The teaching paradigm remained unclear and research into teaching in this area would be a welcome development.

In sum any vision for the development of networked learning and teaching needs to be realistic enough to take note of the university's mission as a research-led university:

"The mission of the University is to maintain the highest standards of excellence as a research-led institution, whose staff work at the frontiers of academic enquiry and educate students in a research environment".

As such it is acknowledged that the university already engages in core activities of teaching and research and that the harnessing of networked technologies needs to be seen as extending and improving the current provision and core activities of the university.   Factors, both enabling and constraining, which affect the development of networked learning at the university, are discussed in the following section.

Enabling and Constraining Factors

For academics, enabling factors include the ability to demonstrate something to the institution that works. In this respect the subject orientation of the university *i.e.* science and engineering was considered to be important. Hence a 'winner', which acted as a showcase for the successful deployment of networked learning for the whole institution was considered to be more persuasive if created in a medical or an engineering context rather than, for example, a humanities or social sciences context. Not only resources but also recognition (and hence the question of incentives) were also seen to be important factors. In this respect quality (external accountability) was seen to be important, if not more so, than innovation. It was also suggested that resources needed to accompany debate. Nearly all aspects of any development process were considered to be potential constraints: hardware, software, resources, academic time, and the perceived lack of reward for innovations in teaching over and above that accorded to the publishing of research. Indeed it could also be argued that the university's success in teaching quality assessments also represents a constraint to action. The organization of learning and teaching was also raised:

> *"If you are going to be responding to students...through the web...I'm not sure that our notion of what is teaching is kind of geared up to that because it is pretty much geared around the idea of you go into the lecture or class and a certain amount of time set aside for tutoring also but this is a much more fluid and open ended time commitment and...I am not aware of much discussion about that".*

It was felt that the new 'contract' between teachers and the institution that networked learning and teaching involves has yet to be generally debated and that such a contract would need debate ahead of any implementation.

For support staff enabling factors included a focus on infrastructure and strategy in order to harness the current expertize latent within the organization. A shared environment for both academics and students was also viewed as an important factor in order for the former to be aware of the problems of the latter. And the need for top-down management to "draw upon ... and acknowledge the skills of those who have the competence to develop this area of work" within the university was identified. Constraints included questions of access and the current volatility of online material and resistance to change.

For management enabling factors included shifts in an external funding regime more focused on regions and a focus internally on a tranche of different strategies. These included an information technology strategy; a strategy for an appropriate infrastructure for the development of networked learning, an infrastructure designed for learning and teaching; a strategy for rewards and incentives; a staff development strategy; and support from the vice-chancellor and his senior management team. For one commentator the university has, as of Spring 1999, support from the vice-chancellor and his senior management team; but with regard to strategies in the other areas mentioned "you can start with any one of those and say we are at year zero". The university's mission as a research-led university, as well as its pride in traditional methods of teaching built on the Oxbridge tutorial model, shape and constrain the type of development which can be embedded and sustained within the institution. As such there is seen to be no "crisis of confidence about conventional teaching", such that the developmental opportunity is not there; there is no perceived need for new markets and "there isn't that kind of coherent space within which learning and teaching initiatives develop". Further, in terms of curriculum development "the main drivers leading towards take-up of communication and information technology for teaching and learning tend to be efficiencies and cost savings, not enhancement and enrichment". The science-oriented nature of the university and its implications for how knowledge is viewed within the university was also seen as a constraint on the development of networked learning methods. In sum important issues included traditionalism (along with established practices as to how to develop a mechanism for identifying key actors and champions in this area) and the need for a vision as to how information technology can "inform research, administration, learning and teaching". Strategy would also help to formalize and bring together the informal and disparate developments that currently constitute the state of networked learning within the university.

The University Learning about Networked Learning

In answer to a question as to how the university might learn about networked learning, an academic member of staff responded in the following way:

> "I think my feeling at the moment is that there is still a kind of dual thing going on, that there are researchers doing things and generating kind of information and knowledge and there's sort of a channel for quality making and reflecting on practice and I am not sure that the two things completely come together [...] I'm not sure whether there is a kind of a link across".

Such a feeling highlights the need for organizations to explore ways of disseminating research conducted into their own institution. Among support staff students were considered to be a source of knowledgeability and hence a source of learning for the institution. University performance is currently measured by two main methods: the Research Assessment Exercize (RAE) and the Teaching Quality Assessment (TQA). The university performs well in both areas and hence, paradoxically, this may represent a constraint on institutionalized innovation in learning and teaching. Hence, from a management viewpoint, the fact of the university learning about networked learning will be influenced by the university's external 'regime of accountability' (Wenger, 1998).

If one conceives of an organization as a monolithic entity then it may appear that facilitating a process whereby a university learns about networked learning is a difficult issue to address.   If one conceives of a university however as a combination of institutional design and overlapping communities of practice e.g. students, teachers, researchers, managers, support services, then it may be said that the university is indeed responding to, and learning about issues connected with, an educational agenda that is making increasing use of C&IT.

In July 1999 the CBCGW project hosted a meeting for those stakeholders interviewed. The objectives were (i) to feedback and validate the outcomes of the research and (ii) to initiate a dialog among stakeholders. Both objectives were achieved with broad agreement reached on the issues facing the university. At the head of this section we mentioned that an attempt is made to both survey and grasp the subjective meanings of those involved in the problem situation and to provide an interpretation of the shared meaning for each peer group. The following quotation from a recent monograph on organizational design for learning is pertinent:

> "In the end, it is in the opportunities for negotiating meaning creatively that the learning of an organization resides [...] this focus on the negotiation of meaning is a focus on the potential for new meanings embedded in an organization. It is a focus not on knowledge as an accumulated commodity – as the ability to repeat the past – but on learning as a social system productive of new meanings" (Wenger, 1998:262).

Our analysis has attempted to illuminate some of the subjective and objective meanings associated with developments in networked learning at one institution.

8.7   Evaluation of Institutional Readiness

The university's readiness to implement networked learning is generally considered to be at an early stage. By implication, much capacity-building e.g. motivation, resources, skills (Fullan, 1999) needs to take place. There is also the need to draw together in a co-ordinated fashion the motivation, resources and skills that already exist within the organization. More formal incentives are needed to capitalize on and extend the width of those individuals within the organization who have initiated developments in networked learning within their own teaching practice. Not only are financial resources required but also a cultural shift that would recognize and reward quality improvement. Networked learning occurs within the university but is conducted in the main by interested but isolated academics with little central support. The expertize that does currently exist within the university is uncoordinated.

Support staff view readiness less in terms of local practice than in terms of top-down direction. There is a need for vision and an implementation strategy as well as resources. An understanding of what are quality-produced materials is also seen to be important. There is a need to move the institution to a situation where networked access is the expected mode. This should be accompanied by strategic planning in the following areas: the effective utilization of information technology, staff development, curriculum development and learning opportunities for students as well as planning with regard to how such strategies are to be implemented.

For management organizational capacity building for networked learning included attention to cultural shifts, student attitudes and provision of technical support for students. The university would also have strategies in relation to information technology, learning and teaching, staff development and a system of rewards and incentives. Indeed, a focus on incentives and implementation would further contribute, in Fullan's (1991) terms, to a process of institutionalization. It was also considered that the university would have a vision (and most probably a top-down one) that is owned by 'very senior' university staff. This claim on ownership is supported by Gibbs' (1999) research that provides some pointers as to how such a vision might be organized. Indeed, the institution would have resources, it would be ready technically, but networked learning and teaching would also be part of the fabric of the institution, 'part of the institution's ethos'. Leadership was seen as important and it was perceived that the university had got to its current position in research over the past decade through top-down leadership and that the same should happen for teaching.

Our analysis provides a window on the views of different stakeholders as to the readiness of their institution for developing networked learning. The views of academic staff are informed and shaped by their own individual experiences and practice. They also appear to be aware, informally, of pockets of expertize within the university. There is a feeling however that there has been less promotion of debate on an institutional scale, and that informal practice has yet to be recognized in any systematic way (although the university does currently fund a number of development projects through its Curriculum Development Fund). Networked learning is currently far from becoming routine within the institution. The views of support staff appear to be more focused on materials rather than pedagogic practice, with a concern for the quality production process, a need for organizational and technical infrastructure and a favouring of top-down strategies to push forward development in this area. The views of management are various. Depending on their organizational role, there is, for example, mention of the development of partnerships with industry and the use of information technology in helping to manage and govern an institution[3]. There is further evidence among management views that more sustainable change requires changing concepts and attitudes, and roles, as much as the provision of learning and teaching materials.

One of the main outcomes of the research into institutional readiness for networked learning has been to highlight not only the role of the institution in formally recognizing developments in networked learning but also recognizing the informal nature of on-going developments in academic practice:

"The point of design for learning is to make organizations ready for the emergent by serving the inventiveness of practice and the potential for

---

[3]   See NCIHE (1997) chapter 13 section 9.

innovation inherent in its emergent structure. Institution and practice cannot merge because they are different entities. The relation between them is not one of congruence, but one of negotiated alignment. And the alignment is never secured; it must constantly be negotiated anew, because it is by being of different natures that they complement each other as sources of structure" (Wenger, 1998:245).

As such the problem currently facing the university at this time could be characterized as the need to further engage the formal institutional nature of the organization with the informal nature of academic practice (Foster *et al.*, 2000).

8.8   Conclusions

In innovation terms the picture which emerges is of an institution at the early stages of a change management process and where networked learning is not yet routine. The university is largely at the initiation stage (Fullan, 1991), with some evidence of implementation. Informal practice has yet to be turned into formal procedure. An organizing vision or model of what the university wishes to achieve in this area has yet to be articulated, at least to the wider university community. Once this vision is articulated, it is recognized that implementation strategies need to be drawn up in key areas affecting take up e.g. information technology, learning and teaching and staff development. Networked learning also clearly affords the opportunity for some form of external collaboration, both for pedagogical and for economic reasons. Such external collaboration is consistent both with current educational policy that advocates inter-institutional collaboration (NCIHE, 1997) and with recent academic thinking (Fullan, 1999). Fullan's recent framework of inside-out and outside-in collaboration appears to be applicable to the university's position with regard to the adoption and institutionalization of networked learning. On the one hand, external educational policy advocates the increased use of C&IT in order to facilitate increased participation in education, to reduce costs and to improve teaching. On the other hand, isolated academics unilaterally adopt C&IT in their teaching, driven by both personal interest and individual careerism. An institution can mediate between the external, global, and internal, local, levels by providing sources of capacity building (e.g. motivational support in the form of incentives, financial resources; and skills in the form of staff development and training). The research-led nature of the university means that the university has no problem with content (Bates, 1999); further emphasis needs to be placed on the internal infrastructure within the institution to support the delivery of networked learning and on collaboration with external agencies.

Such external collaboration crosses national borders. The task of widening participation in UK education is happening not only on a national but also a global scale. Historically the UK's Open University is probably the most well-known example. Witness as well current developments around the UK's e-University initiative (http://www.hefce.ac.uk/partners/euniv/). Thus the institution we studied is currently involved in a newly-established global alliance of universities called the Worldwide Universities Network (WUN) linking British and American universities in a collaboration which extends to research, teaching programs, continuing professional development, and learning materials in general. This push towards external collaboration has also extended to Europe with the Santander (http://www.um.es/sgroup/) and EuroPACE projects (http://www.europace.be/). With both projects having similar aims to develop curricula in common. Perhaps the most well-known of global alliances is Universitas 21 (http://www.universitas.edu.au/) which enables each individual university to "pursue agendas that would be beyond their individual capabilities". Among current projects are aims to

"...capitalize on and extend the capabilities of participating Universitas 21 universities to exploit new teaching and learning technologies, modalities and delivery systems...[and]...consider ways member universities can co-operate to provide mutual access to multimedia courseware".

Indeed if universities are to operate successfully on a global scale it has been argued that they also need to develop a brand image (Newby, 1999). As can be attested from the above alliances universities are responding to the global marketplace by developing partnerships in all aspects of educational provision. Networked learning is no exception and managing institutional change for networked learning will encompass not only the management of internal institutional developments but also inter-institutional and in many cases global developments.

8.9 References

Asensio, M., Foster, J., Hodgson, V. & McConnell, D. (Eds.) (2000) *Networked Learning 2000: innovative approaches to lifelong learning and higher education through the internet, proceedings of the second international conference jointly organized by Lancaster University and the University of Sheffield, and held at Lancaster University 17th-19th April 2000.* Sheffield: University of Sheffield

Bates, A.W. (1999) Restructuring the university for technological change. In Brennan, J., Fedrowitz, J., Huber, M. & Shah, T. (Eds.) *What kind of university? International perspectives on knowledge, participation and governance.* Buckingham: The Society for Research into Higher Education & Open University Press, pp207-228

CBCGW (1998-2001) http://collaborate.shef.ac.uk/

Davis, N. (1997) Strategies for staff and institutional development for IT in education: an integrated approach. In Somekh, B. & Davis, N. (Eds.) (1997) *Using information technology effectively in teaching and learning: studies in pre-service and in-service teacher education.* London: Routledge, pp255-268

Foster, J., Bowskill, N., Lally, V. & McConnell, D. (2000) Negotiating practice: an analysis of an institutional dialog about networked learning. In Asensio, M., Foster, J., Hodgson, V. & McConnell, D. (Eds.) (2000) *Networked Learning 2000: innovative approaches to lifelong learning and higher education through the internet, proceedings of the second international conference jointly organized by Lancaster University and the University of Sheffield, and held at Lancaster University 17t^h-19th April 2000* (pp98-105). Sheffield: University of Sheffield

Fullan, M.G., with Stiegelbauer, S. (1991) *The new meaning of educational change*. (2nd edition) London: Cassell

Fullan, M. (1999) *Change forces: the sequel*. London: Falmer Press

Gibbs, G. (1999) Methodology and key findings of the review of institutional learning and teaching strategies task group [Annex D to HEFCE Invitation 99/48]. http://www.niss.ac.uk/education/hefce/pub99/99_48.html#annd

Griffiths, J-M. & Gatien, G.M. (1999) The role of the traditional research university in the face of the distance-learning onslaught, *The Technology Source*, February 1999. http://horizon.unc.edu/TS/vision/1999-02.asp

HEFCE (1998) Learning and teaching: strategy and funding proposals [Report No. 98/40]. http://www.niss.ac.uk/education/hefce/pub98/98_40.html

HEFCE (1999a) Learning and teaching: strategy and funding [Report No. 99/26]. http://www.niss.ac.uk/education/hefce/pub99/99_26.html

HEFCE (1999b) Teaching quality enhancement funding arrangements [Invitation No. 99/48] http://www.niss.ac.uk/education/hefce/pub99/99_48.html

Hopkins, D., Harris, A. & Jackson, D. (1997) Understanding the school's capacity for development: growth states and strategies, *School Leadership & Management*, 17 (3), pp401-411

JISC (1998) *Deployment of IT within UK HEIs* http://www.jisc.ac.uk/pub98/it_deployment.html

JISC ASSIST (1998a) *C&IT across the institution: a year on from Dearing, Workshop 8 October 1998*. http://www.jisc.ac.uk/pub98/assist6.html

JISC ASSIST (1998b) *Collaborative working, Workshop 1 April 1998*http://www.jisc.ac.uk/pub98/assist2.html

Laurillard, D. (1993) *Rethinking university teaching: a framework for the effective use of educational technology*. London: Routledge

McConnell, D. (1999) Guest editorial: networked learning [Special issue on networked learning], *Journal of Computer Assisted Learning*, 15 (3), pp177-178

MECPOL (1998) The MECPOL Project. http://www.idb.hist.no/mecpol/

NCIHE (1997) *Higher education in the learning society: report of the national committee* [Main report]. London: HMSO

Newby, H. (1999) Higher education in the twenty-first century, *New Reporter*, 16 (14) http://www.soton.ac.uk/~infoserv/pubaff/ newrep/vol16/no14future.html

Somekh, B., Whitty, G. & Coveney, R. (1997) IT and the politics of institutional change. In Somekh, B. & Davis, N. (Eds.) *Using information technology effectively in teaching and learning*. London: Routledge, pp187-209

TLTP (1998) http://www.ncteam.ac.uk/tltp.html

TLTSN (1998) *The Teaching and Learning Support Network (TLTSN) case studies: case study 4, shifting the culture of institutional change*
http://www.tltp.ac.uk/tltsn/cases/csl.pdf

Tearle, P., Davis, N. & Birbeck, N. (1998) Six case studies of information technology-assisted teaching and learning in higher education in England, *Journal of Information Technology in Teacher Education*, 7 (1), pp51-70

Wenger, E. (1998) *Communities of practice: learning, meaning, and identity*. Cambridge: Cambridge University Press

Young, J.R. (1999) Research universities team up to create a 'portal' for online education, *The Chronicle of Higher Education*, 11 June 1999
http://chronicle.merit.edu/free/99/06/99061001t.htm

9. Information Specialists and Networked Learner Support

Philippa Levy

9.1 Introduction

This chapter[1] discusses some aspects of networked learner support, the term adopted here to refer to multidisciplinary support for effective networked learning and teaching, involving staff in a variety of academic support services (Fowell & Levy, 1995). Focusing in particular on the educational role of information specialists, the chapter reflects back on trends and issues addressed by NetLinkS, a national training and awareness project which ran from 1995 to 1998 as part of the UK Electronic Libraries (eLib)[2] development program. Other eLib projects, particularly those which have explored cultural change in academic libraries (IMPEL2)[3], the technology-related training needs of 'hybrid' library staff (SKIP)[4], and the roles of librarians in academic liaison and support (see Flatten, 2000) also provide valuable insights into relevant issues in the UK context. The chapter reviews the impact of recent changes in the educational environment on the work practice of librarians in learner support roles in the UK, against the background of international trends, and draws attention to new perspectives on the contribution of these staff to educational development and delivery. A range of professional and other issues, which continue to bear on the development of librarians' and information specialists' roles in networked learner support, are highlighted.

Developing learner support practice in the networked environment is partly a matter of building on the purposes and methods of well-established traditions in librarianship, for example in the areas of information skills training, advisory work and academic liaison on which this chapter focuses. However, more is at issue than straightforward extension of traditional approaches through the application of new technology. The professional framework in many academic support services is in transition as learner support practice becomes more integrated and

---

[1] The chapter is based on Levy, P. (2000) Information specialists supporting learning in the networked environment: a review of trends and issues in higher education. The New Review of Libraries and Lifelong Learning 1:35-64. The New Review of Libraries and Lifelong Learning is published by Taylor Graham Publishing, 48 Regent Street, Cambridge, CB2 1FD, UK. For full details, see: http://www.taylorgraham.com

[2] eLib http://www.ukoln.ac.uk/services/elib/

[3] IMPEL2 http://ilm.unn.ac.uk/impel

[4] SKIP http://www.plym.ac.uk/faculties/research/skip1.htm

collaborative, and assuring the effective use of electronic information resources is seen increasingly as part of a broader strategic agenda in institutions to contribute to innovation and good practice in learning and teaching. At the same time, the changing environment has a de-stabilizing effect, in that librarians' traditional ownership of areas related to information access and support is, potentially, called into question. These factors mean that in addition to embracing the need to extend their knowledge and expertize into new areas, librarians are challenged to develop new understandings of their professional roles and relationships, and to become active in forging new opportunities both to support learning and to contribute to educational development.

Between 1995-8, these issues were the focus of the NetLinkS project. In its first phase, NetLinkS set out to conduct exploratory research into conceptions of the educational role of information staff in the light of trends in networked learning, and to investigate national and international initiatives in the use of new communication and information technologies (C&IT) in their advisory, teaching and training activities. Focus group discussions were held in nineteen universities and colleges of higher education in the UK, bringing together – usually for the first time – cross-disciplinary groups of colleagues who were interested in networked learning issues, including teachers and staff from library, computing and educational development services. The aim was to gain an understanding of emerging views on networked learning and learner support from a variety of professional perspectives, and to stimulate interaction and new initiatives across functional boundaries. A number of issues relating to information specialists' potential contribution to developing good practice in networked learning and teaching emerged from this and associated research, and feedback was gained about librarians' professional development needs and interests in relation to networked learner support. In its second phase, NetLinkS developed a web-based collection of information resources and ran a number of events, including a series of workshops, a program of 'mini-conferences' led by guest speakers on the project's discussion list, *nls-forum*, and an intensive, networked professional development course in which thirty-three participants from information services in universities and colleges of higher education across the UK participated for a period of seventeen weeks between September 1997 and February 1998. Further details of all NetLinkS research and development activities can be found online in annual and research reports[5] and in a number of papers (Levy, *et al.*, 1996; Levy, 1997; 1998; 1999). Although a relatively small-scale initiative, NetLinkS was successful in establishing an international community of interest in the area of networked learner support for the duration of the project, and in feeding in to a number of concrete initiatives in information services. Within the eLib training and awareness strand, it aimed to complement Netskills[6], a large-scale training project focusing on skills in C&IT, and Edulib[7], a project focusing on expertize in

---

[5]   NetLinkS http://netways.shef.ac.uk
[6]   Netskills http://www.netskills.ac.uk
[7]   EduLib http://www.tay.ac.uk/edulib/index.html

face-to-face teaching and, to some extent, open and distance learning techniques. Based on the premise that librarians should become trained and qualified educationalists and that the special nature of their educational role warrants a tailored approach to staff development (McNamara, 1998), Edulib devised and ran a workshop program which attracted participants from most information services in the university sector.

9.2   The Networked Learning Environment

The question of how best to facilitate subject-domain learning using the resources of the networked environment and, at the same time, to enable students to develop relevant, 'transferable' learning skills, raises numerous issues for both teaching and learner support staff in higher education. From a technical point of view, it is already possible to identify many learners on higher education programs as 'networked'. Such a definition encompasses the majority of students whose use of C&IT for formal or informal learning purposes is relatively *ad hoc* and may, for example, be restricted to accessing course web-pages or the library catalogue, as well as the growing minority who are enrolled on courses designed specifically – in different ways – to take full advantage of electronic resources and facilities. At present, in the UK as elsewhere, the extent and impact of strategic planning related to networked learning varies widely between institutions, and parts of the higher education system are changing more rapidly than others in this respect. Nevertheless, whilst future patterns will no doubt continue to vary, C&IT is becoming increasingly embedded into the experience of participation in higher education and is expected to play a central role in helping many institutions to achieve their targets for cost-effective access and expansion. National and international policies which promote the principles of flexible, lifelong learning, coupled with economic pressures to deliver higher education more cost-effectively to larger numbers of students, point the way towards the continuing integration of C&IT into both campus-based and distance learning in the majority of institutions as rapidly as local circumstances will allow.

The networked 'space' resulting from technological convergence has rapidly come to offer a rich variety of possibilities for electronic interaction between people, as well as access to multimedia information resources and electronic document sharing and publishing. Approaches to the use of C&IT in curriculum design and delivery vary considerably, as reflected, for example, in differences in the extent to which networked learning tasks are intended to entail collaborative as opposed to individual effort, or to encourage independent approaches to the use of information resources. However, there is increasing interest in facilitating electronic interaction and collaboration in learning, in addition to providing access to electronic resources. Already a wide range of media for supporting interaction between learners, teachers and support staff is being exploited, including electronic mail (e-mail), asynchronous text-based conferencing systems, synchronous 'chat', multi-user domains (MOOs), shared workspace tools and groupware packages, and desktop and studio-based video-conferencing. The production of multimedia content for networked learning, in the form of generic or course-based learning materials, is an area of expansion and is a priority of many national and international development initiatives, many of which are being taken forward through partnerships between educational providers and commercial publishers. The characteristics of hypermedia are being exploited with increasing sophistication in the design of online learning materials, and new software and technical standards are being developed to enable easy management of online learning resources, for instance as regards resource-sharing across institutions and harmonization of content from different publishers. The new generation of 'virtual learning environment' shells which interface with, or are based on, the web enable the creation of 'local' learning settings which are, technically at least, boundaryless, in that their users are only a few clicks away from the resources and facilities of the wider electronic communications and information landscape. For example, it is a relatively easy matter in technical terms to tap in to discussions on mailing lists, visit 'virtual communities' using synchronous or asynchronous communications media, participate in discussions hosted by a new generation of interactive electronic journals, or simply to e-mail subject experts directly in the hope of engaging them in debate.

Within the same environment – often via the same interface – individuals are connected to the wider digital information landscape that is available to the higher education community. This too is evolving rapidly, offering a vast array of web pages of varying quality alongside a growing number of stable, high-quality sources including full-text monographs and journals, library catalogs, bibliographic databases, quality-assured subject 'gateways' and numerous resources in graphic and video formats. Digital information developments in the UK have been stimulated in particular by the eLib program. Building originally on the recommendations of the Follett Report (1993), which established early directions for the sector's electronic library infrastructure, eLib has supported a wide range of initiatives aiming to encourage the exploitation of information technology by higher education libraries, including projects in the areas of networked resource access, electronic publishing, digitization, preservation, and training and awareness for library staff and end-users. A key aim of the program has been to mobilize cultural change within the sector as regards electronic information resource use, with the training and awareness projects intended to be major instigators of such change. In its third phase, eLib has funded consortium-based projects to develop model 'hybrid library' services, designed to offer integrated access to a wide range of resources based on both digital and other media. On a broader scale, the Distributed National Electronic Resource[8] has developed a national strategy for provision of integrated access to hybrid information resources.

---

[8]   DNER http://www.jisc.ac.uk:8080/dner/

9.3   Changing Learner Support Roles and Practice

A number of commentators (e.g., Edwards *et al.*, 1998) have suggested that the impact of recent changes in the higher education environment is particularly acute in information services. Widespread reformulation of the role of these services as central to the educational mission of institutions – expressed, broadly speaking, in a shift of ethos from traditional librarianship to learner support – has been identified as part of a far-reaching process of cultural change which has begun to have significant consequences in many services in the UK, affecting underlying assumptions about professional purposes and roles as well as organizational structures, work practice and relationships. Whilst the pace of change is uneven across the sector, with some services relatively untouched by trends which are influential in others, cultural change is especially evident in those services in which continuing efforts are being made to offer 'seamless' support for learning and teaching, and in the renewed emphasis on the teaching, training and awareness-raising roles of information specialists within a collaborative professional framework. As anticipated by the Follett Report (1993) a considerable proportion of UK institutions seeking a cost-effective means of supporting the combined technology and information needs of users have over the last few years merged their library and IT services, often adopting the 'learning resource center' model. New 'converged' services may also include others – such as audio-visual services, educational technology, and teaching and learning development – under the same organizational umbrella. The Learning Center at Sheffield Hallam University is an example of this trend, aiming to provide integrated support for teaching and learning in areas related to information resources, computing, media production, curriculum development, educational research and project management. Multimedia learning resources production is an increasingly important activity of the Center, and here, as elsewhere, efforts are being made both to integrate 'front-line' support for the use of information and computing resources and to enable staff to work in multi-disciplinary project teams (Bulpitt, 1998). Formal operational convergence has not occurred throughout the sector – nor would this always be appropriate (Edwards *et al,.* 1998) – but there is a general move towards greater co-operation between services, in tandem with increasing emphasis on forging closer links between learner support services and academic departments to promote the use of electronic resources in teaching, link skills development activities more closely with the curriculum, and respond to information needs associated with resource-based and distance learning. Recognizing that the library is no longer necessarily the principal physical location or focus of students' information-related activity in the networked environment, there is an effort to shift perceptions of both library and academic staff towards seeing information specialists as part of academic support rather than as part of the library *per se*. In some cases, academic liaison is being strengthened by including library staff in collaborative learner support structures based outside the library (e.g., May 1998);

a NetLinkS focus group participant envisaged an extended form of this approach for her own role in the future: "A long way ahead we can see where this library is no bigger than an office with all our subject librarians distributed into departments... and either double up as, or collaborate with, IT staff as technical help."

The need to adopt a proactive approach to teaching, training and other forms of end-user assistance was a key theme of the Fielden Report (1993), which considered the human resource issues associated with electronic library developments, and this topic has been widely discussed in the international and national electronic library field since then (see, for example: Barry, 1997; Burge & Snow, 2000; Day et al., 1996; Garrod, 1997; Kelly & Robbins, 1996; Rice-Lively & Racine, 1997; Slade, 2000; Stoffle, 1996). The view of a much more interventionist – and empowered – educational role for library staff in the networked environment was, for example, vigorously promoted in an early Follett (eLib) lecture:

"The central and essential role for librarians as teachers cannot be over-emphasized ... the new paradigm of the teaching library, librarian as teacher, is one in which librarians actively seek out users in a variety of settings to provide instruction about information resources and to assist them in acquiring skills in locating and evaluating information. Using a variety of methods and locations for teaching (e.g., classrooms, interactive networks, multimedia presentations and computer-assisted instruction), librarians will create a 'library without walls'... The teaching librarian embodies an outreach mindset ...[and] should also be available to provide training and general support to faculty as they explore both networked and multimedia resources for the redesign of the curriculum" (Creth, 1996).

Information services in the UK, as elsewhere, are responding to the explosion in electronic information resources, and to the widespread awareness and training needs within their user communities, by increasing their teaching and training activities (Edwards, et al., 1998; Garrod, 1998). A survey of information skills training in over fifty per cent of UK university libraries has reported both a significant increase in demand for training in recent years and a widening in the scope of what is delivered, in terms of the range of participants involved and the subject-matter covered (Flett, 1999). Subject librarians are often at the forefront of developing new learner support initiatives (Parker & Jackson, 1998), becoming increasingly involved in end-user training, staff development, learning resource design, course development and validation. They, like others in similar roles, have been envisaged as agents of change in the new learning environment, with an important part to play in ensuring positive scenarios for higher education of the future; this view (e.g., Flatten, 1997) was a fundamental premise of the NetLinkS project. Information literacy is promoted increasingly in the library and information literature as a key element of the 'process' dimension of new modes of university learning (e.g., Webber & Johnston, 2000) – a perspective which has emerged especially strongly in the USA and, as in the example below, Australia:

"Information literacy plays a major role in addressing the process concerns of education. It is seen as an enabling process, a meta-skilling which is crucial to flexible delivery methods in formal contexts and the ongoing personal pursuit of knowledge beyond the walls of the university... The process approach is a major challenge to traditional ways of teaching and requires genuinely collaborative work practices between academics and librarians." (George & Luke, 1996:207, 209)

The need to collaborate in order to ensure integration of electronic information resources and the 'information curriculum' into programs of learning is also widely promulgated in the literature. Librarians are perceived, potentially, as full partners in the curriculum process, working with both teaching and technical staff in curriculum design and delivery to develop appropriate models of support for diverse types of learner, course and information need; see for example, Jones (1997), Kamhi-Stein and Stein (1998) and Ottewill and Hudson (1997). In the USA, the UWired project at the University of Washington is an example of a pioneering initiative that reflects this perspective. Aiming to create a campus-wide electronic community in which communication, collaboration and information technologies are integral to learning and teaching, the project established a standardized information literacy and technology program for entry-level students, and increased subject librarians' involvement in mainstream courses in a range of disciplines. UWired is reported to have brought dramatic role changes for the librarians involved, based on the development of much closer partnerships with other support staff and academic colleagues (Williams & Zald, 1997). There are similar reports of multi-disciplinary projects in the UK which, in bringing together professionals with complementary expertize in C&IT-based learning, librarianship, computing and teaching, offer opportunities to break down traditional client-provider relationships between different professional groups, typically through the development of web resources tailored to specific courses, student groups or subject disciplines (e.g. Biddiscombe, 1999; Needham, O'Sullivan & Ramsden, 2000).

The exploitation of new C&IT has rapidly become part and parcel of learner support practice. At the inception of the eLib program in 1995, early adopters had already begun to use networked technologies in user education, training, guidance and advisory work, for example using e-mail, the web and CD ROMs for enquiry services, disseminating current awareness information, and providing access to subject guides and information skills tutorials. The potential advantages of a variety of new technologies were being discussed, for example, by Cochrane (1996) and Heseltine (1995) and plans for innovative service initiatives were underway (e.g., Carty, et al., 1996). Part of the role of the NetLinkS project was to raise awareness of new learner support developments across the sector. In focus groups and other discussions hosted by the project, information specialists considered the potential impact of new technologies on their practice. Many viewed the introduction of C&IT into both teaching and learning generally, and into their own work, with caution. Ambivalence on this issue is not, of course, necessarily negative; participants in NetLinkS activities often expressed what could be seen as healthy scepticism about the extent to which C&IT will help to make resource savings or will replace effective traditional methods of support successfully. However, although by no means seen as a panacea, it was hoped that technology would alleviate some of the problems caused by rising student numbers and under-resourcing, and would contribute to developing cost-effective, flexible learner support provision. It was anticipated that online open learning resources would be of particular value as refresher or back-up resources to traditional teaching or training sessions, and that C&IT would help to accommodate different learning styles more effectively and facilitate peer support amongst end-users. The limitations of common approaches to user education and training – for example, library tours at the start of academic programs, or generic, lecture-based sessions only loosely related to students' immediate learning needs – were frequently acknowledged, and participants hoped that technology would enable them to provide more effective support at the time of need. Since then, a good deal of progress has been made in terms of the exploitation of technology, although evaluation studies investigating the achievement of goals such as these are as yet scarce. The following paragraphs highlight key trends in the use of C&IT in teaching, training and advisory activities in information services during and beyond the life of the NetLinkS project, both within the UK and on the international scene.

Reference and enquiry services, assistance in online searching. Online reference and enquiry services, often staffed jointly by computing and library staff, have become commonplace, ranging from *ad-hoc* e-mail responses to individual queries, to formal e-mail help desks and services using specialized software; Sloan (1997) offers a comprehensive review of approaches to remote reference to that date. Web-based lists of 'frequently-asked-questions', local Usenet newsgroups and bulletin boards are also common. There has been some experimentation with synchronous communication technologies, for example, the use of video-conferencing (Pagell, 1996) and MOOs (Cook & Stanley, 1999). Initiatives in real-time, online support for information searching are exploring the potential of computer-supported collaborative work applications which enable information staff to interact with users during the search process, as discussed for example by Proctor and Davenport (1997).

Open learning resources. As anticipated by participants in NetLinkS focus groups, information staff have become increasingly involved in in-house authoring and maintenance of online open learning resources, whether generic or tailored to the needs of specific user groups. 'Virtual library tours' are common and web-based guides and tutorials based on straightforward conversion of paper-based documentation are gradually being replaced by more sophisticated resources which exploit the technical interactivity of hypermedia and the capabilities of new web applications, often incorporating assignments and computer-based assessment.

Examples of web-based open learning resources include an interactive information skills 'Webbook' for engineers at the University of Queensland (Cribb & Woodall, 1997) and the CALAIS tutorials produced for the local academic community and for the commercial market at the University of Aberdeen[9]. Computer-based video has been suggested as a means of demonstrating online searching procedures, with explanatory voice-over, for learners to use at their own convenience (Jackson, 1999). A range of free or commercial open learning resources offers an alternative to in-house production, and many resources can be tailored easily for use in different contexts. Commercial packages come in both CD ROM and web formats; an example of the latter is the EC-funded 'Into-Info' series of information literacy resources in a variety of subject areas, which are designed for self-paced use in formal or informal learning settings and as continuing professional development resources for library staff (Fjallbrant, 2000; Thomasson & Fjallbrant, 1996). For discussions of other pioneering initiatives in open learning in information skills tuition, see also Chamberlain and Mitchell (1996), Scholtz (1996) and Vishwanatham (1997).

Information literacy and key skills courses. Credit-bearing 'key skills' courses targeted at undergraduates and delivered wholly or in part by means of C&IT have been initiated in a number of UK institutions recently. Information skills tend, in this context, to be addressed alongside a range of other learning skills, and it seems likely that this approach will become more widely adopted in the short to medium term. An early example was the intranet-based 'Effective Learning Program' at the University of Lincolnshire and Humberside, which covers information retrieval alongside a range of other topics relating to skills in lifelong learning. Linked closely to the subject curriculum across the disciplines, the program is delivered in mixed-mode format by information specialists – 'Learning Advisors' – working alongside academic tutors (Hunter, 1997). University-wide research training programs are also increasingly common and likewise offer opportunities to include a focus on information skills alongside other topics, as at the University of Sheffield where a module on information skills is based on a combination of face-to-face lectures, self-paced web guides, e-mail and computer-conferencing.

Input into mainstream course design and delivery. Input into the design and delivery of academic courses which are adopting C&IT takes a variety of forms; for example, library involvement in the first offering of an online, distance learning program at the University of Southern Queensland included developing a quality assured resource base of Internet materials, providing online access to licensed electronic resources, and *ad-hoc* online enquiry assistance (McPherson, 1997). Areas of involvement include:

- *Selection, adaptation or design of online learning resources.* Typically, this entails advising on the availability and suitability of networked resources for particular courses, and developing tailored, web-based 'meta-resources' to provide access to information sources and guidance on their use.

---

9   CALAIS http://www.abdn.ac.uk/~lib083/calais/dbe.html

- *Online tutorial or advisory assistance to support learners' information-seeking activities.* Courses which use online communication are offering opportunities for information specialists to interact with learners within their 'virtual classrooms', for example as a means of providing guidance for project work. Banks (1997) proposes a role for library staff as online facilitators helping to direct students to appropriate resources and monitoring their learning, whilst Schreiber and Moring (1997) suggest that competencies associated with online group facilitation may become important if librarians develop online intermediary roles in networked learning communities.

- *Advice on the design and exploitation of online learning environments and resource management software; assistance with copyright, metadata and resource-sharing issues.* In the light of current developments in the design of integrated learning environment and resource management systems, it is likely that this will become an area of increasing involvement for information professionals, who are already involved in assisting academic staff with the use of learning environment software such as WebCT, and with metadata and intellectual property issues associated with the creation and use of online learning resources.

Staff development and awareness-raising. Librarians in many institutions are becoming increasingly active in information awareness and training provision for academic staff. Some staff development initiatives exploit C&IT; institution-based mailing lists have for some time been adopted to disseminate current awareness information to academic staff on Internet developments and resources (e.g., McNab, 1995) and web-based open learning resources are, of course, available to staff as well as to students. However, staff development for academics is often a spin-off of collaborative work on learning resource development, or is carried out mainly through face-to-face training workshops and one-to-one consultancy. The latter is perhaps especially effective, as demonstrated by the TAPin project (Flatten, 2000), although its model of librarian-led assistance for academics is also highly resource-intensive in terms of library staff time. TAPin supplemented face-to-face support for academics with various online services, including electronic enquiry services, FAQ databases, individually tailored web pages and online current awareness services.

9.4   Development Issues

The following sections discuss a number of educational, professional and organizational issues, which in recent years have emerged as particularly significant to the development of information specialists' contribution to networked learner support.

9.4.1   Information Literacy, Pedagogy and Educational Development

As teaching staff begin to incorporate network capabilities and resources into their courses and institutional policies place greater emphasis on 'transferable' learning skills, especially in more vocationally-oriented institutions, information staff have fresh opportunities to encourage an explicit focus on information literacy at the level of the mainstream subject curriculum. The principle of embedding skills training into academic programs is a well-established orthodoxy in user education circles (Fleming, 1996), but has often proven difficult to achieve in practice. There are indications of change here; for example, Flett's (1999) UK-based survey shows that the proportion of academic departments which include information skills training as an integral element of their programs has increased recently in many institutions, especially in relation to postgraduate and distance learning courses. It may be assumed that models for 'academic integration' vary from one setting to another; however, there is a strong rationale for ensuring that skills development initiatives are not only subject-related in a general sense but, more specifically, course- and project-related. The view that information skills are most effectively developed when related to learning needs arising directly from academic work underpins some recent approaches to C&IT-based information literacy support and in the UK is also reflected in the Dearing Report (1997), which in establishing medium-term national goals for higher education favours embedding key skills in the subject curriculum rather than tackling them through parallel courses.

This raises significant questions for both librarians and teaching staff. If information skills are to be developed within rather than alongside academic courses, the question arises as to whose responsibility it is to take information literacy initiatives forward. The success of strengthened collaborative partnerships between library and academic staff in some institutions suggests that there will be value in promoting further realignment of professional relationships across the academic/support divide in others, and in information professionals contributing much more to educational development. It is well-accepted that the extent to which students engage independently with information resources and develop information skills of relevance to their subject domain varies from one educational context to another and depends largely on the way information issues are addressed (explicitly or implicitly) by the educational models adopted by academic staff. Models based on the principles of problem-based, active learning are more likely to seek to facilitate learning in contexts which retain complexity and help students develop 'process' awareness and skills which are essential to independent learning (e.g., Grabinger & Dunlap, 1995; Grabinger, Dunlap & Duffield, 1997). Linking skills development closely to subject domain learning is a central tenet of theories of active learning; for example, constructivist perspectives, which are becoming influential in shaping emerging practice in the use of new C&IT, suggest that networked learners should be encouraged to engage independently with the richness of the information landscape in their subject domain and that courses should build in – rather than 'bolt-on' – support for developing relevant skills through authentic, contextualized learning tasks (e.g., Duffy & Jonassen, 1992; Brown, Collins & Duguid, 1989; Oliver & Oliver, 1997). Moreover, the complexity and volatility of the information landscape, and the fact that different information needs emerge at different levels of academic work, suggest that relevant knowledge and skills cannot be acquired in one-off learning events but need to be tackled incrementally as part of a developmental process over time. These issues are starting to be addressed in the educational literature related to networked learning (e.g., Grabinger & Higginson, 1998), as it becomes more widely recognized that skills related to information literacy are fundamental to active learning in the new environment, alongside skills in online communication and group-work, technology access and manipulation, and other aspects of self-managed, independent learning.

On the other hand, many approaches to the use of C&IT in learning present online resources in packaged form and place little emphasis on the process dimensions of learning. There is also a strong tradition of packaged information resource provision in traditional distance learning, which can serve to limit learners' engagement with the resources of the wider information environment. Research into library provision for post-graduate distance learning has identified a mismatch between the values of librarians – to whom the importance of encouraging independent use of information resources in learning is a core professional belief – and those of many course providers, who failed to recognize this issue or for a number of reasons were ambivalent about it (Stephens & Unwin, 1997a). Phenomenographic research into information literacy in higher education has suggested both that conceptions of information literacy are context-dependent and that the understandings of information professionals may not be shared by teaching staff (Bruce, 1997). These findings suggest that more local and system-wide research into educators' attitudes to, and conceptions of, information literacy as they incorporate C&IT into their practice will be of value for librarians and other stakeholders in educational development. However, in the light of their findings, Stephens and Unwin (1997b) suggest that unless information services play a central role in educational design and delivery in the future, many students on distance and open learning courses which exploit C&IT may continue to be presented with tightly constrained models of learning:

"We are sceptical that advances in technology will necessarily help distance learners become more autonomous, and fearful that electronic access might compound the trend towards narrowly prescribed reading, leading to even greater student isolation as teachers are pushed further into becoming designers of pre-packaged programed learning. Instead, we envision a more hopeful and exciting future, in which *librarians collaborate to expand the pedagogic boundaries of distance learning*, ensuring that electronic developments are integrated with traditional concerns for wide reading, student autonomy and independent thinking" (emphasis added).

If information specialists are to promote information literacy in networked learning, as part of their role in learner support, they and their senior managers will need to engage critically with pedagogic issues associated with the adoption of new technologies, and to participate actively in institutional debates and strategic planning related to taking networked learning forward. In order to develop models of practice which are sensitive to learners' needs in specific educational contexts, they will need to understand more about the ways in which networked learners interact with information resources in the context of different learning activities, and about teaching purposes and styles in different disciplines and local educational settings. The scope of their role in course development and, where appropriate, delivery, might then involve contributions in the following areas:

- raising awareness about information literacy issues amongst teaching staff and others involved in developing online resources and courses, including C&IT staff and educational developers;
- promoting the value of the independent use of information resources in learning, and encouraging pedagogic strategies which engage learners fully with the electronic information environment in their subject areas;
- ensuring that information literacy development is part of mainstream courses, and advising on ways of putting appropriate learning strategies into practice using C&IT;
- participating in the design, facilitation and assessment of learning activities related to information literacy for different learning purposes and levels of study, including activities which will be carried out online.

It would appear therefore that a case can be made for librarians to establish a strong profile in networked curriculum development and delivery, and some recent initiatives point in this direction. However, despite the emphasis on the importance of information specialists' educational role in the light of current developments in higher education, it is noteworthy that there is no consensus on how this may best be fulfilled (Brophy *et al.*, 1998). Models of practice are far from well established in many institutions and it is worth remembering past difficulties encountered by efforts to resource the work of teacher-librarians adequately, and to integrate their contribution into institutional structures. Cost-effectiveness and scalability will no doubt be key determinants of directions taken in local contexts and, as outlined below, a range of other factors may also serve to limit librarians' contribution to networked learning initiatives.

9.5   Collaboration, Role Convergence and Hybridization

Many information professionals are embracing opportunities to develop new areas of expertize and models of service with energy and enthusiasm. Nevertheless, feedback from participants in the NetLinkS project alongside evidence from other research suggests that new perspectives on librarians' professional roles may present a significant challenge to the expectations and attitudes of many information specialists and their colleagues. The question of how to strengthen cross-disciplinary partnerships wás a key concern of many librarians who participated in NetLinkS activities. Frustration was sometimes expressed at what was perceived to be a lack of understanding amongst colleagues with computing backgrounds of information specialists' roles in user support; however, fostering new partnerships between support services and teaching departments was often perceived to be the more significant hurdle. Academics' interest in the Internet offers new opportunities for collaborative work – as described, for example, by Leckie and Fullerton (1999) – but in practice liaison between information and academic staff is often weak, with librarians having little connection with the educational process other than responding to students' assignment-related enquiries and ensuring the availability of recommended items on reading lists. Librarians in NetLinkS focus groups often expressed fears about being overlooked by academic staff who might not perceive them as an obvious source of assistance in relation to learning, teaching or even electronic resources. Moreover, wrongly or rightly, academics were sometimes perceived as threatened by, even hostile to, librarians' involvement in supporting curriculum design and delivery, leading to strong reservations amongst some library staff about the possibility of closer partnerships. There is some support for this view of the perspectives of teaching staff in the findings of other research (e.g., Garrod 1998); on the other hand, a number of academic liaison initiatives, including the TAPin project's approach, have demonstrated the positive effects of promoting awareness of the nature and value of information expertize within academic departments (Flatten, 2000).

The grey areas between information, technology, and teaching and learning expertize in the electronic environment, and the overlapping roles and responsibilities of staff involved, were also key concerns for NetLinkS participants. Librarians working in reference and enquiry roles were increasingly required to respond to queries in which 'information' and 'technology' content was difficult to distinguish, or which were plainly technical rather than information-related; at the same time, computing staff were becoming more involved in information matters. The concept of hybridization was beginning to be used in the context of convergence between IT and information roles. Thus, in an *nls-forum* discussion on this topic in late 1996, a Senior Learning Resources Officer from a converged library/IT service commented that:

> "...coming from an IT support background and moving into a library environment... I find I have become a hybrid, neither IT person nor librarian".

It was being noticed, too, that information-related aspects of learner support were sometimes being addressed by staff with professional backgrounds in neither librarianship nor technology, but in educational technology. New types of post –

in terms of traditional boundaries between IT, information and educational expertize – were being created and, as described during one focus group discussion, were not always filled by information or technology specialists:

"We have a post here which was the result of an evolution – the Humanities IT Development Officer... That person could have been based in the computer center, the department, or the information service, but the actual recruitment has challenged us ever since, as they have neither a computing nor a library background, but an education background; a teaching and pedagogic background. This has challenged us to break down barriers... The departments are delighted and their use of IT has gone up immeasurably in the past year. The post was originally to have been a technician post... then it was thought that they needed someone to do more than just plug the machine in!"

Finally, concerns were voiced that with the break-down of the traditional divide between teaching and provision of access to information resources, in future it might fall to teaching staff, rather than librarians, to take on a good deal of responsibility for information resource management and information literacy support.

The indications are that learner support roles within and outside the library service have indeed been changing in response to network user needs, and new roles are emerging in different parts of institutions to support staff and students. 'Role convergence' – between library and computing staff, library and academic staff, library and educational development staff *and* between traditional library roles – has been identified as a key feature of the impact of the electronic library on people (Day *et al.,* 1997). Familiar divisions of labor between distinct professional groups are under pressure, as expertize in technology and information becomes less easy to differentiate, and as academics create web resources and online learning environments that offer direct access to electronic resources. Moreover, where information skills development is embedded into mainstream academic courses, assumptions in the information profession that librarians are ultimately the most appropriate staff to 'teach' information skills, as discussed, for example, by Pacey (1995), may well be challenged.

Against this background, it is unclear how the roles and responsibilities of the various stakeholders in the educational arena will shake out in the longer term. The extent to which role hybridization will affect librarians across the sector is a matter of some speculation, and uncertainty about this issue raises questions for those with responsibility for staff development in information services. As one participant in NetLinkS research put it, *"Does the all-purpose beast exist, and if so, to what level? Or should we be training people to work in teams?"* Decisions about this are likely to vary according to local circumstances and needs. However, it is recognized that a new type of learner support expertize is required for the networked environment, which is seen increasingly in terms of a blend of C&IT,

information *and* teaching/learning expertize. This, for example, is the view of the Dean of Information Services of one UK college of higher education:

> "Information services contribute to institutional development through the activities of information management, information technology and learning support. At the intersections of these areas are the signposts to the most valuable skill blends for the future. Many IS staff have good skills as information managers and also as information technologists. However, staff who position themselves at the junctions of information management, C&IT, *and most crucially learning development,* will be best placed to make the most significant future contribution. They will need an understanding of information-based activities, including C&IT, combined with a knowledge of, and active involvement in, student learning" (Watson, 1998; emphasis added).

It is sometimes suggested that for librarians, the capacity to adopt a new, hybrid form of professional expertize, is becoming a matter of species survival in a rapidly evolving 'information ecology' (e.g., Garrod, 1999). Brophy (2001) argues that given the disintermediatory impact of networked access to information resources, many information specialists are faced with a stark choice between, on the one hand, developing an educational role and, on the other, settling for the lesser challenge of the role of technician. In this context, it is perhaps unsurprising to find that research offers evidence of stress and insecurity about role identity, status, expertize, and overall professional and service direction within information services (Edwards, 1997). The new "melting pot" of professional skills and responsibilities in learner support (Garrod, 1997) adds a further twist to well-rehearsed concerns that traditional library expertize may become redundant when end-user access to both local and global resources is direct from the desktop. Moreover, where strategic direction in relation to networked learning and learner support is lacking at senior levels – an issue which was a prominent theme in discussions hosted by NetLinkS and which has also been noted elsewhere (Brophy, *et al.,* 1998) – librarians are more likely to be unaware of, or unclear about, their potential roles in the educational process. As illustrated by some of the NetLinkS findings, information specialists do not always welcome the prospect of becoming more active in teaching, training and the use of technology, and do not necessarily relate their training or advisory work to its wider educational context. SKIP revealed a tendency amongst many librarians to conceive of their own training and development needs solely in terms of technical proficiencies (Garrod 1998), and TAPin demonstrated that whilst training in the use of C&IT is an essential foundation in equipping librarians to take on new roles in learner support, by itself it is unlikely to lead to new perspectives on roles in skills transfer, or in educational change and innovation (Williams & Reid, 2000).

9.6   Professional Development

In the light of these issues, NetLinkS asked librarians in focus groups about their views on professional development as regards networked learner support, and subsequently hosted a number of workshop-based and online discussions on this subject; this question was also explored with librarians with special responsibility for staff development in a small-scale interview survey. Wide-scale training and awareness-raising needs were identified, if information staff across the sector were to develop the confidence and expertize to develop their educational roles in the ways suggested in the literature and by innovative practitioner initiatives.

Information and C&IT. As an extension of expertize in using and evaluating networked information resources, staff envisaged a need to gain a more solid foundation in C&IT skills, for example in basic technical problem-solving and HTML authoring. Whilst some saw a need to acquire advanced technical skills, others tended instead to highlight the importance of fostering openness to technological change and of becoming familiar with the range of new educational technologies and their general functionality, in order to be capable of offering advice to academic staff and of implementing ideas successfully in collaboration with more technical colleagues. A need was identified for opportunities to experiment with a number of technologies that were beginning to have an impact on the educational scene, including text-based conferencing, synchronous chat, educational MOOs, and desktop videoconferencing.

Trends in educational uses of C&IT. The need for general awareness raising about the use of C&IT in teaching and learning, both nationally and locally, was consistently emphasized. Involvement in the wider educational community, for example through online forums dealing with networked learning issues or through conference attendance, was seen as important. Lack of awareness about *local* innovations in teaching and learning was a dominant theme of the research; librarians anticipated that in order to work closely with academic staff and to tailor information support to the needs of specific networked learning initiatives, they would need considerably more awareness of the ways in which C&IT were being adopted in different contexts.

Learning theory. Library staff expressed a need to gain more understanding of educational theory in relation to learning with technology, with theory relating to 'learning styles' sometimes a particular area of interest in relation to the aim to accommodate different cognitive styles in the design of online learning resources.

C&IT in learner support. At a time when most institutions were just starting to use the web and other technologies for enquiry services and user education, staff were keen to have access to illustrations of emerging practice and to gain support for immediate practical initiatives at work. The value of 'people-networking' and of capitalizing on the experience of early adopters of new technologies was frequently mentioned, and a preference was sometimes expressed for exchanging ideas and information with peers over looking in detail at the literature. The 'mini-conference' model adopted by the NetLinkS project's *nls-forum* – in which staff with experience of, or strong views on, innovations were invited to lead an online discussion over a three-week period – proved to be a success in this respect.

Web-based instructional design. The need for librarians to become proficient in web-based instructional design was anticipated in some focus groups and over the life of the project became increasingly clear. There is a growing literature on the pedagogy of web-based instruction for information literacy; see, for example, Cox (1997), Dewald (1999a) and Fouad (1997). Typical recommendations are that online, open learning methods should be combined with face-to-face interaction with an expert and that learning resources should invite interactivity, defined by Dewald (1999b) as 'thoughtful action or feedback by the learner'. In practice, this generally means providing opportunities for learners to practise skills online and receive feedback on performance and knowledge.

Online course facilitation and design. At the outset of the NetLinkS project, there was interest in learning about the design and facilitation of participative online courses and about the online tutoring role amongst some library staff in focus groups, although none were at that time involved in this type of online course delivery. As new software for supporting participative networked learning emerged and the emphasis on this approach to the use of C&IT in learning gathered momentum during the life of the project, these areas became a stronger focus of interest within the NetLinkS community of interest.

Online communication. The question of communication skills for a variety of online media was often raised in relation to enquiry services, online tutoring, and encouraging online peer support amongst students. Early adopters of computer-mediated communication in learner support signalled difficulties associated with the lack of face-to-face cues, for example in relation to correctly pitching advice and understanding information user needs in conferencing forums.

Multi-disciplinary team-work and promotion of change and innovation. The need to take initiative in team-building and to work in multi-disciplinary groups in relation to educational objectives was perceived to require particular understandings and skills, and library staff frequently commented on the importance of increasing their awareness of issues related to cultural change, and of approaches to encouraging teaching and learning innovation.

Beyond the areas outlined above, feedback from participants in NetLinkS and associated research made it clear that developing the capacity to support networked learning should be perceived more as a matter of *"moving to a new plane of operation"* – in the words of one librarian – than as a straightforward matter of plugging a knowledge or skills 'gap'. The importance of providing opportunities for staff to explore attitudes and assumptions about educational practice, professional roles and relationships, in addition to expanding the scope of their technical expertize or theoretical knowledge, was confirmed. A need was identified, for example, for professional development opportunities that could communicate 'vision' in addition to providing practical support for new initiatives; as one staff development librarian commented during an interview, *"we need professional development to make people think and question their roles. Better to start them thinking than to expect to start teaching them skills"*.

Opportunities to engage with new perspectives by participating in debate and collaborative learning were seen as important in this respect. It was also emphasized that professional development initiatives in this area must be timely and relevant in relation to the pace and direction of local institutional and service developments, so that new understandings and expertize would be supported by managers and put into practice immediately. Given the variation in their organizational and professional backgrounds – for example, in the extent and nature of strategic direction in institutions, the nature of organizational structures, the rate of change, individual roles, prior awareness and expertize in relevant areas – staff involved in NetLinkS activities had different perspectives on their professional roles and potential directions for the future. It became clear that continuing professional development opportunities must be sensitive to a wide diversity of needs and interests. Finally, since networked learner support cannot be taken forward by librarians in isolation, either from colleagues in other support services or from academic staff, professional development initiatives – whether local or national – need to be designed to take this into account.

The NetLinkS project aimed to respond to the points outlined above through its range of development activities. In particular, the online, distance learning course it piloted (Levy 1999) suggests potential directions for other professional development initiatives in this area. The course aimed to enable information services staff to pursue interests in a range of areas associated with their roles in networked learner support in an integrated way, alongside the development of technical and other skills. Offering an environment for pursuing individual interests and projects within a collaborative framework, participants were invited to explore three major areas:

- the emerging educational role of information services and staff in the networked learning environment, and current trends in online approaches to learner support;
- trends in networked learning pedagogy and practice, and the use of a range of new technologies in designing learning materials and environments;
- directions for networked learner support in local contexts, and organizational and professional issues related to change and innovation.

There was a strong emphasis on the course of the value of experiential learning, in terms of gaining direct personal experience of active learning in the networked environment, and on taking a collaborative approach to developing knowledge and expertize related to new professional practice. New perspectives were explored through online discussion and group-work, and participants were encouraged to develop work-based projects which might catalyze new professional collaborations. The course's learning environment and design were evaluated positively by participants. DEDICATE, a European Commission funded project, subsequently designed a networked professional development course in information literacy and learner support, based partly on the NetLinkS learning model, to a mixed group of librarians, researchers and academic staff (Fjallbrant 2000; Fjallbrant & Levy 1998, 1999).

The need for both informal and formal professional development opportunities related to educational matters is a continuing theme of discussions in the networked library context. Other eLib projects such as SKIP and IMPEL2 confirmed the need for a broad portfolio of skills and knowledge for learner support staff in information services, as well as personal qualities such as adaptability and openness to change (Parker & Jackson, 1998; Garrod, 1997). Curriculum development initiatives which require staff with different professional backgrounds to work together challenge all parties to work in new ways and provide valuable informal opportunities for staff development (Biddiscombe, 1998). It is likely that professional development for library staff in the UK will continue to be affected by the increasing emphasis on teaching quality and qualifications in the higher education system as a whole. The recent establishment of the national Institute for Learning and Teaching (ILT) may encourage librarians in learner support and teaching roles to gain formal teaching qualifications, and to gain membership of the new professional body. At the institutional level, staff development initiatives accredited by the ILT will be able to exploit the advantages of bringing together staff with different perspectives on, and roles in, teaching and learner support.

9.7   Conclusion

The issues with which the NetLinkS project was concerned are of continuing relevance in the light of UK and international innovation in networked learning. This chapter has reviewed the changing educational role and practice of information specialists involved in supporting networked learning and has identified issues of relevance to taking new initiatives forward. It has suggested that information specialists need opportunities to extend their knowledge and expertize into new areas, especially in relation to the use of C&IT for educational purposes, but has indicated that professional development in this area cannot be considered separately from strategic development at an institutional level and has emphasized that adapting to – and shaping – the new learning environment is more than a matter of adopting new tools and techniques. In order to participate in defining and supporting new models of educational practice for the new environment, librarians need opportunities to explore new perspectives on their professional roles and relationships, to become confident in relation to relevant aspects of learning theory and of the use of new educational technology, and to extend management and personal skills into new areas of multidisciplinary teamwork and innovation. Despite uncertainties associated with the changing professional environment and the need for clearer strategic planning and leadership in many institutions, current trends suggest that many information professionals will play an important role in developing and sustaining good educational practice in the new environment. Changes in some job titles – for example, from subject librarian to 'learning advisor' – already indicate that information staff at the learning interface may come to define their professional identity largely – perhaps primarily – in terms of *educational* practice in the future. This view suggests an agenda for professional development providers, whose programs must be able to meet the needs of information specialists working in roles that are increasingly oriented towards exploiting the network as a positive environment for learning. At the same time, themes highlighted in this chapter indicate possible avenues for interdisciplinary research that can bring both educational and information perspectives to bear on questions of good practice in networked learner support, especially in relation to conceptions and models of information literacy, and networked pedagogy for information literacy development.

9.8   References

Banks, B. (1997) Beyond the online library: supporting learning with the Learning Environment. *International Journal of Electronic Library Research 1*(3) pp235-252

Barry, C.A. (1997) Information skills for an electronic world: training doctoral research students. *Journal of Information Science 23*(3) pp225-238

Biddiscombe, R. (1998) Coming to an understanding: staff development and training in a multi-skilled team environment. In Heikell, M. (Ed.) *Training for change: new skills for the electronic library.* Proceedings of a seminar organized by NORDINFO and the British Library Research and Innovation Center, York, England, 25th-28th September 1997. Helsingfors: NORDINFO-Publikation pp67-82

Biddiscombe, R. (1999) Managing the learning agenda in a converged services environment. In *Proceedings of the 1999 IATUL Conference*, Technical University of Crete, Greece, 17th-21st May 1999
http://educate.lib.chalmers.se/IATUL/proceedcontents/chanpap/biddisco.html

Brophy, P. (2001) Networked learning. *Journal of Documentation 57*(1) pp130-156

Brophy, P., Craven, J. & Fisher, S. (1998) *The development of UK academic library services in the context of lifelong learning. A Supporting Study in the JISC Electronic Libraries (eLib) Program.* London: Library Information Technology Center

Brown, J.S., Collins, A. & Duguid, S. (1989) Situated cognition and the culture of learning. *Educational Researcher 18*(1) pp32-42

Bruce, C.S. (1997) The relational approach: a new model for information literacy. *New Review of Information and Library Research 3*, pp1-22

Bulpitt, G. (1998) Case study: Sheffield Hallam University. In Hanson, T., Day, J. (Eds.) *Managing the electronic library: a practical guide for information professionals.* London: Bowker Saur, pp 227-243

Burge, E.J. & Snow, J.E. (2000) Candles, corks and contracts: essential relationships between learners and librarians. *The New Review of Libraries and Lifelong Learning 1*, pp19-34

Carty, J., Stark, I., van der Zwan, R. & Whitsed, N. (1996) Towards a strategy for supporting distance-learning students through networked access to information: issues and challenges in preparing to support the Doctorate in Education. *Education for Information 14* (4) pp305-316

Chamberlain, E. & Mitchell, M. (1996) BCK2SKOL: a networked learning model classroom. *Education for Information 14* (4) pp279-295

Cochrane, C. (1996) The use of videoconferencing to support learning: an overview of issues relevant to the library and information profession. *Education for Information 14* (4) pp317-330

Cook, N. & Stanley, T. (1999) MUD/MOO environments in the delivery of user support and training. *Vine 109*, pp53-58

Cox, A. (1997) Using the world wide web for library user education: a review article. *Journal of Librarianship and Information Science 29* (1) pp39-44

Creth, S.D. (1996) *The electronic library: slouching toward the future, or creating a new information environment?* Follett Lecture Series
http://www.ukoln.ac.uk/services/papers/follett/creth/paper.html

Cribb, G. & Woodall, L. (1997) Web book for engineers: an interactive information skills program. *New Review of Information Networking 3*, pp245-253.

Day, J.M., Walton, G. & Edwards, C. (1997) The culture of convergence. *International Journal of Electronic Library Research 1* (1) pp43-62

Day, J.M., Walton, G., Bent, M., Curry, S., Edwards, C. & Jackson, M. (1996) Higher education, teaching, learning and the electronic library: a review of the literature for the IMPEL2 project: monitoring organizational and cultural change. *The New Review of Academic Librarianship 1*, pp131-204

Dearing Report (1997) *Higher education in the learning society. Report of the National Committee of Inquiry into Higher Education.* London: NCIHE Publications (HMSO)

Dewald, N.H. (1999a) Transporting good library instruction practice into the web environment: an analysis of online tutorials. *The Journal of Academic Librarianship 25* (1) pp26-32

Dewald, N.H. (1999b) Web-based library instruction: what is good pedagogy? *Information Technology and Libraries 18* (1) pp26-31

Duffy, T.M. & Jonassen, D.J. (Eds) (1992) *Constructivism and the technology of instruction: a conversation.* Hillsdale, NJ: Lawrence Erlbaum Associates

Edwards, C. (1997) Change and uncertainty in academic libraries. *Ariadne: the Internet magazine for librarians and information specialists 11*, pp6-8
http://www.ariadne.ac.uk/issue11/

Edwards, C., Day, J.M. & Walton, G. (Eds) (1998) *Monitoring organizational and cultural change: the impact of people on electronic libraries. Report of the IMPEL2 Project.* London: Library Information Technology Center

Fielden Report (1993) *Supporting expansion: a report on human resources management in academic libraries, for the Joint Funding Councils' Libraries Review Group (John Fielden Consultancy).* Bristol: Higher Education Funding Council for England

Fjallbrant, N. (2000) Information literacy for scientists and engineers: experiences of EDUCATE and DEDICATE. *Program 34* (3) pp257-268

Fjallbrant, N. & Levy, P. (1998) DEDICATE: distance education courses with access through networks. *Ariadne: the Internet journal for librarians and information specialists, 17* http://www.ariadne.ac.uk/issue17/

Fjallbrant, N. & Levy, P. (1999) Information literacy courses in engineering and science: the design and implementation of the DEDICATE courses. In *Proceedings of the 1999 IATUL Conference*, Technical University of Crete, http://educate.lib.chalmers.se/IATUL/proceedcontents/chanpap/fjall.html

Flatten, K. (1997) Librarians as change agents in the HE community. In Layzell Ward, P. & Weingard, D.E. (Eds.) *Human development: competencies for the twenty-first century. Papers from the IFLA CPERT Third International Conference on Continuing Professional Education for the Library and Information Professions.* Munich: K.G. Saur, pp118-121

Flatten, K. (2000) The TAPin model. In Reid, B.J., Foster, W. (Eds.) *Achieving cultural change in networked libraries.* Aldershot: Gower, pp173-190

Fleming, H. (1996) User education in academic libraries in the United Kingdom. *British Journal of Academic Librarianship 1* (1) pp18-40

Flett, M. (1999) *Information skills training in UK universities: an overview of current practice and future trends, with a particular focus on networked delivery, academic integration and the role of the librarian.* Unpublished Masters dissertation. Sheffield: University of Sheffield

Follett Report (1993) *Report of the Joint Funding Councils' Libraries Review Group.* Bristol: Higher Education Funding Council for England

Fouad, R.H. (1997) Interactive teaching methods in relation to electronic information access. *LIBER Quarterly 7*, pp474-489

Fowell, S.P. & Levy, P. (1995) Developing a new professional practice: a model for networked learner support in higher education. *Journal of Documentation 51* (3) pp271-280

Garrod, P. (1997) New skills for information professionals. *Information UK Outlooks 22.* London: British Library and South Bank University

Garrod, P. (1998) Skills for new information professionals (SKIP): an evaluation of the key findings. *Program 32* (3) pp241-263

Garrod, P. (1999) Survival strategies in the Learning Age – hybrid staff and hybrid libraries. *ASLIB Proceedings 51* (6) pp187-94

George, R. & Luke, R. (1996) The critical place of information literacy in the trend towards flexible delivery in higher education contexts. *Australian Academic and Research Libraries 27* (3) pp204-212

Grabinger, S.R. & Dunlap, J.C. (1995) Rich environments for active learning: a definition. *ALT-J, Journal of the Association for Learning Technology 3*(2) pp5-34

Grabinger, S.R. & Higginson, C. (1998) REALs for Alt-C. *Active Learning 9*, pp57-60

Grabinger, S.R., Dunlap, J.C. & Duffield, J.A. (1997) Rich environments for active learning in action: problem-based learning. *ALT-J, Journal of the Association for Learning Technology 5* (2) pp5-17

Heseltine, R. (1995) The challenge of learning in cyberspace. *Library Association Record, 97* (8) pp432-433

Hunter, B. (1997) The role of learning support in the development and implementation of a key skills program and an Intranet to support it. *Electronic Library 15* (5) pp357-62

Jackson, C. (1999) Computer-based video – a tool for information skills training? *Aslib Proceedings 51* (7) pp213-223

Jones, M. (1997) High five for the next five: librarians and distance education, *Journal of Library Services for Distance Education 1* (1) http://www.westga.edu/library/jlsde/

Kamhi-Stein, L. & Stein, A.P. (1998) Teaching information competency as a third language: a new model for library instruction. *Reference and User Services Quarterly 38* (2) pp173-79

Kelly, J. & Robbins, K. (1996) Changing roles for reference librarians. *Journal of Library Administration 22* (2/3) pp111-121

Leckie, G.J. & Fullerton, A. (1999) Information literacy in science and engineering undergraduate education: faculty attitudes and pedagogical practices. *College and Research Libraries 60* (1) pp9-29

Levy, P. (1997) Continuing professional development for networked learner support. *International Journal of Electronic Library Research 1* (3) pp267-282

Levy, P. (1998) Developing networked learner support in UK academic libraries. In Heikell, M. (Ed) *Proceedings of a seminar organized by NORDINFO and the British Library Research and Innovation Center, York, England*, 25th-28th September 1997. Helsingfors: NORDINFO, pp37-46

Levy, P. (1999) An example of internet-based continuing professional development: perspectives on course design and participation. *Education for Information 17*, pp45-58

Levy, P., Fowell, S.P., Bowskill, N. & Worsfold, E. (1996) NetLinkS: a national professional development project for networked learner support. *Education for Information 14* (4) pp261-278

May, N. (1998) *Changing staff roles and the concept of the Curriculum Support Team: a case study of the science faculty at the University of Plymouth.* Science Education Enhancement and Development (SEED) Working Paper Series. Plymouth: University of Plymouth

McNab, A.S. (1995) Creating the virtual community: supporting internet users by e-mail. *The New Review of Information Networking 1*, pp185-189

McNamara, D. (1998) *Teaching for learning in libraries and information services: a series of educational development workshops.* Hull: EduLib/University of Hull and University of Abertay Dundee

McPherson, M. (1997) Practising the paradigm shift: real-world experience of online support. *International Journal of Electronic Library Research 1*(3) pp219-234

Needham, G., O'Sullivan, U. & Ramsden, A. (2000) ROUTES: a virtual collection of resources for Open University teachers and students. In Brophy, P., Fisher, S. & Clarke, Z. (Eds.) *Libraries without walls 3: the delivery of library services to distant users.* London: Library Association Publishing, pp115-120

Oliver, R. & Oliver, H. (1997) Using context to promote learning from information-seeking tasks. *Journal of the American Society for Information Science 48* (6) pp519-526

Ottewill, R. & Hudson, A. (1997) Electronic information resource use: implications for teaching and library staff. *ALT-J, Journal of the Association for Learning Technology 5* (2) pp31-41

Pacey, P. (1995) Teaching user education, learning information skills; or, towards the self-explanatory library. *New Review of Academic Librarianship 1*, pp95-103

Pagell, R.A. (1996) The virtual reference librarian: using desktop videoconferencing for distance reference. *The Electronic Library 14* (1) pp21-26

Parker, S. & Jackson, M. (1998) The importance of the subject librarian in resource based learning: some findings of the IMPEL2 Project. *Education Libraries Journal 41* (2) pp21-26

Proctor, R. & Davenport, E. (1997) Distributed expertize: remote reference services on a metropolitan area network. *The Electronic Library, 15* (4) pp271-78

Rice-Lively, M.L. & Racine, J.D. (1997) The role of academic librarians in the era of information technology. *Journal of Academic Librarianship*, January, pp31-41

Scholtz, A. (1996) PLUTO: interactive instruction on the web. *College and Research Library News 57* (6) pp346-349

Schreiber, T. & Moring, C. (1997) The communicative and organizational competencies of the librarian in networked learner support: a comparative analysis of the roles of the facilitator and the librarian. *International Journal of Electronic Library Research, 1* (3) pp299-310

Slade, A.L. (2000) International trends and issues in library services for distance learning: present and future. In Brophy, P., Fisher, S. & Clarke, Z. (Eds.) *Libraries without walls 3: the delivery of library services to distant users.* London: Library Association Publishing, pp6-48

Sloan, B. (1997) Service perspectives for digital remote reference services. *Library Trends 47* (1) pp117-143

Stephens, K. & Unwin, L. (1997a) Postgraduate distance education and libraries: educational principles versus pragmatic course design. *Teaching in Higher Education 2*(2) pp153-165

Stephens, K. & Unwin, L. (1997b) The heart of the matter: libraries, distance education and independent thinking. *Journal of Library Services for Distance Education 1* (1) http://www.westga.edu/~library/jlsde/jlsde1.1.html

Stoffle, C.J. (1996) *The emergence of education and knowledge management as major functions of the digital library.* Follett Lecture Series http://www.ukoln.ac.uk/services/papers/follett/stoffle/paper.html

Thomasson, G. & Fjallbrant, N. (1996) EDUCATE: the design and development of a networked end-user education program. *Education for Information 14* (4) pp295-304

Vishwanatham, R., Wilkins, W. & Jevec, T. (1997) The Internet as a medium for online instruction. *College and Research Libraries 58* (5) pp433-444

Watson, L. (1998) Information services: a mission and a vision. *Ariadne: the Internet magazine for librarians and information specialists 14* http://www.ariadne.ac.uk/issue14/

Webber, S. & Johnston, B. (2000) Conceptions of information literacy: new perspectives and implications. *Journal of Information Science 26* (6) pp381-397

Williams, H. & Reid, B. (2000) The impact of the TAPin project on LIS staff. In Reid, B.J. & Foster, W. (Eds.) *Achieving cultural change in networked libraries* Aldershot: Gower, pp191-206

Williams, H. & Zald, A. (1997) Redefining roles: librarians as partners in information literacy education. *International Journal of Electronic Library Research 1*(3) pp253-266

10. Evaluating Networked Learning: Developing A Multi-Disciplinary, Multi-Method Approach

Charles Anderson, Kate Day, Denise Haywood, Jeff Haywood, Ray Land and Hamish Macleod

10.1 Introduction

There has been considerable interest and activity throughout the last decade in the design and implementation of networked learning initiatives in higher education. Many of these initiatives have been evaluated subsequently at institutional or consortial/regional level and the findings disseminated. It is more unusual however to find evaluation of networked learning innovation being undertaken at sectoral level on a nationwide basis. This chapter charts the development and outlines the key characteristics of a research methodology for evaluating large-scale networked learning initiatives. The methodology was developed, and subsequently refined and adapted, through a series of evaluative research commissions undertaken by the Learning Technology in Higher Education (LTHE) Research Group in the Department of Higher and Community Education at the University of Edinburgh.

The instances of use of this methodology are presented here as a series of three case studies. These studies are intended to demonstrate the contextualization and adaptation of the methodology to meet the needs of specific commissions. The first context of use of the methodology involved an evaluation of the Learning Technology Dissemination Initiative (LTDI) which was a Scottish-wide initiative to disseminate the TLTP Program (Teaching and Learning Technology Program). This evaluation was commissioned by the Scottish Higher Education Funding Council (SHEFC). The second context was a commission from the Higher Education Funding Council for England (HEFCE) to evaluate the penetration and impact of Phases 1 and 2 of the TLTP Program. This was followed by the PUSHE Project (Promoting the Use of SCRAN Materials for Teaching and Learning in Higher Education) a formative evaluation commissioned by the Scottish Cultural Resources Access Network, a UK Millennium Fund project. The focus of discussion within these case studies is their methodology. The findings of the various evaluations are not discussed here and are either published elsewhere as indicated below or remain confidential to the commissioners of the research. Each of these evaluations presented the research team with a set of general concerns that the research evaluation strategy would have to address. Certain of these concerns were evident from the outset of the work whilst others emerged and were subsequently addressed whilst work was in progress.

10.2 General Concerns in Undertaking the Evaluations

Each of the evaluative tasks discussed in this chapter was characterized by an underlying complexity which made any initial formulation of the tasks to be undertaken problematic. Each study was large scale, involving all HEIs in Scotland, or in the case of TLTP all HEIs in the UK. Each was of the 'short, fat' variety, operating within tight time frames and resource allocations. Our task was to find ways in which we might measure the extent to which various initiatives had found their respective ways into the host of institutions, faculties, departments, course and modules in Scottish or UK higher education where they might then have an effect on teaching and learning practice. These initiatives ranged from a set of networked learning activities and publications (LTDI), a considerable array of learning materials disseminated from seventy-six networked learning projects (TLTP), or the thousands of cultural and historical multimedia artefacts within the Scottish Cultural Research Access Network (PUSHE).

"Even within a single university setting it would rarely be a straightforward matter to obtain an accurate picture of academic and managerial views about the appropriate role of C&IT, of what was taking place in diverse classrooms, and the uses made of specific teaching and learning resources. There would also be a large number of possible contextual variables, operating independently and interactively at several levels, which could account for the particular patterns uncovered." (Anderson *et al.*, 2000:2)

Matters were not helped by the lack in each instance of appropriate 'baseline' data, as relatively little systematic information was available to assist our understanding of the prevailing situation prior to the work of the initiatives whose impact we were seeking to evaluate.

A further complication arose from the fact that two of the evaluations (LTDI, TLTP) were retrospective in nature, whilst the third (PUSHE) had many retrospective elements. All of the evaluations had to cope with the problem of changes over time. This meant, for example, that potentially useful informants had often moved on to new positions or institutions, or no longer had the same institutional responsibilities that they had once had in relation to networked learning, support for teaching, or running particular courses or projects. Memories tended to fade. Events or activities might be perceived or interpreted differently with the passage of time, leading to concerns about the reliability of recall, and the vagaries of personal hindsight and post-hoc rationalization. The UK HE sector is also characterized by a high degree of diversity. We were aware that any data we sought would be highly dependent on the vantage point and perspective of different observers across a widely varied sector. Such respondents might be expected to have only a partial view of the impact of the initiatives we were evaluating. This required us to be realistic in relation to the limits of knowledge and understanding we might reasonably expect from the different groups of respondents.

There was a continuing need also, at all stages of each of the evaluations to distinguish 'figure' from 'ground' in that it was necessary for us to clearly distinguish the objects of our enquiry from the broader contexts of knowledge, attitudes and developments concerning the use of learning technologies in higher education. At the same time, however, it was necessary carefully to situate the objects of our enquiry within those same contexts.

Finally, in reporting these complex phenomena we were concerned to deal with the requirements of different audiences. We wished to ensure that our research was presented in ways that would be useful to a broad range of stakeholders including not just the commissioners of the research (funding agencies, policy makers, *etc.*) but also academic and related staff in higher education as well as other researchers in the field. As House (1993:128) argues "Evaluations should serve the interests not only of the sponsors but also of the larger society". To employ the distinction coined by Shadish and Epstein (1987), though commissioned in the role of 'service evaluators' we wished to serve also as 'academic evaluators'. Considerations of audience need have implications not only at the reporting stage but also, importantly, during data gathering and analysis. A more detailed analysis of these issues in specific relation to the evaluation of TLTP can be found in Anderson *et al.* (1999b).

10.3 Developing a Research Strategy: Using a Multi-Disciplinary, Multi-Method Approach

We therefore had to develop a strategy that would enable us to access a range of diverse sources of information and help us gain a purchase on different perspectives on innovation. To be effective it was clear that we would need to tailor our research to match various vantage points and to secure a representative range of opinion across the sector.

> "We clearly needed to obtain a complementary (and maybe contrasting) mix of viewpoints, 'takes' on situations, and reactions to initiatives – not simply in terms of going right across the disciplines and types of institutions, but in terms of producers and consumers, academic and support staff, policy makers and chalk-face workers, insiders and outsiders, bottom up and top-down." (Anderson *et al.*, 2000:3)

Two valuable characteristics of our approach in addressing these general challenges were, on the one hand, the formation of a multi-disciplinary research team and, on the other, the adoption of a multi-method research design.

10.4   Working in a Multi-Disciplinary Team

The varied academic backgrounds of the research team members included biochemistry, education, history, information management, psychology, sociology and the humanities, as well as shared interests and experience in learning technologies. The team members also had substantial experience of educational development activity. Hence in the understandings that they brought to the various evaluations discussed below they were able to complement their knowledge of learning technology, evaluation and teaching and learning in higher education with distinctive sets of research skills and approaches. The advantages of a team based approach to evaluation identified by Guba and Lincoln (1983), namely the enhanced potential for multiple roles, perspectives and strategies as well as increased rigour, methodological and substantive representation, and mutual support, were all borne out in our own team experience. Though our team membership was predicated on a firm basis of continuity, trust and familiarity, the multi-disciplinarity that we brought to research meetings manifested itself in a rich difference of assumptions, perspectives and discourses. This ensured that at all strategic points in the development of these various projects there was significant debate and challenge, close scrutiny of proposals and refinement of all design specifications and materials. The fact that all suggestions and interpretations would be routinely submitted to processes of contestation, query and elaboration ensured that any ensuing collective judgement was not prone to an overly facile consensus. The multi-disciplinary team based approach was undoubtedly an asset in the conceptual framing of tasks, in the sharing of practical tasks and in the reviewing and editing of each other's work in the final stages of writing. Contestation, of course, can easily become dysfunctional. Needless to say such lively interrogation and contestation at all stages of the project required reciprocally firm team leadership to ensure that such interrogation was fostering the progress of the work rather than distracting from it.

10.5   Using a Multi-Method Research Design

Our second broad strategy to enable us to address the general concerns discussed earlier was to have a multi-method research design. This would allow us both to optimize access to a range of sources of information as well as to gain different perspectives on innovation. We sought to capitalize on the different perspectives that would be afforded by differently situated vantage points. Acquisition of data from a range of viewpoints would permit us to create fuller, and more nuanced, pictures of the impact and patterns of penetration into HE of the various initiatives we were surveying. In pursuit of such diverse perspectives and richer accounts we were able to access documentary, statistical and bibliographic materials already in the public domain, review records held and reports produced by the projects themselves, as well as devising our own survey questionnaires, interview protocols and user trials in order to elicit new information. At the same time in the interests of efficient resource deployment and busy competing demands on our own academic time and that of our respondents we were concerned that the methods adopted would not result in activity that could be deemed in any way unnecessary.

However, though "The use of multiple methods, often referred to as 'triangulation'" can, as Rossi and Freeman (1993:437) have argued, be 'a means of off-setting different kinds of bias and measurement error' such an approach neither guarantees congruent findings when the data from different methods is combined nor confirms, as Trend (1978:68) points out, 'the notion that using multiple methods will lead to sounder explanations in an easy additive fashion'. Indeed, as Clarke and Dawson (1999:35) find, 'different methods may produce contradictory results when applied to the same evaluation problem'. Our own experience was often in keeping with the latter's findings but the value of drawing on the varied insights of a multidisciplinary team was again borne out in the various reconceptualizings and reformulations that such an approach affords. We would concur with Trend (1978:69) that 'if the accounts mesh this provides an independent test of the validity of the research. If they do not, the areas of disagreement provide points at which further analytic leverage can be exerted'.

In the various studies undertaken therefore we sought to tailor our enquiries to match the vantage points available. In whatever method we adopted at any specific point, be it the analysis of documentary materials, the use of large scale surveys, the use of telephone interviews to develop case studies or the conduct of user trials, we were guided by the content and substance of what each source could reasonably be expected to yield. What those sources were in relation to the particular evaluations undertaken the remainder of the chapter will now illustrate through more detailed and fine-grained accounts of our approaches in the three commissioned evaluations mentioned earlier.

10.6 Case Study 1 - The Learning Technology Dissemination Initiative (LTDI)

The initial development of our research approach took place during 1996-7 in relation to a survey which sought to evaluate the impact across Scottish Higher Education of the Learning Technology Dissemination Initiative. The LTDI had been established to enhance awareness and optimize use of the products of the Teaching and Learning Technology Program (TLTP). The latter was a Universities Funding Council initiative in the UK comprising some 76 projects launched between 1992 and 1993 and intended to make teaching and learning more productive and efficient by harnessing modern technology. The LTDI evaluation had four primary aims, namely to assess the extent to which LTDI met its objectives; the value for money given by LTDI; its impact on the Scottish HE sector and options for future Scottish Higher Education Funding Council (SHEFC) support of learning technology.

The research group adopted a multi-stranded approach to the collection of data relating to the first two years of LTDI's activities. We had three main purposes in our broad approach. Firstly we wished to validate the two detailed annual reports presented to SHEFC by LTDI (by cross-checking but not re-collecting the same data) so as to confirm the lack of bias or omissions in LTDI's own reports and internal evaluation. Secondly we wished to obtain data from different sources from those collected by LTDI, specifically to answer questions about impact, effectiveness and value-for-money. Finally we sought to explore with higher education institutions (HEIs) and expert groups the issues surrounding future SHEFC funding in support of learning technology, so that we could present sensible options for consideration by the Council.

In order to obtain the diverse set of perspectives that was mentioned earlier in the general discussion of our research design and to achieve a richer account of issues emerging from the object of our study we used the following sources of data.

10.6.1 Face-To-Face Interviews

All interviews were undertaken by a minimum of two members of the evaluation team. This was to draw on the strengths of working within a multidisciplinary team as discussed above in exploring a wide range of avenues and perspectives within the interview itself and to ensure accuracy in the subsequent written account. The interviews were conducted with a diverse set of stakeholders to provide a variety of focus, from different vantage points, on their experience of working with LTDI. We interviewed the LTDI Director, some present and past staff of LTDI, staff of educational development units and of CAL/LT support units, and LTDI institutional contacts in HEIs. These interviews were arranged by contact and enabled us to gain an informed institution-wide perspective on the state of networked learning within a particular HEI.

10.6.2 Telephone Interviews and E-mail Survey

In order to assess the reliability of LTDI data, and the durability of the effects of their activities, we also conducted a sample of 21 telephone interviews and an e-mail survey. These provided data on 29 LTDI implementations (mostly at third year undergraduate level) around Scotland. These implementations covered a spread of geographical locations, subject areas and types of HEI. Issues discussed during the interviews were the reasons for their decision to explore the use of LT in their course(s); how they knew about the Implementation Support service; their interactions with it and the quality of support obtained; the impact on student learning.

10.6.3   A Paper Questionnaire Survey of Academic Staff in All Departments of All Scottish HEIs

A questionnaire, which sought information on general LT issues as well as those directly related to LTDI, was designed to be completed by all staff ranging from those with little or no interest/involvement in LT through to those who were 'expert'. Given the particular importance of determining the validity of questionnaire survey data, a question always arises as to whether the population sampled is relevant and the returns are representative. Both these issues are addressed in further detail below in the discussion of the second case study (TLTP).

The questionnaire was designed in such a way that it could be completed by staff who had attended workshops, had received literature, had contributed to workshops and had taken part in implementations, thus obviating the need to survey different groups separately, something which time and overload on recipients made undesirable. Respondents simply worked through the questionnaire and exited at the point relevant to their level of experience with respect to LTDI. There were four sections in the questionnaire:

- the first section was completed by all respondents;
- the second by those who were aware of LTDI but had had no direct contact;
- the third by those with direct experience of LTDI to offer comments on it;
- the fourth section afforded the opportunity to provide extended written comments on LT generally and LTDI in particular.

We compiled a database of all academic departments in SHEFC-funded institutions and mailed copies of the questionnaire, accompanied by a covering letter, to each Head of Department (HoD). We asked each Head to distribute a number of questionnaires (equal to 20% of the size of the department), half to staff who were noticeably involved with LT and half to those with little or no involvement. In this way we targeted 'matched pairs' of academic staff across the sector, with the potential to reach around 20% of the c8000 full-time academic staff.

The resultant sample appeared to be reasonably representative of the total population. As a further measure on representativeness we checked the distribution of years of experience in higher education of respondents (which was broadly likely to equate with age). This measure indicated that our survey was taking account of the views of the whole range of experience and did not unduly favour one group. It was clearly possible that those staff who were interested or involved in the use of learning technology would preferentially return forms over their less involved colleagues. We therefore asked respondents to rate themselves in relation to their peers on experience in the use of technology in their teaching. It was clear that there was a slight skew in the distribution in favour of greater experience with respect to colleagues. However, from the perspective of this evaluation, it was not clear whether more experienced staff would be a more sympathetic or a more critical and demanding group with respect to LTDI. The written comments on the questionnaires expressed strong views but these were just as likely to be critical of LTDI as sympathetic to it. We were reasonably confident therefore that the data derived from this survey were robust.

10.6.4 Scottish Subject Specialists

To gain an additional perspective on the penetration of LTDI's activity we conducted an e-mail survey of 29 out of 81 subject specialists who were listed in the LTDI Information Directory. This provided an opportunity to ascertain the extent to which these specialists had been contacted by staff seeking their advice on the use of learning technology.

10.6.5 Documentary Sources

Finally, we analyzed a range of documentary sources as a means of gaining data that would be pertinent to the evaluation. These sources included the Annual Reports provided by LTDI, copies of the original proposals for each year of their activity and feedback forms from workshops and implementations. We consulted SHEFC Quality Assessment Reports for references to learning technology and IT infrastructure. A number of publications from agencies such as CTISS and TLTP provided further pertinent data.

The five sources we used in this evaluation, drawing on personal and telephone interviews, e-mail surveys, questionnaires and published materials, constituted the first application of the multi-method approach that we went on to develop in other contexts, and it formed the basis of the analyzes and options that we presented in the final project report. Further details are available from this published report (Day, Haywood & Macleod, 1997). The next application of our multi-disciplinary, multi-method approach was to be on a much greater scale, across all teaching departments in the UK HE sector, with this new context occasioning further substantial development of our methodology. This is discussed in the following section.

10.7 Case Study 2 - The Teaching and Learning Technology Program (TLTP)

In 1997 the Research Group was commissioned by HEFCE to assess the extent of use of networked learning products that had become available to the UK HE sector through the projects of Phases 1 and 2 of the TLTP. From the outset it was clear that this would be a complex undertaking and that to achieve our purpose of examining the use of TLTP products within the UK higher education sector, we were faced with the following principal tasks:

- to find out where TLTP products were being used;
- to detail how these products were being used;
- to examine the pattern of usage of TLTP courseware in relation to other uses of C&IT within teaching and learning;
- to explore how 'contextual' factors might have influenced the uptake of TLTP products;
- to conduct a bibliographic search to track existing studies of TLTP use.

In order successfully to complete these key tasks we had to establish the range of products that had been produced by TLTP projects, to characterize the nature of these products and as far as possible to gain a sense of which products were still viable.

10.7.1 Methodological Challenges

As mentioned earlier this was to be a larger study than the LTDI survey, conducted across all HEIs in the UK sector and across all teaching departments in those institutions. In carrying out our study we had, in addition, to meet a number of methodological challenges, including difficulties inherent in conducting any retrospective survey. A particular challenge that we faced arose from our objective of gaining a fairly detailed picture of what types of courses were using TLTP products and how individual products had been used within particular courses. Given the diversity of HEIs with respect to course structure and delivery, designing a set of research instruments that would be applicable to all institutions did not prove to be a straightforward matter.

There was an initial problem of diversity of definition and nature of courses and departments across the sector. A key challenge in the construction of the department survey that we decided to undertake – particularly at the level of the course questionnaire – was the diversity in the administration of teaching and the organization of the curriculum across the UK HE sector. Very precise attention had to be given to the wording of individual questions to ensure that they would apply across the sector, given that many institutions still organized their teaching on a departmental basis, while in others teaching responsibilities belonged with schools or with teaching organizations that covered broad disciplinary groupings. Certain institutions had a mixture of all three ways of organizing teaching.

In addition, we had to confront the general difficulty that faces any research study which investigates backwards over time. There are clearly distinct limits on the extent to which data can be retrieved when one is dealing with past events. Memories fade, and the pace of technological change meant that products created in the early phase of TLTP might no longer be as relevant at that point, and hence less salient to respondents. The size of the potential user base might also have changed over the course of the two phases of TLTP that were being investigated.

Many of the Phase 1 projects were no longer active. Both within the projects themselves and in academic departments using TLTP products, some key personnel had moved on. For these reasons the extent and pattern of usage in the earlier years of TLTP could not be fully recalled and represented. We therefore tried to achieve the best possible estimate of usage in one particular period of time, in effect a 'snapshot' taken in the first half of 1998.

10.7.2 Gaining Different Perspectives on the Use of TLTP Products

Given our concerns about the attrition of data over time and the robustness of the data that remained, it was imperative to maximize access to information on the use of TLTP products by employing different routes into different sources. Concentrating effort solely on one main means of gathering facts and opinions would have been an inappropriate way to address our objective. Independently of this aim to maximize access to available data, it appeared important in terms of ensuring the validity and reliability of our research findings to view the usage of TLTP products from a number of different perspectives. This would allow 'cross-checks' to be carried out on the pattern of findings from different perspectives and would also provide a fuller, and thus possibly more nuanced, picture of product use.

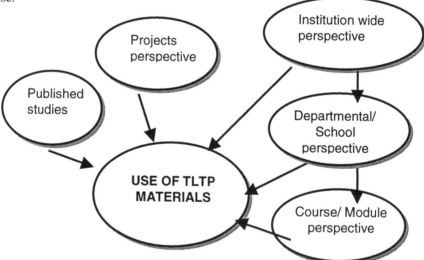

Fig.10.1 Perspectives on the use of TLTP materials

Figure 10.1 shows the main perspectives that we set out to capture. Information was gathered from the following vantage points: from the TLTP projects themselves; from individual courses; from departments and from key informants with an informed overview of the use of TLTP products within individual HEIs. In addition to allowing for checks on data reliability, gathering data from separate levels within HEIs had the advantage of giving a view from differently located 'fixed points'. Course organizers could provide a fine-grained, more narrowly focused account of the use of TLTP materials, whereas informants with an institution-wide perspective could provide a more broad-brush account, situating the use of TLTP products within the wider context of a university's overall use of C&IT for learning and teaching.

Published articles and reports on the incorporation of TLTP materials into courses added another perspective to the study, given that they, by and large, are written from the viewpoint of developers, enthusiastic adopters and those making innovative use of the products.

10.7.3 Exploring the Context of Use

If the focus of our efforts had been confined simply to the use of TLTP products, the resulting picture would not only have been a very skeletal outline but also misleading. The extent and pattern of use could not have been clearly and appropriately understood until they had been viewed in relation to the wider picture of the use of C&IT for learning and teaching and the contextual resources and constraints influencing both C&IT use and the progress of educational innovation. Accordingly we decided to build up this wider picture within which the use of TLTP materials could be viewed. Measures were taken of departments' reported levels of general C&IT usage and that used in learning and teaching. As a result a clearer summary picture of current C&IT use for teaching and learning in higher education emerged from our survey work.

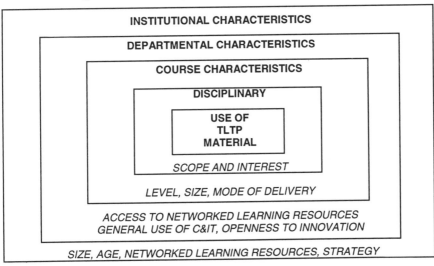

Figure 10.2 TLTP materials in context

With regard to contextual resources and constraints, it was useful to think of context in terms of a number of layers, as Figure 10.2 above illustrates. One possible important determinant of the uptake of TLTP materials can be the discipline/subject area taught by a particular department – the degree to which

TLTP courseware is seen as consonant with the practices of a discipline and the current level of commitment in that discipline to using C&IT in learning and teaching. Course characteristics, including the ones listed in Figure 10.2 of level, size and mode of delivery also needed to be taken into consideration. The use of C&IT within courses is itself in turn affected by a department's general use of C&IT, its access to resources and its openness to innovation. Finally the characteristics of individual higher education institutions, including their particular strategy for supporting C&IT in teaching and learning and the extent to which a defined strategy has been implemented, may impact on the use of TLTP courseware.

10.7.4 Overview of Principal Data Gathering Activities

Translating into action our desire to capture the different perspectives on TLTP use and to delineate the contexts where TLTP products had been used, or had failed to find a place, we made use of various methods of enquiry. These included:

* a survey of all 76 Phase 1 and Phase 2 TLTP projects;
* a survey of all teaching departments in HE institutions within Britain; these were surveyed using a two-tiered approach;
* HEI 'key informant' survey;
* case studies.

We also conducted a search for articles and reports on the use of TLTP materials, and constructed a bibliography from them. A more detailed discussion of the data gathering activities mentioned above is now provided.

10.7.5 Project Survey – General Considerations

The principal objective of the project survey was to gather data on various aspects of their awareness raising/dissemination and distribution activities. We also wished to use this survey to get a very detailed sense from projects of exactly which products they sent where, *i.e.*, to 'track out' from the individual projects to the higher education sector. However, preliminary investigations preparing the way for this survey indicated considerable variability between projects in the nature and quality of record keeping, making this an unattainable goal.

A chief challenge in the construction of this particular survey instrument was the need to take into account: (a) the diversity of the individual projects in terms of size, funding, disciplinary area and the main thrust of their development activities, and (b) the different time scales over which they had operated and technological changes that had occurred over Phases 1 and 2 of TLTP. These challenges required great care to be taken both with the design of the overall set of questions and with the wording of individual items.

10.7.6 Departmental Survey – Why Not Sample?

Surveying all teaching departments within UK higher education institutions is clearly a very large undertaking; but, after careful consideration, it was felt to be a necessary task, given that sampling would have been a very problematic matter in this instance. The chief difficulty lay in the fact that there were many dimensions to sample on. For example, in making sampling decisions, it would have been necessary at institutional level to take account of: the size and type of HEI institution, differences between institutions in C&IT infrastructure, location in the UK, and at departmental level of type of teaching engaged in, TQA rating, research strengths, *etc*. Decisions would also have had to be made concerning sampling by discipline/subject area and factors such as the presence of a TLTP project or a CTI Center within a university that was being considered. Given that there were a large number of relevant sampling dimensions, deciding on a sampling strategy would have been far from straightforward and difficult, if indeed possible at all, to achieve in a principled, justifiable manner. (Viewed from a different angle, some of the TLTP projects covered very small disciplinary areas, and there was a danger that the use of the materials from these projects might have been under-represented, if sampling had been employed.)

Another important reason for deciding against sampling was the concern that both we ourselves and our readers could have confidence in the findings from our survey. To put this point concerning the protection of the validity of our findings in more concrete terms: we wished to be sure that we had no anxiety that a finding which, say, went against received opinion might have been an 'artefact' of a possibly problematic sampling strategy.

10.7.7 Preparatory Work: Assistance from Staff and Educational Development Units

An essential piece of groundwork for the departmental survey was the construction of a database of all teaching departments/schools within UK institutions of higher education. The principal source of the information for this database was Staff and Educational Development Units, whose role would require them to have an up to date, accurate listing of teaching departments within their institution. The heads of these Units were mailed and asked to provide lists of all teaching departments within their institutions.

10.7.8 A Two-Tiered Approach

The survey of departments involved a two-tiered approach, with two quite separate questionnaires, one collecting data at the level of the department as a whole, and the other gathering information on the use of TLTP materials within individual courses. The course level questionnaire aimed to build up a detailed picture of how TLTP materials had been used and to construct a fairly full profile of the courses in which these materials were sited. The construction of the individual items in these two questionnaires, and of the key informants survey which is described below, was guided by the overall research objectives of this evaluation, which were:

- to build up a picture of the extent and nature of the use of TLTP materials;
- to view usage of TLTP products in relation to the wider use of C&IT for learning and teaching;
- to explore 'contextual' features that might influence the general uptake of C&IT in teaching and learning, and more specifically, the use of TLTP materials.

10.7.9 Validity and Reliability of Data

As with all surveys where the return is less than 100% the issue of skew in the nature of the respondents is present, and it is possible that our respondents may have been skewed to those who were most interested in C&IT, with the less interested failing to return questionnaires proportionally. However, it remained less clear what would be the effects on the data of such a skewed distribution. It was not necessarily the case that it would put 'a positive spin' on the data. 'Experts' can be more critical than 'non-experts' of lack of progress or resources: They may be less inclined to see the progress that has been made and look instead to targets still to achieve. We found this to be clearly the case in the LTDI study discussed earlier of C&IT use across the Scottish HE sector. In that study we found positive views of the use of C&IT in teaching emerging just as much from those who felt themselves to be less experienced than their peers about this topic.

10.7.10 Dual Focus in the Survey Design

The research team tried to follow a number of general guidelines while constructing individual instruments. The task of survey construction had to be guided by a 'dual focus' of attention. In other words, there was a need to ensure that concentration was minutely focused on ensuring that each survey instrument was fit for its individual purpose. At the same time, however, it was important not to lose sight of the place that each individual survey would play within the overall scheme of data collection. Attention had to be given to ensuring that the design of individual instruments contributed to an overall data collection strategy that would have coherence. More specifically there was also a concern to be alert to exploit opportunities for using data collected by one survey as a 'cross-check' on the reliability of the data gathered from a similar item in another survey. This was a particularly strong consideration with respect to the construction of the department and Higher Education Institution key informants surveys.

10.7.11 Position, History and Mind Set of Respondents

The need always to be alert to the position, history and mind set of respondents is a standard part of good practice in survey design; and it was a particularly necessary injunction in the case of this current project, where we had been trying to capture a number of separate 'perspectives' on the topic of study and were dealing with a very diverse constituency of respondents. A particular constraint that had constantly to be kept in mind was the need to appreciate how memories fade over time. In other words, we had to be 'realistic' about the amount and the nature of information that could be obtained concerning development or teaching activities that had taken place several years in the past. The task of ensuring that respondents' possible understanding of the thrust of a questionnaire as a whole and that their interpretation of individual items was constantly kept in view was assisted by the existence of a fairly large design team. On this and other aspects of survey construction, critical scrutiny and debate in the research team meetings over tactics and wording of items helped to keep the design work 'on track'.

10.7.12 Diversity in Administration and Curriculum Organization

A key challenge in the construction of the department survey, particularly at the level of the course questionnaire was the diversity in the administration of teaching and the organization of the curriculum across the UK higher education sector. Very precise attention had to be given to the wording of individual questions to ensure that they would apply across the higher education sector, given that many institutions still organize their teaching on a departmental basis, while in others teaching responsibilities belong with schools or with teaching organizations that cover broad disciplinary groupings (indeed certain institutions had a mixture of all three ways of organizing teaching).

One specific difficulty related to this diversity needs to be highlighted. This was a problem for which, we would suggest, there could not be any completely satisfactory resolution. Different institutions structure the courses that their students will take during an academic year in quite different ways. In one institution, for example, a first year student might take only three courses, whereas in another institution a first year student might take a quite large number of individual modules. There is a danger, therefore, that in asking questions of an individual department about the number of its courses/modules that employ TLTP materials, one took a measure not solely of TLTP usage but also of the way in which that department happened to organize its teaching. The wording of individual items in the departmental level and course level questionnaires was designed to 'manage' this problem, as far as is possible; and the course level questionnaire asked respondents who identified a course as using TLTP materials to state: "What percentage of a full-time student's annual workload does the course/module comprise?" However, it is a problem which could not be side-stepped. Accordingly, we were appropriately cautious in our analysis and conservative in our interpretation of questions which asked about the number of students enrolled on courses/modules using TLTP materials and about the number of a department's courses/modules which had taken up TLTP materials.

10.7.13 Gathering the Data

The departmental and course level questionnaires were mailed to all departments with a return date of some six weeks later. As a point of entry the questionnaires were addressed to the head of department who was asked to forward them to the individual in the department who was deemed to be the 'most knowledgeable' on the use of C&IT in teaching and learning. This 'most knowledgeable person' was asked to fill in the departmental level questionnaire herself or himself. Multiple copies of the course questionnaire were sent to the department to be distributed by the most knowledgeable person for completion by the organizers of courses and modules, currently using (or with a history of using) TLTP materials. The most knowledgeable person was then responsible for collecting in any completed course level questionnaires and returning them and the departmental level questionnaire to us. This particular mechanism for organizing the distribution and return of questionnaires was chosen as it appeared to provide a clear cut solution to the logistical problems posed by gathering data from departments at two 'levels', and as one which would not be too burdensome to respondents.

10.7.14 HEI Key Informants Survey

To meet its objective of providing an institution wide view of the use of TLTP materials – a view which could place the use of TLTP products within the wider context of institutional strategy for, and developments within the use of C&IT for learning and teaching – care had to be taken in the selection of appropriate informants. The 102 informants in this survey were drawn from what might be termed as the C&IT in teaching and learning support community. We chose informants from our own experience and knowledge base of the individuals who were best placed to give this institution wide perspective, or identified through our network of connections.

10.7.15 Case Studies – Why Case Studies?

There has tended to be a divergence in the meaning attached to 'case studies' by social science researchers on the one hand and by the community of practitioners involved in the use of C&IT for teaching and learning on the other. Although the definitions attached to case study research by social scientists vary considerably, it seems safe to claim that as a common core of meaning, there is an emphasis on gaining a clearer, more analytical understanding of a particular topic or innovation or at least a new perspective on that topic. In contrast, case study work as practised by the C&IT teaching and learning community has tended often to involve a more descriptive account of how an innovation has been implemented and how it has worked out in practice. Given the potential for different audiences of this report to have rather different expectations of what a case study entails, it is necessary to give an account of exactly what our objectives were in this evaluation in conducting case studies.

A primary purpose in conducting case studies was the desire to give a more fine-grained account of the use of materials from selected projects than could be achieved through a survey. Whatever their general merits, surveys are necessarily a somewhat 'top-down' method of conducting research. Case studies allowed the possibility to take a more 'bottom-up' approach to research, to stay closer to the experience of the users of TLTP materials and to be alert to any insights or issues that might emerge from the more exploratory approach that case studies usually entail. There was thus the aim of achieving, potentially, new ways of viewing and framing the use of TLTP materials and of recognizing issues that otherwise might have escaped us.

10.7.16 Constructing the Case Studies

The specific procedures used in the five case studies of an individual TLTP project or projects had to be tailored to fit the nature of that project and to address the issues that emerged in the course of the investigation. All of the TLTP project case studies, however, involved a core set of research tasks:

- building a profile of the objectives, and history of, the project;
- examining the nature of the materials that the project had produced;
- conducting telephone interviews with 'users', 'non-users' and 'abandoners' of the materials of the project.

To provide a measure of commonality in the issues and topics that were addressed across all of the project case studies, guidance schedules were constructed for the semi-structured interviews with 'users', 'non-users' and 'abandoners'. The projects chosen for case study analysis were largely selected on the grounds that it was clear from our surveys that their products had achieved relatively widespread uptake. It therefore seemed likely that these projects might provide interesting pointers to factors which might make for successful uptake and continuity of use of courseware.

10.7.17 General Considerations in Analysis of the Data: Issues Concerning Validity

Two general aspects of the way in which the analysis of data within this project was handled need to be highlighted, as they were intended to make a substantial contribution to our efforts to ensure that the work of analysis and interpretation was conducted in a trustworthy manner. One aspect was that it was judged important to look at the findings from each survey quite separately first, so that they could be examined and judged on their own terms, before there was any move to synthesize findings from different sources. Once individual sources had been looked at separately, the reliability of the data was examined by conducting 'cross-checks' between findings derived from different sources.

The second aspect of the procedures employed at the stages of analysis and interpretation that is worth noting was the way in which the research team as a whole was used. Individuals had analytical tasks assigned to them. At certain stages of the work of analysis and reporting, another individual was assigned to an 'editing', critiquing role on the work of the person who had primary responsibility for a particular analytical or writing task. Once an analytical task was completed, an individual would bring his or her findings back to the group as a whole for debate and scrutiny. The fact that (often quite lengthy) group meetings were held on a regular basis also meant that a common knowledge base was built up within the group and, therefore, all members of the team were well placed to challenge any pre-formed, or 'immature' judgements.

10.7.18 Analysis of the Qualitative Data

It seems useful to look in more detail at one part of the analysis in this study in order to clarify the approach that was taken to analyzing qualitative data. Given the variety of methods that potentially can be employed when analyzing qualitative data, it seemed important to make transparent the procedures that were used in our study to analyze the data that was collected from the open-ended response questions in the projects and HEI key informants' surveys. As a first step all of the responses were collected, and composite ones split up and the whole set was made available to the whole research team, not just the person primarily responsible for the qualitative analysis, so that all members could read the 'tone' of individual statements. The individual responses were then categorized into themes. This work of categorization was largely a 'bottom-up' process, driven by the data, but it was also done with an eye on the key research aims of the study as a whole. An attempt was made to pace this work of categorization patiently to prevent any hasty classification. The earlier stages of the 'theming-up' of the qualitative data were also performed, as far as was practicable, independently of a consideration of the picture that was emerging from analysis of the quantitative data, to avoid any analytical set. Once a provisional categorization scheme had been created by the researcher responsible for the qualitative analysis, it was then subjected to scrutiny by other team members. In analyzing and reporting the qualitative data, frequency counts were used, wherever appropriate, so that particularly arresting expressions of a point of view were not given undue weight.

10.7.19 Interpretation, Issues and Practice

The preceding section on analysis of the data has detailed how not only the process of analyzing the data but also any emerging interpretations were subject to the scrutiny of the research group as a whole. In terms of reporting strategy, we tried to ensure that where we presented an interpretation of findings that might be subject to debate, we had supplied enough evidence, either in the main report itself or in the data appendices, to allow a reader to make his or her own judgement about the validity of our interpretation and possibly to arrive at a different viewpoint. A published account of this study is available in Anderson *et al.* (1999a). Further accounts of the methodological aspects of the study can be found in Anderson *et al.* (1999b) and Anderson *et al.* (2000).

10.8 Case Study Three: The PUSHE Project (Promoting the Use of SCRAN Materials for Learning and Teaching in Higher Education)

The experience we gained in the Learning Technology Research Group whilst undertaking the LTDI and TLTP surveys considerably informed the methodology we subsequently adopted when commissioned to undertake a formative evaluation of SCRAN – The Scottish Cultural Resources Access Network. This was a project funded by the UK Millennium Commission. As its title suggests, the SCRAN network provides educational access to a vast range of multimedia resources covering many aspects of Scottish culture and history (www.scran.ac.uk). The remit of our group was to consider the potential use of this rich database in relation to the HE sector.

10.8.1 Project Aims

The aims of the PUSHE Project were twofold:

- To assist SCRAN in optimizing the utility of SCRAN materials and online tools for adoption within teaching and learning in higher education;
- To assist SCRAN in maximizing penetration of the UK higher education sector through identification of appropriate communication channels, informed targets and professional networks.

The broader research questions which the project sought to address and which provided continuing direction throughout the duration of the project were as follows:

- What levels and kinds of use of the SCRAN materials were currently to be found in Scottish higher education?
- What reasons explained the current apparent level of usage?
- What potential was there for enhanced usage of the SCRAN materials in HE?

10.8.2 Levels of Use

In order to help us address these questions we identified a set of 'levels of use' of SCRAN materials, in terms of a local 'ecology', that would provide an informing framework for the project. These levels were as follows:

1. **Awareness** of the materials (in relation to such user characteristics as role, experience, awareness of other databases, tools and potential).
2. **Access** to and **Exploration** of the materials (in terms of general interest).
3. **Evaluation of Potential** of the materials (in terms of specific applications).
4. **Educational Adoption/Usage** of the materials (within particular curricula and in terms of the pragmatics of instructional design).

The levels were used to help determine the following:

*   Priorities in terms of activities within the project schedule and milestones;
*   Clarification of different target groups and their respective client characteristics;
*   Identification of appropriate research instruments and methods for each of the levels.

The approach of the LTRG team, whilst remaining multi-disciplinary and multi-method as exemplified in the earlier evaluations was therefore, in this new undertaking, also to be essentially 'layered'. Four distinct operational levels or contexts were identified, for each of which appropriate methods of information gathering were employed. The main methods were as follows.

10.8.3 Survey of Academic Departments

The first stage of the project was concerned primarily with levels 1 and 2 of this informing framework. Planning meetings involved the project team in identifying postal surveys as the most effective method for gaining understanding of the scope and scale of *awareness* and *access*. After a detailed consideration of alternatives which drew on the project team's experience of the other large-scale surveys of C&IT usage discussed earlier in this chapter, it was decided to send questions to all academic departments in Scottish universities, the larger further education colleges and the University of the Highlands and Islands Millennium Institute (UHIMI). Contact was through an entry route (via the Head of Department) developed by the team in the large-scale studies mentioned earlier (Day *et al.*, 1997, Anderson *et al.* 1999). The responses to this survey of academic staff constituted the first data set.

10.8.4 Survey of Librarian Staff

In order to gain an alternative perspective on the four levels of usage identified earlier a second survey was undertaken of librarian staff in Scottish HEIs. Academic librarians with responsibility for visual databases were identified as having a potentially important 'gatekeeper' function in this respect. Some 39 academic libraries in 38 institutions were sent a different questionnaire to provide an alternative perspective on aspects of access and awareness. The data gained from the librarian survey constituted the second data set from which the PUSHE project drew its findings.

10.8.5 User Trials and Key Informant Interviews

A third data set was drawn from a series of user trials with individual subject specialists in higher education and from interviews with key informants working in the staff development and learning technologist communities. Volunteer respondents from a range of disciplinary backgrounds with experience of using the SCRAN database were interviewed by project team members to gain insights into levels 3 and 4 of the framework in relation to the *evaluation of potential* of SCRAN materials and their *adoption* in higher education.

10.8.6 Data Analysis

Analysis of data followed a similar pattern to that which had been undertaken and found effective in the earlier studies with the survey responses (both open comments and tick boxes) again being entered into a Filemaker Pro database, exported into MS Excel, and the numerical data then analyzed using Statview. Again, similarly, notes from interviews were logged later according to the question areas in the interview schedule and subsequently re-analyzed in the light of emerging themes. The open comments were, once more, listed according to thematic content and in priority order.

10.8.7 Networked Learning and Academic Practice in Higher Education

As the study got under way, and we addressed the brief we had been commissioned to undertake it soon became apparent that a defining feature of higher education, which distinguishes it from its primary, secondary and further counterparts, is that it is not easily characterized in terms of core curricular activity. There is clearly a convergence of trends taking place in terms of the promotion and facilitation of use of powerful information and communication technologies in higher education and this convergence provides significant opportunities (and tensions) for the academic and staff development communities in higher education. Yet academic and scholarly practice in higher education, by its very nature, renders problematic the wholesale uptake of resource-based, networked learning though web-mediated technology. Though there are in some large first year classes, within particular disciplines, strong similarities in terms of broad coverage and aims, it remains misleading to speak of 'the higher education curriculum'. This is owing to the fact that the delivery and process of higher education is mediated through the specialist knowledge, expertize and experience of specialist academics and remains highly personalized and idiosyncratic. As students in higher education progress through three- or four-year programs of study they are likely to encounter courses that branch into ever-increasing specialization and depth.

Academics in higher education tend to frame their teaching within a rich and complex set of reference points – scientific, technical, literary, cultural, depending on the discipline – which arise from their deep familiarity with a specialized knowledge domain. Their resource base of choice is consequently often that of specialized, comprehensive and extensively cataloged reference collections which permit the detailed and fine-grained comparison of, and refined discrimination between texts, artefacts, examples or cases. Such juxtaposition and contrast mirrors and arises from their own deep and comprehensive mastery of a specialized knowledge domain but is perceived as crucial in the maintenance of their critical purview of an area of research expertise. Academics, of course, also seek to foster the adoption of such values and approaches in the practice of their own students. Such representative and authoritative understandings are usually the result of years of meticulous personal research and specific resource gathering from a myriad of disparate sources, and the construction and maintenance of such particularized resource-based knowledge is a somewhat daunting process to emulate. This does however explain the dissatisfaction sometimes expressed by academics with tailored electronic (or even print-based) resource collections, even though the availability of such resources is, paradoxically, commonly requested by academics. Any consideration of a multi-disciplinary, non-specific resource database such as SCRAN had therefore to take into account the low levels of core curricular activity that were likely to be found in teaching and learning in higher education, and the high levels of disciplinary specialization and contextualization that were demanded.

The higher education sector, moreover, is characterized by its heterogeneity and caters for diverse educational markets at undergraduate and postgraduate levels, in vocational areas, continuing education and continuing professional development. This diversity also had to be recognized and addressed in the design and execution of this evaluation.

10.9 Conclusion

The multidisciplinary, multi-method research approach that has evolved through these projects has proved to be of continuing and flexible use in the work of the Learning Technology Research Group. Our self-evidently eclectic approach is clearly not situated within purist paradigms of either a quantitative or qualitative nature. Such eclecticism, we feel, is no longer regarded as the contentious issue it might once have been. Over two decades ago Cook and Reichardt (1979:19) encouraged evaluators to be 'flexible and adaptable; why not use both qualitative and quantitative methods?' More recently Patton (1990:38) has advocated a 'paradigm of choices', which 'rejects methodological orthodoxy in favour of methodological appropriateness as the primary criterion for judging methodological quality'. Working, as we have demonstrated, as a multi-disciplinary team, we would further endorse Patton's view that evaluative researchers need to be 'aware of their methodological biases and paradigmatic assumptions so that they can make flexible, sophisticated, and adaptive methodological choices' (Patton, 1988:119).

The discussion that has been presented here of our different evaluations has drawn attention to the methodological features that they have in common. However it must be emphasized that the multi-disciplinary, multi-method approach described here is not intended as a recipe book for large-scale evaluation of networked learning. It has been found to be a useful and flexible approach to the evaluation of complex, multi-faceted and often changing environments. However we would argue that what remains crucial is the constant interplay between method and context in such environments, and that our approach to evaluation is continually informed by that concern. Any evaluative project, if it is to be effective, needs to address the challenges of its specific context in a principled manner that is appropriate to its specific set of purposes, object(s) of study and audience(s). This requires an appropriate matching up and detailed tailoring of specific research tools and tasks, as well as the overall configuration of the different methodologies and instruments employed. As Stufflebeam and Shinkfield (1984:12-21) remind us:

'An evaluation is a place for every kind of investigation ... The difficulty for evaluators ... is that they must decide on the distribution of investigative effort in a particular project at a particular time; so the trade-offs in design must be very much the center of concern'.

10.10 References

Anderson, C., Day, K., Haywood, J., Land, R. & Macleod, H. (1999a) *Use of TLTP materials in UK Higher Education*, HEFCE Report June 99/39. Higher Education Funding Council for England, Bristol. http://www.flp.ed.ac.uk/LTRG/TLTP.html

Anderson, C., Day, K., Haywood, J., Land, R. & Macleod, H. (1999b) *Going with the grain? Issues in the evaluation of educational innovations*. Paper presented at the European Conference for Research on Learning and Instruction (EARLI), 24-28 August, Gothenburg, Sweden

Anderson, C., Day, K., Haywood, J., Land, R. & Macleod, H. (2000) 'Mapping the territory: issues in evaluating large-scale learning technology initiatives', *Educational Technology & Society 3*(4)

Clarke, A. & Dawson, R. (1999) *Evaluation research: an introduction to principles, methods and practice.* London: Sage

Cook, T.D. & Reichardt, C.S. (1979) *Qualitative and quantitative methods in evaluation research,* London: Sage

Day, K., Haywood, J. & Macleod, H. (1997) *Evaluation of the Learning Technology Dissemination Initiative.* Edinburgh: Scottish Higher Education Funding Council

Guba, E.G. & Lincoln, Y.S. (1983) *Effective evaluation.* San Francisco: Jossey Bass

House, E.R. (1993) *Professional evaluation: social impact and political consequences.* Newbury Park: Sage

Patton, M.Q. (1988) Paradigms and pragmatism. In Fetterman, D.M. (Ed) *Qualitative approaches to evaluation in education: the silent scientific revolution.* New York: Praeger, pp116-137

Patton, M.Q. (1990) *Qualitative Evaluation and Research Methods* (2nd. Edition), Newbury Park: Sage

Rossi, P.H. & Freeman, H.F. (1993) *Evaluation: a systematic approach* (5th edition), London: Sage

Shadish, W.R. & Epstein, L. (1987) Practice of program evaluation practice among members of the Evaluation Research Society and Evaluation Network. *Evaluation Review, 11,* pp55-90

Stufflebeam, D.L. & Shinkfield, A.J. (1984) *Systematic evaluation.* Lancaster: Kluwer-Nijhoff

Trend, M.G. (1978) On the reconciliation of qualitative and quantitative analysis: a case study. *Human Organization, 37,* pp34-54. Reprinted in Cook, T.D. & Reichardt, C.S. (Eds) (1979) *Qualitative and quantitative methods in evaluation research,* London: Sage

Section 2

Studies of Networked Learning

11. Approaches to Researching Teaching and Learning Online

Gilly Salmon

11.1 The Need to Consider Approaches to Researching Teaching and Learning Online

This chapter is set in the context of the rapid development and combination of Communication and Information Technologies (C&IT) at the turn of the century and the wide impact these are having on teaching and learning at a distance. It focuses, as an example, on computer mediated conferencing (CMC). CMC is the transmission and reception of messages using a terminal or personal computer, a telecommunications system to connect to a central server and a software system to store and organize the messages. Typical software platforms used are FirstClass, Blackboard, Web CT or Lotus Notes. The asynchronous nature of CMC is a particular characteristic of the medium since users can log onto and take part in a conference at any time and from any location where they have access to the necessary hardware and software. The asynchronous characteristic is also known to promote in users both reflection before a response to a conference message and reflection on conferencing practice itself (Salmon, 2000b). CMC presents, however, a major challenge for educators and researchers to harness its potential for teaching and learning in a productive and successful way.

I began a study of CMC practice in 1993. At that time, CMC as a field for research was in its infancy. Even now, because of rapid growth and change in the field, some key insights, ideas or concepts come from relatively informal sources such as conference papers and Web sites rather than from books and journals.

The continually growing use of networked computers for online communication, coupled with the potential of the medium for co-operative learning and teaching, demands that we continue to look closely at ways to research and exploit that potential. It is important that we focus immediate feedback and dissemination of understandings and that results focus on exploring practice where the greatest impacts may lie in the short term. In this way the potential of C&IT may be harnessed by the educational practitioners. Later in this article, therefore, I provide examples where researchers are providing opportunities for teachers and trainers – (typically called e-moderators in the online environment) to benefit from the results of studies into CMC.

11.2   CMC Research

The undertaking of effective CMC research is not a straightforward process. Throughout the 1990s there was debate about the rapidly increasing use of C&IT in education and appropriateness of methodologies for research on CMC (Tolmie & Boyle, 2000). There was criticism of evaluation studies for their focus on the nature of students' reactions rather than learning outcomes (Alexander, 1999; Gunn, 1999). Further critiques included the emphasis on quantitative analysis, *i.e.* "everything that could be measured" (Mason, 1992; Rudy, 1995; Newman *et al,.* 1996); the limitations of descriptions of applications in very specific contexts (Newman *et al.,* 1995; Dede, 1996); the lack of account of contextual factors (Reynolds, 1994); the focus on human-computer interaction, rather than on the quality of communication and learning (Collis, 1994); and the dearth of research on the receivers' perspective rather than on that of the senders of messages (Mantovani, 1994). Commentators now suggest that research should emphasize the role of the learner and teacher, rather than the role of the technology (Oliver & Reeves, 1996). Recent studies point out that CMC does not provide a given environment with intrinsic outcomes for teaching and learning but instead that "CMC offers a *customizable* networked learning environment, *tailorable* to a wide range of different purposes" (Light *et al.,* 2000:266). We need, therefore to have effective ways of researching, understanding and applying the customizing and tailoring process.

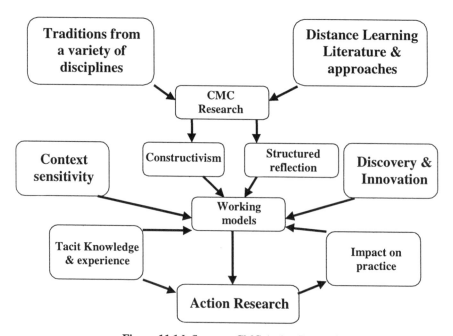

Figure 11.1 Influences: CMC Action Research

11.3   Methodological Considerations

Writing about the field of adult education, Brookfield pleads for the surfacing and exploration of what constitutes good educational practice and for the demonstration of its validity, accuracy and applicability (Brookfield, 1992). He suggests that the way to frame practice is through the use of "people's experience as the raw material" (p.13). Oliver and Reeves suggest that in-depth case and ethnographic studies are appropriate for knowledge development about CMC and teaching (Oliver & Reeves, 1996). Finally, Wild argues that interpretivist and developmental studies (rather than analytical and comparative research) are likely to shed light on this area of enquiry (Wild, 1996).

CMC studies for teaching and learning, when rooted in positivist perspectives can lead to research that is less sensitive to context and less suited to the exploration of meanings attributed by human actors to their purposes than are more qualitative approaches. Such positivist research perspectives also miss the "discovery dimension" and the interactive and subjective role of the inquirer. It may not address fully the pervasiveness of the paradigm's impact on the ontology (*i.e.* the form and nature of reality); the epistemology (the relationship between the subject and inquirer in terms of their knowing); and the methodology (how the inquiry can be achieved appropriately from within the chosen paradigm) (Guba & Lincoln, 1994). Lincoln and Guba argue that in any case all paradigms of research are themselves human constructions and advocates must rely on "persuasiveness and utility rather than proof".

A different approach from that of positivism is constructivism. Constructivism calls for participants to explore their own thinking and knowledge building processes (Biggs, 1995). This personal knowledge includes not only ideas about the topic area under study, but also the teachers' and participants' responses to the experiences of teaching and learning themselves (Hendry, 1996). Constructivism has grown in importance as an underlying paradigm for teaching, especially in the online teaching and learning environment (Jonassen *et al.,* 1995; Murphy, 1999). Concerns about the shortcomings of positivist research have led researchers in the field of CMC to draw on the strengths of constructivism, both as a research perspective and a pedagogical approach.

11.4   Educational Research Traditions

Disciplines from which research in distance education have been drawn include psychology, adult education, systems, sociology, business and educational technology. Within the already wide and continually widening distance education field, both qualitative and quantitative studies have been used, with more qualitative approaches in the last decade (Burt, 1997), although distance education in the US has traditionally focused on technologies (Tait, 1994). More recently there have been calls for emphasis on outcomes and debate surrounding the usefulness of evaluation (Calder, 1995). There is a tradition of grassroots research and of action research in distance learning (Morgan, 1984; Cooper, 1992; Stevenson *et al.*, 1996; Salmon, 2000a). It is worthy of note that much of the distance learning literature is illuminative rather than a reflection of the approaches of traditional scientific paradigms.

CMC is still a new medium, at least to large scale teaching, learning and training at a distance. Because of its freshness, neither following intuition nor basing researching on previous histories appears appropriate (Tolmie & Barbieri, 1997). As CMC is still new, we need to be open rather than closed in our approaches. We may benefit from wider educational research (rather than the study of technology). I explore these ideas further below. For example, Bassey's view of educational research rejects "playing hunches" or using "historical" drivers. He advocates the slower, more time consuming way of "creating education through research" (Bassey, 1992). This involves asking questions, searching for evidence, asking about intentions, determining their worth, appraising resources, identifying alternative strategies and monitoring and evaluating outcomes.

11.5   The Role of Theory and Models in CMC Research

In order to start to build coherent bodies of knowledge and shared practice, we need to explore underlying concepts, whether these are models or theories. Theory has held a central place in educational inquiry, despite the emergence of strong anti-theoretical strands in post-modern thought. However, Thomas (1997) suggests that, with so many different meanings attached to theory, it is difficult to see its value, or its utility may be camouflaged. He argues that theory encourages certain kinds of focused thinking and discourages diversity in thought and ideas. It works as a way of institutionalizing and bestowing legitimacy on a study and therefore reinforcing or promulgating certain types of studies, practices and methods. Thomas therefore makes the plea for "methodological anarchy" in educational research (Thomas, 1997:76). Glaser and Strauss's (1967) inductivist position has produced the idea of "grounded theory" and similarly, students of education have been encouraged to develop their own personal or practical theories (Carr, 1995; McIntyre, 1995).

Carr's view of theory in education suggests any kind of *structured* reflection and "a capacity to explore a particular range of problems in systematic and rigorous manner" (Carr, 1995:32). Smith argues for a "new vision of practice", a view reflected in Polyani's (1962) view of the importance of tacit knowledge. Smith suggests avoiding a "theory- first" view of the world, not only for philosophical reasons but because in the field of CMC there are no major theories to draw on. We cannot therefore build on previous knowledge at this stage. The research approach has of necessity to be practical and personal (Smith, 1995). This is a view of practical theory related to reflection on practice and it provides direction and underpinning for study of the experience of CMC.

CMC research is part of the constant flux being experienced in the world of information and communication technology (C&IT) and C&IT's impact on educational practice. Central to progress in CMC research is the notion of "problem solving" (as opposed to theory development) particularly of the kind engaged in by educationalists (Thomas, 1997). A considerable amount of creativity needs to go into the building of the environments for online research, not only by the designers and educationalists responsible but also by the participants and respondents.

We may conclude then that Dewey's words seem to hold true for online research in the 21st century, just as they did for the world at the beginning of the 20th:

"The critical issue for human sciences such as psychology and education is whether the strategy will work under the actual work requirements of daily life." (Lee, 1988:146, quoting Dewey)

11.6 Building and Using Models

If we reject, at this stage of CMC development, the role of overarching theory, we need then to consider the benefit of models of CMC use. CMC research can lead to working models and their development and testing under a variety of conditions.

One major criticism of CMC is that the majority of findings are descriptive rather than empirical (Oliver & Reeves, 1996:54). And to echo Henri "a framework and an analytical model could be used by educators for a better understanding of the learning processes" (Henri, 1992:117). Newman *et al.,* in turn, encourage CMC researchers to avoid descriptions of applications and to focus on natural or unstructured use of CMC in order to develop basic models of understanding (Newman *et al.,* 1996). The role of model building is now important for CMC research to provide an overall framework around which to hang the action research processes and to explore critically research questions. Models can then act as developing and iterative frameworks.

11.7 Action Research and CMC

In developing his argument for CMC to be researched as a *context* rather than simply as a channel of communication, Metz insists that an action research perspective is the most useful (Metz, 1994). The term *action research* was first attributed to social psychologist Kurt Lewin who examined social issues and provided techniques for examining relationships. Lewin stressed the importance of collaboration and participation and developed the notion of action research as a series of spirals involving planning, acting, observing, reflecting, revising and implementing (Lewin, 1946). Action research is therefore a process involving a diagnostic stage in which problems are analyzed and hypotheses developed, and a therapeutic stage during which the hypotheses are tested through action in the educational context (Kemmis, 1982; Cohen & Manion, 1996).

Research is an activity performed within communities. The behaviour of human beings consists in the main of their actions, and a distinctive feature of human actions is that they are meaningful. This social nature of actions implies that present actions arise from the networks of meaning that are constructed by individuals from their past history and which structure their interpretations of "reality" in a certain way (Kelly, 1955). To this extent, meanings which guide the actions of individuals are predetermined by the "forms of life" into which they are initiated (Carr & Kemmis, 1986:89). Carr suggests that interpreting human behaviour can then influence practice by eliciting the ways in which practitioners comprehend themselves and their situation. In this sense, the action researcher may comprehend and describe practice using new concepts. This offers practitioners a way of becoming self-conscious about the basic patterns which frame their own actions, the means and opportunity to reconsider their inherent beliefs and thereby contribute to choices and change. The aim, whether of a large or small-scale action research project, is typically to add to a practitioner's functional knowledge. Therefore the basis of action research is involvement, improvement, change and action (McNiff, 1988). Everyone in CMC is his or her own researcher.

Action research is considered to be an approach to carrying out an inquiry that is closely linked to practice in teaching and learning, and typically based in one institution, involving the researcher as an active participant. It is usually in response to a particular problem or issue that arises out of teaching practice involving a number of participants, is self-evaluative and continuously monitored (Cohen & Manion, 1996). There is a considerable body of published work on action research in schools and in teacher education but less on Higher Education. There also has been increasing research interest in collaborative learning (Baker & Lund, 1997) which is accelerating with the advent of C&IT use for teaching and learning in Higher Education. The newness of the medium of CMC and its apparent role in changing educational practice suggests that an action research approach which enables the "voices" of as many participants to come through is thus appropriate for many studies.

The following figure is a framework for action research, which I developed and used successfully for a large-scale online action research study in a Higher Education business school. It is based on Kemmis' framework:

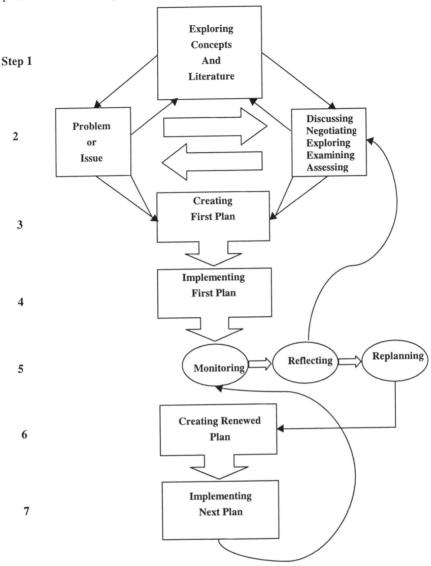

Figure 11.2 Action Research Process

11.8   Limitations and Problems of Action Research

Cohen and Manion suggest a wide variety of mechanisms are appropriate for data collection for action research, though typically observational and behavioural data are used. The key feature of data collection for action research is that the ensuing feedback can usefully be implemented, often immediately. This has led to a critique of the methodology that focuses on its lack of scientific rigor and generalizable concepts (Cohen & Manion, 1996). Some commentators suggest that there are problems related to attempting research and action in one study especially in terms of the differing objectives of each (Cohen & Manion, 1996). However, some researchers consider that openness and the full-scale participation in the research findings address these criticisms. McNiff raises the issue that problems do not present themselves sequentially for solution in the action research cycle and that there are likely to be "spin off" spirals (McNiff, 1988).

The limitations and problems of action research suggested by the literature are that action research may be resource hungry and time consuming and yet be carried out whilst staff are continuing their normal duties. A high degree of motivation is needed. Validity and naturalism is gained but at the expense of control. It is difficult to manipulate the independent variables. There may be ethical dilemmas in carrying out research and teaching simultaneously with students and other participants online. Latent conflict and tensions that come into the open. In researching online, we should use the computer for data collection and analysis since the problems of "data overload" are even greater than usual with thousands of online messages. There is also a need to ensure that the researcher has excellent, supported, reliable online access.

These difficulties should not prevent a committed action researcher, teacher or professional from proceeding successfully. However, they should be taken into account and planned for from the beginning of the study.

11.9   The Role of the Researcher

The role of the researcher in action research is partly that of participant observer, which has special qualities in the online medium. With ethnographic methodology, the observer is typically from a different culture (Agar, 1980) whereas with action research the researcher is full involved. Becker defined participant observation as:

> "... [observers] participating in the daily life of the group or organizations they study. They watch the people they are studying to see what situations they ordinarily meet and how they behave in them...[and they] enter into conversations with them to discover their interpretations of events" (Becker, 1958:652)

In online terms this means having access to conferences and online discussion and logging on very regularly as conferencing develops, twists and turns.

11.10 Reflection as Intrinsic to Constructivism and Action Research

The earliest approaches to professional education aimed to offer information largely related to technical skills. Reflective practice can be seen to be a reaction to the more technical and competency based teaching and learning strategies. The notion of the reflective practitioner is linked with learning and action, research and inquiry (Rose, 1992). The idea is not new however, and forms of it go back as far as Dewey's thinking (Dewey, 1910). Reflective practice suggests that skills cannot be gained in isolation from context, a further reinforcement of the notion that the study of online interactions should best take place online rather than through reliance on more regular traditional, standard procedures such as postal questionnaires. Reflective thinking acknowledges the complex, situation-specific, perhaps contradictory nature of a professional task and emphasizes the experience of undertaking that task. Schön distinguished between reflection on action (reflection after practice has been completed) and reflection in action (thinking that takes place in the midst of practice) and thereby acknowledged the cycles of thought that take place and their link with and impact on action (Schön, 1983). The practitioner, him or herself, is viewed therefore as a *constructor* rather than a technician (Rose, 1992) and the most in depth research therefore views the construction process rather than the outcome or a later view of it as of central concern.

Reflective practice therefore focuses on the individual interpretation of events and the framing of these into suitable actions. Reflection, therefore, has broad implications for teachers and for researchers. The study of the reflective practitioner has become part of the movement towards qualitative research as well as the result of it (Rose, 1992). Such research has been tied to action research, *i.e.,* that which actively involves the researcher as the part of the problem solving and the interpretation of events. Reflective practice also implies process – from novice to expert in a field – and through reflection the development of a personal cognitive map or schema for understanding particular situations. These frameworks build on an individual's previous knowledge and experience and by building connections. The schemas are *constructed* through experience, providing a link with the more philosophical approach to constructivism in teaching.

Brookfield describes critical reflection as "hunting assumptions" and suggests that this involves examining our thoughts and actions in a questioning way (Brookfield, 1995). However, critical reflection is much harder to research than technical practice (Rose, 1992). Some writers argue that reflection is essentially an independent activity. Others stress the importance of collaboration in the reflective process (Rose, 1992). The characteristic of being able to reflect on messages and on the topic under discussion, before replying, has always seemed important to researchers into CMC. Since CMC is believed to promote reflection, it provides a particularly suitable context for researching reflective practice through action research.

More recently, the close links between teaching, learning and research in online environments have been explored (Mann & Stewart, 2000; Stein, 2000). As experience of online researching increases, the importance of reflection and a broad framework of constructivism online are recognized:

> "... helping teachers improve their teaching is best done using a theory that helps teachers reflect on what they are doing.... To my mind, this means constructivism" (Biggs, 1999:60).

In the case studies that follow, reflection on practice was explored as both a teaching process and a research tool.

11.11   Examples of Online Action Research

11.11.1   Action Research with Management E-Moderators in Europe

Notions of reflection and collaboration, especially related to experience, have a central place in management education (Reynolds, 1998). The Open University Business School (OUBS) is at the forefront of introducing C&IT into the distance learning media mix for managers, and has implemented CMC on a large scale (Salmon, 1999, 2000a, 2000b).

From 1993 to 1995 I conducted an online study by modelling how management students used computer mediated conferencing. From 1996 to 1999, from this grounded model, I developed online training programs for OUBS management tutors and incorporated action research into the structure of the programs.

The underlying principles shown in the diagram in Figure 11.1 provided a framework for the cycles of planning, action, monitoring, reflection and re-planning for the various parts of the study over time. This framework imposed a loose structure and process to the variety of literature, instructional and constructivist concepts deployed throughout the study. Simple quantitative data collection was combined with more sophisticated analysis of qualitative sources. The "voices" of the participants involved in the tutor training were explored through extensive use of their conference message texts. In that sense, the methodology lent itself to developmental and interpretative analysis. The framework accommodated this broad directional structure whilst allowing for pathways, ideas and feedback to be explored.

The action research was aimed at specific problem solving rather than at establishing theory. However, in addition, the models that were created and developed at each stage of the research provided a set of propositional constructs that enabled testing as well as a base for the online training and induction programs. These working models proved highly practical and useful in the OUBS context and at that point in time were used in the practical manner that Carr suggests (Carr, 1995). Both content analysis and focus groups contributed to the development of the basic model at the start of the action research. This first model was developed in the spirit of grounded theory. This model provided the basis for the first action cycle of providing an online tutor training program. The model was tested empirically and developed through the feedback from the training program. A second model was then developed and underpinned the second tutor training program as well as a large-scale online student induction program. Both online programs allowed qualitative and quantitative data to be collected from the participants and this data was further developed into Model 3. Details of the model are explored in (Salmon, 2000a).

Specific "reflection points" were built into the online training programs. They encouraged the trainees to stop to reflect in the middle of their action online and to record their thoughts, their progress and any critical incidents. Since all messages were then available to other participants, they could read the messages and respond to each other. These responses enabled extensive qualitative analysis to be undertaken. The understanding derived from the qualitative analysis contributed to the building of further frameworks of understanding and to continual incremental improvements to the training programs. The final version of the Model provides a base upon which further webs of knowledge and practice could be built and the model continues to be developed in a variety of ways. The third model provided a representation of what occurred when learners and tutors used CMC and it provides a framework for understanding the online learning process.

In 1999, we provided OUBS tutors with an online training program to enable them to become fully familiar with the use of FirstClass software, to become comfortable as users and communicators within online conferencing and to develop competence as e-moderators. The training is entirely interactive and online and is divided into five stages. At each of the first four stages, the participant is invited to stop and reflect on his or experience of the online training to date before moving on to the next stage. At the fifth and final stage, there is a short questionnaire and invitation to comment on the training as a whole.

Here are our question messages:

Reflections on Level One

Please ensure that you have completed all the tasks at this level. Then send a message to this conference reflecting on:
The key learning points from your initial experiences in the Associate Lecturer Training.

Reflections on Level Two

Please ensure that you have completed all tasks at this level, especially those on developing skills with FirstClass and learning about appropriate styles of communication online.
Then send a message to this conference reflecting on:
What key learning points from your progress on the training so far would you pass on to your students?

Reflections on Level Three

Please ensure that you have completed all tasks at this level, especially those with a direct relevance to the use of CMC for teaching purposes.
Then send a message to this conference reflecting on:
What key learning points from your progress on the training so far would you pass on to colleagues from a teaching (or rather online tutoring) use perspective?

Reflections on Level Four

How do you feel about working with Computer Mediated Conferencing (CMC) with your students, based on your experience of the training so far?
Please send your contribution to this conference.

A powerful aspect of the validity testing was the feeding back of collated data and interpretation to the tutors who had taken part in the training, completed the questionnaires and given their reflections at each level of the training. The democratic and participatory nature of this approach convinced tutors of the value of their contributions and their involvement led to their greater interest in improving their online practice. In view of the grounded nature of the working model and the feeding back at each stage of the findings into the actions, the model is persuasive in terms of its practicality and workability rather than in terms of "proof".

11.11.2   Action Research with Teachers in Vermont

At the School for International Training in Brattleboro, Vermont, US, the Master of Arts in Teaching program is using online asynchronous dialog to help teachers understand theory and develop skills in reflective practice. As part of their work, graduate students (who are also practising teachers) submit reflective journal entries to an online conference, and their instructor responds with feedback on the art and science of reflective thinking and reflective practice. In other items on the conference site, a cohort group of the participants discuss content issues such as classroom management, student initiative, and feedback.

Linked with the learning of the participants, an action research project is underway to trace the evolution of the teachers' skills in learning to think reflectively, apply their thinking to investigate what happens in their classrooms and make changes that will serve their students' learning. Since the course runs from September to June, *i.e.,* over a 9-month period, it is possible to trace and see changes in the teachers' practical skills and conceptual understanding of reflective practice.

Data is collected from the asynchronous dialog in the online course. There are two points at which the teacher participants give feedback on their experiences. The first is at the mid-point of the course. Here the reflection is invited by questions:

- What have you learned about reflection up until now?
- How has the medium helped you?
- How has the instructor helped you?
- What do you need to continue?

Then at the end of the course, the participants undertake an extensive review of the year and their learning about reflection. The review takes place entirely online. Students submit their final papers to the reflective journal conference and they are available for everyone to read.

The study has strongly impacted this entire faculty's understanding of the development of reflective thinking skills and how it is applied to reflective teaching. Members of faculty are now, more readily and easily, able to assess the students' grasp of theory and skill in reflection. This results in better teaching responses to the student's work online and impacts on the students' teaching practice.

11.11.3 Action Research with Pilot Instructors in Europe

The Lilienthal Project is collaboration between various flight schools and universities in Europe (http://www.pilotschool.net) and offers another example of using online research to explore teaching and learning. The project partners have co-operated in developing a shared distance learning platform for training students towards a private pilot licence (PPL), the first stage of any pilot training (Sandberg *et al.*, 2001). Until recently, theoretical pilot training used only conventional forms of education, predominantly classroom teaching. The Lilienthal Distance learning platform provides various synchronous and asynchronous electronic means of communication for students and tutors, such as e-mail, electronic discussion groups and bulletin boards and a synchronous chat facility.

One of the challenges of this approach is to enable flight instructors to change their teaching style from conventional classroom teaching to tutoring via the CMC. The Lilienthal project calls these new-style instructors "tele-tutors". The tele-tutors are trained on three occasions, in both face-to-face situations and through distant education. Each training occasion serves as a stepping stone, after which time is allowed for tele-tutors to practise at their own pace at the flight school. Evaluation studies are carried out during each training session to explore the instructors' acquisition of appropriate knowledge and the quality and nature of the computer mediated communication. Results of the studies are used to further develop the training sessions.

The first tele-tutor training deals mainly with getting instructors acquainted with the functionality of the Distance Learning Platform (DLP), especially the electronic communication services. This takes place during a two-day face-to-face instruction period. The participants undertake a range of practical exercizes. A pre-test/post-test design is used for evaluation. The pre- and post-test consist of self-assessment multiple-choice questions concerning declarative, procedural and strategic knowledge in the training subjects (Sandberg *et al,* 2001). Additionally, free-format observations are carried out to obtain qualitative data on the performances of tele-tutors. The second training event is developed based on the learning outcomes of the first training event and a working model of 'when to use which communication' is created.

The second training activity is the 'summer-school' event, which comprises a simulation of the future instructing situation. Tele-tutors are assigned to a "virtual class" of students. The virtual student is either another tele-tutor playing the role of a student or a non-aviation person who has shown interest in the course and with similar background to future students. The virtual students are at different geographical locations from their tele-tutor so no face-to-face communication is possible. The flight instructors therefore perform the role of tele-tutor and student. This gives them the opportunity to experience being a distant student for themselves. Experiencing the role as a learner serves as an eye-opener and gives the opportunity to observe the teaching strategy of another tele-tutor.

The virtual students study a few modules with the support of their tele-tutor. The tele-tutors welcome the students in the class by e-mail on the first trial day and start and develop a discussion on a relevant topic in an asynchronous electronic discussion group, for example, about meteorology. Advice concerning the subjects to study is posted on the class bulletin board. The bulletin board is used to announce administrative messages. A weekly chat hour is offered during which students and tutors interact synchronously.

The messages sent to the discussion groups by the students are analyzed through a content analysis process. The category system assigns a function to each interpretable unit in the discourse, such as reflection, initiating or ending a discussion or summarizing or adding knowledge. The content analysis also explores the different moderating roles – such as adding content or "smoothing" the discussion.

Results of the content analysis indicate that most messages are about organizational and content issues (Christoph & Emans, 1999). Online discussions where the tele-tutor identifies with the process-facilitating role prove to be most useful and satisfying kind for the students. Other analysis showed that asynchronous discussion is the preferred communication mode, whereas the synchronous chat facility was hardly used.

The main finding from the research is that a distinction in online tele-tutor styles can be made: a pro-active and a reactive tutor style. The reactive tele-tutor responds to communication initiated by the students. S/he starts off the course, welcomes the students and provides feedback but only after the students have contacted the tele-tutor and have actively asked for feedback. The pro-active tele-tutor style thinks and plans the CMC ahead of time. Pro-active tele-tutors spent more time, compared to the reactive tele-tutors, in planning for the communication, choosing when to intervene and which media to use.

During the third and final training session, the students' attention is drawn towards this pro-active tutor style. An idealized learning path for students is developed and points in time are identified when communication through a particular medium is most appropriate. Results from the ongoing research with the students will indicate whether this pro-active tutor style has a positive effect on the quality of the learning process and the learning success of the students and whether CMC is a viable alternative to classroom discourse for PPL instructing.

11.12 Conclusions

This chapter asserts that underlying approaches for the study of CMC are likely to need to be interpretivist, developmental and based on practice over time. Special opportunities for reflection and rapid action exist in working online. Through action research and constructivism a convergence between theory and practice of online learning and teaching may be achieved.

The examples show that a variety of productive approaches can be taken, which support teaching and learning online, in addition to research into practice. Action research, which includes opportunities for participants to reflect on their learning and its impact, can prove especially useful in exploring the use of CMC for teaching and learning.

The literature is developing but is currently best used for interpreting and understanding findings rather than for hypothesis building. The literature used needs to be drawn from a variety of disciplines. In my view, researchers should aim to provide basic models of understanding from their action research. These can then provide frameworks that can be shared and developed through creative and constructivist approaches. A careful approach to action research is needed which enables the "voices" of all the participants to be articulated and methods and approaches are needed that enable participants to reflect on the experience of action.

11.13 Acknowledgements

The author acknowledges the help and reflections of Claire Stanley, Associate Professor of Applied Linguistics in the Department of Language Teacher Education at the School for International Training in Brattleboro, Vermont and Noor Christoph of the Social Science Informatics, University of Amsterdam.

11.14 References

Agar, M.H. (1980) *The Professional Stranger: An Informal Introduction to Ethnography* New York, Academic Press

Alexander, S. (1999) An evaluation of innovative projects involving communication and information technology in Higher Education *Higher Education Research & Development 18* (2) pp173–183

Baker, M. & Lund, K. (1997) Promoting reflective interactions in a CSCL environment *Journal Computer Assisted Learning 13* (3 September) pp163–174

Bassey, M. (1992) Creating Education through Research *British Educational Journal 18* (1) pp4–16

Becker, H.S. (1958) Problem of Inference and Proof in Participant Observation *American Sociological Review 23*, pp652–60

Biggs, J. (1995) The Role of Meta-learning in Study Processes *British Journal of Educational Psychology 55*, pp185–212

Biggs, J. (1999) What the student does: teaching for enhanced learning *Higher Education Research & Development 18* (1) p75

Brookfield, S.D. (1992) *Uncovering Assumptions: The Key to Reflective Practice* The Reflective Practitioner, pp13–18 January

Brookfield, S.D. (1995) *Becoming a Critically Reflective Teacher* San Francisco: Jossey-Bass

Burt, G. (1997) *Face to Face With Distance Education* Milton Keynes: Open and Distance Education Statistics

Calder, J. (1995) Evaluation & self-improving systems. In Lockwood, F. (Ed.) *Open & distance learning today* London: Routledge

Carr, W. (1995) *For Education: towards critical educational enquiry* Milton Keynes: OU Press

Carr, W. & Kemmis, S. (1986) *Becoming Critical: Education, Knowledge & Action Research.* Falmer

Christoph, L.H. & Emans, B.S. (1999) *Tutor training: Results of a course for distance tutors* Proceedings of Online Educa, Berlin 25–26th November

Cohen, L. & Manion, L. (1996) *Research Methods in Education* London: Routledge

Collis, B.A. (1994) Collaborative learning and CSCW: research perspectives for interworked educational environments *IFIP transactions A-Computer Science & Technology 46*, pp81–104

Cooper, D. (1992) Action research-student perspectives on tutor-marked assignments and tutorials *Open Learning 8* (3), pp3–11

Dede, C. (1996) Evolution of Distance Education: Emerging Technologies & Distributed Learning *AJDE 10* (2), pp4–36

Dewey, J. (1910) *How Do We Think?* London: Heath

Glaser, B.G. & Strauss, A.L. (1967) *The discovery of grounded theory: Strategies for qualitative research,* New York: Aldine

Guba, E.G. & Lincoln, S.Y. (1994) Competing Paradigms in Qualitative Research. In Denzin, N.K. & Lincoln, Y.S. (Eds.) *Handbook of Qualitative Research* Thousand Oaks: Sage

Gunn, C. (1999) They love it, but do they learn from it? Evaluating the educational impact of innovations *Higher Education Research & Development 18* (2), pp185–199

Hendry, G. (1996) Constructivism & Educational Practice *Australian Journal of Education 40*(1) pp19–45

Henri, F. (1992) Computer Conferencing and Content Analysis. In Kaye, A. (Ed.) *Collaborative Learning Through Computer Conferencing: The Najaden Papers* Heidelberg: Springer-Verlag

Jonassen, D.M., Davidson, M., Collins, C., Campbell & Haag, B.B. (1995) Constructivism and Computer-mediated Communication in Distance Education *American Journal of Distance Education 9*(2) pp7–25

Kelly, G.A. (1955) *The Psychology of Personal Constructs* New York: Norton

Kemmis, S. (1982) *The Action Research Planner* Geelong: Deakin University Press

Lee, V.L. (1988) *Beyond Behaviourism,* Hillsdale NJ: Lawrence Erlbaum

Lewin, K. (1946) *Resolving Social Conflicts* New York: Harper

Light, P., Nesbitt, E., Light, V. & White, S. (2000) Variety is the spice of life: student use of CMC in the context of campus based study. *Computers & Education 34*, pp257–267

Mann, C. & Stewart, F. (2000) *Internet Communication and Qualitative Research* London: Sage

Mantovani, G. (1994) Is computer-mediated communication intrinsically apt to enhance democracy in organizations? *Human Relations 47* (1), pp45–62

Mason, R. (1992) Evaluation Methodologies for Computer Conferencing Applications. In Kaye, A.R. (Ed.) *Collaborative Learning Through Computer Conferencing: The Najaden Papers* Berlin: Springer-Vaerlag

McIntyre, D. (1995) Initial teacher education as practical theorizing: A response to Paul Hirst *British Journal of Educational Studies 43*, pp365–383

McNiff, J. (1988) *Action Research: Principles & Practice* London: Macmillan

Metz, M. (1994) Computer-Mediated Communication:Literature Review of a New Context *International Computing & Technology 2* (2), pp31–49

Morgan, A. (1984) A report on qualitative methodologies in research in distance education *Distance Education 5*(2), pp252–267

Murphy, D. (1999) *Still 'getting the mixture right': Increasing interaction on the Internet* Proceedings of 8th Conference on Open and Distance-Learning, 'Learning and Teaching with New Technologies', Cambridge, UK, 28th Sept–1st Oct

Newman, R., Cochrane, C., Johnson, C. & Webb, B. (1995) A Content Analysis Method to Measure Critical Thinking in Face to Face and Computer Supported Group Learning *Interpersonal Computing and Technology 2*, pp56–77

Newman, R., Cochrane, C., Johnson, C. & Webb, B. (1996) An Experiment in Group Learning Technology: Evaluating Critical Thinking Face to Face and Computer Supported Seminars *Interpersonal Computing and Technology 4*(1), pp57–74

Oliver, R. & Reeves, T.C. (1996) Dimensions of Effective Interactive Learning with Telematics for Distance Education *ETR&D 44* (4), pp45–56

Polyani, M. (1962) *Personal Knowledge: Towards a Post-critical Philosophy* Chicago: University of Chicago Press

Reynolds, M. (1994) Decision-making using computer conferencing: a case study *Behaviour & Information Technology 13* (3), pp239–252

Reynolds, M. (1998) Reflection and Critical Reflection in Management Learning. *Management Learning 29* (2), pp183–200

Rose, A. (1992) Framing Our Experience: Research Notes on Reflective Practice *Adult Learning* (January), p5

Rudy, I.A. (1995) *A Critical Review of Research on Electronic Mail* Cambridge: Judge Institute of Management Studies

Salmon, G. (1999) Computer Mediated Conferencing in Large Scale Management Education *Open Learning* (June), pp45–54

Salmon, G. (2000a) Computer Mediated Conferencing for Management Learning at the Open University *Management Learning 31* (4)

Salmon, G. (2000b) *E-moderating: the key to teaching and learning online* London: Kogan Page

Sandberg, J.A.C., Christoph, L.H. & Emans, B.S. (2001) Tutor training: a systematic investigation of tutor requirements and an evaluation of a training British journal of educational technology *British Journal of Educational Technology, 32* (1), pp69-90

Schön, D. (1983) *The Reflective Practitioner; How Professionals Think in Action* London: Basic Books

Smith, J.E. (1995) Expanding the Potential of Distance Education *Adult Learning 7* (1)

Stein, S. (2000) *Learning, Teaching and Researching on the Internet; A practical guide for social scientists* London: Addison Wesley Longman

Stevenson, K.P., Sander, P. & Naylor, P. (1996) Student perceptions of the tutor's role in distance learning *Open Learning 11*(1), pp22–30

Tait, A. (1994) Speaking personally with Alan Tait *AJDE 8* (3), pp74–80

Thomas, G. (1997) What's the Use of Theory? *Harvard Educational Review 67* (No.1 Spring)

Tolmie, A. & Barbieri, S. (1997) Computer-mediated Communication in Higher Education *JCAL 13* (4 December)

Tolmie, A. & Boyle, J. (2000) Factors influencing the success of computer mediated communication (CMC) environments in university teaching: a review and a case study *Computers & Education 34*, pp120–140

Wild, M. (1996) Technology refusal: Rationalizing the failure of student and beginning teachers to use computers *British Journal of Educational Technology 27* (2), pp134–143

12. Learning from Watching Others Learn

Terry Mayes, Finbar Dineen, Jean McKendree and John Lee

12.1 Introduction

This chapter outlines the ideas and assumptions on which the 'Vicarious Learner' project is based, describes some attempts to test the ideas empirically, and considers the exploitation of the approach in education. The basic idea – expressed in our use of Bandura's (1986) term vicarious learning – is that through technology we are now able to capture, store and retrieve the records and outputs of real learning episodes, and to make these available for new learners. One important question is whether a database of such material might essentially represent a new kind of courseware, easier and less expensive to generate than conventional courseware. Our project has attempted to demonstrate how the idea might be exploited in practice, and we describe our design of a system, called Dissemination, which compiled such courseware from the recordings of students and tutors engaged in a specially-devised set of 'task-directed discussions'. In an experiment comparing subjects who were offered this material in addition to conventional courseware we found that those students who chose to use the vicarious resources tended to model in their own performance the tasks, language and approaches used in the discussions they had viewed vicariously. We tentatively conclude that the experience of watching other students learn helped the new learners to model the basic task of learning more effectively. We ask: is this an effective way of 'learning how to learn'? Certainly, though, this is only part of the story, and in the latter part of the paper we consider how the approach might be effectively exploited.

12.2 The Vicarious Learner Project

Our research program on vicarious learning, part of which we report in this chapter, has been aimed at exploring the idea that learning can be facilitated by providing learners with access to the experiences of other learners. We borrowed Bandura's term vicarious learning to describe this, and as our research progressed our sense of what was most important about the paradigm came closer to Bandura's original use of the term (see Bandura, 1986). We now want to

213

emphasize a process of social learning, in which the learner's approach to learning something is shaped by the observation of others attempting to learn it. This is a slight change of emphasis from our original focus on providing answers to learners' questions about the subject matter by compiling lots of examples of learner questions and tutor answers from previously recorded spontaneous dialogs. Originally we considered that the advantage of vicarious learning would lie in the relevance of the dialog generated by other learners. The unique benefit would derive from making visible a learner's perspective on the subject matter, revealing misconceptions or highlighting questions raised by the primary material for learners at a particular level of conceptual understanding of the particular material. It would capitalize on the experience we all have in classroom episodes, where we often recognize a question asked by a fellow learner as closely articulating our own struggle to understand. However, with this conception of vicarious learning we emphasized the direct benefit for learning specific subject matter. We would still expect this kind of benefit to occur with suitable vicarious material, but our emphasis now is on the more generalized benefits, for the vicarious learner, of seeing how to engage in learning dialogs. One of the keys to successful learning, of course, is being able to ask appropriate questions. It may be that this involves confidence as much as skill or knowledge, and observing other learners engaged in such dialogs has its effect by providing a model of good learning behaviour.

12.3 The Role of Dialog in Learning

In the work we report here we have departed from the mainstream tradition of computers in education where the technology is placed in the role of tutor. The principles which underpin the conventional computer-based learning view of dialog, including that of intelligent tutoring systems (ITS), focus directly on the gaining of comprehension in the subject matter. Thus, a tutorial in a discursive subject will explore misconceptions or areas of particular difficulty, will make explicit links to other areas of knowledge, and will point to implications or alternative accounts. It will seem essentially to involve a deeper elaboration of the meaning of the subject matter. This, of course, in one sense defines learning. It can be viewed simply as a by-product of comprehension (Mayes, 1992). The main point of a tutorial is to improve the comprehensibility of the subject matter for the individual learner by encouraging him or her to think more deeply or more analytically about the subject matter. Part of this process involves the making explicit of assumptions and inferences which would normally remain implicit. An important problem faced by all learners is that they make assumptions which often turn out not to be those held by the tutors, not to be part of the common ground needed for understanding (Clark, 1996). An effective tutorial dialog should result in the underlying assumptions being aligned.

There is, of course, more to an effective tutorial than making the implicit meaning of the subject matter more explicit. Indeed McKendree *et al.* (1998) have argued that dialog is central to the learner's "enculturation" into the patterns of language and thought, discussion and criticism, that are characteristic of an academic discipline. This can be thought of as a higher-level alignment. The learner acquires a new set of norms and procedures, as well as a new framework of knowledge. So there are two rather different ways in which we can think about tutorials. In one way they involve the mutual alignment of individual meanings about some subject matter. In the other, less cognitive sense, tutorials serve social and cultural ends: the learner is given a model of what it means to become an expert in the subject. Importantly for our present purposes we can regard vicarious learning as a paradigm for becoming an expert in *learning*. The student observes the outcomes of many different styles and approaches to the task of becoming an expert. Such observation should encourage reflection on the process of learning, and provide the student with different models of how to behave as a successful learner.

The vicarious learning paradigm offers the prospect of a real alternative to the building of intelligent tutors. Of course the computer-as-tutor would, if successfully designed and implemented, provide the learner with a tutorial dialog, but the immense difficulties of building such systems have forced the adoption of a very restricted definition of what constitutes a tutorial. The vicarious learning approach allows us to come at the problem from a different direction: rather than programing computers to mimic effective tutorial dialogs we start by collecting real examples. This still leaves a big problem of accessing the right example at the right moment, but it avoids the most intractable problem of having to design systems that can achieve the understanding by which to generate spontaneous language.

The context for the vicarious learning project is higher education (HE). Since the UK expansion of HE began in the 1960s, we have witnessed a gradual shift away from the tutorial dialog as the cornerstone of the learning and teaching experience, towards a notion of teaching through the effective delivery of information, particularly through the timetabled lecture, and then, as hopes for a new efficiency based on technology gained ground, through multimedia presentation. We can observe this trend by noting a subtle shift in the language used to describe education and training. Increasingly, it is described in terms of the 'delivery of materials', or even as the 'delivery of *learning*'. Gradually, we see the burden of teaching falling onto the primary presentation of subject matter. While this can become effectively elaborated to include self-assessment tests and a rich variety of pathways the key question is whether it can substitute for real dialog. Is it possible that through really good design of the presentation of the subject matter, the majority of learner questions can be anticipated and built in, and through a series of questions posed to the learner by the material, an efficient level of detail for the learners' current level of understanding can be chosen? Thus, the really important question is posed: is it possible, by building effective interactivity into the primary courseware, to achieve a measure of genuine automation in teaching? If a kind of dialog can be achieved through interactivity which is embedded in the materials then it would represent a solution to the obvious problem that there are now in HE too few tutors for too many learners. A recent report about the setting up of a UK e-university (HEFCE, 2000) has rightly focused on this as a key question. Not only is the nature of the e-pedagogy at stake, but the basic validity of the business model depends on the answer to this question. The report states:

"...the next major step forward is that the technology now also allows a high degree of interactive tutorial support and student choice to be built into the material itself – sufficient for it to be self-standing with little or no further support ... we would not expect face-to-face tutorial support to be a normal part of the e-U provision. Current expectations of the need for it are not based on the high level of interactivity which will be a key feature of e-U material."

The main challenge, for campus-based teaching as well as for e-learning, is to sustain the individual dialog between student and tutor as a major teaching method. A real danger with the introduction of new learning technologies is that they are associated with a confounding reduction in human-human dialog, and a consequent impoverishment in the quality of understanding. An important assumption on which the vicarious learning research is based, then, is that learning can occur not only through direct participation in dialog, but also through observing others participating in it.

Given the potential importance of this approach we need research to establish the ways in which we can take advantage of it and build on these to create an advanced prototype system for use in educational settings. The method we favored was to create, as a resource for new learners, databases of re-usable dialogs and discussions which have arisen from other learners who have been faced with similar issues or problems in understanding the subject matter. In both experimental laboratory studies and in real university courses, we have developed our understanding of how to design, capture, store, index, retrieve and re-use educational discussions. This research should underpin some of the attempts to develop online learning on a large scale. It should be particularly relevant for isolated or distance learners, and for students who might need greater exposure to the language and concepts than they are likely to get in traditional educational encounters in the classroom and lecture theatre.

12.4   The Concept of Tertiary Courseware

In work funded by BT prior to the present project, (Mayes *et al.*, 1995; Fowler & Mayes, 1997) a framework was described in which types of supporting technology could be mapped onto stages of learning. This gave a principled way of distinguishing three kinds of courseware: primary, secondary and tertiary. The term 'courseware' usually refers to the representation, explanation and presentation of the subject matter content, as in a textbook. This is what we term *primary* courseware, and it encompasses many forms – text, hypertext, graphics, multimedia, most Web material. This maps onto the stage of learning we have termed *conceptualization*, the learner's attempt to relate the new material to what is already known. In contrast, *secondary* courseware comprises tools which learners use to operate on this primary material, and the products of these operations. These can be presentation or concept-mapping tools; they might be applications with which students compose multimedia essays, or problem solving environments, or self-assessment tools. Essentially, secondary courseware supports learning by doing, and maps onto construction, so called to emphasize constructivist assumptions about the need to situate learning in meaningful, task-based activity. The third sort of courseware, the focus of our project, comprises structures to support discussion between learners and tutors, and allows us to capture these dialogs in order to render them reusable for the next group of students. We refer to this as *tertiary* courseware and it is intended to offer at least some of the benefits of small-group teaching.

12.5   Experiments on Vicarious Learning

Our starting point was to explore how easy it would be to capture suitable dialogs. Initial attempts to exploit CMC (computer-mediated communication) technologies led us to design a (at that time) novel web-based learning environment involving an SGML-based integration of primary and secondary courseware, with the HyperNews system which provided a forum maintaining persistent discussion threads accessible through a Web browser. We twice taught a module on 'Computers in Teaching and Learning' to students who were taking a Masters level course on Human-Computer Interaction. In the first of these the discussion environment was used relatively loosely. Students were prompted by a few seed questions, but then were left to develop the discussion as they chose, with some conventional moderation from the course tutors. Over the two occasions of running the course our findings anticipated what has now become well established in online learning. There were large differences in the way the discussion was approached, with some students being very reluctant to enter into discussion at all. Questions that were aimed at a clarification of concepts were surprisingly infrequent. However, based on the experience in the first course, and suggestions in the literature on conducting online discussions (Sproull & Keisler, 1993), we made the discussions in the second running of the module more structured, and participation in them compulsory. We required tutors to post specific questions and to summarize the main points at the end of each week's discussion. Overall, these changes were not successful in enhancing the effectiveness of the discussions. Although all students now participated, the number of questions raised was actually fewer, with students restricting their questions to a more shallow 'text-based' level. An important conclusion from these trials was the difficulty of eliciting dialog that had any of the characteristics that we judged to be necessary for reuse. These results are discussed in further detail by Lee, Dineen and McKendree (1998).

Having established that dialog at a suitable level is hard to capture spontaneously we decided to devise a way to facilitate its production. Before embarking on this, however, we needed to establish that vicarious dialogs really help to promote learning. If tertiary courseware has no particular benefit over primary courseware in the form of the usual expository materials, then it would seem hardly worth the effort of capturing and storing such resources. We therefore designed an initial study to compare primary expositions – text and worksheets – to versions annotated with captured dialog.

12.5.1 Formal Grammar Analysis Experiment

Students on our course on Human Communication had particular difficulty with the problem of learning formal techniques for analyzing English sentences. In particular they found it difficult to complete exercizes in constructing syntax-trees depicting the grammar of sentences and other kinds of formal diagrams. To help with this, a computer-based tool was developed to assist the students in creating and editing these diagrams. This could be regarded as a typical piece of instructional courseware (in our terms it could be used as either primary or secondary courseware). Using this as the basic learning task we now experimented with different kinds of vicarious material.

We looked at the difference between expert monologue and student-tutor dialog (Cox *et al.,* 1999). In the one case, a tutor constructed a diagram while explaining the activity for the benefit of students; this was captured as a movie of the manipulation of the computer tool, along with a transcript of the tutor's commentary. In another case, a novice student constructed the diagram, with assistance from the tutor where needed – which was often. These materials were presented to the students also as animated diagrams accompanied by transcripts of the recorded speech. We observed that although there was no clear difference between students given the dialogs and those given the "direct instruction" tutorial monologues, both of these produced significantly better results than conditions where students were given only animations of the diagrams or only "primary text" materials. So it does seem that these dialogic materials can increase students' understanding when attached to more traditional instructional material.

12.5.2 Turning Discussions into Learning Tasks

Encouraged by this we now turned to the need to find a way of generating suitable dialog. We decided to investigate an area of teaching where discussion is paramount: the learning of a foreign language. Based on approaches used in second language acquisition (Skehan, 1998), we have developed a series of structured activities that we call Task Directed Discussions (TDDs). These are tasks that *require* learners to engage in meaningful structured discussion. The learners are engaged task by task in deeper thinking about the domain concepts and are required to participate in a variety of discussion forms. These TDDs are in themselves constructivist learning tasks in which the learners' developing understanding of the material is made visible. The idea is that from the recorded content of these tasks other learners may learn vicariously.

In itself, each TDD was a discrete language activity with a set goal, with all discussions being based upon discursive manipulations of a common set of domain concepts. Altogether eleven Task Directed Discussions were devised ranging in discursive focus from single concepts to groups of concepts, with varying manipulations of these. The discussions varied in the specificity and form of the concepts that they aimed to elicit and make explicit and observable to others. Each discussion task focused the learners' attention on an explicit and shared set of concepts that have been derived from the primary courseware (*i.e.*, the course content). Thus the primary courseware remained the target for each discussion task, but the form and scope of each discussion was controlled through specified manipulations of these concepts. So, each discussion form was based around a simple cognitive task and acted as an example of secondary courseware. Tertiary courseware was produced as an outcome of these TDDs in the form of recorded discussions about the course content. Finally, these discussions were then indexed into a multimedia database which linked to the primary courseware.

We devised eleven Task Directed Discussions:

1. *Amphibolic TDD*: the goal is to examine the multiple interpretations offered by the primary courseware.
2. *Common Denominator TDD*: given a concept, name examples of its application.
3. *Comparison TDD*: describe the connection between two concepts relative to a given criterion.
4. *Defining Terms TDD*: one student attempts to describe a concept well enough for another to guess what this concept is.
5. *Depiction TDD*: explore the multiple representational structures, styles or media in which a concept or argument may be depicted (e.g. charts, text, graphs).
6. *Gestalt TDD*: the explicit goal is to highlight the underlying assumptions made by another student as part of one of their explanations of a concept or argument using a given concept.
7. *Hypothetical TDD*: Encourage learners to reason to and from precepts, conjecturing to and from 'possible worlds'. Examples would be counterfactual arguments.
8. *Ranking TDD*: rank a given set of concepts in terms of level of importance along a given dimension.
9. *Reconstruct TDD*: have learners re-organize the order and propositional structure of sections of the primary courseware to explore the conceptual and functional structure implicit.
10. *Repertory Grid TDD*: select three concepts and describe in what way two are similar, but different from the other one along a common dimension (construct).
11. *Scanning TDD*: select from a designated section of the primary courseware a specified number of factors that are the most relevant examples of a given criterion.

TDDs are good examples of constructivist pedagogy in practice and there would be a strong case for developing tools that encourage the general use of these tasks for online learning environments. Through engaging in tasks of this kind learners are implicitly encouraged to achieve deep learning: effort is directed towards an underlying conceptual clarity. More than this, however, learners are helped to develop their 'epistemic fluency' (Morrison & Collins, 1995) by being asked to communicate their understanding when it is still incomplete. In trialing these tasks we were struck by their social impact – there is a compelling social effect of participating in a collaborative endeavour to achieve a joint understanding through revealing one's own processes of constructing meaning. While we have only qualitative observation and anecdote to support this conclusion it has emphasized the potential importance of using such tasks in online distance learning, in which the need to feel part of a larger group is so important for isolated learners. However, the question for our research was not the relative importance of materials and tasks (*i.e.,* primary and secondary courseware) for the learners directly involved, but the effectiveness of allowing other learners to observe some of the outputs of the process later (*i.e.,* tertiary).

We next turned to exploring issues relating directly to tertiary courseware. How can pedagogical discourse best be made available to, and accessed by, new learners? In order to explore issues of multimedia indexing and modality presentation we developed and implemented an indexed multimedia database of TDDs in a system we called 'Dissemination'. A logical representation of the interface structure of Dissemination can be seen in Figure 12.1 below, while an example of the actual system is shown in Figure 12.2, also below.

12.5.3 Dissemination: An Indexed Multimedia Database of Tertiary Courseware

The experimental system used as primary courseware a portion of the course material from our module on Computers in Teaching and Learning. A self-contained section on Models of Learning with Technology was extracted containing approximately 14,400 words on 45 Web pages ranging from a few paragraphs to a page and a half in length. Integrated with this online material was the tertiary material. This consisted of dialogs edited from the over-30 hours of tapes recorded from the face-to-face TDDs: 108 video clips, 13 audio clips, 43 text transcriptions, and 27 audio annotated graphics. Any one of these could be accessed by clicking on highlighted keywords in the primary text, or by searching on keywords or the type of discussion task.

Using Dissemination a study was undertaken in which 37 undergraduate subjects were required to undergo a 10-hour learning experiment. The subjects' task was to learn and understand enough of the primary courseware to achieve 70% on a post-test about it. Subjects were motivated to perform this task by being offered a financial reward for achieving this score. The subjects were divided into two groups based on their pre-test scores on a knowledge test of the domain and on two questionnaires, one about their frequency of use of various types of media for learning, and another on their views about various aspects of peer discussion as a useful source of learning, as well as matching for gender. This resulted in two groups who did not differ significantly on knowledge, stated media preferences, or attitude toward discussion. One group saw the primary learning material only; the other had additional access to the Dissemination database of TDD-derived discussions. There was no requirement on the subjects in the latter condition actually to use this tertiary courseware. The assumption was that subjects would only attempt to retrieve those examples of discourse from the database that would help them in the interpretation and understanding of the course content. In fact, subjects' own stated comments confirmed that they only made use of this material when they found it useful to do so. It should be noted that all the items on the knowledge tests could be attempted having read the primary material only.

Each media clip in the tertiary courseware could be retrieved along three orthogonal dimensions:

1. The concept or focus topic of the TDD.
2. The form of the discourse as determined by the discourse goal specified in the TDD.
3. The medium of discourse. This is the dimension along which the discourse is captured and entered into the database (video, audio, text, graphic).

The relationship of the primary courseware to the tertiary courseware can be seen in Figure 12.1. In studying the course notes the learner can access Dissemination through an indexed set of key concepts highlighted directly (top left), or they can access an archived TDD indirectly through a search of the database (bottom left). For each key concept the learner is presented with the indexed set of all TDDs for that key concept in various media (top right). In selecting one of these along the three orthogonal dimensions the learner is shown the desired piece of tertiary courseware (bottom right).

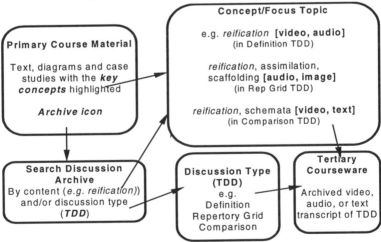

Figure 12.1 The 'Dissemination' Tutoring System: a logical representation of the linking of primary to tertiary courseware

The students spent two hours each day for two days in the lab studying the primary courseware and taking notes on paper, resulting in four hours to read the material. Their paper notes were collected at the end of each session and returned to them at the beginning of the next session. The server stored information about each page or resource that was viewed, the amount of time spent on each, and in the case of audio and video files, how much of the clip was played. On the third day, the students had 40 minutes to review the online material and their written notes. They then filled in an HCI questionnaire about the system and a questionnaire about their learning experience followed by the knowledge post-test which was the same as the pre-test.

On the fourth day, the students were divided into groups of either two or three and participated in 40-minute, online, synchronous discussions of the material using Internet Relay Chat. They were simply told to discuss the course content to clear up anything they didn't understand. These discussions were saved for analysis. The subjects were motivated to engage in peer discussion for the purpose of improving their understanding of the subject matter by being offered a further financial incentive if they could improve their performance on a final test.

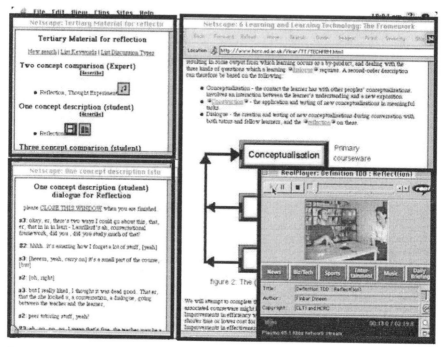

Figure 12.2 A Screenshot of the 'Dissemination' Tutoring System, showing the primary courseware (center-right), the indexed database of TDDs for the concept 'reflection' (top left) and tertiary courseware presented as a text transcript (bottom left) and digitized video clip (bottom right)

12.5.4 Tertiary Courseware as a Vicarious Learning Resource: Some Conclusions from the Experiments

Detailed results of the 'Dissemination' experiment are complex. There is no overall effect of whether an individual learner had access to the tertiary material, on the level of understanding achieved. However, this turns out to be because there are very large individual differences in the way the system is used, and in the learning strategies employed. When we look at individual learners we find clear evidence for a 'vicarious learning' effect. Subjects who have chosen to spend most time observing effective discussions subsequently structure their own free discussions of the course materials in ways that resemble what they have observed. Moreover, these subjects then show real learning gains. It is also the case that subjects who had access to tertiary materials are significantly more likely to judge the system as representing an important learning resource, and as providing an 'enjoyable' learning experience. Interestingly, subjects who did not have access to the tertiary material rate the content as more 'correct'.

Analysis of the online discussions, using several dialog mark-up and analysis methods (Newman, Webb & Cochrane, 1995; Henri, 1991; Pilkington, 1996) was undertaken. The analysis showed that the group that were allowed access to tertiary materials showed significant increases in the number of occurrences of several educationally relevant discourse features. This group:

- showed more critical assessment of their own or another person's contribution to discussion;
- exhibited more use of justification – providing proof or examples to ground a statement;
- more often explicitly derived new information from known facts;
- had a tendency to signal recall or exposition of another person's argument or reasoning.

It was also noted that there were significant differences in the amount of discussion generated, averaging 1,075 words for the group with access to tertiary materials and 834 words for the others. When scored by a blind rater for the relevance of each statement, the tertiary group stayed on topic significantly more than the others (82% against 68%). We have here valuable evidence of the power that watching dialogs can have to influence positively the subsequent behaviour of students in discussions. This influence is likely to have beneficial educational consequences in the longer run, if the dialogs watched are well selected.

Overall, the most interesting result is that when the students engage in discussions themselves, we find that those who had seen the vicarious resources have been modelling the tasks and language used in them. For instance, in the groups who had access to tertiary courseware, when the discussants ran out of things to say on a topic, they often suggested trying one of the discussion games they had seen in the resources. These subjects also were significantly faster in returning to an 'on-topic' discussion.

<Discussant1>	OK, perhaps we could just pick a concept and try and describe it to another person.
<Discussant2>	Well you can go first then
<Discussant3>	Accretion?
<Discussant2> form of learning	Adding of new knowledge to existing schema, most common
<Discussant1>	Accretion is the second stage in the learning process, after structuring, and it involves adding bits of knowledge into a schema
<Discussant3>	Ah, I see.

12.6 Vicarious Learning From Educational Dialog

Stenning *et al.* (2000) have provided an account about what aspects of educational dialog make it particularly amenable to capture and reuse for overhearers. An important feature of educational dialogs is the way in which they make explicit inferences which would normally remain unspoken. This involves an explicit process of establishing the common ground needed for understanding (Clark, 1996). Usually, of course, this will involve a dialog between a tutor and a student, or a group of students, which will result in a shift in the assumptions made by the learners bringing them more into line with the tutor. Stenning *et al.* have argued that this process occurs most effectively not through the student(s) simply being told (accepting an exposition) as much as being shown. By working through a more or less logical process of derivation, the authority of the tutor is largely abrogated in favour of the more abstract authority of reasoning norms that can be explicitly discussed and agreed, the procedure can be observed. The student thus learns, not only about the subject matter, but also about the process of argumentation. Stenning *et al.* argue that educational discourse is a special case since conceptual misalignment is the default expectation, unlike most everyday conversations. So educational dialog involves "reasoning to an interpretation", rather than reasoning from a relatively non-problematic initial interpretation. The development of the common ground being thus relatively out in the open, derivational dialogs are well suited to vicarious following of the process by indirect participants or overhearers.

Much real dialog in educational settings involves the indirect participation of other learners. In group tutorial sessions, the tutor may, for the benefit of the indirect participants, be more explicit than would be strictly necessary for an individual student being directly addressed. In cases like these, the dialog participants are well aware that there are overhearers, and they take this into account. In classroom settings most dialogs are of this kind. The very fact that this happens, of course, acts on the one hand as evidence that overhearers are known to have effective interpretative strategies, but on the other as evidence that these strategies require specific assistance from the direct dialog participants.

Nevertheless, the skilled teacher will also choose to have occasional one-to-one dialogs with individual learners where no overhearing at all will occur.

In most educational settings the rules which govern overhearing are well understood and form part of the experience of learning as a member of a group or cohort. In the various forms of online learning, however, where the presence of overhearers may not be obvious, these norms need to be explicitly evolved. In the case of tertiary courseware, where dialogs are recorded and stored for repeated and unspecified future overhearers, we will need to develop a completely new set of rules. Clearly, the original dialogs will themselves be influenced by the nature of the expectations about what use they may be put to. For each possible variety of vicarious learning, dialogs need specifically to be developed in such a way as to facilitate the overhearer's construction of a common understanding. This means that educational dialogs will always be partly shaped by the direct participants' perception of the level of understanding of the indirect participants. However, when the future indirect participants are by definition unknown, as will be the case for stored dialogs which are genuinely reusable, then as much as possible of the context of the original dialog needs to be recorded with it. If we cannot depend on the direct participants to moderate the dialog in a way that takes account of the requirements of the potential overhearers then the burden needs to fall on the system itself for selecting an appropriate dialog for a particular vicarious learner.

Underpinning the idea of vicarious learning is an assumption that learners not only can learn by observing other learners, but will actively want to do so. But why should a learner find vicarious resources any more motivating than conventional subject matter? In fact much of the potential effectiveness of the kind of learning resource we have called tertiary courseware will depend on the potency of the identification the new learner can develop for the original participants, and on the extent to which the the dialog is considered relevant to the achievement of the learner's goals. For us, following Wenger (1998), this identification and this relevance will be largely determined by the extent to which the original participants in the dialog are seen as representative members of a target community of practice. This view encourages us to consider vicarious learning not just in terms of techniques for supporting the overhearing of dialogs, but more generally in terms of its effect on the formation of learning identities. Learning involves social participation – in particular, by being an active participant in the practices of social communities, and by constructing an identity in relation to each community. Wenger's conceptualization of communities of practice gives us a way of defining personal meaning in a way that isn't just circular. However, it is not a description of learning per se, or of how people learn together. It provides a very high level design heuristic and in that sense it tells us where we should start looking for design principles which address the key question of motivation.

Recently, Fowler and Mayes (1999) have discussed the idea that vicarious learning environments should be designed around recognition of the importance of the learner's personal identification with others. This approach takes the notion of a *learning relationship* as central, rather than a community of practice. Our experience of communities is mediated through individual relationships. In an initial attempt to study the nature of these Fowler and Mayes distinguished between explorative, formative and comparative learning relationships, and characteristics of these have been studied in a project observing 16-year-olds attending schools in three different European countries (*i.e.,* UK, Finland and Portugal). The data from this study begins to show the crucial role cultural factors play, and confirms that the shift of emphasis about vicarious learning with which we began this paper – moving from a learning-content view to a learning-how-to-learn account – is probably taking the work in the right direction.

12.7   Conclusion

We do not see vicarious learning as a *replacement* for direct participation in dialog, but we view vicarious learning resources as offering genuinely learner-centered learning materials, providing affective support through increasing the feeling of sharing in a learning community, and a means of more effective immersion into the language and practice of students' chosen areas. However, if the benefits we have identified for vicarious learning are real then time and resources will be freed to allow 'live' tutorial dialogs to be more focused and efficient. As with most technology-based approaches to learning support, the effective exploitation of the research reported here will ultimately depend on the balance of costs for development weighed against the perceived benefits for the learner. In the view of the researchers in the vicarious learning project this balance currently looks much more favourable here than for conventional courseware development.

12.8   Acknowledgements

The research reported here was carried out under the EPSRC grants GR/K72759 and GR/K86930 ('Distributed Learning Dialogs: Deriving tertiary courseware', awarded to Terry Mayes, John Lee, Keith Stenning and Patrick McAndrew) and ESRC grant L127251023 ('The Vicarious Learner', awarded to Terry Mayes and John Lee). Initial teaching trials for the 'Computers in Teaching and Learning' course were conducted at the Institute for Computer Based Learning, Heriot Watt University, Edinburgh. Other members of the Vicarious Learner group were Keith Stenning, Richard Cox, Richard Tobin and Jonathan Kilgour. We are very grateful to Chris Fowler of BT Labs and the Institute of Education for his contribution to this work.

12.9   References

Bandura, A. (1986) *Social Foundations of Thought and Action.* Englewood Cliffs, NJ: Prentice-Hall

Clark, H.H. (1996) *Using Language.* Cambridge: Cambridge University Press

Cox, R., McKendree, J., Tobin, R., Lee, J. & Mayes, J.T. (1999) Vicarious learning from dialog and discourse: A controlled comparison, *Instructional Science, 27*, pp431-458

Fowler, C.J.H. & Mayes, J.T. (1997) Applying telepresence to education. *BT Technology Journal, 15* (4) pp189-196

Fowler, C.J.H. & Mayes, J.T. (1999) Learning relationships: from theory to design. *Association for Learning Technology Journal, 7* (3) pp6-16

Henri, F. (1991) Computer conferencing and content analysis. In O'Malley, C. (Ed.) *Computer Supported Collaborative Learning,* Springer Verlag

Higher Education Funding Council for England (HEFCE) (2000*) Report on a Business Model for the e-University.* http://www.hefce.ac.uk

Lee, J., Dineen, F. & McKendree, J. (1998) Supporting student discussions: it isn't just talk. *Education and Information Technology, 3,* 217-229

Mayes, J.T. (1992) Cognitive Tools: a suitable case for learning. In Kommers, P., Jonassen, D. & Mayes, J.T. (Eds) *Cognitive Tools for Learning* Springer-Verlag

Mayes, J.T., Coventry, L., Thomson, A. & Mason, R. (1995) *Learning through Telematics.* ICBL, Heriot-Watt University and Open University. Report for BT Labs

McKendree, J., Stenning, K., Mayes, T., Lee J. & Cox, R. (1998) Why Observing a Dialog may Benefit Learning: The Vicarious Learner. *Journal of Computer Assisted Learning, 14* (2) pp110-119

Morrison, D. & Collins, A. (1995) Epistemic fluency and constructivist learning environments. In Wilson, B.G. (Ed.), *Constructivist learning environments: Case studies in instructional design.* Englewood Cliffs NJ: Educational Technology Publications

Newman, D.R., Webb, B. & Cochrane, C. (1995) A Content Analysis Method to Measure Critical Thinking in Face-to-Face and Computer Supported Group Learning, *International Computing and Technology : An electronic Journal for the 21st Century 3* (2) pp56-77

Pilkington, R. (1996) Interacting with computer-based simulation: the role of dialog, *Computers and Education, 27* (1) pp1-14

Skehan, P. (1998) *A Cognitive Approach to Language Learning*, Oxford UP, Oxford

Sproull, L. & Kiesler, S. (1993*) Connections: New Ways of Working in the Networked Organization (*3rd edition), London: MIT Press

Stenning, K., McKendree, J., Lee, J., Cox, R., Dineen, F. & Mayes, T. (2000) Vicarous Learning from Educational Dialog. In Hoadley, C. & Roschelle, J. (Eds.) *Proceedings of the Computer-Support for Cooperative Learning (CSCL) 1999 Conference.* Dec. 12 – 15, Stanford University, Calif. Mahwah, N.J.: Lawrence Erlbaum. pp341-347. http://kn.cilt.org/cscl99/A43/A43.htm

Wenger, E. (1998) *Communities of Practice: Learning, Meaning and Identity.* Cambridge: Cambridge University Press

13. Issues for Democracy and Social Identity in Computer Mediated Communication and Networked Learning

Vivien Hodgson

13.1 Introduction

The rapid development in advanced communications and information technology has been accompanied by many claims for the impact that such technology will have upon learning, approaches to education and, indeed, the very nature of the educational process.

Dramatic changes in the potential and possibilities for communication and access to information of the kind that we have seen due to developments such as, in particular, the Web and the Internet inevitably lead to exaggerated claims and anticipated fundamental changes. There is a tendency to liken the tremendous advance and growth of the Internet to the development of the printing press and the way that it led to a different system of education and one that was more accessible and available to more people.

Amongst these claims is the one that advanced or new communications and information technology will, in their own way, help to create a more democratic process of education. Such comments are linked to what Simeon Yates (1997) recently referred to the as 'the democratic theory' of CMC (computer mediated communication). They can be traced to numerous writers such as Sproull and Kiesler (1991a, 1991b) writing on the impact for democratization within organizations, Boyd (1987) and Boshier (1990) on the potential of CMC to emancipate educational processes, Hiltz and Turoff (1978) on the potential for leveling out hierarchical power differentials amongst networked individuals.

More recently within the education literature the emphasis has moved towards how this potential for apparently more egalitarian and democratic forms of communication supports and allows more collaborative and/or constructivist approaches to learning. Riel (1995) e.g., suggests that CMC leads to a reconstruction of the teaching/learning relationship, shifting the role of the teacher from controlling the transmission of information to providing intellectual leadership in 'challenging conversations among a community of learners'. In much the same vein Garrison comments:

"The conventional view that knowledge can be transmitted in whole from the teacher is being replaced by a critical and collaborative approach to constructing meaning and confirming understanding." (Garrison, 1997)

He goes on to explain:

"Individual responsibility and control along with authentic communication is the essence to a constructivist approach to education." (ibid.)

Other related claims made about the potential of CMC for supporting more egalitarian patterns of interaction is that it enables women to speak more easily and without interruption in mixed sex groups than would normally be the case (Graddol, 1989). Kirkup and Von Prummer 1997 also recently suggested a further potential advantage for CMC is to satisfy the desire of distance learning women students to have connection with others.

Whilst I also support the idea of democratic/egalitarian networked learning communities and I am very happy to see in the literature that discussions and interest is moving away from what Richard Boot and myself termed the 'dissemination orientation' to open learning to the 'development orientation' to open learning (Boot & Hodgson, 1987). More recently referred to by Pratt (1998) as the Transmission and Developmental teaching perspectives. I think we need to look a little more critically at some of the claims being made.

13.2 The Theoretical and Practical Assumptions about Computer Mediated Communication

What are the assumptions upon which these claims about CMC are based and to what extent can they be substantiated in practice? Leaving aside for the moment the issue of access to the technology, albeit an essential one, at the theoretical level much of what has been said about the importance of CMC to support educational processes that are both more democratic and collaborative derives from the ideas and thinking of the critical pedagogy school of educational thinking. The proponents of this school advocate that higher levels of learning and knowing are achieved through critical reflexivity and dialogical processes (Freire, 1972; Giroux, 1992; Brookfield, 1993, *etc.*)

Linked to this, is the critical theory concept of 'legitimate discourse' developed by Habermas (1981) or as described by Mezirow 'ideal discourse'. Mezirow describes 'ideal discourse' as that which is:

"Free from coercion or distorting self deception, is open to other perspectives and points of view, is accepting of others as equal partners." (Mezirow, 1988)

Both Boyd (1987) and Boshier (1990) argue that CMC forms of communication begin to make the idea of 'ideal discourse' become a more achievable reality than an impractical ideal.

At the level of practice CMC characteristics which are believed to have the potential to change processes and patterns of interaction between people have been summarized by Hodgson and McConnell (1994) and, in brief, can be said to be:

- it is possible to contribute to a computer medicated interaction or discussion whenever individuals feel they want to without having to wait their 'turn' or without having to interrupt someone else;
- contributions can be made at any time of day or night and on any day of the week;
- contributions can be made wherever the different participants are geographically, from almost any location in the world, and are not dependent on the 'physical' presence in one locality of the discussants;
- discussions are ongoing and continuous in nature for as long or short a period of time as required or desired;
- responses to others do not have to be made instantaneously or immediately but when the respondent is 'ready';
- communication is generally slower and of a more sporadic nature (and thus potentially more reflective) as compared to face to face communication;
- there is a permanent record of a group's work and of every individual contribution which can be referred to at any time and which can be manipulated as any other information held electronically in a database.

These characteristics lead to key assumptions such as within a CMC environment there are no visual clues to reflect status and all participants can contribute on an equal basis to the discussion when they are ready and without having to interrupt others or wait their turn and at what ever time or place that suits their circumstances or situation. All things that are possible because of the characteristics that are specific to CMC and which, it is claimed, facilitate the ability to have discussions on equal terms for all participants.

I think both the theoretical and practical assumptions about interaction in CMC environments just described need to be subjected to closer examination.

Garrison points out that much of the interest in collaborative approaches to learning has its roots in the theories and ideas of social constructivism which claims that what we perceive to be knowledge is not so much a reflection of nature as the outcome of social processes. Garrison explains the relationship between social constructivism and collaborative learning in the following way:

"Collaborative learning has its roots in social constructivisim. That is, establishing a social environment where critical discourse is valued and where students and teachers are encouraged to 'develop theories and ideas of their own which challenge and test the limits of traditional sources of knowledge' (Brody, 1995)." (Garrison, 1997)

explains that people's use of certain ways of talking constructs different social relationships and, in addition, he explains that we construct between ourselves not only a sense of our own identities but also a sense of our 'social worlds'. Similarly, I would suggest, that by analyzing people's use of certain ways of talking 'online' we can examine the processes through which social relationships are constructed and through which each person acquires a sense of their own identity in the social world of an online learning community.

In the next part of this chapter I would, consequently, like to examine in more detail these different concepts and ideas about what is visible and what is 'real' and how certain ways of talking constructs different social relationships and sense of identity in CMC environments

13.3   Analysis of 3 Online Transcripts

The approach taken in this part of the chapter is to closely examine three different excerpts from computer conferences.

The first excerpt looks at a process of negotiation and decision-making taking place in a computer conference between a group of university researchers located in five different countries. The researchers are engaged in a trans-european project which is essentially attempting to create common descriptors (referred to in the conference as 'brevets') for describing the skills and competencies gained by students when successfully completing given academic courses whatever the country. One of the key tasks of the researchers was, through a process of discussion and negotiation, to ascertain those skills or competencies (or brevets) that were in practice essentially the same although gained from taking different courses in different countries and those which were clearly unique to either a particular course and/or country. In the conference transcript the participants refer to particular skills or competencies (*i.e.,* 'brevets') that can be obtained as a result of taking given courses in terms of a number given to each brevet at each of the participating universities, e.g. 211 or 651, *etc.* In the example shown Paola and Maria make their contributions from Sienna and Simon and Val from Lancaster.

Example 1: the 'Nectar' conference
1. **Item 10**   **Labour 02 Sept 7:55**   **Siena: Paola**
2. **10:8**   **Simon   41 lines 10 Oct   14:02**
3. Hi folks!
4. Further to Val's proposal [3:7], this is how we'd 'chair' Labour if you
5. agree:-
6. Re 205 and 651 - we take it that this has been agreed as a merger we
7. report here that Lancaster has deleted
8. 205 and presumes 651 is being kept
9. re211 and 651 we think there is scope for a new merger here
10. We examined 422 and 651 and felt this was not possible, we examined 667
11. and

12. and 212 and felt that this was not possible as a merger but to
13. differentiate
14. differentiate them Lancaster would change its 'context' word from
15. "international' to "organization" OK?
16. we examined 211 and 651 in the light of these examinations and propose
17. the following merger:-
18. That Lancaster changes its 'context' word from "society" to "firm" on
19. 211;
20. the labels will then read:
21. LABOUR   (domain) ANALYZING (action) FIRM (context) ACAD
    RECOGNITION
22. (proof)
23. the Brevet title will then read:
24. "Analyzing Employee Relations" - as in Lancaster's 211, and
25. the Brevet Definition will then read:
26. "Analyzing contemporary industrial relations and their economic and
27. political effects in a national context" - as in Siena's 651.
28. If you agree we will make 211 passive and at Lancaster we will add 651
29. (the proposed version) to our course "BA 315"
30. Please let us know your reactions to this proposed merger!
31. Bye for now!
32. Simon.

33. **10.9 Maria   7 lines   11 Oct   16:52**
34. 651 is still alive and kicking with changes we agreed on sep
35. sept. 12 *i.e.* with contemporary in the def. It seems a good idea
36. to merge 211 and 651 and we will change the title as you
37. suggested
38. bye
40. Maria

41. **10:10   Simon   5 lines   12 Oct   16:28**
42. Hi Maria
43. re merger between 211 and 651: I'll take it that's agreed then?
44. (if so Hurray!)
45. Byeeee
46. Simon

47. **10:11   Maria   6 lines   13 Oct   17:03**
48. Hi again Simon
49. As they say at Cape Canaveral yes we've got a merger!
50. re. brevet 212 ref. 10:8 Did you mean you were going to change the
51. context word from SOCIETY to organization?
52. bye bye

53. Maria
54. **10:12   Val   11 lines 14 Oct   15:46**
55. Yes Maria we intend to change the context of 212 to organization
56. from Society
57. Also we will make 211 passive in preference to your 651 as agreed
58. And that I think concludes the summaries for this week!!
59. Have a good weekend one and all
60. Val

In the conference then they are basically discussing whether a particular competence or academic skill associated with a course or courses at either Sienna or Lancaster are in practice the same or different to ones identified as associated with courses at one of the other institutions in the project. The idea being that where a skill or competence is identified as essentially the same agreement is then negotiated between the institutions concerned on the way to describe the skill so that it is acceptable to, in this case, both Lancaster and Sienna. In each case individual skills or competencies were defined in terms of 4 fields or labels, these being: the domain, the action, the context and the proof. In addition each one was given a title and a brief description. It was each of these that had to be agreed in the negotiations.

A much fuller analysis of the interaction is available in Hodgson and Fox (1995) but the short excerpt presented here shows how the participants in the conference navigate their actions and agreements within the space-time reference of the conference by indexical reference to textual happening and events within the conference e.g. by retrospective indexical references to previous comments in the conference (e.g. line 4, further to Val's proposal) as well as prospective comments which are about to be made (line 4, this is how we'd 'chair' Labour if you agree) – but also to situations and sites not present within the conference itself (e.g. line 7, we report here that Lancaster has deleted 205 and presumes 651 is being kept).

Throughout the negotiation in this conference, external situations outside the conference retained a partial and persuasive character within the conference itself. The emergent, situated conversational-text of the conference was, however, where participants negotiated what the prior situation meant for the current negotiation. The negotiation occurred through a process of sequential turn taking in the conference which had the same properties that Garfinkel *et al.* (1981) characterized as "first time through". That is, it occurred here first and not elsewhere, such as in people's heads or in prior agreements that had taken place in 'real life'.

Consequently, it can be claimed the final agreement can be seen to emerge and that this can only have arisen in the first time through emergent situations of the conversational text of the conference itself. It is woven from the textual, relational, interactions of the four people engaged in a mutual process of editing and is the product of an essentially interactive work practice of 'negotiation'. Moreover this shared meaning is a matter of agreement amongst the participants; the practical accomplishment of which takes numerous performative formulations, reformulation and double checking in order to refine an initial suggestion or proposal until a final one is agreed (for example, see lines 9, 16-27, 28-30, 34-37, 43, 49 and 57).

Thus the persons, activities and situation arose together in the conversational-text, not as a theoretical entity but as a practical entity, which in this case is the decontextualized excerpt analyzed.

The negotiation just examined shows that in many ways that there was no other negotiation process or 'real' world outside of the text of the computer conference, since all prior or external events were, in effect, reconstructed in the emergent 'here and now' of the conversational text. However, as previously mentioned, prior and external events did retain a partial and persuasive character within the interaction taking place. In much the same way as they do in any other conversation or negotiation.

In the following two excerpts which are taken from a different conference it can be seen that the 'experience' of this 'here and now' frequently retain the same patterns of social interaction and dialog that are associated with and reflected in physical face to face interactions. And, as in face to face dialog contributes to the construction of social identities and the social world of the conference. The excerpts are taken from an MA course where computer conferencing, together with occasional residential workshops, was the main environment used for discussion and group work.

The excerpts in this case are specifically chosen in an attempt to illustrate why it was that some of the women course participants had said that the ways in which the some of the men communicated (talked) within the conference was both different to their own preferred ways of communicating (talking) and for some women off-putting for them.

Example 2: MA Conference

7:5   Anne   18 April   20:16
It is strange because already I can feel that I am feeling, feeling like an outsider in Orient. Having just started work.

7:6   Anne   18 April   20:19
Sorry, something went wrong, I was trying to say that I am surprized and very concerned as to why I feel this way. I can feel myself pulling against this interpretation so it does not become self-fulfilling.

7:7   Adam   18 April   21:26
Anne, is it possible to say WHY and HOW that has happened? I've been really enjoying your participation here and don't for a moment think of you as some sort of outsider - in fact I think you are participating much more than I've maybe seen you do for a while and that seems really GREAT to me. But maybe somehow you don't feel so great about it?
Adam

> **7:8   Bob   18 April   23:32**
> Anne - I'd like to endorse what Adam says. I felt you were really 'motoring' here in Lotus (sorry about the pun). I too would be interested in your thoughts about why you feel as you do. Does it have any links with your feelings about set formation? (last time).
> Bob
>
>
> **7:9   Jean   19 April   11:41**
> Anne actually said "in orient" (showing my ignorance) is that the name of your new set guess it must be cos she was in Calypso!
> **7:10   Brian   19 April   18:03**
> I'd really like to find out more about what creates the feeling for you, Anne, cos I felt that what's been said about your participation in Lotus could also be said about Orient.
>
>
> **7:11   Anne   23 April   21:18**
> Help, now I've said it I have to think why. I'll think and get back

There are many points that could be made about social identity and social presence in examining this excerpt. One is the way the three men, Adam, Bob and Brian, all ask Anne to explain to them the reasons for having the feelings of that of an outsider which she expresses at the beginning of the excerpt; why does she have them, how has it happened, what are her thoughts, what has created the feelings? Arguably these are very conventional male type responses in that they, in effect, distance their own feelings from the discussion (they simply do not mention them) and focus on those of their women colleague as an 'object' of interest in its own right. By adopting these 'typically' male approaches to the discussion they also by implication act in a way that assumes that they themselves are 'insiders'.

The net effect of these questions upon Anne is, apparently, to silence her. Whilst she makes the comment that she will think and come back, in the event she never responds to the questions put by Adam, Bob and Brian.

In the next example, again beginning with a response from Anne, the pattern of the discussion is somewhat different. In the example Anne is responding to a general question put to the whole course group, by Brian, about the process that the group had adopted at their last residential workshop for forming tutorial sets/groups.

> **Example 3: MA Conference**
> **3:4   Anne   7 April   23:17**
> In answer to your questions Brian, I was surprized that people had given you their set preference over coffee. It felt a bit secretive, particularly when some were confidential. It left me electing to continue the session without all the info. I thought we had decided that you would decide if you were the only one left. As I and several others had decided to continue. I think it left us in a difficult position. Having said that I am happy with the sets and pleased that we all seemed to agree to go along with it. I'll try to explore more if it would help.

3:5   Lynn   8 April   14:41

My only feeling around set formation was surprize, really! Surprize that we actually went with the proposed grouping.

I can understand Anne's reactions as one who elected to stay on and work on set formation, but as one of those that chose not to stay, I'm happy with the result. Yeah, I guess I'm just a bit flabbergasted that your proposal was actually taken up.

3:6   Adam   8 April   15:30

I think I worked on the assumption Brian that I would go along with what you worked out on our behalf. I didn't like the way it worked out cos I didn't think the last "large set" (lilacs) worked very well at all - but because I had said I would accept your decision I really didn't feel I could challenge it.

That's not to say I can't live with the outcome - but I'm not sure that it can work very well (for me that is!!!).

3:7   Jane   16 April   11:59

About the set formation, Brian .... the part I didn't like (and Anne has already mentioned this in 3:4) was the feeling that things were going on during that coffee break that not everyone was aware of: added to this the fact that some of the expressed preferences were then confidential to you. Maybe its naive to think that it could have all been discussed in the large group. Anyway, I also acknowledge the difficulty of the task you ended up with, I didn't envy you having to do it!

3:8   Jean   16 April   13:50

The most striking aspect of set formation this time around for me was giving someone, in this case you Brian, the authority to "do it" didn't make some of the pain associated with set formation any the less, although it might have relocated it a bit!

3:9   Brian   16 April   21:01

Jean, where did you think the pain may have been relocated from to? By the way, thanks for the response to this - I must remember to weave back through it and pick up discussion.

3:10   Jean   18 April   11:02

Not sure I feel able to say Brian, there was it seemed pain around - perhaps others might be prepared to comment for themselves!

3:11   Anne   18 April   20:13

I think I have already expressed that I felt upset about the agreement changing. There is also something strange about the change going unnoticed and a lack of care. Giving you Brian outside of the meeting stopped me from participating. It left my need and offer to continue rejected. To do this seemed acceptable and yet on other occasions, as a group, we have spent a lot of time avoiding, rejecting people and trying to be sensitive. Have we as a group moved on and become more expedient?

Again there are many things upon which we could focus in this example. In terms of typically male or female ways of talking or interacting it can be seen that, as in the previous example, Brian again asks one of the women, Jean, after her comment about the pain associated with set formation having been relocated but no less there, to explain more precisely her comment about where it had been relocated to. The only other man respondent, Adam, restricts himself to answering directly the question put to the group by Brian and makes no reference to the other contributions already made.

Both of these responses are arguably of a different character or type to those made by the women respondents in the excerpt. In each case the women refer, directly or indirectly, to the feelings being expressed by the other respondents and/or by Anne in particular, by such comments as; "I can understand Anne's reaction", "Anne has already mentioned", "there was it seemed pain around", *etc.* The women respondents are arguably 'including' Anne and by doing so a social identity and/or presence for Anne is constructed within the group whereby she is not silenced through feeling she has to explain her feelings from the position of perceived or experienced outsider to the group.

It could be said that the comments made by the women respondents are representative of what has been referred to by some writers as women's preferred ways of talking and/or knowing (Belenky *et al.*, 1986; Coates & Cameron, 1988; Tannen, 1991; van Nostrand, 1993). The women are using what Deborah Tannen has termed 'rapport' talk, or language that is intended to establish rapport and develop intimacy. The men, on the other hand, when asking for rational explanations of feelings expressed by the women, are using what she has termed 'report' talk, that is language that is intended to reinforce autonomy and maintain status.

It thus seemed that in these two excerpts at least the men and the women were adopting typically gendered ways of talking and interacting and it could be argued that by doing so were constructing within the conference similar kinds of social identities for themselves as in 'real' life.

Examination of these two excerpts from the MA program indicate that through the analysis of online 'conversations' or interactions it is possible to see some of the processes by which social relationships/worlds and, in particular, gendered identities are constructed. In some instances it is also possible to see that the processes are reminiscent of those that take place in 'real life' or physical, face to face interactions. The question remains that if this is the case how realistic is it to claim that more democratic or egalitarian communication can be achieved in CMC or online learning environments than in face to face communication or situations.

We have also seen that what is real or what constitutes 'real life' is debatable. The question whether the virtual world offers an alternative culture (place or space) to that of the real world or is simply a cultural artefact and/or an extension of the physical world requires more reflection and examination.

It is thus too soon to be able to assert that CMC/online communication is more or less able to support democratic or constructionist approaches to learning. CMC does, however, offer an opportunity for detailed analysis of the way social relationships and worlds are constructed in online environments which in turn may well offer us new insights and understandings about the processes whereby social identities and presence are constructed in face to face as well as virtual communities.

13.4 References

Asensio, M. & Hodgson, V. (2000) Working Across Boundaries; Issues for European Education, paper presented at 7th Conference of the International Society for the Study of European Ideas (ISSEI) Bergen, Norway

Baym, N. (1995) The Emergence of Community in Computer-Mediated Communication. In Jones, S. (Ed.) *Cybersociety*. Thousand Oaks, USA

Belenky, M.F., Clichy, B.M., Golberger, N.R. & Tarule, J.M. (1986) *Women's Ways of Knowing. The Development of Self, Voice and Mind*. New York

Boot, R. & Hodgson, V.E. (1987) Open Learning, Meaning and Experience, in Hodgson *et al., Beyond Distance Teaching Towards Open Learning*, Milton Keynes : S.H.R.E./Open University Press

Boshier, R. (1990) Socio-Psychological Factors in Electronic Networking. *International Journal of Lifelong Education, 9*(1) pp49-64

Boyd, G.M (1987) Emanciaptive educational technology. *Canadian Journal Of Educational Communication, 16* (2) pp167-172

Brookfield, S. (1993) Breaking the code: engaging practitioners in critical analysis of adult educational literature, *Studies in the Education of Adult, 25* (1) pp64-91

Coates, J & Cameron, D. (1988) *Women and their Speech Communities*. London: Longman

Cherny, L. (1999) *Conversation and Community: Chat in a Virtual World*. USA: CSLI Publications

Derrida, J. (1978) *Writing and Difference*. A. Bass (trans.), London: Routledge & Kegan Paul

Freire, P. (1972) *Pedagogy of the Oppressed*. London: Penguin

Garfinkel, H., Lynch, M. & Livingstone, E. (1981) The Work of Discovering Science Construed with Materials from Optically Discovered Pulsar. *Philosophy of the Social Sciences*, 11, 2 pp131-158

Garrison D.R. (1997) Computer conferencing: the post-industrial age of distance education *Open Learning*, June 1997, pp3-11

Giroux, H (1992*) Border Crossings: Cultural Workers and the Politics of Education*. London: Routledge

Graddol, D. (1989) Some CMC discourse properties and their educational significance. In Mason, R. & Kaye, A. (Eds.) *Mindweave - Communication, Computers and Distance Education*. Oxford: Pergamon Press

Habermas, J (1981) *The theory of communicative action, volume 11*. Boston: Beacon Press

Hiltz, S.R. & Turoff, M. (1978) *The Network Nation: Human communication via computers*. Reading, MA: Addison Wesley

Hine, C. (2000) *Virtual Ethnography* London: Sage Publications

Hodgson, V. & Fox, S. (1995) *Understanding Networked Learning Communities*. Proceedings of Delta 94 Conference, Dusseldorf, Germany

Hodgson, V.E. & McConnell, D. (1994) Online Education and Development in Prior, J. (Ed.) (2nd edition) *Handbook of Training and Development,* Aldershot: Gower

Kirkup, G. & Von Prummer, C (1997) Distance Education for European Women. *The European Journal of Women's Studies 4,* pp39-62

Marvin, L.E. (1995) Spoof, spam, lurk and lag: The aesthetics of text-based virtual realities, *Journal of Computer-Mediated Communication* 1 (2) http://www.usc.edu/dept/annenberg/vol1/issue2/marvin.html

Mezirow, J. (1988) *Transformation* Theory. In *proceedingsof the Adult Education Research Conference.* Calgary, Alberta, pp223-227

Pratt, D.D. & Associates (1998) *Five Perspectives on Teaching in Adult and Higher Education.* Malabar: F.L. Krieger

Reid, E. (1991) *Electropolis: Communication and Community on the Internet Relay Chat.* Honours Thesis, Department of History, University of Melbourne

Reid, E. (1995) Virtual Worlds: Culture and Imagination. In Jones, S. (Ed.) *Cybersociety.* Thousand Oaks, CA

Riel, M. (1995) Cross classroom collaboration in global learning circles. In Starr, S. (Ed.) *The Culture of Computing,* Oxford: Basil Blackwell

Rheingold, H. (1993) *The Virtual Community, Homesteading on the Electronic Frontier.* New York: Addison-Wesley

Rheingold, H. (1995) A Slice of Life in My Virtual Community. In Harasim, L. (Ed) *Global Networks: Computers and International Communication.* Thousand Oaks, CA: Sage Publications

Shotter, J. (1993) *Conversational Realities: Constructing Life through Language.* London: Sage

Spears & Lea (1992) Social influence in CMC. In Lea, M. (Ed.) *Contexts of Computer-Mediated Communication* pp30-65, London: Harvester Wheatsheaf

Sproull, L. & Kiesler, S. (1991a) Computers, networks and work *Scientific American, 265* (3) pp84-91

Sproull, L. & Kiesler, S. (1991b) *Connections: new ways of working in the networked organization.* Cambridge, MA: MIT Press

Stone, A.R. (1992) Will the Real Body Please Stand Up? Boundary Stories about Virtual Cultures. In Benedikt, M. (Ed.) *Cyberspace: First Steps,* Cambridge, MA: MIT Press

Tannen, D. (1991) *You Just Don't Understand: Women and Men in Conversation.* London: Virago Press

Van Nostrand, C.H. (1993) *Gender-Responsible Leadership.* London: Sage Pubications

Yates, S. (1997) Gender, Identity and CMC. *Journal of Computer Assisted Learning, 13*(4) pp281-90

14. Small Group Teaching across the Disciplines: Setting the Context for Networked Learning

Nick Hammond, Annie Trapp and Catherine Bennett

14.1 Introduction

ASTER is a cross-disciplinary project exploring the use of educational technology to support small-group learning and teaching activities in the Physical Sciences, Psychology and disciplines within the Humanities. The main aims of the ASTER project are to identify the different ways in which communications and information technologies (C&IT) can support small group work, identify similarities and differences between the disciplines and examine the case for cross-disciplinary transfer of good practice.

The term small-group teaching is widely used but open to a number of interpretations. We do not consider group size to be the critical defining feature. Rather, we consider small-group teaching as a situation in which students iteratively interact with each other or a tutor and engage in dialog for analysis, reflection or critical thinking for the purpose of achieving a set of learning goals. Generally speaking, members of the group work together to attain shared goals, although individual learning goals will also be important. Collaboration during group learning may be face-to-face or distant, synchronous or asynchronous, and may be discussion-based or focused around shared external tasks or materials.

When surveying the use of C&IT, the project has looked at the different types of usage and their rationales, for example the use of the web or software to provide content for small group activities, the use of discussion and simulation tools to support the learning process, and the use of web and communication tools to facilitate organization of small group activities. We have considered local versus off-campus use, and the timing of the use relative to small-group activity, whether it is used before, during or after, and of course whether usage is a substitute for face-to-face interaction.

14.2 Issues To Be Discussed

The cross-disciplinary perspective of the ASTER project allows us to document differences between subject areas and to triangulate how different pedagogical approaches combine with educational context (such as subject matter, learning objectives and learning tasks) to determine learning outcomes. From this understanding, the project is developing support for students, lecturers and institutions to make the most effective use of C&IT within small-group learning activities. Networked learning (in which learners, with or without tutors, engage in dialog over an electronic network) is one of several modes of small-group learning activity that we are exploring.

In this chapter we discuss the attributes of networked learning within the wider context of small-group learning activities across the disciplines, calling upon evidence from three types of investigation we have conducted within the ASTER Project. The first is a survey of published literature on small-group learning and teaching within each of the three discipline areas on which the project is focusing (ASTER, 1999a); the second involved questionnaire and interview studies of current practice in small-group learning and teaching (ASTER, 1999b); and the third involved a series of case studies of specific educational interventions, again within the chosen discipline areas (ASTER, 2000). In particular, we wish to make the point that network-based activities are often part of a wider range of learning activities, some individual, some face-to-face, some at a distance, which may be beneficial not only in themselves but also to subsequent non-network-based learning.

Networked learning has an established place within educational theory supporting both co-operative learning (Slavin, 1997) and collaborative inquiry and knowledge building (Doise & Mugny, 1984). Crook (1994) suggests the main cognitive benefits of peer collaboration to be articulation, conflict and co-construction. According to Reeves (1999), collaborative learning is one area in which the use of C&IT excels. However, as with any learning method, networked learning must find its appropriate place within the broader context of the learning environment. This context includes the features of a discipline such as its knowledge base and its culture, the dimensions of the learning environment as defined by Laurillard (1993), individual needs of the student, as well as the organizational and political factors that may influence learning and teaching in higher education. Some of the findings from the ASTER project that address these issues are discussed in this chapter.

One goal of the project has been to define a framework to assist lecturers in determining the appropriate use of C&IT within their particular context and set of constraints (ASTER, 2001). For example, in a distance-learning course, networked learning can contribute to the social support for students as well as to the learning process, but networked learning may serve a different role when supporting conventional teaching where the majority of students are on-campus.

Finally, we discuss some of the organizational and political factors which influence the effective integration of innovative methods, including networked learning, into higher education. For instance, placing low value on pedagogic knowledge and scholarship, as well as the traditions of teaching as a private activity, inevitably stifles debate and change (e.g., Boyer, 1990, Glassik *et al.*, 1997).

14.3 The Educational Context of Networked Learning

We conducted surveys of the current use of C&IT to support small-group teaching in the Physical Sciences, in Psychology and in disciplines related to the Humanities (ASTER, 1999a, 1999b). The first survey identified literature giving examples of C&IT use in small-group teaching, whilst the second survey consisted of a questionnaire sent to lecturers using C&IT to support small-group teaching, followed up by semi-structured interviews with 41 lecturers drawn from the three discipline areas covered by ASTER. Taken together, the surveys showed that C&IT is widely used as a means of providing course information and source material, as an analysis tool and to some degree, at least within Psychology and the Humanities, to support discussion and collaborative working around shared resources or activities.

Where network-based collaborative activity was reported, it tended to be focused on electronic resources or exercizes rather than purely in support of discussion. This pattern is also reflected in the subsequent case studies conducted by the project (ASTER Project, 2000; Bennett *et al.*, 2000). Of 14 case studies involving C&IT support for collaborative activity, four provided support only for discussion, whilst the remaining ten provided support for collaboration over shared resources or exercizes.

The surveys sought to identify the educational rationale for introducing C&IT into small-group teaching. A clear difference in the forms of rationale given was evident when the literature survey and lecturer survey were compared. In the literature survey, reasons for many of the C&IT interventions reported in publications were stated in educational terms, often with some reference to underlying theoretical work. In the lecturer survey, most respondents initially defined their rationale for introducing C&IT pragmatically: addressing class size, providing improved resources, facilitating discussion. In most cases, some prompting was required by the interviewers to get respondents to focus on the type of activities that students were engaging in, on the intended educational goals and in particular on an underlying educational rationale for the approach adopted. Where discussion was the main activity, the educational goals tended towards enhancing knowledge, collaborative learning and deeper understanding. For activities that centered on data analysis, retrieval and handling, the educational goals were more concerned with transfer of information, transferable skills and enhancing knowledge. Team working was only mentioned as a specific educational goal in one instance although this was mentioned as a spin-off in a few cases. Only one respondent claimed that their methods were driven by a particular theory of learning. However it was clear that small-group teaching was considered by most interviewees to be 'a good thing' either from a pedagogical, organizational or transferable skill perspective. Table14.1 summarizes the main reasons given for introducing C&IT support for small-group activities.

Table 14.1 Reasons for introducing C&IT support into small-group activities

Pedagogy
Social constructivist models; improve learning; collaboration; motivation
Organizational
Diversity of students and delivery methods; handling large numbers; need to maintain quality and human contact
Transferable skills
Critical thinking; information access and evaluation; communication skills; understand scientific method; teamwork skills; ethical behaviour; social awareness; integration of knowledge

This difference in emphasis between those that publish on learning technology use and those that practise it is not perhaps surprising, but is important to bear in mind for those wishing to bring about change. The pragmatic reasons for innovating may often be overlooked when discussing educational processes; and, conversely, the immediate demands and constraints on the practitioner may inhibit reflection about pedagogic rationale. This split may be particularly relevant for the introduction of networked learning, both because there may be strong pragmatic pressures to innovate (such as the need to expand courses for remote learners, or institutional pressures) while the educational issues need careful consideration for optimal use of the technology.

14.4   The Discipline Context

Evidence from the surveys suggests a variety in the nature and purposes of small-group teaching and learning across the three discipline areas studied. The most striking difference was between the Physical Sciences and the other discipline areas in the use of C&IT to facilitate dialog. There were no instances reported within our survey of Physical Sciences where the principal use of C&IT was to facilitate discussion. This is in striking contrast to both Psychology and the areas related to the Humanities where such practice was frequently mentioned. In areas associated with Physics, small-group teaching appears to focus on providing students with practical tasks to develop their understanding and analytic skills or on helping with problems and exercizes.

These findings are supported by the subsequent case studies, where the focus of C&IT usage reported in the Physical Science case studies was on the use of simulations and exercizes (occasionally as a collaborative activity) rather than on facilitating dialog. An explanation given by lecturers for the lower usage of discussion within Physics teaching and learning is that the learning aims of deeper understanding and knowledge enhancement are best achieved through the use of computer-based self-study driven by worksheets. However, we would question whether this view is pedagogically justifiable or largely a traditional view widely-held within the UK community of lecturers in Physical Sciences. There are counter-examples. In the US, Novak and colleagues (Novak, Patterson & Gavrin, 1999) have developed a method they term *just-in-time teaching* (or JITT)[1] aimed at integrating individual web-based study of Physics with dialog-based active learning in the classroom. This method has been successfully applied across a range of courses in the Physical Sciences, emphasizing that role that dialog can play in these discipline areas in conjunction with focused self-study and exercizes. The method is applicable in other discipline areas too.

We also noted some differences between the Psychology and Humanities case studies. For instance, there was higher usage within Psychology of discussion environments (virtual learning environments), and more usage within the Humanities of face-to-face discussion based around electronic resources.

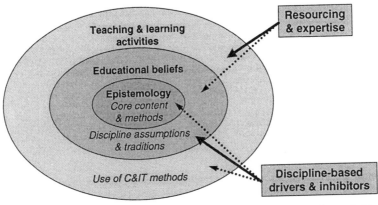

Figure 14.1 Framework for discipline influences on teaching and learning activities

There are probably a number of reasons for these discipline differences in the teaching and learning methods used and the ways in which C&IT is deployed. Figure 14.1 presents a summary of factors likely to be relevant. As indicated by the central ellipse in Figure 14.1, the nature of the core content of the discipline will be important: this includes the conceptual structures and the representational notations used to express concepts and their relationships. Related to this are the forms of discourse and activities deployed within teaching and learning activities, such as text language and notations used in text-books or lectures. The epistemology of the discipline will bring particular constraints. For example, when solving problems in the physical sciences the correct solution path is often well-defined, and more broadly there may be a strong consensus on the 'best way' to conceptualize and understand a given topic area. Learning outcomes may be defined in terms of understanding the correct procedures and processes involved in

---

[1]   Information on the JITT method is at http://webphysics.iupui.edu/jitt/jitt.html

reaching the right answers to a set of problems. In this context, the role for reflection and student-centered definition of the learning path may be quite limited. In the arts and humanities, the student is expected to develop skills for critical analysis of materials, and learning outcomes are more closely related to argumentation skills.

Other differences between discipline areas may lie within the traditions and culture of teaching a particular subject, the beliefs about learning held by students and the contextual factors within an institution and department (this is represented by the middle ellipse in Figure 14.1). Various external factors will also impact the take-up of particular methods: available resources and expertize may well impact teaching and learning activities directly, whereas external pressures on the discipline (such as professional accreditation requirements or research developments) are likely to influence teaching and learning methods through their impact on the curriculum and espoused educational beliefs.

To summarize, the evidence from our survey and case studies supports the view that a range of factors contribute to discipline differences in the use of C&IT to support small-group learning and teaching. Epistemological differences between curricula as well as traditions in teaching and learning methods are influential. Collaborative networked learning is unlikely to be perceived as relevant in those disciplines where little store is put by learning through dialog.

14.5   Characterizing the Impact of Networked Learning

We have structured our case studies around four classes of outcome that a C&IT intervention in teaching or learning might have: on teaching processes and methods of delivery, on the learning process and associated activities, on the learning outcomes and finally on the management of the module or course within the context of the department or institution. In addition, we have prepared a broader educational framework which aims to provide practitioners with an understanding of the questions and issues raised in small-group teaching when using electronic resources and the opportunity to reflect on those issues prior to course development (ASTER, 2001).

Within our case studies we can find examples of networked learning impacting all four of these outcomes: teaching process, learning process, learning outcomes and course management. We can take an example of a Psychology case study on "the use of web pages and WebCT to preserve small-group work in seminars". In this Organizational Psychology course, increasing student numbers had made seminar discussions hard to manage, and the tutor wanted to introduce activity-based seminars with maximum participation by the students. To support this, she used the virtual learning environment WebCT to host the course. Course notes were uploaded into WebCT for the students to access before the class, enabling the face-to-face contact hours to be used more effectively for focused discussion and group work. During the contact time, a short introduction by the lecturer was followed by group activities. Material produced by the students during their group work was also uploaded into WebCT. The electronic communication facilities within WebCT were used to hold class discussions outside the normal contact time.

The intervention influenced the teaching process substantially: considerable effort was required to prepare materials for the WebCT environment and discussions needed to be seeded and moderated. The skills to achieve these tasks successfully may not be possessed by many lecturers. Likewise, the impact on learning processes was substantial, with an increased emphasis on student-centered learning and on group-based activities. This is likely to have promoted reflection and critical thinking, but the changes were not universally popular with students, one commenting, "we did all the work!" There was also likely to have been an impact on learning outcomes (for example resulting from a greater emphasis on discussion of case materials), although outcomes were not specifically measured. Finally, the networked environment substantially changed the management of the course, allowing, for example, better tracking of student participation, better organization of course materials and targeted feedback to individual students.

More generally on distance learning courses, networked learning provides an alternative mode of course delivery, it can facilitate discussion and interactive activities that would not be possible otherwise and it can provide a timely way of delivering and marking course material. But networked learning is also increasingly being used to support conventional courses that take place on-campus. Virtual learning environments allow lecturers to put course content and guidance notes online, use online assessment and to provide novel forms of discussion-based activity not possible in a face-to-face situation. The tools provided with this type of software may therefore be used to support different activities and fulfil a different purpose than their intended one on distance learning courses. For example, it is difficult to get students who meet on campus to spend time talking remotely on online discussion boards. A more effective use of a virtual learning environment may be to put individual activity questions online so that students can answer these individually and their answers can then form the basis for group discussions during face-to-face seminars. The lecturer is using the environment to shift face-to-face sessions towards a more student-led, problem-based style of learning.

Such a shift may not, however, be beneficial to all students. For example, student dissatisfaction was reported on one course using WebCT. The course had a student intake of mixed academic ability, and students said they wanted more face-to-face teaching rather than having their lectures replaced by material on WebCT. Student evaluations from other courses using virtual learning environments in different departments were more positive. Understanding these different reactions to C&IT tools in different contexts will help lecturers to make an informed choice about the appropriate use of a C&IT intervention.

Our point is that lecturers need a framework, illustrated by a variety of examples, that provides insight into how networked learning can support different situations and an understanding of the factors that may influence its success.

Within the ASTER project we are attempting to provide this not only through our educational framework document, but by providing a web-based question interface by means of which lecturers can be led from a questions about teaching to further sub-questions, a summary of accepted practice (with bibliographic references where appropriate) and concrete examples from our case studies.

14.6 The Organizational Context

In an earlier section of this paper we stated that, in conversation, lecturers tended to use pragmatic reasons for introducing C&IT. Even when pushed, many lecturers tended to be reluctant to discuss how an intervention may support the learning process or be underpinned by pedagogic principles. This reluctance may be because lecturers lack the pedagogical knowledge or there may be a more implicit reason to do with the HE culture of teaching as 'a private activity'. As Bass (1999) describes, a problem in research is one to be shared and discussed but a problem in teaching can be regarded as an accusation or weakness.

Whatever the underlying reason, lecturers are unused to talking about their teaching and lack the language to describe the nature of their methods. This itself is an indication of the low status afforded to the practice and profession of teaching within UK Higher Education. Funding has driven lecturers to put their research before their teaching, and excellence in teaching has brought few rewards afforded to other forms of scholarly activity. Back in 1990, Boyer contended that we must move beyond the 'teaching versus research' debate and use the term 'scholarship' to include four distinct but interrelated dimensions: discovery (research), integration (texts and reviews), application (professional service) and teaching. Similarly, Shulman (1993) and others argue that teaching is not just technique but an enactment of our understanding of our disciplinary, interdisciplinary or professional field and what it means to know it deeply.

In reality, lecturers in higher education are poorly trained in appropriate teaching methods and lack the time to reflect on whether their methods were successful (Glassick *et al.*, 1997). A similar view is expressed by Laurillard (1993): "teachers need to know more than just their subject. They need to know the ways it can come to be understood, the ways it can be misunderstood, what counts as understanding: they need to know how individuals experience the subject. But they are neither required nor enabled to know these things".

In order for lecturers to engage in the pedagogy of their discipline there must be a shift both in University and discipline cultures. In some respects, this has started to happen. National UK policy and initiatives, such as subject-based appraisals of teaching quality, the setting up of the Institute for Learning and Teaching in Higher Education and funding initiatives for teaching developments, both reflect the changing culture and provide frameworks and routes for change. The increasing importance of lifelong learning, and initiatives in the UK such as the University for Industry and the e-University place networked learning as a key method within these changes. There must be appropriate mechanisms to encourage innovation, debate and research both within and across disciplines to allow networked learning to find its appropriate level of use within Higher Education.

14.7 Acknowledgements

The ASTER Project is supported under phase 3 of the Teaching and Learning Technology Program (TLTP) funded by the UK HE Funding Councils (HEFCE and DENI). The following members of the ASTER Project team contributed to the work reported here: Dick Bacon, Lena Tostevin and Lee Sproats (University of Surrey); Frances Condron and Stuart Lee (University of Oxford); Sylvia Hogarth (University of York); Chris Colbourn and Ann Jelfs (University College Northampton).

14.8 References

ASTER (1999a) *Report: Online bibliography.* Available from http://cti-psy.york.ac.uk/aster/

ASTER (1999b) *Report: A survey of current practice in the use of C&IT to support small-group teaching activities in disciplines associated with the Humanities, Physics and Psychology.* Available from http://cti-psy.york.ac.uk/aster/

ASTER (2000) *Report: Investigating the use of electronic Resources in small-group learning and teaching.* Available from http://cti-psy.york.ac.uk/aster/

ASTER (2001) *Educational Framework for Reflecting on the use of Electronic Resources.* Available from http://cti-psy.york.ac.uk/aster/

Bass, R. (1999) The Scholarship of Teaching: What's the problem? *Inventio, February, 1*(1)

Bennett, C., Hammond, N., Trapp, A., Condron, F. & Tostevin, M.H. (2000) ASTER: *Examining Networked Collaborative Learning in Small-group Teaching in UK Higher Education.* Paper presented at ECER 2000, University of Edinburgh, September

Boyer, E. (1990) *Scholarship Reconsidered: Priorities of the Professoriate.* Princeton, NJ: The Carnegie Foundation for the Advancement of Teaching

Crook, C. (1994) *Computers and the Collaborative Experience.* London: Routledge

Doise, W. & Mugny, G. (1984) *The social development of the intellect.* Toronto: Pergamon

Glassick, C., Huber, M. & Maeroff, G. (1997) *Scholarship Assessed: Evaluation of the Professoriate.* San Francisco: Jossey-Bass

Novak, G., Patterson, E.T. & Gavrin, A.D. (1999) *Just-in-time teaching: blending active learning with Web technology.* New Jersey: Prentice Hall

Laurillard, D. (1993) Rethinking University Teaching: *A framework for the effective use of educational technology.* London: Routledge

Reeves, T. (1999) A research agenda for interactive learning in the new millennium. In *Proceedings of Ed-MEDIA 99* AACE

Shulman, L. (1993) Teaching as Community Property: putting an end to pedagogical solitude. *Change 25* (6) pp6-7

Slavin, R. E. (1997) *Research on co-operative learning and achievement: a quarter century of research.* Paper presented at the Annual Meeting of Pedagogical Psychology, Frankfurt, September

15. Designs for Networked Learning in Higher Education: A Phenomenographic Investigation of Practitioners' Accounts of Design

Chris Jones and Mireia Asensio

15.1 Introduction

Academics in higher education are coming under increasing pressure, which includes pressure to adapt their teaching practices to accommodate networked learning technologies. In order to incorporate networked learning into teaching and learning in higher education, there has been a search for what may be described as 'good' practice. There has also been discussion of what has been called a new paradigm, a convergence between different modes of teaching and learning enabled by networked technologies. In the search for 'good' pedagogic practice in networked learning there is a need to examine in depth the current practices of educators designing networked learning activities, courses or programs. In particular we need to understand the design process itself and the assumptions about the nature of learning and the learning process that are often implicit in design decisions.

Drawing from a range of academic literature addressing issues of design and particularly design for learning in mainstream higher education, this chapter explores the educational paradigms and learning theories that have been applied to the design of networked learning. This theoretical perspective is examined in relation to the empirical findings from recent phenomenographic research we have conducted into practitioners' design practices. This research is based on interviews with ten practitioners actively involved in the design of networked learning in higher education. The phenomenographic approach is assessed in relation to criticism of its reliance on the unstructured interview and a constructionist revision of phenomenography. We argue that phenomenographic research can adapt to its critics and provide a suitable approach for the investigation of practitioners' design practices.

Preliminary findings indicate that there is a common acceptance of the notion of design for networked learning. There is also evidence of a widespread acceptance of features of what has been called the new paradigm in teaching and learning, a commonality in the educational philosophy and conceptualizations of learning that underpin design. There are clear variations in practitioners' descriptions of the structure and implementation of their designs. This may represent significant differences in the way the process of learning is understood by the practitioners even though they adopt a common language of design.

All the practitioners sought to enhance the design of their networked learning activities, however their motivations varied. Some enhancements aimed to broaden the scope of networked learning itself, innovating with radical new proposals, whereas others attempted to modify existing practice. Refining existing practice was related to concerns that the outcomes of designs often failed to reach the expectations embedded in prior planning. These complementary processes of innovation and refinement represented a design process that is both evolutionary and iterative. In this fluid environment it may prove difficult and challenging to determine what is good practice or good design for networked learning.

15.2   The Nature of Design

The nature of our inquiry into design is not to provide a comprehensive review of ideas about design and practical design procedures or models. Our intention is to understand and situate the practitioners' accounts of design that we have collected in our own research. It is also to sensitize ourselves to the application of the notion of design in education and in particular with the use of new technology. In particular we are curious to know if there is a coherent shared view that might be described in terms of 'good' practice in networked learning and whether that view is indeed a new paradigm.

We do not have to look far to see examples of design. All the things on our desk: the computer, lamp, pens and paper pads have been the original idea and creative efforts of an individual or a group. Design is so embedded in our everyday life that we often tend to overlook it. The Collins English Dictionary (1994) defines design as:

> "...an end aimed at or planned for intention, purpose/a plan, sketch, or preliminary drawing."

We have learned to discriminate a 'good' design from a 'bad' design, this often means that we look at design as an end result and as an outcome of some kind. However the concept of design also involves having an idea, purpose or intention and suggests preparation and planning. This may mean either modifying what is there at present, or introducing something quite new into the situation. Thus understanding design simply as an end product or outcome does not fully capture the intricacy of designing. Any outcome implies that there has been a set of sequential or iterative stages from the original idea, and this is often referred to as the design process, which is intrinsic to every design.

However, in trying to define design and the design process we find that in different contexts this can represent such varied activities and end products that the meaning of design is unclear. Interestingly Cooley (1999) remarks that the notion of design, as we know it today, arose during the fourteenth and fifteenth centuries in Europe and implied the separation of thinking and doing, as he puts it:

"This is not to suggest for a moment that designing was a new activity. Rather it was separated out from a wider productive activity and recognized as an activity in its own right. Design can be said to constitute a separation of hand and brain, of manual and intellectual work, of the conceptual part of a work from the labour process." (1999:59)

Cooley (1999) argues that the Western view of science and the scientific method has highly influenced the predominant characteristics that a process or design must display to be regarded as scientific namely:

"...predictability, repeatability, and mathematical quantifiability. This, is by definition, precludes intuition, subjective judgement, tacit knowledge, dreams, imagination, and purpose." (1999:60)

However ethnographic studies of the design process demonstrate that these characteristics can be challenged (Suchman, 1987; Hughes et al., 1992; Randall et al., 1994). Design in this view is a situated action and cannot have the characteristics outlined for the scientific method. Rather than the formal scientific approach ethnographic studies suggest that design is an iterative process and that the products of design are not outcomes of the design itself but of a deeply social and situated set of work practices. Design in this sense does not have a determining role but is a resource, which informs the working practices of those involved in the design process.

In addition traditional models of design have overlooked the involvement of the designer in the practice of design which inevitably involves subjective value judgements (Lawson, 1980). Whiteley (1993) refers to designs as cultural products that have meanings encoded within them which are decoded by producers, advertizers and consumers according to their own cultural codes.

In relating this to design for learning we have to be aware that the outcome is not a static artefact like a house or a car, but it is itself a learning *process*. In the case of learning not only is design a social process but so is the object of design. In the next section we look at design in the educational context and examine it in the light of the issues concerning design and design process that we have discussed here.

15.3   Design for Learning

The practice of design and design for learning generally involves making a large number of decisions (Boot & Reynolds, 1984). These decisions may be guided by assumptions on the nature of knowledge and learning. In this process some decisions are made on the basis of what is 'best' and most 'effective' for the students' learning experience. As Reynolds (1997) states designing is more than a simple selection from a reservoir of methods and contents believed appropriate for achieving intended purposes. It is also concerned with the beliefs and values held by designers. Designer's values and beliefs about knowledge and learning, which have been formulated through their own experiences, can have a direct influence on decision-making (Boot & Reynolds, 1984).

Toohey (1999) in the mainstream of design for learning in HE refers to the importance of 'mindfulness' in course design.

"This is characterized by willingness to reconceptualize what we are doing, openness' to different perspectives and clarity about what we hope to achieve." (1999:2)

Toohey's (1999) claim for 'openness' and 'clarity' is relevant to the planning and decision making of design for learning. However we still do not know what comprises 'good' design. Lawson (1980) argues that because the design process is iterative and not an end-for-all process, the designer's job is never really done and he or she can always try to improve the design. In fact the end-point of this process is a matter of the designer's judgements. Therefore there can not be an infallibly 'good' design, and there is no logical sequence of operations which will guarantee a specified result.

In conclusion we can speculate that design for learning requires the ability to be 'critically reflective' about practice (Burgoyne & Reynolds, 1997). The critical aspect encourages practitioners to be aware of the larger social processes, assumptions and hidden issues that are part of any design for learning activity. The reflective aspect encourages practitioners to question and revise their practice, including the working theories that underpin their design and may not match with their expectations or outcomes.

Within this context the importance of being a critically reflective practitioner becomes clear.   As Burgoyne and Reynolds argue the critically reflective practitioners play an important role as:

"...they are aware that with every practical action they take they are 'fixing (temporally) their belief' and acting on their current best working theory, but they realize that this may also be open to challenge and improvement." (Burgoyne & Reynolds, 1997:2)

Thus though there is not a recipe for 'good' design, the situation may not be as hopeless as it may seem as critical reflection may offer an approach to design.

In sum, the reviewed literature above indicates that the search for 'good' design may entail clarity about the intentions and assumptions that inform the design process. In so far as design is an iterative approach informed by educational philosophies and learning theories these sometimes tacit and assumed resources require examination. In the next section we look at these assumptions in terms of a new paradigm within the context of design for networked learning.

15.4   Design for Networked Learning

The idea of a new paradigm in education has developed alongside the introduction of new technologies.   Harasim (1989) has claimed that to appreciate the educational options of 'online education', we need to consider this medium as being distinctive from both face to face and conventional distance learning. Robin Mason has elaborated a convergence hypothesis (Mason, 1989).   The convergence hypothesis argued that the distinctions between distance and mainstream education are blurring. These distinctions were identified as applying to both the methods used in education and the clientele addressed. The teaching and learning systems of place based institutions were said to be increasingly coming to resemble those used in distance education. The students in place based centers were also becoming older and more often working students.   The convergence thesis has been further developed by Mason and Kaye into what they call a "New Paradigm" for distance education (1990).

In a more recent consideration of the idea of a new paradigm Tim Koschmann places the idea in the context of a research program in the use of instructional technologies (Koschmann, 1996). Koschmann identifies an 'emerging paradigm', which he calls CSCL. This emerging set of research questions is contrasted with previous outlooks, CAI (Computer Assisted Instruction), ITS (Intelligent Tutoring Systems) and the 'Logo-as-Latin' paradigm associated with Papert's seminal text 'Mindstorms'.   The research conducted in the CSCL paradigm is related by Koschmann to socially oriented constructivist viewpoints, Soviet sociocultural theories and theories of situated cognition. Likening this shift to a gestalt shift in view, he claims that the new paradigm draws attention to the social and cultural context of education as the object for research.

This idea of an emerging paradigm echoes the positions of Mason and Kaye (1990) and also Linda Harasim who has described networked learning as a new educational paradigm for the twenty-first century (Harasim et al., 1995). Though undoubtedly networked learning opens up opportunities for multiple interactions and breaks down barriers such as location and time, there is an interesting underlying (and often unconscious) sense that the technology is the driver of this educational change.

An important literature on design for learning and in particular in relation to the use of technologies is the field of Instructional Design (ID).   The idea of instructional design was and still is, to create a discipline that is concerned with understanding and improving the process of instruction or teaching and to prescribe 'effective' methods of instruction that would induce desired changes in student knowledge and skills (Reigeluth, 1999). Instructional design theories are explicitly design oriented and offer guidelines on what methods might best lead to particular outcomes (Reigeluth, 1999). Instructional design has responded to the emergence of the new paradigm by a revision of instructional design theory. Advocates of ID have tried to engage with the new theories that are identified with the new paradigm whilst still retaining a strong sense of design (Wilson, 1997; Dills & Romiszowski, 1997). The purpose of ID has been to articulate, manage, and systematize the processes involved in designing effective learning environments (Lin *et al.*, 1995). Eastmond and Ziegahn (1995) believe that:

> "...successful course design offers objectives, resources, strategies, timelines, products, and assessment elements that can be flexibly negotiated between faculty and students. However, conventional instructional systems design approaches provide valuable heuristic (rules of thumb) for CMC course designers and should be referred to during the instructional development process." (1995:61)

Thus they argue that the ID model addresses important phases in the creation of a CMC course. Eastmond and Ziegahn claim that the sequential steps in ID's models are a useful system for thinking and planning all the elements that are involved in design.

The emergence of what has been called a new paradigm and its absorption by the Instructional Design tradition brings our attention to those elements that might be available to inform designs for networked learning. These are:

1. Socially oriented theories of learning. (e.g. constructivism, constructionism, situated learning).
2. Communities of Practice/ learning communities.
3. Collaborative learning.

We will examine each of these aspects of the new paradigm in more detail below.

15.4.1 Socially Oriented Theories of Learning

For clarity we concentrate on the much-referenced account of situated learning by Brown, Collins and Duguid (1989) that has had particular importance for computer supported collaborative learning. The idea of situation they propose is summed up in the contrast between 'know what' and 'know how'. Situations are described as co-producing knowledge through activity. The breach between know how and know what is said to be internalized within educational practice in a separation between knowing and doing. Brown *et al.* argue that situations co-produce knowledge so that educational practice would be improved by taking into account the situated nature of learning.

In this account the idea of situation is a means to distinguish authentic from inauthentic settings. Thus, in their paper the position is made clear at the outset:

> "...many methods of didactic education assume a separation between knowing and doing, treating knowledge as an integral, self-sufficient substance, theoretically independent of the situations in which it is learned and used." (Brown *et al.*, 1989:32)

They argue that the primary reason for learning failure is to do with the abstract approach to cognition taken in schooling. They go on to advocate a variety of apprenticeship, whereby learning takes place in a 'real world' context, as more appropriate and effective metaphor. This use of apprenticeship is closely related to the idea that authenticity in learning varies according to how situated the learning is. It is the real world nature of apprenticeship that ensures authenticity.

15.4.2 Communities of Practice/Learning Communities

The re-conceptualized educational practice advanced in the work of Brown *et al.* is a variety of cognitive apprenticeship, an approach that is also to be found in the works of Lave, Wenger and Rogoff (Lave & Wenger, 1991; Rogoff, 1990; Wenger, 1998).

The account they give of cognitive apprenticeship rests upon a distinction between authentic activity, "simply defined as the ordinary practices of the culture" and school activity (Brown *et al.*, 1989:34). Cognitive apprenticeships try to enculture students in 'authentic practices' through activity and social interaction. Authentic practices are ordinary practices as opposed to the 'ersatz' activity found in a school. In a powerful analogy Brown and Duguid (1996) liken learning to theft. The presence of a full context allows the students to 'steal' whatever they find appropriate.

> "Cars are socially so well integrated that the learning becomes almost invisible. The success of learner drivers – with or without instruction – should undoubtedly be the envy and object of many who design far less complex consumer or workplace appliances." (Brown & Duguid, 1996:51)

The use of the idea of 'stolen' knowledge highlights the implicit elements of practice. Brown and Duguid emphasize that a great deal of what comprises a web of practice cannot be made explicit.

Elsewhere Brown and Duguid suggest that:

> "...rather than deciding ahead of time what a learner needs to know and making this explicitly available to the exclusion of everything else, designers and instructors need to make available as much as possible of the whole rich web of practice – explicit and implicit, allowing the learner

to call upon aspects of practice, latent on the periphery, as they are needed." (1989:54)

The idea of learning as apprenticeship and knowledge as learned by peripheral participation, articulated above, has clear implications for design. In particular it would involve less concentration on explicit knowledge and more focus on the engagement of learners in activities that might enable them to draw on implicit as well as explicit elements of authentic practices.

15.4.3 Collaborative Learning

Computer conferencing is an environment that has been identified as inclined towards collaborative use. Collaboration between students and between educators and students would allow for the peripheral participation envisaged as enabling situated learning. Robin Mason cites 'collaborative discussions and peer activities' as features that the 'medium facilitates' and goes on to enumerate a variety of 'social' features that depend upon working together (Mason, 1994). The technology of computer conferencing appears with advantages and disadvantages that rely on the capacity of the conference to 'facilitate' students and staff working together. Collaboration in itself is seen as the unproblematic outcome of the use of the computer conference.

The discussion of the technology merges seamlessly with the discussion of learning methods and the technology is taken to imply in particular a co-operative or collaborative approach. Hiltz and Benbunan-Fich note the confusion of the technology with a particular learning style:

"Most studies have confounded the use of computer-mediated communication as a mode of course delivery, with the use of collaborative learning as a pedagogical technique." (Hiltz & Benbunan-Fich, 1997:3)

Despite their awareness of this confusion the article still linked aspects of the technology directly with teaching and learning style:

"The asynchronous nature of the interaction leads to new paradigms for teaching and learning, with both unique problems of co-ordination and unique opportunities to support active, collaborative (group or team-based) learning. Collaborative learning appears to be crucial to the effectiveness of online learning environments." (Hiltz & Benbunan-Fich, 1997:1)

In this view computer conferencing has features that both enable the use of collaboration and require co-operation as a guarantee of effectiveness.

The association of collaborative learning with computer conferencing and networked learning more generally can be found in a wide range of literature.

Collaboration can be viewed as an outcome of the technology or as a consequence of the technology and its associated educational methods. In either case good design either of the technology itself or of the pedagogic environment, is the key to successful learning.

This brief elaboration of possible assumptions entailed in the adoption of the new paradigm sets an agenda for our analysis of practitioners' accounts. One of the features we will be attentive to is whether the practitioners give accounts in terms of the new paradigm and the assumptions associated with it. We are also interested in how the different assumptions are deployed for design purposes.

15.5   Methodology

The research was informed by a phenomenographic approach. Ference Marton explained phenomenography as a research approach for understanding people's ways of experiencing the world. He defined the approach as:

> "...the empirical study of the differing ways in which people experience, perceive, apprehend, understand, or conceptualize various phenomena in, and aspects of, the world around them." (Marton, 1994:4424)

The aim of phenomenography is to describe the limited number of qualitatively different ways of experiencing phenomena. The objective in our case is to illuminate the variations in the ways that practitioners experience the process of design for networked learning (Marton & Booth, 1997; Laurillard, 1993). This chapter reports the analysis of interview data in terms of the emergent topic of design. The search is for the limited number of ways in which design is understood.

The dominant method for collecting phenomenographic data has been the individual interview. The interview can be complemented by a variety of other methods including observation, stimulated recall and documentary analysis. In the research for this chapter data was collected from one main source, the individual interview. The emphasis in the conduct of the interviews was in stimulating the practitioners' reflection upon their experience. This conforms to Marton's view that the phenomenographic interview provokes a change from unreflected to reflected awareness (Marton, 1994).

The interviewees were all active practitioners and ranged from experts who have used a variety of systems for a long period of time to early adopters who had begun to use networked learning over recent years. This initial report of results relies on ten interviews with practitioners from eight departments in five universities. The interviews were approximately one hour in duration and focused on the practitioners' use of networked learning technology to deliver a particular course. The interviewees all made use of text based systems provided over the internet ranging from individual use of e-mail in one particular case to a variety of conferencing systems. All were available using web access, either primarily or as a supplement to a client server system, and some had web resources that were distinct from the conferencing system itself.

The interviews were largely unstructured though the interviewers had a loose schedule or format that provided some consistency between interviews and acted as a prompt to indicate key areas of interest. The interviews were conducted as a dialog and each interview began with a request for the practitioner to explain a course that they had taught using networked learning. The interviewer tried to intervene as little as possible and concentrated on asking questions that were intended to provoke reflection by the respondent on their own experience.

The interviews were transcribed verbatim from audio recordings. The transcriptions were then analyzed in order to develop categories that identified similarities and differences in the interviewees' experiences and understandings of design. The interviews have been examined for variations in the experiences of the practitioners and to try and identify emergent elements that might be common between them. The analysis focused on both variation and the possibility of a limited number of types of variation being present. The transcripts have been analyzed from the point of view of the phenomena *i.e.*, design, rather than the individual. Indeed it was expected that individual accounts would vary internally and that each transcribed interview might provide variations within itself as well as variation between different interviews.

15.5.1 Phenomenography and Design

Reynolds (1997) when commenting on phenomenographic research in relation to a critique of learning styles, noted that it emphasized 'context', the conditions in which people learn, as a major factor in the choice of a learning approach. This suggests that learning environments could be varied or designed so that they minimize the conditions that encouraging a superficial approach and maximize the conditions that encourage a deep approach to learning. In relation to the connection between teachers' and learners' approaches Prosser and Trigwell comment that:

> "The relation between teachers' experiences and their students' experiences is such that university teachers who adopt a conceptual change/ student-focused approach to teaching are more likely to teach students who adopt a deep approach to their learning, while teachers who adopt an information transmission/ teacher-focused approach to their teaching are more likely to teach students who adopt surface approaches to their study." (Prosser & Trigwell, 1999:162)

This suggests that the phenomenographic emphasis on variation could have implications for the design of learning environments. If the 'context', however that is understood, is a major factor in the choice of learning approach and the approach adopted by the teacher is another key variant then it should be possible for phenomenographic analysis to provide useful information to inform the design of networked learning. An explicit attempt to bring research influenced by phenomenography to bear on the design of learning has previously been made by Entwistle *et al.* (1993).

In our case we are not advocating the use of phenomenographic research as the basis of good design. Though we would note that in the field of CSCW the use of ethnographic studies of work to illuminate design has a long history (see for example Hughes *et al.*, 1992; Randall *et al.*, 1994). The use of ethnographic studies has not been unproblematic and the question has been asked; what are workplace studies for? (Plowman *et al.*, 1995). An answer to this question has been offered by John Bowers who suggests that ethnography can offer up 'design images' (Bowers & Martin, 1999). We would suggest that phenomenographic accounts of practitioners' approaches to design can similarly illuminate the design process in education. Our particular concern is in the description of variations in the way practitioners approach design. We believe it is by no means clear what a practitioner might mean when they provide an account of their experiences in terms of design. We hope that by phenomenographic analysis of the variations in practitioners' accounts we can help clarify the variety of ways design is understood.

15.6   Criticisms of Phenomenography

Our aim is to describe the variations we found in practitioners' accounts of their experiences. In so far as we look at developments in phenomenography we are concerned with criticisms of the use of the interview (Fleming, 1986) and a recent review and critical development of phenomenography written by John Richardson (1999).

Phenomenographic research has been criticized from an ethnomethodological perspective for its reliance upon the interview (Fleming, 1986). Fleming gives an example of 'versions' – that is, of an individual giving a series of accounts of one event to a variety of audiences. Each account is different each is fitted to its particular purpose and might appear to be out of place in another setting. The point being that all accounts are partial, that they point towards something but cannot contain all the information required for a complete description of that which is described. So in the example chosen by Fleming an account given by a student to his mother of the day's events would not be replaceable by the account given to his tutor of the same day's events. The accounts may both be truthful and accurate in the context of their use. This raises the question of the status of the interview and the reliance we have placed upon it in this research and in phenomenography more generally.

A recent critical review of phenomenography offers a 'constructionist' revision of traditional phenomenographic approaches (Richardson, 1999). Richardson argues that conceptions of reality are discursive practices, which may be used as resources in particular communicative encounters, rather than psychological entities that reside in the minds of individuals (1999:72). Richardson argues for more attention to be paid to accounts given by participants in real-life situations.

We would agree with this point but would argue further that viewing interviews as situational and paying attention to the context in which the interview was given will help to deal with Fleming's criticism of interview based data.

Unlike much phenomenographic research we adopt a sceptical stance towards statements made by interviewees, accepting that the accounts given are indeed versions fit for the purpose of the interview. We will point to some ways in which we believe the contextual nature of the interview has affected the research we have conducted. Nonetheless we believe that the accounts given by practitioners, examined in the ways we have outlined, can provide us with some valuable insights. In particular we believe interviews can be treated as reports of the resources that practitioners have available for action, in particular for design. In order to demonstrate this we set out below some preliminary findings.

15.7 Findings

Design was a term used freely by all our respondents. This was in part prompted by the interview structure itself, which began with a request to outline details of a particular course for which the respondent had been responsible. Nevertheless we believe it a finding worthy of note that every interview contained a reference to design prior to the use of the term by the interviewer. We believe this indicates that the practitioners use design as a term that loosely covers a variety of issues concerning the planning and deployment of a course. When talking about design the interviews show a number of different understandings of the term. So while there is a common usage of the term design it is not clear that there is a single or simple understanding of what the expression might mean.

To illustrate this point we include below a variety of the uses we found:

"We are now planning to design a Networked Learning MA which will be more Web based and more of information rich..."

"We've been using particularly Lotus Notes. We've done an awful lot of work of designing it to our specific needs and tailoring it..."

"It's designed to help people who want to develop an open learning, a networked open learning, course of their own and so they go through the experience of learning online about online learning..."

"Now when you said that you were involved in the design of this course, what do you mean by design exactly?" (Interviewer)
"Um, I mean everything by it, I mean in terms of the content and of the interface in particular, um, we actually started this course from having some funding..."

"It did seem that it went on too long so we shortened it. Which meant that obviously we've got to re-design how many themes we have. So it went down to a 12-week course and we added in time for people to catch up. So the idea of it is that although you can get to any of the materials, start discussions about any part of the course at any time to fit in with the principles of flexible learning there is a sense of progression..."

"The tutors would write or set up notes about why this particular theme is important – introducing it. There would be tasks for the learners to do so that their learning is driven by them. Doing things that are useful to them, you know, and that there would be a set of reading attached to the topic to help them with those tasks. So those are the kind of first principles in the terms of the design and obviously having the discussion space so that the students can share."

It is possible that from a reading of the above examples, the usage of the word design could be grouped into references to 'pedagogical design', 'technical design', or 'interface design'. What is clear from the interviews was that respondents used the term design unhindered, without explicitly noting the different uses that we found.

One respondent reserved the term design for discussion of the course materials and his students. When referring to the very same activities undertaken by himself he talked about 'developing' the course. This use of development and design to cover the same understandings was not uncommon and several practitioners used design and development as interchangeable terms.

Whilst our respondents were clear that they undertook design of their courses and programs they were equally clear that this was a complex and difficult task. Below we include a particularly clear and illuminating example of the experience of difficulties and complexities in designing for networked learning.

"What else ... um ... I certainly haven't yet learnt how to do it, so I, so I still don't know how to create an online learning environment that would work in the way I imagined it might. There are probably trivial examples where I can get things to pan out the way I want but I think you find this quite common that people however much experience they have developed, how ever many articles they write about good ways of doing things, however much they analyze student experiences it's still extremely difficult to design an online environment and online course online activities in ways where you are not surprised and/or disappointed by the output." John

The first conception we developed to describe this experience was in terms of the expression of disappointment. On further reflection and in the light of the additional evidence provided by further interviews, we would like to suggest disappointment as a sub-category of a wider phenomenon, the difficulty in a networked environment of accurately predicting outcomes. The expression of this problem of prediction was stated in a variety of ways, two examples of which are given below:

> *"My background is in teaching so schools teaching, training teachers, training with xxxx University, designing courses and so you think you've got some feel for it maybe in terms of workload ... er ... and if you were to talk to me about a conventional ... er ... I have no problem in estimating how long it will take you to design that course, how long it will take you to learn that course to (inaudible) that course but suddenly moving into this area a lot of those estimates they seem out by a factor of three, four and five."* Frank

> *"Both Brian and I started with fairly liberal minded constructed learning like that and you have two years of experience like this and you want to say no, what you're going to do is, I'm going to record every page you learn, um, everything you look at, I'm going to assess you at every point and I'm going to let you know as soon as you fall out of line. I'm going to hit you with a stick until you get back into line. You sort of lose that, certainly for the on-site students I certainly lost a lot of things I thought I believed in two years ago and rather than learn things I certainly think I've had to re-think things that I believed in."* Robert

This second example is a strong case, but this level of reaction was found with at least one other practitioner. It is interesting to note that the unexpected outcomes are challenging the practitioner above to re-think his educational beliefs, his assumptions, because they do not match his experience. Levels of surprize, being unable to predict, and disappointment were closely related to practitioners' experiences of levels of participation. The levels of participation by students were reported as both too high and too low. In both cases they revealed concerns about how levels of participation could be managed so that outcomes could be related to expectations that had been built into the course designs. The issue for all respondents in terms of design was a problem of linking planned outcomes to actual results.

15.7.1 Participation

> *"Um, I'm concerned about the level of participation, we always are with these things."* Alice

Two respondents stood out as not experiencing the same feeling of disappointment as others. Their use of networked learning was at postgraduate level and was informed by a very consistent educational theory that had initial 'tight' structures, for example participation in residential sessions, but then allowed a greater degree of freedom in course dynamics once the base expectations were set. The educational philosophy they had was similar and both programs embodied a strong group ethos. Participation in these courses was also obligatory:

> *"How is participation - is it high is it low?" (Interviewer)*
> *"Well it varies I think um from person to person but no one can get through the course without participating and they know that so that's one factor. I think in some courses that use computer conferencing, at the OU for instance, you can take the course and do nothing in the computer conference and still get through the course. In ours you couldn't that's a difference but it's incredibly high I mean sometimes it's just too much, sometimes people say this is just too much I can't keep up with it all."*
> *Tim*

The concern expressed by this respondent about high participation being 'too much' was mirrored elsewhere:

> *"We actually say on page 7/9 I forget 'we are expecting you as the student to read the bulletin board a couple of times a week a couple of hours. We expect you as a tutor to be online six times a week' – fantasy, fantasy – I'm here Saturday morning, nine hours on a Saturday desperately trying to keep up to date with these guys. We are talking an average over twenty hours a week online. Now that may not sound a lot, but when like you I have a work-time and I'm paid to work, that's work and six hours is six hours. Twenty is like fourteen hours extra. Now I only put in seven hour days cause I like to go to the loo, I like a cup of coffee and have my lunch and leave before seven o'clock at night, so that's got to find two person days well seven has gone for a start by ... where do you find the other day, Sunday? Sorry I'm not going to work Saturday and Sunday so I'll get here a bit earlier and I'll sit here a bit longer and I'll work a bit faster so what is a very low resource course initially is an **incredibly** intensive teaching/learning experience for all of us." Frank (bold added to indicate speech emphasis)*

The level of activity had clearly overwhelmed this respondent, while other practitioners reported managing high levels. Management of the perceived problems that arose from high participation was 'hands on', not pre-course planning or design, a good example is found in the following response:

> *"It has to be very carefully managed because that can explode ... um ... I know a lot of people who say 'Oh well don't you just get flooded by e-mails'. The answer is there are periods where you get quite a bundle ... um ... but usually it's earlier on when they are starting out on this, they are actually worried about this they are apprehensive once you've managed to send reassuring responses the sort of flood of e-mail dries well it doesn't dry up but it's perfectly manageable." Norman*

Generally participation was a problem, either through a lack of participation or the high rates reported above. For the following practitioners the problem was of low participation even though a high level of participation had been anticipated in the design:

"In this module there is a very clear design assumption that everyone would participate in the online environment and that they will do that in quite a highly structured way. The last module that the students where involved in the online activity, I may be wrong about the last module, but it's not uncommon in previous modules for the online activity to be seen by the students as entirely optional. The majority of them wouldn't participate at all in any one module and if you look back over the last two years on the program under half of the students that could participate in the online activity did so. So this is actually better than that, but it's not as good as I hoped for when I was designing it." John

The concern with low rates of participation was often related to a discussion of structure, in particular with 'tighter' structures, which is an issue we will return to later. An illustration of this link can be found in the following comment:

"I'm reasonably happy with, um, but obviously getting feedback from the students does make one question about the way that the course is designed and what we need to do with it and the fundamental questions of student participation and participation by all the students in it, um, remain unresolved as they ever were in some ways so (inaudible) of it. It's making me question, um, whether the structure is the way to encourage participation, so by having set tasks and activities and demanding that the students or even making this stronger and saying you must contribute is that the way to go forward? I don't know, it's certainly making me question about it, um, there are different views. Typically what is happening with networked learning courses is that people believe that the way to get participation levels up is by giving more structure, there are some of us who would question that and whether it is appropriate." Alice

Our analysis of participation leads us to question the expectations that inform the reactions our participants have. Disappointment was related to a failure to control levels of generally poor participation. High participation was conceived of as a problem for the tutor, one that in some cases could be managed day to day though not planned for. The quality of participation was often discussed in relation to levels of activity and quality seemed to be conceived of as a secondary or dependent factor.

15.7.2 Expectations

An underlying issue behind expressions of surprize and disappointment was the type and level of expectations of our practitioners. As interviewers we had our own expectations and one was that the practitioners might vary between those who were pioneers and had become expert in the use of networked learning and those who were more recent early adopters. It became apparent on reading the transcripts that there was a more or less common 'philosophy' or educational approach that underpinned their work. This could be reduced to a series of points, which would include:

- people learn collaboratively by articulating and sharing their ideas, experience and expertize through discussion and dialog;
- people learn by linking ideas from literature, online contributions and their own practice and experience;
- people learn by doing, by engaging with the activity or task;
- people learn from experience, either positive or negative and from exposure to different tutoring and learning styles.

It can be seen from this list that the practitioners have a relatively common educational outlook that is similar to the approach described earlier as the emergent or new paradigm.

The types of assumptions about learning that we found are illustrated below:

"One of the things that we want is for people to learn from each other, get insights into their own work by hearing about other peoples' work, um, actually giving some of their background is really quite useful." John

"We encourage students to use it {the online environment} to share their experiences and their expertize." Alice

"{The program} is very much focused around the personal development or professional development and works a lot in the area of relationships and discussion and dialog..." Penny

"We decided we were going to develop a course like this and what we wanted to do was we wanted to sort of turn in on itself so they could learn about developing teaching and learning systems by experiencing a number of teaching and learning systems, um, from a variety of backgrounds that were based on a variety of different theories." Robert

All the practitioners except one either mentioned constructivist or collaborative approaches to learning; some expressed their ideas in terms of learning communities or communities of practice. Generally the concept of learning through collaboration was strongly expressed. The one respondent who made no mention of such approaches was using a combination of web pages and individual e-mail to promote a dialog in the form of philosophical letters with the students. A wide variety of pedagogical techniques have been associated with networked learning and it is perhaps surprising to find such a narrow range of underlying approaches adopted by the practitioners (see, for example, Paulsen, 1995).

In relation to expectations we have found that practitioners often referred to students as being 'good students', 'compliant students', and 'motivated students'. We found that these descriptions of students were related to whether the student matched or not with the educational approach of the course/program. Thus for instance when discussing assessment a practitioner said the following:

"This is another issue I find very difficult about assignment marking. Students who feed back the party line about collaborative learning and whatever and I don't mean just feed it back in a sense of hype and stuff but people who have clearly seen the benefits of collaborative learning. It's hard not give them high marks because this is what we are trying to teach people, the value of collaborative learning. However people who don't see it and don't want to and stand out against collaborative learning and say well you know it isn't so (inaudible) and are resistant to it. I would like to see a student like that, that I could still give 90 to but I haven't. I've only seen ones that I could, you know bending over backwards, give 60 to because I'm trying to not be biased against them." Elaine

Several practitioners described collaborative learning as a 'problem'. Student resistance concerned some whilst others were concerned by a lack of clarity amongst other practitioners about what 'collaboration' meant. Overall practitioners identified collaboration as an aim but were concerned that it was difficult to achieve and difficult to conceptualize. Collaboration and participation were both features that exemplify the gap between expectations and outcomes. They provided incentives for practitioners to re-visit their initial course designs.

15.7.3 Innovation and Refinement

When discussing change and future iterations in the design of course and programs we distinguished between two distinct approaches in terms of innovation and refinement. Practitioners clearly had distinct ideas about elements of existing courses that might be altered and in other cases of a more radical type of re-design that had a speculative quality. Both examples given below were thoughts on design for courses that were not yet ready for deployment.

"I'm beginning to get the sense, erm, about moving to much shorter and I don't even want to use the word course because I want to move away from the notion of a course which I think is the new model. The new world we are moving into it's sort of learning bites, learning moments,

um, and which could be longer or shorter but, um, I'm not saying that there's no place for a course, um, a course with a beginning and middle and an exam at the end kind of concept but particularly for undergraduates but for the lifelong learning market and the professional updating market, um, I think we need to be coming up with a new concept and for me it has these elements and I'm only really you know these are just ideas I'm working on myself at the moment they're not worked out at al.... " Elaine*

This quote illustrates an idea we found expressed elsewhere, that 'course' structure is not fitted to the sorts of environments that are becoming available for networked learning. The idea of learning bits and learning bites had a resonance with other descriptions. The second example reconceptualizes the idea of a field of knowledge but similarly questions the topic and theme format of previous presentations.

"From my point of view it's trying to introduce some new ideas about how you should see a field of study anyway, rather than in terms of topics and themes. I mean even on the part-time although the themes they are only loose focuses for the workshops there are themes to each workshop. Whereas on the Networked Learning MA the starting principle is more in terms of, er, actors in the field and the way they see the field and the field is defined by the people who are actors and students you know in the broadest sense like scholars in that field and the field is more pre-determined in terms of themes and focus but in terms of peoples' interests and boundaries are located in a series of nodes within and with those nodes saying to each other that becomes the loose definition of that field. " Penny

In terms of refinement the interviews were peppered with minor revisions to course structures, technical interfaces and minor organizational features. Some of these revisions had a more comprehensive character as is illustrated below:

"Now we have recently been overhauling the whole program that we offer and this is the first module in the revised version of the program. So the larger framework has changed but also the way we do individual modules has changed and this module has always been seen as having a transitional character to it, so that it doesn't represent all of our ideas about how we are going to do the next module for example. " John

The above example is interesting as it spans the innovation – revision divide. It is a revision in so far as the change over is gradual between one form of the course and another and as the new course is based on revision of the previous presentation. It is an innovation in so far as it is a new course presented for the first time.

The more usual form of revision is illustrated below:

> *"We've got these four basic essays and so those have been revised, revised in light of reaction to comments that we had while those measures were being studies so they've been changed, they're in the process of being re-edited and printed ready for circulation and that's a minor part of the course you know if you think of 400 hours study time you could study that stuff in a couple of hours so not a major part of the course." Frank*

Revision was a common response and indicated an iterative approach to minor elements of design. The inclination to revision was not simply driven by factors internal to the course and the match between expectations and outcomes. There are some particular reasons why revision is a common response as illustrated below:

> *"I have to say it's very daunting to me as Program Director to go through all the hoops that I'll have to go through if I'm going to make any changes to the MA. Some part of me wants to say oh just let the thing just let it tick over because it is so wearing, the kind of bureaucratic stuff which I don't enjoy and I'm not very good at. So I guess that is an element in course design that can't be ignored working with the structures of higher education." Elaine*

The bureaucratic problems are complemented by some good pragmatic reasons connected to design:

> *"I think looking back on that it's a pretty good way of putting a larger course together by trialling the different elements of it and making sure they work and then you're more confident that the whole thing will work." Murielle*

We found that refining of existing practice is related to concerns that the outcomes of designs often fail to reach the expectations embedded in prior planning. However, as indicated above, it is also related to a design process that is both evolutionary and iterative. This is not to say that the practitioners interviewed were either 'innovators' or 'refiners' but that at particular times in their designs they experience different concerns and interests. Revision and an iterative approach to design may be initiated by the gap between expectation and outcome but the institutional context and a strong pragmatic orientation also condition it.

15.7.4 Tight and Loose Structures

One aspect of design revision related to practitioners' concerns about 'structure'. They were concerned with how to organize students' activity and how much to organize their activity. For example:

"...so the structuring of the exercizes in terms of the time schedule has been and I think necessitated in order to actually save them from wasting their time going to a PC lab checking, finding nothing, going away and getting frustrated and annoyed about it. We've tried to structure it fairly tightly and we may tighten that up even more this year because ultimately that means they are actually using their time more effectively and efficiently. Erm the downside of that I think is that with the tighter the schedule the more structured the exercize is and there is a danger that you're damping down on the potential for creativity and the extra time of the research that might be produced in that extra time, if you see what I mean, but there's a fine balance to be drawn there..." Norman

Within the respondents' accounts the issue was often seen as either tight or loose structures. Practitioners had often experienced courses that had not run as expected and in later iterations, or in plans for future iterations, referred to changes in the structures of enforcement. Assessment criteria and course requirements, such attendance at face to face sessions or active participation on line, were the common examples.

The problem was identified in a number of ways. Two illustrative quotes are given below of characteristic responses.

"Part of the point of having a very tight structure was to encourage people to participate in, in a much more, well in a way in which the mutual expectations are more clearly understood." John

"The reason for setting the deadlines and structuring a timetable has been in response to one of the problems which arose the previous year which was that one team would post a load of messages to the other teams and then have to sit and wait for three days before the others bothered to reply because that team happened to be better organized so the structuring of the exercizes in terms of the time schedule has been and I think necessitated in order to actually save them from wasting their time." Norman

Loose structure was often associated with assessment. Practitioners that had experience of assessment being used to engineer participation or interaction were concerned about its consequences:

"One of the dominant issues was that we began to believe that our program was heavily over assessing students, that created more work for them and more work for us." John

"What they begin to see is or what they seem to see is the fact that the tutor wants to see them interacting online and our experience has been

that they will work together off-line and then come into the lab and they'll put the stuff up onto the conferencing system which is supposed to show that they are learning online, but they're not they're doing that for your benefit or because that's what their perception is this is what the assessment is based on and this is what the tutor wants to see so they've actually done it somewhere else and then brought it in or fabricated it or simulation might be a better phrase." Jack

Looser structures were, at least in part, responses to the effects that previous structured interventions had produced. In particular when outcomes had undermined the designers' intentions. They provide another illustration of the overall design issue of expectations. The concern with structure was a response to gaps between design intentions and actual outcomes.

15.8 Discussion and Conclusions

We question whether the common use of design that we found amongst practitioners of networked learning would be found amongst HE staff more generally. Higher education in the United Kingdom has not until recently concerned itself with training its practitioners to teach. Many HE practitioners are discipline experts who may find the idea of design alien to their current practice. When asked to discuss teaching issues, they may do so in terms of their shared tacit or craft knowledge (Van Driel *et al.*, 1997). This knowledge might not even be thought of as professional as until the formation of the Institute for Learning and Teaching in HE there was no professional body able to licence or guard standards. The documentation that is currently required for validation of courses is often cut off from teaching and learning. A recent study investigated the connections between, on the one hand validation procedures and course documentation and on the other teaching and learning. The research found considerable confusion in the process between quality control and what they called 'curriculum and pedagogical development' with the former threatening to imperil the latter (Woodman & Redley, 1996).

In traditional and face to face setting expectations are in some ways common sense or common knowledge (Edwards & Mercer, 1987). Participation in lectures and seminars, whilst not unproblematic, has a set of commonly understood assumptions about attendance and behaviour. This should not be taken to imply that we fully understand face to face settings or that we endorse common sense views of such settings, only that such shared expectations are present in face to face contexts. The boundaries within a networked setting appear to be less commonly understood. Each practitioner had comments to make about how they had varied their own practices. On the other hand we note that while there is not currently a common sense or common knowledge about networked learning there appears to be a common educational philosophy that both expert practitioners and early adopters display. We wonder whether this would be well understood or accepted outside of this narrow and possibly self-selected group. Their explicit use of design and references to component assumptions of the new paradigm suggest that networked learning practitioners are not currently 'typical' academics or teachers in HE.

The assumption amongst the practitioners derived from a particular set of learning theories and this may have implications for a large-scale roll out and future take-up of new technologies. The developing common philosophy may lead to what Boot and Hodgson (1987) described as a mismatch between program orientation or philosophy and student orientation. They argue that learning can arise with either a match or mismatch but that participants will either have to cope with the mismatch or be 'socialized' into the orientation of the program or course. If there is a mismatch between educators and students then students may need to be 'socialized' into the program philosophy or the orientation expected on networked learning courses. There may also be a mismatch between staff orientations and the orientations expected of staff when deploying networked learning courses. The educational philosophy and theories that provide the rationale for networked learning may be absent from the staff required to make use of such technologies. This would raise questions of staff development requiring significantly more than simple training.   Without staff and student development of this type disappointment, if widely experienced, could lead to resistance to the adoption of networked learning in the future.

The accounts provided by the practitioners were in terms of design though the term was used to cover a variety of discrete activities.   The respondents were reflective practitioners refining their existing practice and being prepared to consider considerable innovation.   There was not a stable basis for design and practitioners were concerned that outcomes did not match expectations.   Tacit knowledge and common sense approaches to design were not apparent amongst the practitioners.   On the other hand there was evidence of a common philosophy, a new paradigm, that provided a language for the design process and a set of criteria from which judgements could be made.   This emergent paradigm may yet settle down into a tacit practice, a new common knowledge.   At this stage whilst common principles inform design, practice reveals clear tensions between intentions and outcomes.

Our findings help us to comment on the general approach of phenomenography. The accounts we were given make us cautious in what we claim interview data represents. We do not believe for example that the interview reveals any fixed internal state in the practitioner. Rather we would claim the interview reveals some of the resources for action available to the respondent. These resources may or may not be used to inform practice and may provide after-the-event rationalized accounts rather than motives prior to action.   The interviewees display the characteristics of reflective practitioners and we cannot be sure that a movement from unreflected to reflected awareness was achieved during the interviews. This is an important finding as Marton has relied on this transition from unreflected to reflected or meta- awareness in his defence of the interview from its critics (Marton, 1994:4427; Marton & Booth 1997:129-132). Most of the interviewees have written about their experiences prior to the interview and had previously reflected upon the issues that the interview raised. The accounts we heard were in some senses a performance of previously rehearsed ideas.

Finally we would like to comment on the idea of 'good' design. Practitioners generally expressed a concern that they did not fully understand the relationship between their educational designs and their outcomes. It might be that there is not yet sufficient understanding for an easy match between planning and expectations and outcomes. There is certainly no common agreement or a common sense view of educational practice in a networked environment, though there is evidence of such a common sense view emerging in terms of a new paradigm amongst practitioners. In this sense the craft knowledge relied upon elsewhere in HE is reduced or restricted in a networked learning environment. This may mean that rather than a singular good design we may find various good designs, and that each design was fit for its own particular purposes. In which case the best we may be able to distil from practitioners' reports of their practice will be rules of thumb. Design of learning environments may well be revealed as an iterative process in which there is continuous identification of problems and modifications of practice.

15.9   Acknowledgements

This work was part-funded by a grant from the Committee for Awareness Liaison and Training of JISC (the Joint Information Systems Committee of the UK higher education funding councils). The views expressed here are not necessarily those of JISC or CALT. Further information about the project can be obtained from the project's website (http://csalt.lancs.ac.uk/jisc/). We would like to acknowledge the contributions of other members of the project team: Vivien Hodgson, Peter Goodyear,   Christine Steeples,   Susan Armitage,   Mark Bryson, Michael O'Donoghue and David Hutchison.

15.10 References

Boot, R.L. & Hodgson, V.E. (1987) Open Learning: Meaning and Experience. In Hodgson, V.E., Mann, S. & Snell, R. (Eds.) *Beyond Distance Teaching Towards Open Learning.* Buckingham: SRHE/ Open University Press

Boot, R. & Reynolds, M. (1984) Rethinking Experience Based Events. In Cox, C. & Beck, J. (Eds.) *Management Developments: Advances in Practice and Theory.* Chichester: John Wiley and Sons

Brown, J.S., Collins, A. & Duguid, P. (1989) Situated Cognition and the Culture of Learning. *Educational Researcher*, 18(1) pp32-42

Brown, J.S. & Duguid, P. (1996) Stolen Knowledge. In McLellan, H. (Ed) *Situated Learning Perspectives*. Englewood Cliffs, N.J.: Educational Technology Publications

Bowers, J. & Martin, D. (1999) Informing Collaborative Information Visualization Through an Ethnography of Ambulance Control. In Bodker, S., Kyng, M. & Schmidt, K. *ECSCW '99: The Proceedings of the Sixth European Conference on Computer Supported Cooperative Work.* Dordrecht: Kluwer Academic Publishers

Burgoyne, J. & Reynolds, M. (Eds) (1997*) Management Learning. Integrating Perspectives in Theory and Practice.* London: Sage publications

Cooley, M. (1999) Human-Centered Design. In Jacobson, R. (Ed.) *Information Design.* Cambridge MA: MIT Press, pp59-83

Dills, C.R. & Romiszowski, A.J. (1997) *Instructional Development Paradigms.* Englewood Cliffs NJ: Educational Technology Publications

Eastmond, D. & Ziegahn, L. (1995) Instructional Design for the Online Classroom. In Berge, Z. & Collins, M. (Eds) *Computer Mediated Communication and the Online Classroom* (Vol. 3: Distance Learning) pp59-80. New Jersey: Hampton Press

Edwards, D. & Mercer, N. (1987) *Common Knowledge: The Development Of Understanding In the Classroom.* London: Routledge

Enwistle, N., Entwistle, A. & Tait, H. (1993) Academic Understanding and Contexts to Enhance It: A Perspective from Research on Student Learning. In Duffy, T.M., Lowyck, J. & Jonassen, D.H. (Eds) (1993) *Designing Environments for Constructive Learning.* Berlin: Springer-Verlag

Fleming, W.G. (1986) The Interview: A Neglected Issue in Research on Student Learning. *Higher Education 15*, pp547-563

Harasim, L. (1989) Online Education: A New Domain. In Mason, R. & Kaye, A.R. (Eds) *Mindweave: Communication, Computer and Distance Education.* Oxford: Pergamon

Harasim, L., Hiltz, S.R., Teles, L. & Turoff, M. (1995) *Learning Networks: A Field Guide to Teaching and Learning Online.* Cambridge, MA. MIT Press

Hiltz, S.R. & Benbunan-Fich, R. (1997) Supporting Collaborative Learning in Asynchronous Learning Networks. In *UNESCO/OPEN UNIVERSITY International Colloquium: Virtual Learning Environments and the Role of the Teacher. Milton Keynes: Open University.* http://eies.njit.edu/~hiltz

Hughes, J., Randall, D. & Shapiro, D. (1992) Faltering from Ethnography to Design. In *Proceedings of the ACM 1992 Conference on CSCW.* New York: ACM Press

Koschmann, T. (Ed) (1996) *CSCL: Theory and Practice of an Emerging Paradigm.* Mahwah, NJ. Lawrence Erlbaum Associates

Laurillard, D. (1993) *Rethinking University Teaching: A Framework for the Effective Use of Educational Technology.* London: Routledge

Lave, J. & Wenger, E. (1991) *Situated Learning: Legitimate peripheral participation.* Cambridge: Cambridge University Press

Lawson, B. (1980) *How Designers Think.* London: The Architectural Press Ltd

Lin *et al.* (1995) Instructional Design and Development of Learning Communities: An invitation to Dialog, *Educational Technology* Sep-Oct 1995, p53

Marton, F. (1994) Phenomenography. In Husen, T. & Postlethwaite, T.N. *The International Encyclopaedia of Education* (2nd edition). Oxford: Pergamon, pp4424-4429

Marton, F. & Booth, S. (1997) *Learning and Awareness.* Mahwah,NJ: Lawrence Erlbaum Associates

Mason, R.D. (1989) A Case Study of the Use of Computer Conferencing at the Open University. PhD, Open University

Mason, R. & Kaye, A. (1990) Towards a New Paradigm for Distance Education. In Harasim, L. (Ed) *Online Education: Perspectives on a New Environment*. New York: Praeger

Mason, R. (1994) *Using Communications Media in Open and Flexible Learning*. London; Kogan Page

Paulsen, M.F. (1995) The Online Report on Pedagogical Techniques for Computer-Mediated Communication. http://home.nettskolen.nki.no/~morten/

Plowman, L., Rogers, Y. & Ramage, M. (1995) What Are Workplace Studies for? In *ECSCW '95: The Proceedings of the Fourth European Conference on Computer Supported Co-operative Work*. Dordrecht: Kluwer Academic Publishers

Prosser, M. & Trigwell, K. (1999) *Understanding Learning and Teaching: The Experience in Higher Education*. Buckingham: SRHE and Open University Press

Randall, D., Hughes, J.A. & Shapiro, D. (1994) Using Ethnography to Inform System Design. *Journal of Intelligent Systems 4*, (1-2), pp9-28

Reynolds, M. (1997). Learning Styles: A Critique. *Management Learning. 28*, (6) pp115-133

Richardson, J.E.T. (1999) The Concepts and Methods of Phenomenographic Research. *Review of Educational Research 69*, (1) pp53-82

Reigeluth, C. (Ed) (1999) *Instructional-Design Theories and Models Volume II. A New Paradigm of Instructional Design*. London: Lawrence Erlbaum Associates

Rogoff, B. (Ed) (1990) *Apprenticeship in Thinking: Cognitive Development in Social Context*. New York: Oxford University Press

Suchman, L. (1987) *Plans and Situated Actions: The Problem of Human-Machine Communication*. Cambridge: Cambridge University Press

Toohey, S (1999) *Designing Courses for Higher Education*. Buckingham: SRHE and Open University

Van Driel, J.H., Verloop, N., Van Werven, H.I. & Dekkers, H. (1997) Teachers' Craft Knowledge and Curriculum Innovation in Higher Engineering Education. *Higher Education, 34*, pp105-122

Wenger, E. (1998) *Communities of Practice: Learning, Meaning, and Identity*. Cambridge: Cambridge University Press

Wilson, B.T. (1997) Reflections on Constructivism and Instructional Design. In Dills, C.R. & Romiszowski, A.J. (1997) *Instructional Development Paradigms*. Englewood Cliffs NJ: Educational Technology Publications

Whiteley, N (1993) *Design for Society*. London: Reaktion Books

Woodman, D. & Redley, M. (1996) The wretched document: an analysis of the talk and perceptions of staff on the process and procedure of validation and review, course planning and teaching preparation. In Gibbs, G. (Ed) *Improving Student Learning: Using Research to Improve Student Learning*. Oxford: Oxford Center For Staff Development

16. Online Collaborative Assessment: Power Relations and 'Critical Learning'[1]

Kiran Trehan and Michael Reynolds

16.1 Introduction

Online collaborative forms of assessment occupy unusual education territory. In addition to challenging conventional canons of academic assessment, such approaches offer the potential to generate insights into individual and group behavior in a crucial area of educational practice. This chapter attempts to expand the potential of collaborative assessment, especially online collaborative assessment, by examining its rationale from a critical perspective.

Our intention is to explore the dynamics involved in operationalizing online collaborative assessment. First we review alternative assessment practices, their rationale and the influences of participative pedagogies more generally. We then describe the MA in Management Learning at Lancaster University and the way in which online collaborative assessment is undertaken on this program. From this we present an analysis of students' views on the outcomes and impacts of being involved in online assessment. The next section questions the assumption that such an approach necessarily empowers the students taking part, and explores the significance of power relations encountered during the process. The final section examines the implications for online assessment practice and the role of tutors, particularly in the context of 'critical' management education.

We will argue that by illuminating social and power relations embedded within collaborative forms of assessment, it is possible to present a more contextual and processual account than the idealistic prescriptions that have dominated the study of this practice.

16.2 Collaborative Assessment: An Overview

In adult and professional education there has been significant interest in developing more participative approaches to assessment, whether peer (carried out by fellow students), collaborative (jointly evaluated by learners and the tutor), or consultative

---

[1] Acknowledgement: This chapter draws on an earlier paper published in *Studies in Higher Education* (Reynolds & Trehan, 2000).

(collectively between self, peer and tutor but with ultimate responsibility resting with the tutor). These developments are particularly appropriate in the case of participative courses which are designed more generally to provide students with opportunities for influencing – for example – the content of the curriculum, the educational methods used, or the choice of topics for assignments.

Given the rapid pace of development and innovation in educational technologies, coupled with alternative approaches to learning, a re-evaluation of assessment methods might be expected to be a prominent feature of a critically-based educational program[2] involving less hierarchical procedures and relationships – particularly one which aims for pedagogical consistency between the curriculum and the teaching methodology. Yet, while examples of critical pedagogies, including those situated online, are accumulating, they seldom exhibit corresponding changes in assessment practices. Where assessment does depart from mainstream practice, alternatives are typically based on humanistic, student-centered aspirations for social equality, rather than on an analysis of assessment in terms of institutional power and control over educational procedures.

The concept of collaborative assessment in online learning environments is based on several assumptions according to McConnell (1999). In collaborative assessment students are actively involved in decisions about how to learn, what to learn and why they are learning. They are also involved in decisions about criteria for assessment and the process of judging their own and other learner's work. Boud (1986) argues that engagement in more collaborative practices helps to encourage critical faculties and wean students from dependence on the assessment of others. Rowntree (1987), in his critique of mainstream practice, argues that traditional assessment processes are in any case contradictory. The notion of the assessor as an all-knowing, all-powerful entity is fundamentally flawed, because it fails to take sufficient account of the biases of the assessor and of the potentially prejudicial nature of the process. He argues that conventional assessment practices make the measurable important instead of making the important measurable.

As a consequence of these concerns, the 1980s saw a growth in the literature on self and peer assessment, albeit often in the context of otherwise traditional teaching methods. In a number of publications, attention was drawn to such issues as comparisons of teachers/student ratings (Boud, 1986; Falchikov, 1989); the introduction of self-assessment practices into undergraduate courses (Boud, 1986); work on peer, self and tutor assessment (Stefani, 1994); peer tutoring (Saunder, 1992); and self and peer assessment (Howard, 1991). During this period, the topic of self, peer and collaborative assessment began to be studied more critically (see, for example, Boud, 1981, 1989; Cunningham, 1991; Heron, 1981; Somervell, 1993).

The practice of online learning has also raised critical debate with reference to program design (McConnell, 1999), the role of tutors (Hardy, 1993) and gender differences in online groups (Hardy & Hodgson, 1994; McConnell, 1997). However, attention to issues specifically concerned with assessment is to be found to only a limited extent. McConnell (1999) argues that collaborative assessment in

---

2   For more detailed accounts of applications of critical perspectives see Fox (this volume) and Reynolds & Trehan (2000).

online learning environments is often a difficult process for students and staff to implement. Online collaborative assessment involves learners having to assess their own and others' learning through the negotiation of criteria and methods of assessment. Whilst this approach is designed to enhance learning and to be developmental, it can also create anxiety, uncertainty and stress (Reynolds & Trehan, 2000). Students are often concerned about their lack of knowledge and experience in relation to assessment and feel uncomfortable with the prospect of assessing their own work, and the work of others. Yet as we have observed earlier, whilst these are important issues, there is limited discussion of the implications and impact such issues have within online learning environments. In the main the literature on online assessment tends to focus on practicalities of online assessment and on offering guidelines for future practitioners.

16.3 Critical Perspectives and Online Assessment

For the most part, the critical curriculum in management education has been disseminated through traditional methods, but increasingly there is interest in the contribution which online methods could make to a critical pedagogy. Giroux (1981) has emphasized the value of earlier androgogists because they have 'called into question the political and normative underpinnings of traditional classroom pedagogical styles' (1981:65). More recently there are a growing number of propositions for pedagogies which apply a critical perspective to method as well as to content. So, for example, the Learning Community (Reynolds, 1999) and Virtual Learning Communities (Fox, this volume), are participative in that they offer an opportunity for choice in the direction and content of learning through shared decision-making within the course. Students involved in this approach, as they would be in Willmott's (1997) proposal for 'critical action learning', have an opportunity to base their learning on their professional experience and to select the ideas with which to make sense of it. The 'learning community' and 'critical action learning' therefore, illustrate possibilities for both a methodology and a curriculum which reflect a critical perspective. Not only is conceptual content and its application based on critical perspectives but methods, procedures and relationships are developed in ways which are consistent with them.

Recent influences from radical education (Giroux, 1992), feminist pedagogy (Weiler, 1991) and from critical theory (French & Grey, 1996) have given fresh impetus to the development of more participative, less hierarchical approaches to teaching and learning – the expression of a critical perspective in both content and methodology. Arguably, in such a context, some form of collaborative assessment might be expected as a prerequisite. Yet, as we observed at the outset, while there are some examples of a critical pedagogy affecting content and method, corresponding changes in the practice of assessment are harder to find, both in face to face and online learning environments. This omission reflects perhaps, a tendency within the social reconstructionist tradition in education, to be stronger on political vision than on practical propositions (Gore, 1993).

Our interest in the assessment process is because if it is not critically addressed, attempts to provide a less hierarchical milieu are undermined by reinforcement of the institution's unilateral control over the granting of qualifications and through unquestioned acceptance of the tutor's authority. Collaborative assessment would be more consistent with the aims and principles of a critical pedagogy than top-down or unilateral grading systems and could be incorporated into the online course design. Conversely, while criticality may be claimed in content and method, if assessment, the clearest manifestation of power within an educational context, is itself unquestioned and unchanged, such claims are open to doubt.

There are those who are aware of this contradiction and the constraints imposed by 'the institutional hierarchical structure which teachers and students typically inhabit' (Grey et al., 1996:105). Similarly, Gore (1993) has emphasized that the relationship between teacher and students is 'at some fundamental level, one in which the teacher is able to exercize power in ways unavailable to students' (p68). Some educators have seen these disparities of power as placing inevitable limitations on what can be done with the assessment process (Tisdell, 1993). Others have addressed the inherent contradiction with 'expedient' modifications to procedures: such as group assignments and contracts for grades (Weiler, 1991); ensuring that examinations are used to 'test the quality of thinking, not the quantity of what is thought' (Grey et al., 1996:104); or by advocating that students are involved in dialog with tutors over 'the criteria, function and consequences of the system of evaluation' (Giroux, 1988:39).

It seems, however, that critical pedagogies have yet to make any significant impact on the essentially hierarchical nature of traditional assessment or online assessment. This might at first seem puzzling, given earlier examples of collaborative assessment developed within the 'student-centered' learning movement. Perhaps it is because of critical educationalists' general mistrust of the humanist discourse which characterizes student-centered approaches, often to the neglect of the more social and political processes involved in classroom relations.

So while some form of collaborative assessment would seem necessary for any critically based approach to education, it is equally important to take account of the social and cultural bases of power which influence relationships among students themselves and which are likely to be central to their experience of collaborative assessment online. In the same way, it should not be assumed that even if the tutor was *not* involved – as in peer assessment – equality would be ensured. While collaborative assessment is often advanced as a corrective to more hierarchical methods, students' experience of it suggests that the application is far from straightforward – desirable as it remains as a pedagogical objective.

In the rest of this chapter we examine the aims of collaborative online assessment in the light of the experiences of students on a postgraduate program in order to illustrate the interaction between assessment and the complex political and social dynamics of learning groups.

16.4   Setting the Scene: Online Assessment in Practice

The computer mediated MA in Management Learning at Lancaster University is a two year part-time program for professionals in management education and development. The design of the program can be summarized as follows. The course consists of six intensive residential workshops spread over a two-year period. In between these workshops, participants and staff are supported by a networked learning environment made up of computer conferencing and electronic mail. Participants log on to the system several times a week over periods of between three and seven months in between workshops. They work in small groups ('learning sets') made up of four to six participants and a tutor. The learning sets focus on each student's chosen piece of work that is to be assessed. Each participant helps the others in thinking through the topic of their assignment and offering relevant advice, support and references to the literature.

There is also an opportunity for larger 'community' conferences, open to all members of the program – students and tutors – where discussions of a more general nature take place relating to the program, to the design of the forthcoming workshop, to work problems, to career planning, or for purely social exchange. The program claims to be highly participatory. Course members are involved in the design of the program and they make decisions about the focus of their work over the two years, as well as being involved in the assessment of their own and each other's work.

In the learning sets, the students and the tutor contribute comments on each paper or project and agree a mark. Some criteria are 'given' but interpretation of them and the addition of other criteria related to each student's learning goals are areas for negotiation and ones with which each group will engage. The tutor is ultimately responsible for ensuring that the learning group agrees a mark and for recording both marks and a summary of the procedure adopted by the group and of subsequent discussion. A singular advantage of online assessment is that much of this is in any case recorded. Rarely, a disputed case is carried forward to the examining board for resolution[3].

If we are to accept that students' ability to assess their own work as well as others' work is an important element in the learning process, then questions of power and authority deserve particular attention. In what sense is the tutor a 'member' let alone an equal member of the group? Does each group member – including the tutor – make an equal contribution to the 'agreed' mark? In the next section, and as a way of furthering understanding and development of a more critical approach, we will review such questions in the light of students' experiences of online collaborative assessment throughout the program, while drawing on ideas from critical and feminist pedagogies. The research was phenomenographic, data being collected from both online discussions and interviews in which students described their experiences and feelings before,

---

[3]   We have used 'collaborative' as a generic term throughout this chapter. On the MA, assessment is described as 'consultative' reflecting the tutor's ultimate responsibility.

during and after the assessment process. Marton (1994) explains phenomenography as a research approach for understanding peoples' way of experiencing the world. He defined it as:

"The empirical study of the differing ways in which people experience, perceive, apprehend, understand, or conceptualize various phenomena in, and aspects of, the world around them." (Marton 1994:424)

The aim of phenomenography is thus to describe qualitatively different ways of experiencing phenomena and was particularly suited to this inquiry, as we intended to examine students' individual experiences of participating in collaborative assessment and to compare this material with the rationale and ideals which had originally informed the course design.

16.5   Power, Authority and the Online Experience

It might be assumed that questions of power and authority are chiefly confined to traditional assessment methods, and that they are not so problematic in more collaborative approaches. The nature of the dynamics of collaborative methods generally would suggest otherwise (Reynolds & Trehan, 2000). Ellsworth (1992) points out, contrary to the rhetoric of critical pedagogy, concepts of power, empowerment and student voice have become myths that perpetuate relations of domination. If for example interpretations of 'participative' education result in an increased emphasis on self-awareness, consciousness-raising or reflexivity in the assessment process, but power, authority and judgement-making are not examined, students have even less control than in more traditional methods. At least within traditional methods the notion of the assessor as an all-knowing, all-powerful entity who has the intellectual authority to make assessment decisions is transparent, with the tutor-student role clearly defined. In collaborative online assessment the individual boundaries are not so clearly defined, and this can lead to feelings of disempowerment.

Vince (1996) has suggested that individuals can respond to their anxiety either by entering a cycle that promotes learning, achieving insight through struggle and by being prepared to take risks, or – if the uncertainties are too great – a cycle that discourages learning by way of resistance, denial or defensiveness, ultimately maintaining 'willing ignorance' (pp122-133). Not only, therefore, should power and authority be central foci of analysis in the context of a critical pedagogy (Gore, 1993), but such an analysis might be expected to result in visible changes in assessment procedures.

Certainly in practice, a participative approach is unlikely to be straightforward whether in taking part generally (Reynolds & Trehan, in press) or in taking part in collaborative assessment. The tutor's intention may be that students will share in evaluating and grading work, even to the extent of collectively managing the entire process. Initially, however, such freedom may cause anxiety and frustration, as the following extracts illustrate:

"The whole experience was very emotive, I felt pretty distressed about it."
(extract from interview)

"When I think about it, it was just intense, quite emotionally charged. I
just felt this ringing headache." (extract from interview)

The above accounts show the dissonance experienced by some participants, in the sense that they felt unsettled and experienced uncertainty and anxiety. However, what is interesting to observe is that with the online discussion, some participants ultimately viewed the learning provoked by their experiences very positively.

> "On reflection it allowed me to develop two things, ...the ability to self-assess subjectively, objectively and to think about the process...this sponsored interesting debates." (extract from online discussion)

As Vince (1996) argues, any consideration of learning needs to take account of the emotions experienced by learners in the learning context. A collaborative course is likely, as a result of the level of social engagement it entails, to touch participants' emotions. Changes to learner-teacher power relations may have similar consequences, as Vince writes:

> "Approaches to learning that break free of dependency on the teacher, and place emphasis on the responsibilities of the learner, always create anxiety" (1996:121).

From our experience, active engagement in collaborative assessment can be painful and, contrary to its intention, can be disempowering. We should not expect it to be comfortable, whether face to face or online. Indeed as has been observed more generally, learning cannot take place without anxiety or critical learning without personal struggle (hooks, 1993).

Equally important is to address the question of how students' assessment of each other online might be affected by power relations amongst themselves. Dearden (1972), in his critique of non-directive facilitation, argues that the granting of freedoms by a teacher can result in that source of control merely being replaced 'by that of some other agency' (p451). Operating assessment methods which encourage learners to be supportive to fellow learners, whilst at the same time developing their skills in critically evaluating each others' work is a challenging process further complicated by power relations between students as well as between students and tutors. As the following extracts suggest:

"The picture in my head regarding evaluation is around what are the
criteria by which work will be judged as good or otherwise, and making
those explicit ... The alternative is to cruise along, doing our own thing
and applying our own unstated criteria, and then being hurt and

surprized that it wasn't what.... the [tutors] were expecting." (extract from interview)

"There seem to be a number of issues all jumbled up to do with the mark, how it is arrived at, how fair, the judgement of one piece of work against another, quality, standards, etc. alongside the process and the emotions of the feedback itself, fear of failure etc. as well as the dynamic of the group, personalities, styles, interests, the tutor's perceived and real role etc." (extract from interview)

16.6 Online Collaborative Assessment: Unravelling Tutor and Student Roles

When applying critical thinking to online assessment, a critique of the student-tutor relationship needs to be addressed. It seems crucial that tutors are constantly reflexive, so as to question their motives, their style of facilitation, and their awareness of the potential impacts of a critical learning approach to online assessment. In particular, it must be important that tutors are aware of the power they have over resources, structuring the agenda, or controlling assessment. So for example, within the philosophy of the MA, it is hoped that learning will be initiated by the student exchanging ideas freely with the tutor. This exchange echoes the process described by Freire (1972) as 'problem posing', where the traditional assumption of teacher supremacy and student compliance is dismantled.

Our research suggests however, that although tutors may support this model of learning from the outset, it can take some time before the student fully adapts to it. One could argue therefore, that within this problem posing approach there is a point in time where the student feels there is still a power imbalance, because while the tutor understands the philosophy, the student, initially at least, is to a great extent 'in the dark'. There is an underlying belief that some form of unspoken but expected authority is still present. This belief is particularly reinforced through the experience of assessment.

In practice therefore, clarifying the role of the tutor in collaborative approaches is unlikely to be straightforward, because of the ambiguities that result from the redefinition of the tutor's role. Bilimoria (1995) notes the shift which takes place, from a tutor's role based on the 'exercize of control, expertize, and evaluation' to a concept of authority as shared among participants, expressed through collective generation of knowledge and in the 'ownership' of its evaluation (p448). But this is not necessarily how students experience it, as the following extracts illustrate:

> "... the assessment process in my case was quite short, principally because there was a tutor who was a member of the group and she put her marks in first, which everybody then kind of fell in with because, you know, we just weren't experienced, not up to arguing, and actually I still have quite unpleasant feelings about that." (extract from online discussion)

> "There is also the tutor/student bit where there is a leaning on the tutor's mark over others. To what extent is this collaboration!" (extract from online discussion)

Without recognition of such ambiguities and support in making sense of them, Race (1991) argues students will expect tutors to intervene if they think the marking is unsatisfactory, therefore the procedure cannot be claimed to be either collaborative or empowering. The following quotations illustrate that, whilst online assessment may provide the opportunity for and perhaps the illusion of equality, hierarchical relationships remain intact.

"I was thinking about this whole question of collaboration and being equal and then thinking about marks, which isn't easy, and yes the tutors marks were lower than I would have expected and I didn't feel that I could challenge them, because I know that the tutors always argue that they need to justify the marks to an external examiner, so I didn't feel I could argue" (extract from interview).

"The tutors role was important and powerful, it was not overtly stated but that certainly was my view of how the group worked ... there are university criteria in which you are not well-versed" (extract from interview).

For collaborative assessment to realize in practice what it promises in principle, it is important to be alert to the tendencies for hierarchical relations to persist in the shape of disciplines which students come to impose on themselves and on each other. This, it could be argued, is a form of governmentality (Foucault, 1979) exercized through the action of 'being one's own policeman', of managing one's own practices.

"There was one paper that was noticeably weaker than the others. I felt some anxiety as to whether it should be a pass or not, we all felt it was a fail really but in the end we chose to moderate it and push the mark up." *(extract from interview)*

These extracts from online discussions and interviews highlight the complexities associated with collaborative methods of assessment. The change from traditional assessment where the tutor unilaterally attributes a mark to a method which places the emphasis on a devolved or shared process, attaching value to understanding and defending how marks are attributed and criteria applied is demanding on students and tutors alike.

16.7   Discussion

We have argued that one of the necessary but difficult aspects of a participative program is to introduce a correspondingly collaborative approach to assessment. Assessment is a critical part of the formal learning process in any educational method, traditionally exercized by the tutor but in participative learning by the student also. But as we have illustrated, such *apparent* transition of power may not necessarily be empowering.

Ellsworth (1992) points out that in the literature on critical pedagogy, there are central concepts – namely power, empowerment and student voice – which have become myths that, contrary to the rhetoric, perpetuate relations of domination. Dispenza (1996) voices the concern that by *talking* empowerment into existence we are adding to the politically correct language of the more modern educational philosophies and that the articulation of such language often diagnoses a lack of imagination at an operational level in the classroom, and an unwillingness to change more comfortable didactic methods. (p241 – author's italics).

It would appear from these ideas that offering students more control over the assessment process is not necessarily or inherently more liberating. Even when empowerment, self-awareness, 'raising consciousness' and reflexivity are introduced into the assessment process, issues of power, authority and judgement remain problematic. The more collaborative approaches to assessment can also represent a more subtle disciplining technique for introducing power relations into play.

Orner (1992) argues that discourses of 'liberatory' pedagogy which claim to empower students do not overtly support relations in which students are monitored by others as they discipline themselves. Ball (1990) states that confessional techniques used in pedagogical practices which encourage students to view the procedures of appraisal as part of the process of self understanding, self betterment and professional development is simply a more complex mechanism of monitoring and control.

Hardy (1993) has commented on the difficulties experienced by tutors in collaborative assessment. She highlights two paradoxes, the first of which is that of trying to work democratically while at the same time being responsible for maintaining the accepted academic standards of the university embodied in the assessment process. Here the tutor encounters, more clearly than in any other aspect of the program, the potential imbalance of power between themselves and the student. The second paradox is in evaluating a person's work in a context where one is normally trying to be supportive and encouraging. As McConnell (1997) argues:

"... we are constantly confronted with the contradiction in playing the dual role of 'tutor participants'. This is especially so in the assessment process. Any intervention we make has the likelihood of being received differently from interventions made by other participants. Our wish to remove the inequality of power relationships takes some considerable time" (p287).

16.8 Conclusion

We have highlighted that collaborative forms of assessment are not *necessarily* empowering and might even be dis-empowering in that they can potentially create a hidden curriculum of hierarchical authority. As Vince (1996) observes, learning environments are a powerful and contained arena for viewing negotiations on autonomy and dependence. Within collaborative assessment therefore, it is important to acknowledge the inequalities of power which assessment can generate and which in any case can develop between students. Learning groups are permeated with relations of power, which contribute to the construction of individual and group identity. As McGill and Beaty say of a related approach:

"Action learning sets have a political dimension in that they replicate interpersonally and in the set, the sense of power and powerlessness that is found in any other group or organization." (1995:191)

All groups develop norms and establish a dynamic of influence and hierarchy which will be in tension with any attempts towards equality. Our observations reinforce the criticisms of feminist pedagogy, that participative learning cannot lightly be assumed to give rise to a non-hierarchical environment.

The challenge of working with online collaborative assessment means we must include a frank look at the power of the tutor. Rather than spurious or exaggerated claims for collaborative assessment, its value is as a location where power relations can be examined and – ideally perhaps – negotiated. As Shrewsbury (1987) argues:

"Empowering pedagogy does not dissolve the authority or power of the instructor. It does move from power as domination to power as creative energy...a view of power as creative community energy would suggest that strategies be developed to counteract unequal power arrangements. Such strategies recognize the potentiality for changing traditional unequal relationships. Our classrooms need not always reflect an equality of power, but they must reflect movement in that direction." (p9)

Gore (1993) points out that the institutional context may militate against changes such as these, begging the question as to how much freedom academic institutions really have to question and challenge existing structures. Brookfield (1986) has highlighted how a number of institutional variables seem repeatedly to skew, distort, or prevent the application of empowerment and self-directed learning principles. This is because the realities of curricular imperatives, grading policies and institutionally devised evaluative criteria preclude student involvement.

Similarly, within critical pedagogy, whilst there is an acknowledgement of the socially constructed and legitimated authority that teachers hold over students, there has been a failure to analyze in any depth the institutionalized power imbalances between themselves and their students, giving the illusion of equality while leaving the authoritarian nature of the teacher/student relationship intact. As Ellsworth (1992) argues 'empowerment is a key concept... which treats the symptoms but leaves the disease unnamed and untouched' (p98).

What implications does this raise for online collaborative assessment? If we are to believe that students have been given a greater measure of control over their learning and over educational processes, if the nature of the underlying power relationships remain significantly unaffected, how much control do they really have over the judgement of work produced for assessment and evaluation?

Where online collaborative assessment of some degree is practised, there is just as much need for open examination of what it entails. These are questions which are not often asked either during course design or during the course itself – but ought to be. The procedures and processes of assessment extend further than the negotiations between tutors and students. Whose views are subsequently represented at of examiners meetings? How and where are disputes resolved? Which other processes of power are involved which affect students' evaluation of their own and others' work? What is the tutor's role and responsibility in drawing attention to all this?

These complexities cannot be reduced to a simplified set of guidelines but it does seem as if there is an argument for tutors being willing and capable of recognizing them and openly working with them. From a critical perspective this would entail a reflexive understanding of the processes involved – including the tutor's own part in them, and the skill to support students in working through the implications for the judgements which are being made.

When implementing online assessment our experience reminds us of the power that tutors can have to influence students' grades, which clearly indicates responsibilities we have for questioning our own intents, motives and practices to be reflexive. Tutors have to be prepared for emotionality and conflict, and be aware of their own needs and biases, and above all to develop an informed understanding of the power situated in their roles and the procedures traditionally associated with them. They need to be constantly developing themselves, in a sense mirroring the task they ask the students to engage in.

16.9   References

Ball, S. (1990) *Foucault And Education* New York: Routledge

Bilimoria, D. (1995) Modernism, Postmodernism, and Contemporary Grading Practices. *Journal Of Management Education, 19,pp* 440-457

Boud, D. (1981) *Developing Student Autonomy In Learning (2nd* edition) London: Kogan Page

Boud, D. (1986) Implementing Student Self-Assessment. *Higher Education Research And Development Society 5*, pp3-10

Boud, D. (1989) The Role Of Self-Assessment In Student Grading. *Assessment And Evaluation In Higher Education 14* (1) pp20-30

Brookfield, S. (1986) *Understanding And Facilitating Adult Learning* Milton Keynes: Open University

Cunningham, I. (1991) Case studies in collaborative assessment. In Brown, S. & Dove, P. (Eds.) *Standing Conference On Education Development*, SCEA 63 Newcastle: Newcastle Polytechnic

Dearden, R.F. (1972) Autonomy and Education. In Dearden, R.F. (Ed.) *Education And The Development Of Reason* London: Routledge

Dispenza, V. (1996) Empowering students: a pragmatic philosophical approach to management education. *Management Learning 27*, pp238-250

Ellsworth, E. (1992) Why doesn't this feel empowering? Working through the repressive myths of critical pedagogy. In Luke, C. & Gore, J.M. (Eds.) *Feminisms And Critical Pedagogy* New York: Routledge

Falchikov, N. (1989) Student self-assessment in Higher Education: a meta-analysis. *Review Of Educational Research, 59*(4) pp395-430

Foucault, M. (1979) *Discipline And Punish: The Birth Of The Prison* Penguin Books

Freire, P. (1972) *Pedagogy Of The Oppressed.* Harmondsworth: Penguin

French, R. & Grey, C. (Eds.) (1996) *Rethinking Management Education,* London: Sage

Giroux, H.A. (1981) *Ideology, Culture and the Process of Schooling.* Philadelphia: Temple University Press

Giroux, H.A. (1988) *Teachers as Intellectuals: Towards a Critical Pedagogy of Learning.* New York: Bergin & Gravey

Giroux, H.A. (1992) *Border Crossings: Cultural Workers And The Politics Of Education.* New York: Routledge

Gore, J M (1993) *The Struggle For Pedagogies.* New York: Routledge

Grey, C., Knights, D. & Willmott, H. (1996) Is a critical pedagogy of management possible? In French, R. & Grey, C. (Eds.) *Rethinking Management Education* London: Sage

Hardy, V. (1993) Introducing computer mediated communications into participative management education: the impact on the tutors' role. *ETTI 29* (4) pp325-331

Hardy, V. & Hodgson, V. (1994) Computer conferencing: a new medium for investigating issues in gender learning. *Higher Education 28*, pp403-1

Heron, J. (1981) Self and Peer Assessment. In Boydell, T. & Pedler, M. (Eds.) *Management Self Development, Concerns And Practices* Westmead Farnborough: Gower

hooks, b. (1993) bell hooks Speaking About Paulo Freire – The Man, His Work. In McLaren, P. and Leonard, P. (Eds) *Paulo Freire: A Critical Encounter* New York: Routledge

Howard, J. (1991) Self and Peer Assessment. *Standing Conference On Educational Development SCED 63* Newcastle: Newcastle Polytechnic

Marton, F. (1994) Phenomenography. In Husen, T. & Postlethwaite, T.N. *The International Encyclopaedia Of Education* (2nd edition). Oxford: Pergamon

McConnell, D. (1997) Computer support for management learning. In Burgoyne, J. & Reynolds, M. (Eds.) *Management Learning: Integrating Perspectives In Theory And Practice*. London: Sage

McConnell, D. (1999) *Implementing Computer Supported Co-operative Learning* (2nd. edition) London: Kogan Page

McGill, I. & Beaty, L. (1995) *Action Learning* London: Kogan Page

Orner, M. (1992) Interrupting the call for student voice in liberatory education: a feminist post-structuralist perspective. In Luke, C. & Gore, J. (Eds.) *Feminism And Critical Pedagogy* London: Routledge

Race, P. (1991) Learning through assessing: *Standing Conference On Education Development SCED 63*

Reynolds, M. (1999) Critical reflection and management education: rehabilitating less hierarchical approaches. *Journal of Management Education 23*, pp537-553

Reynolds, M. & Trehan, K. (2000) Assessment: a critical perspective. *Studies In Higher Education 25* (3) pp267-278

Reynolds, M. & Trehan, K. (In Press) Classroom as real world: towards a pedagogy of difference. *Gender and Education*

Rowntree, D. (1987) *Assessing Students: How Shall We Know Them?* London: Kogan Page

Saunder, D. (1992) Peer tutoring in Higher Education: *Studies in Higher Education 17*(2), pp211-217

Shrewsbury, C. (1987) What is feminist pedagogy? *Women Studies Quarterly 15* (3/4), pp6-14

Somervell, H. (1993) Issues in assessment. *Assessment and Evaluation in Higher Education. 18* (3) pp221-232

Stefani, L. (1994) Peer, self and tutor assessment: relative reliabilities. *Studies In Higher Education 19* (1) pp69-75

Tisdell, E.J. (1993) Interlocking systems of power, privilege and oppression in adult Higher Education classes, *Adult Education Quarterly, 43*, pp203-226

Vince, R. (1996) Experiential management education as the practice of change. In French, R. & Grey, C. (Eds.) *Rethinking Management Education* London: Sage

Weiler, K. (1991) Freire and a feminist pedagogy of difference *Harvard Educational Review 61*, pp449-474

Willmott, H. (1997) Critical management learning. In Burgoyne, J. & Reynolds, M. (Eds) *Management Learning: Integrating Perspectives In Theory And Practice* London: Sage

17. The Campus Experience of Networked Learning

Charles Crook

17.1 Introduction

During the course of a collaborative project about virtual universities, Vivienne Light started to refer to student study-bedrooms as 'nests'. There was something engaging about her metaphor. Cosy, personalized spaces: private, yet securely embedded in a larger community. If equipped with networked computers, these rooms become *'learning nests'*. I suspect this particular theme resonated well with our romantic image of learning. It suggested contented young scholars, absorbed in research, insulated from distraction, yet reinforced by a slightly monastic community around them.

Of course, all good terms of this sort invite the construction of an acronym. My idea for acronymic expansion was "networked environments for student tenancy". Despite vigorous exposure at conferences, this verbal trick did not seem to catch on. Eventually, we ourselves became disenchanted with it. Possibly, there was some tension between the agreeable conviviality of 'nest' and the soulessness of 'networked environments' or the subservience of 'tenancy'. However, perhaps such semantic tensions alert us to a risk of idealizing the learner. Implementing a campus-wide computer network *may* create our romantic 'learning nests'. For it may release existing obstructions to effective study and thereby resource "the insatiable desire of students for more and more information at a higher level of complexity" (Cole, 1972:143). On the other hand, such networked learning may simply foster a "knowledge-delivery view...[that] portrays students as vessels into which the university pours information" (Brown & Duguid, 1998:40).

It is seductive to think that learners are held back by various sorts of institutional 'obstruction' to their enthusiasms. The idea encourages a search for new techniques to unblock their path or to somehow re-route them. Yet the history of innovation with educational technology tends to suggest that obstructions to effective study are not so easily dislodged (Cuban, 1986). At the time of encountering the learning nest metaphor, David Barrowcliff and I were wondering about the potential of campus computer networking in this regard. At Loughborough University we were studying just the sort of learning nests that such networking seems to afford. There seemed to be good reasons for investigating what goes on in these new spaces of networked study bedrooms.

Two particular reasons for studying this seemed clear. First, extensive campus networking had become a resource that residential universities feel under strong pressure to provide. As discussed further below, much enthusiasm for the computer as an educational tool assumes that it is equipped with fast and easy access to local and global networks. So universities will feel compelled to invest in such networking and research must help clarify what follows in terms of educational practice. Second, enthusiastic projection of these networking initiatives promises more radical visions for the future of higher education. Such visions question the necessity of traditional, full-time, residential universities (Duderstadt, 1999; Tiffin & Rajasingham, 1995). For computer networking invites the fragmentation of educational provision such that it can be distributed in both time and space. The virtual learner will have no need to congregate in set places at set times. There is evidently a need to evaluate the prospects for such developments.

It is very unclear how far the virtualization of higher education could be pursued. At the time of writing there are certainly commentators who are sceptical of both the reach and appeal of so-called "e-learning" (Economist, 2001). Research such as that discussed here on the virtualization of residential provision may be our most helpful empirical window onto these prospects. The basis for such a claim is as follows. Society may continue to expect higher education to be contiguous with secondary education. So we may still wish to invest in furnishing an intense period of organized learning prior to encouraging learners to embark on their careers of employment (albeit careers with greater openings for continuing and flexible learning). In which case, what is happening now in networked study bedrooms becomes particularly interesting. For the occupants of these spaces are the current representatives of the very constituency who will be lined up for the de-schooled future of virtual learning. For this reason, we need to make visible the experiences of these 'partially virtualized' learners and consider how readily they take to this mode of education.

The structure of the present chapter is as follows. I shall first review some opportunities that are expected to arise from access to networked learning on a traditional residential campus. I shall then introduce the context of the research reported here: a study which documents reactions within one community of staff and students to such a networked resource. After summarizing certain of these reactions the chapter will conclude with some conjectures about how networked learning could be designed to have a more productive impact within a residential university context.

17.2   The Opportunities of Networking

It can be claimed that no media (such as a local computer network) itself has an effect on learning. If there is an impact associated with some technical innovation then – or so it has been argued – this will be because "learning is caused by the instructional methods embedded in the media presentation" (Clark, 1994:26). Yet certain technologies will invite certain instructional methods more readily than others. In which case, making a technology institutionally accessible and creating pressure to use it must mean that the methods easily afforded by that technology will become more widely visible. It is not necessary that such possibilities of a technology are immediately obvious to potential users. Sometimes the practices that follow are propagated more by the particular enthusiasms of professional advocates for that technology.

One construction of the networked computer is that it provides the basis for readily distributing rich sources of information and, it is claimed, this is what students lack. As one academic commentator expresses this, the university's role now "is no longer to provide the main conduit for knowledge transmission. Technology does that more efficiently" (Delvin, 1997). The author of an influential report on technology in higher education (CSUP, 1992) exercizes the same slippage between 'information' and 'knowledge' in celebrating the prospects of "richly structured, highly-accessible and interactive machine-resident knowledge" (MacFarlane, 1998:83). In short, it is anticipated that learners on a fully-networked campus will enjoy extended access to a rich array of learning resources.

It is also expected that a consequence of this should be a greater degree of autonomy for the learner. "The classroom institution has historically centralized power and influence in the hands of the instructor ... asynchronous learning networks in contrast, shift a considerable amount of power, authority, and control from the faculty to the students" (Jaffee, 1998). The success of this shift may depend on the networked resources conforming to a certain design: they may need to be fashioned into a learning 'package'. As two senior practitioner/researchers put it: "Online self-learning packages fundamentally question the traditional role of the educator by giving students greater individual control. Effective learning can be realized by providing a student with a computer, loading the educational software and walking away" (Gell & Cochrane, 1996:252). In the environment to be discussed below there were available computer-aided learning packages of the sort that Gell and Cochrane are perhaps contemplating. However, even more modest web-based course material is claimed also to offer this liberating potential of autonomy also. So, it is not unusual for enthusiastic developers of networked learning material to frame their activity as an affirmative one in relation to student identity: "by cancelling traditional lectures as we have done and making the material available online we are supporting the ideals of having student-directed and student-controlled learning." (Smeaton & Keogh, 1999:84)

Associated with these projections there is often a theme of network resources offering a greater individualization of learning. Even if it is not always clear how such customizing is to be designed into materials. The MacFarlance report proposes that: "supportive learning environments would be created by using educational technology where appropriate, in many cases after the groundwork had been prepared through lectures and hard copy materials. *As used here, the term supportive learning environment implies a shift to selfpaced teacher supported learning"* (CSUP, 1992:26-27 italics in original). The implication seems to be that technology again offers a potential to provide rich materials, with customizing of study programs merely requiring some individual routes to be designed by teachers.

However, the promise that distinguishes networked learning from mere 'electronic learning' is the promise of interpersonal communication. Students linked by a common computer network are empowered to interact with their peers and their tutors through this infrastructure. At present the commonplace realization of this potential is asynchronous text messaging – electronic mail – but in the longer term it is reasonable to expect more synchronous communication and more vivid modalities, such as audio and video transmission. This feature of networking is much advertized as it seems to challenge the widespread worry that computer-based learning must necessarily be a solitary experience.

In sum, we might expect the extension of networked learning to a traditional campus setting to have a number of impacts. We might expect students to find new motivation in the scope and depth of learning materials that will now be readily accessible at their workstation. This, in turn, might encourage greater autonomy of study. We might also expect that new and extended conversations will be prompted by the ease with which tutors and fellow-students can be contacted in this networked space. Changes of this kind were sought in research to be described next: a study of networking in a classically campus and residential setting.

17.3   Research Context

The research described here took place at a large UK university comprising a self-contained campus located on the edge of a medium-sized town. The university enjoys particular strength in engineering and computing and, thus, had developed good IT facilities and a positive attitude within management to the use of technology for teaching and learning. Fifty-two per cent of undergraduates were resident on campus: a situation that had encouraged extensive networking of the environment. At the time of recruiting participants for the present research, approximately 800 study bedrooms had been networked for 1.5 years. The university had also created a specialized web server (the 'Learn Server') which provided disc space for all 2,555 taught modules. Each module could be accessed by students through a hierarchical system of menus, individual module areas had substantial storage space as well their own e-mail discussion boards. Staff were vigorously encouraged to use this server. Each lecturer's module file space was easily mounted as a directory icon on their own office computers. Thus, managing web space was relatively easy. Moreover, a variety of courses and workshops had been organized to promote both technical and pedagogic understanding of the resource.

In addition, a support unit in the university maintained a 'CAL Server'. This acted as a single and central repository for specialized teaching and learning packages including a number of generic items relating to numeracy and study skills. In fact it is claimed to be "one of the UK's largest collections of fully-functional,   networked   LT   [learning   technology]   materials" (http://www.lboro.ac.uk/service/fli/services/lt/matl/lt2.html). Finally, at the time of the present research, the university was part of the Acorn project which empowered the library to make full text of any recommended reading available on local networked computers. In short, while this site hardly defined a virtual university, it had taken a number of infra-structural steps that should permit the evolution of more virtual practices. The research discussed below considered the impact of these developments through conversations and observations involving a group of students either living in networked study bedrooms or – for comparison – a group living in a student room with no such PC facility. Attention has also been directed towards what staff have done with their opportunities to create web-based learning environments.

Matched groups of undergraduates were recruited. It was intended that half would be in networked rooms and half would not. All 'networked' participants were required to have had use of this service for at least one full semester. A total of 168 letters were sent to a random selection of residential students stratified by their university Faculty assignment. Letters explained the project and the possibility that they may be visited to invite participation. The aim was to recruit 28 students in networked rooms and 28 in non-networked rooms. .

Students were then visited. Where an individual was not available, two further visits were made. Of the 168 potential recruits, 69 were unavailable after three visits and 20 declined to take part. Finally, administrative problems and difficulties of timetabling interviews led to a total of 26 networked students being interviewed and 19 non-networked students. Arguably, compared to typical work of this kind, the sampling can be regarded as furnishing a good cross section of the community. Selection was paced to include all academic departments; reasons for not taking part were usually good-natured and typically to do with arbitrary circumstances at that time.

The focus in what follows is upon an interview carried out individually with each of these students. It lasted for approximately an hour. Reference will also be made to summaries of study-related activity that were derived from parallel research projects based on diaries and computer system logs. As it happens, much of the innovation within this networked environment is accessible in web-based format because of the increased versatility of the web browser as a network tool. Accordingly, much of the present report concentrates on web activity on the so-called Learn Server. However, before commenting on how students' use of this material, it is necessary to examine what staff have provided. I shall do this next.

17.4   What Teaching Staff Do with the Web

The first thing to observe about Learn Server activity by staff is that it was surprisingly underused. Of the 2,555 modules catered for, only 29% currently contain any resources. Moreover a significant number of those have only a minimal set of materials. This is the case despite three years of availability and, as yet, no constraints on the amount of file space available to developers. Deering recognized the modest uptake of teaching technology by university staff, noting that it was "far from being embedded in the day to day practice of learning and teaching in most higher education institutions ... the main reason is that many academics have had no training and little experience in the use of communications and information technology as an educational tool" (Deering *et al.*, 1997, Chapter 3 Section 61). It is hard to accept this as an adequate explanation of the present case. Certainly, for most academics, composing and organizing even simple HTML will require some instruction. However, this university had been very generous in offering such support, and would do so at a very intense tutorial level where that was invited. Moreover, being in the midst of quality auditing, individual departments would have been highly motivated to display innovative practices.

Clearly academics do master other information technology tools routinely – where they are perceived as powerful resources for their work. So, one is bound to suppose that many teachers are not convinced that the investment in this case is a particularly good one. Learning resource development of this kind does not become a high priority for them. I shall not dwell further on the issue of modest uptake. Except to note that it may be naïve to dispose of it in terms of inexperience coupled with indifference to training. This may be part of an explanation but it will also be important to research just how academics do perceive this form of educational innovation and, perhaps, learn from whatever reservations they express.

We may turn instead to what staff users actually did offer students. I base the summary here on a random sampling of 10% of the modules that did have material available. The single most commonly provided resource was notes arising from lectures. Forty-five per cent of module websites offered these. (Here, and in other cases, percentages need careful interpretation. Some modules had such minimal amounts of material that a more telling sample for a percentage calculation might be the number of modules where the amount of provision suggested a more serious intent to develop the site.) Often lecturers would supply sizeable Word files of their notes, others provided the PowerPoint slides used in a session and a small number merely supplied some annotated diagrams and images that had been used to support a lecture. The next most commonly provided resources related to assessment. This would take the form of old exam papers (41% of sites) and details of coursework assignments or problems (35%).

Some sites (21%) provided reading lists although it was unusual for individual items in these to be hotlinked to the library catalogue. Only 3% of sites provided full texts of supplementary material although a fair proportion (24%) did include mention of some useful URLs. Otherwise, content was characterized by timetable information (23%), course outlines (37%) and other administrative details such as membership of tutorial groups (11%). On the whole, sites were visually simple in construction with only 7% using frames and 15% using any kind of graphic design.

In many ways these sites are telling for what they do *not* offer, and I shall return to comment more on this towards the end of the chapter. At this point it might be claimed that the rather pedestrian content undermines any further research on what the students do in this networked environment. It might be claimed that this case study furnishes too inadequate a model of networked-supported learning. Yet, as illustrated more below, it seems that the sorts of things that are being provided are very much what the students say they want. This observation may, in turn, invite a retort along the lines of "but they don't yet know how it could be better". However, what it is in this environment that is 'better' may not be easy to get accepted. Observations below about student's typical study practices suggest that some features of the existing learning culture may be in tension with the kinds of networked innovation we may be contemplating for the 'better' learning environment.

Whatever conclusions get drawn about these matters, at this point what is emerging does seem to justify yet further exploration of students perceptions and activities within this particular setting. To that end, I shall next comment on the specific issue of what students understand by virtual forms of education, and whether they find it an attractive notion.

17.5   Students' Perceptions of Networked Resources

Perhaps the most striking outcome of interviewing these students concerned their general attitude towards the prospect of virtualizing higher education. This part of the conversation was organized around three questions. The first concerned whether they believed that virtual universities would become commonplace. The second concerned whether they believed this to be desirable. The third concerned whether they themselves would be prepared to study in a virtual university.

Twenty per cent clearly thought that higher education would eventually come to take this form. Fifty-two per cent did not see this as a realistic development and the remainder were uncertain or thought that some partial form of virtualization might occur. The question as to whether it was desirable was reacted to in objective terms. That is, answers did not reflect the students' own preferences but were an opportunity to rehearse the accepted public arguments for and against such developments. In these terms, the students showed themselves to be very comfortable with the claims that are commonly deployed in support of virtualization. They referred to the potential freedom associated with being able to study at times the learner wished. They referred to the financial benefits of distributed education and the social benefits of a potentially more inclusive system. Although only 11% invoked the idea that such education might involve a richer learning resource base.

However, these generally positive explanations of the advantages of virtual learning contrasted with students' responses to the question of whether they themselves would be happy to study at a virtual university. Not a single student interviewed found this prospect appealing. Many vigorously dismissed it and defended enthusiastically the character of their present undergraduate experience. Their responses suggested five themes that underpinned the feeling that virtual education was an unwelcome prospect.

Not congruent with the nature of learning. Forty-nine per cent of students invoked the idea that learning was an inherently social process. It worked because of the intensity of interaction made possible by involvement in educational discourse. In replies to these questions and also from their own experience of using networks, they revealed that they understood the potential for computer-mediated interaction. However, clearly there was a view that the intensity, spontaneity and serendipity of face-to-face conversation could not be captured within the virtual university scenario.

Limited bandwidth of the medium. Fifty-one per cent of students made a variety of specific points to identify perceived limitations in the technologies of virtualization. For example, 18% believed that the quality of their present hands-on or practical experience could not be reproduced in a virtual university. Similar numbers claimed feedback and support inevitably would be less prompt and that tutorial support only worked well when it was based on closer and more personal familiarity with the individual student.

Problems of sustaining motivation. Forty per cent of students predicted that they would not find adequate sources of motivation to persist with studying in this way. Around half appealed to the expected lack of explicit structuring. They noted the discipline that was imposed by the present university curriculum: for example, the corporate nature of lectures and tutorials, the deadlines, and the organized pace or routine of institutional life. Instead, they expected the autonomy of virtual learning would make them vulnerable to a whole range of distractions and, consequently, studying would suffer. Around half made reference to the particular benefit of being in close contact with student peers. In the traditional system, participating in this community provided the subtle benchmarks, challenges and standards that students felt were important to remaining self-confident and engaged.

Lack of adequate social life. Forty-two per cent of the sample cited the importance of the social life they enjoyed at university. The potency of moving away from home was often mentioned in this context. Clearly, the opportunities for socializing with a wide range of peers was a very significant part of what these students valued about being at university.

Narrowness of personal experience. Related to the above point about socializing, 29% developed the idea that university gave you a breadth of experience that went beyond the official curriculum. University was seen as an arena providing rich opportunities for personal development – opportunities over and above the possibilities of intellectual growth. Sport and recreation were cited in this context but also the challenges of adapting to and learning from a wide variety of same-aged peers. The advantages of a controlled move towards greater everyday independence was also recognized. These were all features of traditional university experience that were regarded as precious and not likely to be protected by any virtualized alternative.

The percentages above are merely to give credibility to the status of these themes as central issues. These conversations were not surveys and no attempt was made to press students for a position on all the possible issues of virtualization. Accordingly, some students made perhaps one strong point and felt no need to list any further reservations. It remains for future research to determine the exact priority of concerns among the basic reservations that were expressed. Whatever the detailed picture looks like, these interviews do give a strong signal that the traditional constituency of higher education – young people who have recently left school – is unlikely to be easily seduced by the prospect of independent learning that is decoupled from the bricks-and-mortar world of institutional learning.

It could be argued that a cohort of young people such as this will not have an adequate grasp of the technical and institutional possibilities of more virtual education. Students may be unfamiliar with the visionary detail of such developments and, accordingly, their reservations about it may be unfounded. Yet in other things they said, these students did reveal themselves to be quite sophisticated in their understanding of computer-supported activities. Remember, half of them had their own PC and had elected to connect it to the campus network in their room. Our records of what these students did on their computers (Crook & Barrowcliff, in press) suggests that they were very comfortable with a wide range of tools including video-mediated communication, instant messaging, text conferencing and more general internet browsing strategies. Finally, some of their reservations are unquestionably a problem for any future de-schooling of higher education. These include issues of enjoying a richly orchestrated social life, of taking part in extra-curricular recreation or creative activity, and of controlled opportunities for independence. These are all experiences that depend upon the face-to-face circumstances of organized community life.

However, other comments were made in the responses summarized above that do refer more directly to the experience of an academic curriculum. For instance, points were made about the basis of motivation for study, the potency of peer or tutor discourse, and the significance of teachers having a more thorough personal familiarity with learners and their predicament – all such learner perceptions deserve more careful scrutiny. Optimistic claims about the ease with which learners will engage with networked resources, will function independently, and will sustain their motivation are all claims that are poorly researched. The simple fact that, at the present time, there are successful distance and continuing education students is not in itself a good basis for wholesale projections of what is possible on a grand scale. Success in such educational niches provides no strong promise that distance modes of education will work comprehensively, such as to be attractive to *all* learners. We must attend in particular to the more reluctant scholars – many of whom may perhaps be found among the young school-leavers that make up the bulk of current university students.

17.6   Students' Use of their Own Networked Environment

Reservations about joining a virtual university should not imply these students had some general unease about computer-supported learning. Over half (56%) of them thought that the university should be making *more* use of information technology in teaching. Moreover, many of those who said "no" to this question were not necessarily negative about computers – often they simply believed that the present level was about right. When asked exactly where any future institutional investment should be made, they were fairly conservative in their preferences. Eighteen per cent thought that the basic infrastructure should be better; either in terms of public access points or in terms of network delivery speeds. Only 11% thought there should be more specialist discipline-relevant software and only 4% cited the need for more computer-mediated communication structures. On the other hand, 36% said that more lecturers should put their notes and lecture slides onto module web pages. Sixteen per cent suggested that staff should provide more direction in using internet resources.

This pattern of student preferences could be seen as reflecting the pattern of what staff have so far developed on the network (Although there is no evidence that student opinion had been polled prior to the development of network resources). So the somewhat scorned policy of putting lecture notes on web pages is a practice that is welcomed by many students. On the other hand, computer-mediated communication is largely neglected. There was virtually no use of the discussion boards associated with each module site; what use can be found was often restricted to two-turn exchanges with staff regarding problems over assignments. Moreover, in a study of a parallel student cohort, David Barrowcliff and I have found that e-mail gets very little use for academic purposes in this community. Mail that contains study-related advice or help accounts for only 5% of incoming mail for students in networked rooms and 7% for a matched group not networked. Certainly, there are respectable proportions of e-mails that are more broadly about academic matters (28% or 26%). However these tend to be impersonal announcements about course administration – many of them are lecturer-to-class general mailings. On the other hand over 60% of networked students made heavy use of instant messaging. Often they used the program ICQ to exchange short text messages, files or URLs according to who of their friends they could 'see' was online at a particular moment. Interestingly, no one within the whole fabric of teaching and computer administration had recognized the student preference for this style of communication over traditional e-mail.

During the interviews, students were asked explicitly about the role of computers in their collaborative experience of learning. Only two mentioned ICQ in this context and it was clear that the use of this tool was largely limited to playful purposes. On the other hand 35% reported that they had used e-mail to send work-related files to their friends. Typically this applied to the sharing of lecture notes although there was some passing around of 'used' essays. Finally, listservs concerned with their disciplinary studies were not represented in our survey of student incoming mail. Thus, although these students were very comfortable with the various formats of electronic mail mentioned above, they were not making any strikingly novel use of these tools to support their study. Computer-mediated communication was largely limited to matters of course administration and to the occasional peer-to-peer circulation of lecture-related material.

However, networked computers afford another species of collaborative activity. Students may elect to assemble and interact "around" them (Crook, 1994, Chapter 8). In this sense, they could be regarded as a resource-intensive and interactive site for joint study. Such congregating does happen, although not necessarily that often. Thirty-six per cent of networked students reported working with others in their room around their computer. On the other hand, even more (63%) of the non-networked students reported periodic collaboration of this kind.

In their case, the work would involve gathering around a terminal in a public room. Computer rooms have a bustle that actually may encourage this more than would happen in domestic residences. At any given moment public computer rooms may also be more likely to be populated by same-course peers.

A networked computer in ones own room may not, therefore, confer any great extra advantage as a catalyst for joint work. There is another sense in which the ready-to-hand quality of the study bedroom PC may be suspect. These students were asked about the style of working they adopted when using computers. Most of those with networked computers in their room reported intensive use of network facilities. They would typically multi-task and move in and out of applications quite frequently. Of course, many of those applications were of more recreational than study-related interest: media players, games, messaging boards, e-mail, news tickers, websites and so forth. Elsewhere (Crook & Barrowcliff, in press) we have documented this animated style of working more fully. It was not typical of the way students worked on PCs in public spaces. A crude measure of this difference is found in what students said about having e-mail available as they worked. Eighty-five per cent of networked students reported that they always had their e-mail active on the Windows desktop as they worked. While, only 21% of students who normally worked in computer rooms said this would be typical practice for them.

The observations made in this section do not suggest that access to networked facilities is radically reconfiguring patterns of study. Students' own vision about resourcing remains focused on lecture notes. They actively use computer-based communication but it hardly transforms their collaborative study or tutorial contact. Finally, easy access to a networked computer in one's own study space prompts intensive use of that facility (Crook & Barrowcliff, in press) but by no means for purposes that are well focused on the curriculum. In fact, the highly interactive character of the networked PC may make it a somewhat problematic single site to focus so many tools. While study may always be vulnerable to the distractions of a student's own living space, the peculiar concentration of such distractions in one physical site for working (the Windows desktop) may serve to undermine habits of more sustained engagement with work-related projects.

Some of the observations made here may be clarified further by consideration of how students describe their study habits more generally. It is the resilience of this background of teaching and learning practice that may account for much of the difficulty of establishing and sustaining new forms of network-based learning.

17.7 The Established Framework of Study Practice

I am not concerned here to document the curriculum and, in particular, the specification of exactly how time is allocated between different teaching and learning arenas. Nevertheless, it is interesting to note that the profile of this investment changes noticeably as you move from the images portrayed in undergraduate prospectuses, to the official institutional statement of modular teaching/learning hours, to the diary records of how students actually do spend their study time (Crook, 1999). Just in terms of central priorities, prospectus students will be mainly doing practical things, the institutionalized reality will have them immersed in private study to reinforce teaching, and the actual student seems preoccupied with completing coursework assignments.

I shall focus here on the raw materials of study and how they are made visible within the interactions that students have with their peers. Thus, the summary observations in this section largely arise from responses to interview questions about study contacts with other students. This is a particularly pertinent domain for questioning as it is the communal dimension of existing higher education that may appear to be threatened by more networked learning. We do need to understand more of how current experiences of participating in such a community does or does not support study.

Comments made earlier in this chapter about modest levels of computer-based collaboration might predict that students generally were not very active in orchestrating informal study-related meetings with their peers. While some students did occasionally work together in networked study bedrooms, they were in a minority. Accordingly, these students were asked whether and where they did have *any* work-related discussion with their peers. Certainly, some of this took place in their own rooms (29% reported this) and some took place in the context of routine social interaction, such as over cafeteria meals (18%). Neither of these frequencies is very high and, together, they might imply that students were not typically active in regard to informal collaboration (Crook, 2000). This, in turn, implies that the campus-based community was not catalyzing the sort of productive social exchange typically claimed for it.

However, the fact that students did not routinely congregate for organized collaboration does not mean that participation in an institutional community did not serve their study in other ways. Thus 62% of these students said they routinely discussed work in and around the time-tabled teaching sessions of their course. "Walking between lectures" was a regular occasion upon which work would get discussed. When students were asked to think through the preceding 24 hours and identify any occasions when they had discussed work with peers, 60% cited chance meetings. Twenty-eight per cent of examples were specifically between two scheduled teaching sessions. Only 15% of encounters involved an active effort or arrangement to meet another student. Thus, the way this community largely 'works' to give a social texture to private study is more through providing an everyday routine within which improvized opportunities for (perhaps short) exchanges can occur. The same may apply to contact with staff. Forty-two per cent of these students reported an unscheduled exchange with a member of teaching staff in the preceding 24 hours. Most of these were serendipitous encounters exploited during peoples' movement through the shared spaces of the institution.

What gets talked about during these contacts that involve student peers? It seems usually to be coursework. Seventy-three per cent of students cited the management of such assignments as their main topic of discussion. Thirty-three per cent were more specific in citing "reassurance" as often the basis for launching such conversations. Arguably, the ecology of the institution affords a particular sort of social opportunity to students whereby they can be repeatedly checking their own status and progress with coursework by means of chance conversations with relevant peers. It was less usual for students to report talking about lectures in this manner. Twenty-seven per cent of respondents did mention lectures as a conversational topic although several students qualified this by suggesting that such occasions might be more talk about *lecturers* than lectures: in particular, shared gripes about delivery and demands.

If coursework is the main currency of conversation, lectures are the main currency of material exchanges. That is, when students were asked what kind of documents they passed among each other, then 80% identified lecture notes: particularly to support their friends who had missed sessions. Forty-four per cent reported the sharing of books and 29% the exchange of essays. It could be concluded that lectures and coursework surface in the traffic between these students in opposing ways. Lectures are not experiences that promote a lot of discussion, but they are occasions that students wish to have fully documented: thus students pass around written records of the events (and seek web-based versions of these). Coursework, however, is something that is talked about more (albeit often with benchmarking motives) but the written products are either guarded more carefully or perhaps are seen as less useful to others.

These observations about the established context of study do echo some of what was witnessed happening on the computer network. The apparent significance or authority of lectures locates them as events that need documenting on course websites and so this is what students are requesting. Their own notes from lectures then become important records to circulate electronically and this is what we find. In a learning culture strongly driven by assessed assignments and examinations, possibly there is a resistance against technologies that provide yet more resources. Accordingly, these students want clear, authoritative and bounded versions of what it is that is being tested. They are not asking for specialist disciplinary tools to be circulated on the network and they are not attracted by self-pacing computer-aided learning packages. In a parallel study (Crook & Barrowcliff, in press), we found only 2 out of 34 students making use of CAL server software within a week of sampling usage patterns on their networked PCs (an apparently higher level of traffic with this server merely reflected its easy use as a gateway to the library catalogue).

The observations above concerning routine collaborative activity also complement what is emerging as the social patterns of network use. Organized face-to-face meetings with other students and with tutorial staff are relatively rare and yet both peers and tutors remain valued resources for learning. However, the nature, timing and location of face-to-face contacts typically is improvized and unstructured – that is, not organized. Students value this style of work-related interaction and, among the various benefits, it seems discretely to deliver the kind of progress benchmarks that motivate learners and give them self-confidence. It is therefore unsurprising that text conferencing discussion boards – with their formality and lasting visibility – are unattractive to networked students from this community. Neither would we expect much person-to-person e-mail debate, given that most face-to-face initiations of academic discussion avoid too conspicuous an intentionality (Crook & Webster, 1998).

17.8   Looking Forward

Notions of learning as 'networked', 'virtual' or 'electronic' have not been carefully distinguished in this chapter. However, I take "networked" to invite a focus on the infrastructure that might deliver a form of learning that is intended to be more paced by the student, richer in resources for study, and affording new varieties of interpersonal communication. These are generous promises: understanding whether an investment in networking will shift the culture of conventional campus life is important. Not least, it will give enthusiasts for radically virtual universities some basis for predicting how virtual students will cope with their learning life on the network. Insofar as virtual universities will continue to be populated by the constituency of school-leaving young people, then how such individuals are reacting now to networked resources is very significant.

Given this framework, the observations made here surely represent a credible case study of 'virtualization'. Yet the observed impact of networked resources and opportunities is hardly dramatic. Students do welcome this infrastructure within the context of their familiar experience of study. Yet they have no taste for comprehensively virtual education and their comments alert us to the breadth and drama of experience that is associated with being a full-time undergraduate. While they are quite comfortable using their computers to locate network resources or to engage in person-to-person communication, little of this activity seems particularly focused on their studies. Indeed, the convergence of both study and recreational resources on one site for activity (the Windows desktop) may be disruptive of learning for some. When asked if they felt they might spend too much time doing playful things on their networked computers, 50% of these students said that they did and, for many, this was a matter of concern.

One analysis of this situation would claim that the present case study is constrained by the unimaginative resources so far fashioned by the staff. Yet at least the circumstances of this case remind us that the enthusiasm of lecturers for working in this way can not be taken for granted. It also reminds us that taking seriously the students' own resource preferences may lead to rather pedestrian forms of web-based material. Arguably, this will be a problem as long as the curriculum is driven by a relentless pace of modularized and competitive assessments. Ironically, enthusiasts for networking educational technology often are also enthusiasts for the model of student-as-customer and the procedures of highly formalized quality management. This package of ideas tends dangerously towards a commodity view of educational resources. Networking can thereby conjure up a setting in which "...information technology would be used to provide self-paced and asynchronously-accessed learning support delivered as, when and where the learner needed it. Such support, delivered at a user's request and convenience, would be paid for like any other commodity" (MacFarlane, 1998:86).

Networking is not necessarily bound to the acquisition metaphor of learning, to the commodity metaphor of knowledge, and to the delivery metaphor of teaching. There is a set of alternatives based on conceptions of learning as 'participation'; such that education is viewed as an inherently community-oriented activity (Sfard, 1998). There is no space here to develop this acquisition/participation distinction. However, raising it does provide an opportunity to close the chapter by returning to the observations above of what lecturers were choosing to do with their websites. Further consideration does indicate that there is little in what they are doing that much strengthens a student's sense of identity as someone participating in a community of disciplinary practice.

Of the 71 course websites examined only one adopted a conversational manner in relation to the potential user. Not that familiarity of this kind is essential to building a sense of student participation. However, it may not be helpful if material offered to support learning is written in a prescriptive or directive tone. Moreover, there were few other signs of author-lecturers conceptualizing courses as social communities. So, it was not typical for the WebPages author actively to invite personal tutorial contact (only 18% of course sites had a live 'mailto': link that allowed e-mail to be launched from within the website). No sites gave indications of times that staff might be available for 'office hour' consultation. Only one site drew attention to the possibility of using the associated e-mail discussion board. Most significantly, there were no opportunities taken to make reference to students' own work. Whatever a module was producing in this sense was not celebrated in the web space context. Even if this was not possible for ongoing projects, it would surely be possible to present outcomes from *previous* presentations of a course. Membership of a community does entail a sense of history and progression that can be captured if members are able to 'leave tracks' in this sense.

In sum, there is much in these reactions of 'traditional' staff and undergraduates for future observers and commentators to consider. Appropriating networked learning may not be willingly or comfortably done by those students who currently make up the bulk of our undergraduate population. Moreover, what it is that networks get appropriated to may turn out to be a model of teaching and learning that could be in need of some repair. One important focus for more vigorous debate is the distinction raised above between learning as acquisition and learning as participation. Whether networks are to become the conduit-of-delivery or the arena-for-community is an issue requiring a deeper level of pedagogic discussion than is commonplace within current university management.

17.9   References

Brown, J.S. & Duguid, P. (1998) Universities in the digital age. In Hawkins, B. & Battin, P. (Eds.) *The Mirage of Continuity: Reconfiguring Academic Information Resources for the 21st Century*. Washington, D.C.: Council on Library and Information Resources, pp39-60

Committee of Scottish University Principals (1992*). Teaching and learning in an expanded higher education system*. Edinburgh: SCFC

Clark, R. E. (1994) Media will never influence learning, *Educational Technology Research and Development, 42*, pp21-29

Cole, R.I. (1972) Some reflections concerning the future of society, computers and education. In Chartrand, R. (Ed.) *Computers in the Service of Society*. New York, Pergammon Press. pp135-145

Crook, C.K. (1994) *Computers and the collaborative experience of learning*. London: Routledge

Crook, C.K. (1999) Learning Nests. Paper presented at Conference: New Media in Higher Education and Learning, UCS Los Angeles, October. http://www-rcf.usc.edu/~ics/HigherEd.html

Crook, C.K. (2000) Motivation and the ecology of collaborative learning. In Joiner, R., Littleton, K., Faulkner, D. & Miell, D. (Eds.) *Rethinking collaborative learning*. London: Free Association Press, pp161-178

Crook, C.K. & Barrowcliff, D.M. (in press) Ubiquitous computing on campus: patterns of engagement by university students. *International Journal of Human-Computer Interaction*

Crook, C.K. & Webster, D. (1998) Designing for informal undergraduate computer mediated communication, *Active Learning*. 7, pp47-51

Cuban, L. (1986) *Teachers and machines*. New York: Teachers College

Deering, R. *et al.* (1997) *Higher education in the learning society: Report of the National Committee of Inquiry into Higher Education*. London: HMSO and NCIHE Publications

Delvin, K. (1997) University challenge. *Guardian online* June 11th

Duderstadt, J.J. (1999) Can colleges and universities survive in the information age? In Katz, R. (Ed.) *Dancing with the devil. Information technology and the new competition in higher education*. San Francisco: Jossey-Bass

Economist (2001) Lessons of a virtual timetable. Feb 15th (Also at URL http://economist.com/printedition/PrinterFriendly.cfm?Story_ID=505047)

Gell, M. & Cochrane, P. (1996) Learning and education in an information society. In Dutton, W. (Ed.) *Information and communication technologies*. Oxford: Oxford University Press, pp249-263

Jaffee, D. (1998) Institutionalized resistance to asynchronous learning networks. *Journal Asynchronous Learning Networks* http://www.aln.org/alnweb/journal/jaln_vol2issue2.htm#jaffee

MacFarlane, A. (1998) Information, knowledge and learning. *Higher Education Quarterly, 52*, pp77-92

Sfard, A. (1998) On two metaphors for learning and the dangers of choosing just one. *Educational Researcher, 27*, pp4-13

Smeaton, A.F. & Keogh, G. (1999) An analysis of the use of virtual delivery of undergraduate lectures. *Computers and education, 32* pp83-94

Tiffin, J. & Rajasingham, L. (1995) *In search of the virtual class*. London: Routledge

18. Learning Networks and the Issue of Communication Skills[1]

Erica McAteer, Andrew Tolmie, Charles Crook,
Hamish Macleod and Kerry Musselbrook

18.1 Introduction

The expansion of UK further and higher education over the last decade has been accompanied by increased use of communication and information technologies (C&ITs) to aid the management of teaching and learning amongst the resulting larger and more diverse student communities. Various forms of C&IT support have been developed, but one type of growing importance is the use of conferencing systems to enable interactions between teachers and learners that would otherwise be unlikely to occur, because of constraints of time and/or distance. Video conferencing (one to one, one to many, many to many), text-based communication (e-mail, bulletin boards, synchronous and asynchronous conferencing,) and audio conferencing (telephone tutoring, shared workspace plus audio link) are the principle technologies that have emerged to serve these mediated forms of learning interaction.

In some respects, the advent of these systems seems to place educators in the enviable position of having a variety of media to choose from in the organization of teaching and learning. On the face of it, all that is necessary is to gather some hard data on the relative advantages and disadvantages of different media for different types of learning activity. These features can then be matched up against course methods and objectives, and an appropriate array of technology put in place. However, such a perspective is too simplistic. In the first place, any assumption that the main issue involved in implementing delivery technologies and media is that of choice based on pedagogical quality is by and large mistaken. The real situation is more typically one of necessity rather than choice, with technologies only getting brought into use when there is some overriding reason for doing so

---

[1] The work discussed in this chapter was undertaken during the Learning Networks: Communication Skills (LNCS) project, funded by the UK Joint Information Systems Committee (JISC) between January 1999 and March 2000, as part of the Committee on Awareness, Liaison and Training (CALT) Networked Learning initiative. The web deliverable described in the chapter can be viewed at http://www.gla.ac.uk/lncs/

(e.g. students being unable to be in the same physical classroom at the same time), and being strictly subject to the limitations of what is affordable.

Moreover, the perception of many experienced users of these technologies is that they are not in any case amenable to a 'plug in and play' approach. Their effective use for educational communication depends on staff and students possessing certain skills, especially those that allow them to unambiguously convey what they mean across a range of potentially complex interactions. Thus there is a need to help lecturers and their students to acquire the communication skills and strategies necessary to adapt to the technologies that happen to be available to them in their own particular circumstances. With this need in mind, the Learning Networks: Communication Skills (LNCS) project was set up to examine educational usage of video, text-based and audio conferencing, in order to identify effective communication practices and consider how best to develop these in current and new communities of use.

18.2   Communication and Communication Skills

A crucial first step in this task was to define what 'communication skills' consist of, since this had major implications for how the project was conducted. This is not in fact a straightforward issue, and a number of alternative conceptualizations are possible, although there is a basic division between what might be termed 'individual difference' and 'contextual' approaches. These are outlined briefly in turn below.

It is generally accepted that human communicative behaviour developed to support face-to-face exchange, and that this remains the default condition under which most communicative experience occurs, and under which ways of communicating are learnt and refined. Face-to-face encounters are informationally very rich (at least for those with reasonable sight and hearing) in terms of verbal signals and paralinguistic accompaniments, and communicative behaviour makes much use of that richness to convey subtle distinctions in meaning and attitude. One definition of communication skills that appears to follow from this is that these skills comprise knowledge of the meanings conveyed to others by different words, tones, gestures and expressions, and the ability to use this knowledge to communicate intended messages and all their nuances as exactly as possible. In this framework, skill resides within individuals, who may vary in their knowledge and ability to deploy it.

Applying this approach to use of conferencing technologies, it has long been argued that when communication shifts to media which allow exchanges over distance, some subset of the informational elements available in face-to-face encounters is lost, with potentially deleterious effects (Rutter, Stephenson & Dewley, 1981). So, for example, Abbott (1994) reports that during audio conferencing, the lack of visual cues restricts interaction, and participants experience difficulty in concentrating. With video conferencing, tutors report difficulties in managing groups across sites, due to the absence of coherent visual feedback and a consequent lack of confidence on the part of both teachers and students about how communications have been received (Cannon & Martin, 1995). Text-based conferencing, which lacks the turn-taking of face-to-face exchange, is frequently associated with failure to co-ordinate perspectives between participants (Collis, 1997). Communication skills under any of these 'reduced' conditions, could be considered to consist of face-to face skills plus the ability to compensate deliberately for the loss of informational elements (e.g. by substituting verbal statements for gestures and expressions), so that as far as possible intended messages are still conveyed in an exact fashion. Again, individuals may differ in this compensatory ability.

With regard to the object of the LNCS project, it seems from this standpoint as though it ought to be possible to identify a series of generally applicable do's and don'ts that encapsulate the compensatory behaviours required for different types of conferencing technology. Promoting the acquisition of communication skills for these media would then be a matter of making users aware of what these do's and don'ts were, and helping them to enact them. This is, in fact, exactly what many guidelines for conferencing technology use have attempted to do in the past (Butters et al., 1994).

However, there is good reason to suppose that this individual differences approach is based on a limited and inaccurate conceptualization of communication and therefore communication skills. The main problem is that it portrays communication as a one-sided process of transmission or 'broadcast' from sender to receiver: provided the message has been 'encoded' appropriately by the sender for the medium being used, it will be received as intended. In fact, as Clark and Wilkes-Gibbs (1986) point out, for an utterance to be understood as intended requires effort on the part of the receiver as well as the sender. In particular, the receiver's prior knowledge of the 'matter' of the message, as shaped by their past experience and their educational and cultural background, will guide their judgement as to what the sender is likely to mean, and thus what actually gets conveyed.

The result of this is that effective communication actually depends in practice on a process of *collaboration*, in which senders emit messages that attempt to take into account the receiver's assumed knowledge; and receivers attempt to interpret these messages in accordance with what they assume the sender's knowledge to be. This process may encompass a number of exchanges during which senders and receivers seek and present evidence (e.g. by asking questions or by elaborating on previous statements) that an acceptable level of shared understanding of what an initial message meant has been established. In essence, then, communication involves sender and receiver endeavouring to 'triangulate' upon the meaning of messages to their mutual satisfaction. Communication skills can be considered to include use of any behaviour to increase the efficiency of this process.

18.3 Implications for Investigating and Promoting the Effective Use of Conferencing Technologies

This collaborative model places an emphasis on the importance of *context* which carries a variety of implications for both the investigation and the promotion of effective communication practices using conferencing technologies. First of all, communication skill can no longer be seen solely as a function of individuals, since the effectiveness of any behaviour depends not only on the sender's ability to execute it, but also on what the receiver makes of it. It follows that communication skills are not generally applicable either, because what is effective for one combination of sender and receiver may well not be for another where, for instance, their background knowledge differs. In addition, communication skills must be seen as encompassing not just short term communicative tactics, such as use of explicit verbal statements, but also longer term strategies relating to *any* factor that influences the process of establishing agreed meanings. This might include, for example, tackling the stages of a joint activity in a particular sequence in order to allow the growth early on of the background knowledge needed for later communication.

As far as the use of conferencing technology is concerned, then, it is inappropriate to think about communication skills as compensatory extensions of individual behaviour in face-to-face encounters. Whether or not efficient, meaningful communication takes place depends on the extent to which effective *practices* (of whatever kind) have been established – and not necessarily consciously or deliberately – *across* participants in a given context. It is therefore the context, not the individual which is the correct level of analysis. Cataloging which practices are effective and which are less so remains an exercize of considerable value, since there may be some commonality between contexts, and what is effective in one might prove to be so in others that are similar. This does entail, however, a need to be sensitive to the broad sweep of factors that communication practices in different contexts might be attempting to address, and to examine a representative *range* of instances.

A sensitivity to context also means that the product of this cataloging will not be a general set of do's and don'ts for use of a particular conferencing technology. On the one hand, the information it provides should allow identification of perceived constraints on the success of technologically-mediated communication, and ways of bringing these constraints under users' control. However, what issues matter and what it might be possible to do about them will still vary from context to context. Conferencing technologies may require adaptations in all participants' behaviour for successful communication to take place, but such adaptations will be effective primarily in terms of how well they allow the task in hand to proceed. In other words, they are 'what works' in a specific context, as defined by characteristics of the technology, the people using it, their cultural background, the physical and social environment of usage, the nature and purpose of the messages themselves, and, as far as educational use is concerned, the course learning aims and teaching objectives.

From this perspective, general rules of thumb of the kind produced previously are of limited value for several reasons. Firstly, if they are pitched at the level of individual action, they will have little impact unless taken up by the majority of participants: it is performance at the community, not the individual level that is critical. Secondly, any attempt to impose a specific rule without consideration of how it will affect other behaviour may have unforeseen and even negative consequences, since effective communication practices are likely to be a response to the demands of a number of interrelated factors. Rigidly introducing a new strategy may therefore disrupt other adaptations that are already in place, or it may fail to work because certain conditions do not obtain. Thirdly, if teachers and students are to make use of the communication practices developed by others, not only must these be broadly appropriate to their own context, they must be *recognized* by them as such. Abstract rules without contextual detail are unlikely to resonate with users' personal circumstances, however relevant they may be.

Taking these points into consideration, it was evident that, to meet its overall aim, the LNCS project had to achieve two principal objectives:

- document and examine both tactical and strategic communication practices using video, text and audio conferencing across a sample of contexts which reflected the range found within UK higher and further education, and examine as thoroughly as possible the issues and constraints these practices were an attempt to respond to within each context;
- encapsulate the findings of this research in such a fashion as to preserve a sense of the contexts from which they were drawn, and employ this as a point of connection to intending users' own experiences and needs.

18.4 Methodology: Design and Data Collection

These objectives informed both the design and the data collection procedures used to conduct the project research. With regard to design, the key consideration was that the research should examine information drawn from as wide a range of teaching and learning sites as possible within the time available. It was also important that these sites had two or more years' experience of incorporating conferencing technologies into their teaching, so that there had been time for effective adaptations to develop. The main focus of the research was therefore on fieldwork involving visits (physical and virtual) to each of fifteen teaching sites. These fifteen sites (see Table 18.1) were asked to take part in the research because they constituted a representative spread of conferencing technology use in terms of type of institution, subject discipline, course level, purpose served by conferencing, and actual technology involved. This sample enabled different kinds of experience to be accessed in a relatively systematic fashion, and thus increased the likelihood of other users in the further and higher education community being able to recognize circumstances and issues similar to their own in subsequent reports on these experiences.

Table 18.1 Teaching sites participating in the LNCS project

Course	Students	Conferencing technology
Product design engineering (ICON)	Third year undergraduates	Video conferencing, text-based conferencing & audio conferencing
Foreign policy and analysis	Postgraduates (masters)	Video conferencing
Rural development	First, second and third year undergraduates	Video conferencing
Accrediting prior learning	Lecturers undergoing continuing professional development	Video conferencing
Elective in cultural studies	Second and third year undergraduates	Video conferencing
Physics and environmental sciences	Final year undergraduates and postgraduates	Video conferencing
Arts Faculty lectures	First year undergraduates	Video conferencing
Open and distance education	Postgraduates (masters/professional development)	Text-based conferencing
Introduction to cultural studies	First year undergraduates	Text-based conferencing
Computer mediated communication and education	Postgraduates (masters)	Text-based conferencing
Computer mediated communication and psychology	Third year undergraduates	Text-based conferencing
Psychology and information technology	Final year undergraduates	Text-based conferencing
Engineering	Postgraduates (masters/professional development)	Text-based conferencing
Educational psychology	Postgraduates (masters/professional training)	Text-based conferencing
Telephone tutorials in distance learning	Various	Audio conferencing

So, for instance, the courses listed in Table 18.1 were based at a variety of institutions including traditional and post-1992 universities (*i.e.,* former polytechnics), and those with a major remit in distance education. A range of disciplines (arts, humanities, social sciences, engineering and natural sciences), and of undergraduate and postgraduate courses were also represented. In some courses, conferencing technologies were an 'interesting add on', or were one of several teaching and learning components. In others, they were essential to the actual functioning of the course, since they provided the only means of interaction and discussion, or they enabled the grouping of enough students to make it viable and cost-effective to run. In some cases, conferencing technologies were the focus of students' studies as well as the means of delivery or a channel for communicating. Product design students at the ICON site, for example, were using the tools of their future profession as part of their project work, and also reflecting on the adequacy of these tools. Finally, the spread of the technologies and the purposes to which they were applied reflected current implementations. Thus text conferencing sites were included more often than any other type because this was the most commonly used technology. Similarly, video conferencing was represented primarily in its use for remote lecturing, since this was typically how it was employed. Audio conferencing on its own was represented by only one site (albeit by several courses from this site), since it was comparatively rare. The same was true of sites making use of a battery of mixed technologies.

Turning to data collection, once each teaching site had agreed to participate, detail on the courses was gathered from teachers and also from written documentation (e.g. course statements). The information sought at this stage concerned the course format and timetable, the technology in use, and the background of the students, including their familiarity with the technology. This information provided an important contextual backdrop to the material garnered during the subsequent fieldwork. The object of the field work itself was to collect data at each site on the communications that took place using conferencing technology, and, crucially, on teacher and student *perceptions* of these communications and how they felt these served the activities in which they were embedded. This data took the form of conference archives, notes of observations made by researchers while communication was ongoing, records of individual interviews and focus groups with both students and teachers, and questionnaire responses.

Conference archives provided some detail of the communication strategies used by teachers and students, as did notes of observations. However, these were necessarily limited sources of information, and could only provide partial records of interaction. In text-based conferencing, for example, much communication takes place off-line, for instance via telephone or fax. A record of this surrounding activity may be critical to forming an understanding of what is happening online (Tolmie & Boyle, 2000). More importantly, recordings and observations could not capture individuals' internal responses to and interpretations of communicative events, a critical part of the communication process. In 'virtual lectures', for instance, mismatches between sender and receiver on the meaning of communicative content may be hard to detect, and yet participants' awareness or lack of awareness of these may have a considerable impact on learning and on subsequent communication. Similarly, how a text-based message has been received may not always be self-evident from a rejoinder to it, especially if more than two people are part of the 'conversation' and protocol requires politeness. For these reasons, individual interviews with students and teachers, in which they could voice these more hidden reactions, were considered to be a fundamental part of the research. These interviews provided a central means of identifying successful and unsuccessful communication events and communications practices, the reasons for success or failure, and thus the underlying issues that effective practices needed to address.

A total of 75 interviews were conducted across the fifteen sites. Most of these took place on a face-to-face basis, but for practical reasons a small number of students and teachers were interviewed by telephone or videoconference link. These interviews (which were essentially the same in each case) comprised an initial exploratory stage, in which interviewees were simply asked to describe and evaluate in their own words their experiences of the conferencing systems they had used. A 'critical incident' approach was used to aid memory, with interviewees being asked to recall instances where communication was particularly successful and particularly unsuccessful, and to give their understanding of the reasons why. Where possible, archives were used to assist in this process, by, for example, giving interviewees access to conferences they had taken part in, in order to illustrate, check and qualify their comments. After this initial free response stage, the interviewer moved on to ask targeted questions about other factors that might have influenced interviewees' experiences, but which had not been dealt with up to that point. These factors were drawn from a list identified by a preliminary literature review as being potentially important to the effective use of conferencing, and included, for example, implicit and explicit rules of exchange, perceptions of relative status and the constraints imposed by the technology itself.

The one-to-one interviews allowed students and teachers to discuss their experiences without being influenced in what they said by other participants' reports. In some cases, however, additional focus group sessions were used as a convenient means of cross-checking data obtained from individual interviews, and identifying similarities and differences between experiences. These sessions followed the same format in terms of their content as the interviews, and in some instances were arranged to follow on from e.g. videoconference sessions that a project researcher had also attended and observed. This provided an approximate parallel to the critical incident plus archive approach aimed at in the interviews.

Finally, questionnaires along similar lines to the interviews were circulated to students at two sites where time-tabling and other restrictions meant that this was the only practical means of gathering individual data. In addition, the postgraduate students on the Open and Distance Education course were mailed a set of open-ended questions and a list of emergent issues from our preceding fieldwork for comment, at the end of the continuous assessment period of their own course.

18.5   Methodology: Analysis and Dissemination

The first stage of the project research gathered in-depth data on communication via conferencing technology from a range of representative teaching sites, in line with the first project objective.   As a crucial step towards achieving the second objective, it was necessary to find a means of systematically capturing the full detail of the issues and practices revealed in that data, whilst maintaining a sense of the contexts in which these issues and practices arose.   To meet this need, analysis was conducted using a linked case study approach to data from each of the teaching sites.   This enabled the requisite level of contextualized detail to be preserved, but within a framework that facilitated comparison across sites.

As a first stage in this analysis, recordings of interviews were either transcribed, or digitized directly from tape.   The resulting files were then organized by teaching site, and stored on CDs. These CDs, along with archive data and other site information, were made available to all members of the research group for initial inspection at a 'scanning and sampling' level.   On the basis of this, a set of issue codes was agreed upon, where each code designated a factor or a set of related factors that was a) reported by respondents to affect successful conferencing communication, and/or b) apparently addressed in one means or another by the practices employed at a given site.   This set of codes provided a standardized framework for subsequent analysis.

Each member of the research group then took responsibility for fully analyzing all the data from a subset of sites.   This entailed examining the available archives and interviews for each site, noting all instances of a particular issue being mentioned and what was said about it, together with all instances of an issue being evident as a concern in the records of actual interactions.   From this data, the first draft of a case study summary was compiled for each site. These summaries then formed the core of further, comparative analysis.

This was achieved in the following fashion.   First of all, the full set of issue codes used to analyze the case study material was reduced to a set of eight overarching 'issues to manage', representing broad areas of emergent concern encompassing all the original, more specific issues.   These eight issues were as follows:

- *characteristics of the communication technology* (technical specification, capacities and limitations, reliability);
- *stated purpose of the technology* (what users have been told it is there to achieve);
- *stated principles of use* (the 'rules of engagement');
- *character of the communication* (interactional style, spontaneity, presence, strategies and patterns of behaviour);
- *self-perceptions* (self-consciousness, motivation, benchmarking);
- *learning and teaching relationships* (roles, attributions about others, social patterns);

- *getting things done* (task grounding, preparation, establishing the purpose and function of activities, co-ordination of group work);
- *continuity with curricula* (context, co-ordination, integration, assessment).

These issues were used as the basis for organizing all the draft case summaries; *i.e.*, each consisted of a report under these eight headings detailing the specific issues raised in that context, and how, if at all, these were managed. These points were accompanied by illustrative material in the form of quotations from interviews and focus groups, or extracts from archives. This meant that as far as possible the voices of actual users were preserved as an integral part of the case summaries, whilst at the same time being organized to form part of a bigger picture.

Once compiled, the draft case summaries were checked by other members of the project team and by staff at the relevant teaching sites for correspondence to their own knowledge and perceptions. Final versions were prepared in the light of feedback from this process. However, because the eight issues to manage formed a common structure across the case summaries, they enabled assessments to be made of the extent to which issues, and strategies for dealing with them, were similar or different across contexts and across technologies. Thus the exercize of checking the case summaries also became an occasion for members of the project team to carry out comparative assessments with respect to points which appeared to them to be significant. These analyses formed the basis of what were termed "educational theme narratives". These were essays authored by individual members of the team, which dealt with issues that were common across at least some contexts and technologies, anchored once again, however, in illustrative quotations and archive extracts from specific sites.

Six such theme narratives were identified in the first instance, as follows:

- *Grounding* – the facilitatory role played by previous experience of the activity to be conducted online;
- *Reliability* – the patterns of consequences associated with unreliable systems;
- *Common knowledge* – the mobilization and construction of shared knowledge in online environments;
- *Collaboration* – problems of using collaborative exercizes as a means of promoting conferencing;
- *Experience* – the influence of past experience of conferencing technologies;
- *Audience* – the role of a sense of audience in online communication.

These six narratives were by no means seen as exhausting the identifiable common themes, but rather as constituting the first of a set of similar reflections that might be generated over time from further examination of the case material, by those outside as well as within the research team. Presentations of project findings up to this point at conferences and workshops, both face-to-face and online, provided an opportunity to gain feedback and to refine the output from the research, but perhaps also served as a first step towards encouraging these further reflections.

Both the case summaries and the theme narratives were explicitly designed to meet the objective of reporting on existing conferencing users' experiences in such a way as to maximize the possibility of new users being able to pick out those points which were most relevant to their own circumstances. One further strand of work was seen as necessary, however, to complete this effort. Not surprisingly, the eight overarching issues to manage identified by the research were similar to the issues which emerged during the preliminary literature review, and which fed into the interview schedule – although not all of these were given the emphasis that the LNCS data indicated they should have. This similarity suggested a means of expanding the scope of the project output without impairing its sense of being anchored in concrete contexts and experiences, by distilling existing research and practice literature (e.g. conferencing guidelines) into a general set of messages, focused on the same eight issues to manage as the case summaries.

Three literature summaries were drafted on this basis, one for videoconferencing, one for text-based conferencing, and one for audio conferencing. These differed somewhat in scope and content, reflecting differences in the material that was available in each instance. So, for example, the summary for text-based conferencing covered both a practice and a research strand by dint of being the focus of an extensive literature of both types. The videoconferencing summary had more of a practice flavour, due to the relative lack of previous research in educational settings, whilst the audio conferencing summary was smaller in scale since there was less background literature of any kind. However, each of the summaries was designed to serve an identical function; *i.e.,* that of presenting an overview of what the literature had to say about the same issues and constraints on technology-mediated communication as were apparent in the project teaching sites, and about how these issues might be managed. In this sense, they constituted general 'guides' to use of the three broad types of conferencing technology, but guides that were still at root connected to specific contexts because the issues they addressed were exemplified by one or more of the sites.

Once these guides had been drafted and cross-checked by members of the project team, the final piece of a dissemination vehicle aimed at supporting and promoting the development of effective communication practices fell into place. This vehicle takes the form of a web-based hypertext focused on the three conferencing guides, the case summaries from the fifteen teaching sites, and the educational theme narratives. The *conferencing guides* are each directly accessible via a straightforward choice of technology from a menu. As indicated above, they are organized to discuss each of the eight issues to manage emergent from the field research and past literature, and in this way they define the range of points where attention may need to be concentrated in developing effective usage of a particular technology. They also provide links to a list of the research and practice references on which they are based, and to other web sites covering related material.

The *case summaries* are clustered under separate menu headings for each of the three technologies, and have titles which indicate the level and subject discipline of the course concerned. This serves to signal the basic contextual parameters that apply in each case, as an aid to selection. The sites relevant to each technology are also directly accessible from the corresponding conferencing guide. As with the conferencing guides, the narrative of the case summaries is organized according to the eight management issues, but in this instance the text contains optional hypertext links to the words of participants (teachers, students and support staff) in the fieldwork study, and to archived examples of conference activity. Specific sections of both the conferencing guides and the case summaries can also be accessed from a separate, cross-indexed menu for each of the eight management issues.

The *educational theme* narratives are accessible from a further menu presenting a choice of titles. These deal with specific areas of concern within one or other of the eight issues to manage, and so are organized along different lines to the guides and the case summaries. They are, however, still connected conceptually to the other material via the links they contain to illustrative interview and archive extracts, since these provide in turn a link identifying the specific case and technology from which they are drawn. Finally, the site also provides access to a project report detailing how the data was collected and analyzed, and to a user guide outlining the structure of the site and how it is envisaged it might be employed.

The key characteristic of this web site is that rather than presenting the project output in linear fashion, with beginning, middle and end, it quite deliberately allows multiple points of entry to, and routes through the material. For instance, a teacher newly involved in setting up videoconferencing provision for a course in history might choose to look first at the videoconferencing guide in order to examine and consider the full range of issues that could come up, and how these might be dealt with. They might follow this up by linking through to the case summary on the foreign policy course, as providing the closest parallel to their own circumstances, in order to check on the specific issues that arose in that context and about which they might therefore need to be especially sensitive. They might then look to see whether the educational themes provided any more material relevant to these identified issues. In contrast, a more experienced user of conferencing technology might work through the material in the opposite direction, starting with the cross-technology issues identified by the educational themes, using these as an aid to interpreting their own experiences, and working down to specific cases that might provide further insights. An educational researcher, on the other hand, might find it more useful to access the material through the issues to manage, exploring the impact of those issues that are of particular concern across a variety of contexts.

This dissemination strategy therefore makes it possible, crucially, for users to determine for themselves what point and level of contact with the material makes most sense to them, given their own objectives, circumstances, and past experience. Underpinning this strategy is the central concept of *grounded guidelines*, which merits some elucidation. It was noted above that not only must information relating to communication practices using conferencing technology be relevant to users for them to capitalize on it, but that it must also be recognized by them as such. This point was emphasized because users often report feeling that they have difficulty identifying how abstract, general guidelines might apply to them, and thus whether and how the principles embodied in them should be implemented. The implication is that they require some measure of contextual detail before they can grasp (even if only intuitively) the issues and processes being pointed at, and make a judgement as to whether or not these are likely to apply to their own circumstances.

The corollary of this is that guidelines need to be grounded in the sense of providing exactly this kind of contextual detail. This is not entirely straightforward if it is in fact desirable to make some generalized set of statements, as with the conferencing guides described above. The solution adopted here is to provide grounding by ensuring that all points can be *traced back* to specific contexts, and ultimately to the voices of specific individuals recounting their own experiences. Of course, achieving this also has the effect of ensuring that the guidelines are grounded in a second sense, that of providing the grounds on which general statements or claims are based, something that has typically not been the case either with previous conferencing guidelines. A final point to make is that grounded guidelines, because of their appeal to context as a means of judging relevance, can never constitute strict recommendations for action, but merely an outline of issues and strategies that might be relevant. In other words, the user must necessarily engage in active extrapolation to their own situation.

It is for this reason that visitors to the LNCS dissemination site are given no firm prescription as to usage, though some description of potential routes through the material is provided as an aid to orientation. The aim instead is to resource users in making their own judgement about the information from which, for them, such extrapolation is possible. However, systematic patterns of usage of the site material may still emerge over time, and these might usefully be captured and fed back to others. In particular, it was envisaged throughout the project that the final output would be capable of forming part of institutional staff development courses in good practice within networked learning environments, as well as being used independently by academic and research staff. The intention is that members of the project team will themselves be involved in organizing such institutional provision, and will make reports on their experiences available via the web site as a guide to future use by others. This highlights one final point, that the dissemination package is regarded as dynamic, not static, and capable of being added to over time as further data and analyses, including educational theme narratives, become available.

18.6 Acknowledgements

The authors would like to thank the Joint Information Systems Committee for funding this research project as part of their CALT (Committee for Awareness of Learning and Teaching) Networked Learning Initiative. We also owe much to the teachers, support staff and students at our collaborative sites, to colleagues concerned in the development of good practice with conferencing technologies across the HE sector and, particularly, to participants in the various workshops and conference sessions at which the LNCS material has been presented, for their input, then and afterwards.

18.7 References

Abbott, L. (1994) The application of video-conferencing to the advancement of independent group learning for professional development. *Educational Training and Technology International 31,* pp85-92

Butters, L., Clarke, A., Hewson, T. & Pomfrett, S. (1994*) The do's and don'ts of video conferencing in higher education: A report to the advisory group on computer graphics.* Support Initiative for Multimedia Applications Report Series No.4

Cannon, R. & Martin, J. (1995) *Survey of user experience of the University of Wales video network.* Support Initiative for Multimedia Applications Report Series No.15

Clark, H.H. & Wilkes-Gibbs, D. (1986) Referring as a collaborative process. *Cognition 22,* pp1-39

Collis, B. (1997) Supporting project-based collaborative learning via a world wide web environment. In Khan, B. (Ed) *Web-based instruction.* New Jersey: Educational Technology Publications

Rutter, D.R., Stephenson, G.M. & Dewley, M.E. (1981) Visual communication and the content and style of conversation. *British Journal of Social Psychology 20,* pp41-52

Tolmie, A. & Boyle, J. (2000) Factors influencing the success of computer mediated communication (CMC) environments in university teaching: a review and case study. *Computers and Education 34,* pp119-140

19. Beyond E-Learning: A Future For Networked Learning

Christine Steeples, Chris Jones and Peter Goodyear

19.1 Introduction

Where are we going with e-learning, online learning, networked learning? In the chapters of this book you will have found references to and discussion of networked learning, e-learning, online learning, and computer-mediated communications amongst others. While we do not propose to spend time in this concluding chapter interpreting each of these terms again (since we would argue our fellow authors have already clarified their terminology anyway), instead what we do want to do here is acknowledge that there is an abundance of such terms. This profusion of closely associated terms can be confusing to the reader trying to find their way around this area of learning technology. One of the currently most used but confusing and troublesome terms we feel is *e-learning*. Confusing, because this term is being used in very loose ways that we feel will be unhelpful for improving the scientific rigour of this field of research and practice. Troublesome, because it is sadly often found to be representative of a highly impoverished form of learning support.

Yet e-learning is a term that seems to have captured widespread support and enthusiasm, and so we would like to discuss it in this chapter, in relation to our own selected term of *networked learning*, chosen quite intentionally for this book. We do this from a standpoint that e-learning is currently being used as a blanket term, in a variety of manners that are quite distinct from each other and, at worst, include a form of learning support that we believe is deeply concerning for the advancement of qualitatively rich and supportive learning experiences to people in higher education.

What currently seems to be offered under this banner of e-learning includes 'quick-fix' forms of provision and support for learning in so-called online courses that are little more than an online provision of the course support materials that would otherwise be provided as part of a face-to-face traditional course. Offered online to remote learners such courses operate at the level of transmission of information, providing little or no opportunities for the learners to engage with tutors or peers. We feel that the proliferation of e-learning in this form will do little good either for the long-term take-up of technologically-mediated forms of learning support, nor more crucially for the learners that encounter this form of learning. Indeed Noble refers to institutions caught up in this kind of growth of online courses as operating as 'digital diploma mills' (Noble, 1998). Preece (2000) further claims that putting up lecture notes on the web, and thereby using online education as a forum for dissemination of knowledge, is an uninspiring method of teaching. Sadly too this is being welcomed by some learners as a quick way to get a degree or qualification.

The push to e-learning also comes from economic perspectives (Ash & Bacsich, Chapter 3 this volume). Macdonald (2000) asserts that the deciding factor, setting the pattern for the form of higher education in the future will be cost, and cost effectiveness. Leaving quality aside, he suggests virtual universities will:

> "... provide 'university education' at dramatically lower cost than traditional universities – and a cost that will proportionately decrease as the online audience expands .. [and] this ... will weaken existing universities' hold on higher education" (Macdonald, 2000:193).

The picture of what seems to be happening under the name of e-learning is quite startling. There were 79,400 links to e-learning from Google found in April 2001, giving links primarily to a raft of business enterprizes and institutions that are offering e-learning 'solutions' primarily in the form of online training courses or programs. The New York Times in 1999 estimated there are thousands of courses online in the US alone and according to the BBC news, the number of universities in the US providing internet-based courses leading to degrees more than doubled in the 1999 academic year, from 15% to 34% (BBC, 2000). As a specific example, Illinois Governor George Ryan announced in May 2001 that enrollments in distance courses offered through the Illinois Virtual Campus (IVC) rose to nearly 38,000 by late 2000, an increase of 44% on figures in Spring 2000. 2,615 different courses are offered through some form of distance learning by the IVC. Overall, US figures suggest that technology-based training is projected to represent 55% of all training by 2002, up from 21% in 1998 and the largest proportion of this is likely to be online. Indeed, web-based training is expected to expand from US$197 million in 1997 to US$5.5 billion by 2002, representing an explosive growth of 95% annually (Moe, Bailey and Lau (1999) in Berge, 2001). In the UK, the Open University is said to have 100,000 students working online of its 250,000 total enrollment (Scigliano, 2000)

We must also point to what's happening with online learning in terms of empirical evidence about teacher and learners' use and particularly from studies on the experiences of teachers and learners of networked learning. In terms of *use* in the UK, we found on the Networked Learning in HE project[1] in our survey sample (of around 90 teaching staff across nine different subject areas) that 94% of the teachers use e-mail on a daily basis and 59% use the web on a daily basis (with 83% using the web 'every couple of days'). Seventy-nine per cent of the students in our case study sample agreed that the technology was helping them to learn.

---

[1]   Networked Learning in HE project: csalt.lancs.ac.uk/jisc

Eighty-eight per cent felt that they were given autonomy and responsibility for their own learning in the networked learning environment. Fifty-nine per cent felt the technology was helping them achieve their personal aims. Sixty-one per cent felt the technology helped them study more effectively. (All of these responses were given *after* their networked learning experiences.)

Part of the growing image being portrayed for universities in the future is as 'ubiquitous mobile computing environments' (see also Crook, Chapter 17 this volume on learners' ambivalence to communicating with their peers via their learning nests). The image portrays students downloading e-mail as they walk about the campus, with wireless technology often substantially cheaper than fixed network access points, especially in older buildings. As an example, Buena Vista University in Iowa claims to have realized savings on time for installation and savings on costs at around $4000 per room, by hanging one or two access points rather than drilling out walls to add a number of wall-jack ports. However such a policy necessarily requires students to have their own laptops and Buena Vista are covering this by charging a higher fee to cover the lease of laptops (Carlson, 2000).

The rapid development and interest in e-learning highlights some of the key concerns and issues that are confronting higher education staff (faculty) today. We are probably all too aware of cases of institutional online learning failures, with HE teachers struggling with acceptance and implementation of new technologies and cases where learners are rejecting the use of learning technologies. HE institutions are under pressure to create strategies/polices for using learning technologies to extend their reach to new constituencies across the globe and to allocate budgets for remaining viable. Yet HE institutions need to be able to demonstrate qualitative advantages for using networked technologies and as Darby has noted the inadequacies in much of the current provision stems from the lack of significant investment in creation of a substantial underlying infrastructure (Darby, Chapter 2, this volume).

While we are critical that many institutions are putting their course pages on the web and calling them 'e-learning', there are some salutary examples to highlight. For example, the Chronicle of Higher Education (1 March 2001) describes the OpenCourseware@MIT project. This MIT effort is estimated at around US$100 million, and is concerned with creating web pages for every course (around 2000 courses) that the university offers. It is estimated it will take over 10 years to complete the work. Assurance comes from a further statement that this putting up of web pages is not education, 'education is what you do with the materials'. The work will create *transparency* about the institution, through 'a public window into MIT ... to see the sorts of things we're teaching'. More cynically it is probably intended to act as a counter to competition from the raft of new, virtual universities besetting US higher education.

Goodyear (draft) has also problematized this issue of e-learning but he suggests e-learning can be rich and 'empowering' if the following interpretation is applied:

"... the systematic use of networked multimedia computer technologies
- to empower learners;

- improve learning;
- connect learners to people and resources supportive of their needs; and to
- integrate learning with performance and
- individual with organizational goals" (Goodyear, draft).

This is a sophisticated definition and one that clearly places considerable and complex demands on HE faculty/staff to operationalize, if it is to be interpreted into the design of successful and effective e-learning or networked learning programs. As Goodyear suggests we can use this interpretation as a way to move forward with e-learning in a positive and pedagogically-informed manner.

If we are to talk about futures, then this chapter must comment also on some of the new developments that are emerging in the field of networked technologies that might offer pedagogical advantage. We focus on the significant advances that have been made in the capability of personal computers to incorporate multimedia. Multimedia can allow information and ideas to be communicated in more naturalistic, expressive and intuitive ways than has hitherto been possible with just text characters. In particular we present some ideas from using multimedia elements in e-learning or networked learning,, where we see some new exciting possibilities for closer and more naturalistic collaboration for learning and development among distributed professional communities. But first we wish to examine more closely the implications for practice, when attempting to design for e-learning from a pedagogical perspective. We do this by looking first at aspects of design and then propose the use of a pedagogical framework for networked learning.

19.2   Preparing for Networked Learning Design

We assert attention to design for e-learning is critical. If we are to predict a future for e-learning or networked learning as a qualitatively better educational provision than the base resource-oriented form of e-learning, then attention to aspects of pedagogical design would seem to us to be paramount in this future.

What we want to suggest here is some initial ways to prepare for design for networked learning or e-learning. We therefore suggest a continuum for e-learning provision that at one end of the scale is attuned to transmission of information and therefore is largely associated with more passive responses from the learner or with more shallow forms learning. At the other end, we would suggest the design leads to highly interactive and supportive provision that is geared to support of deeper approaches to learning or what Goodyear has referred to as 'good learning' (Goodyear, Chapter 4, this volume). Figure 19.1 below attempts to capture the design aspects of online learning provision that constitute this continuum, that can be combined in different ways within an online learning environment. Varying degrees of depth of provision are also possible in each of these design aspects, *i.e.*, within each of the boxes in the figure. We suggest this continuum as a device for practitioners in the upstream stages of designing an online environment, to clarify two polarized forms of e-learning and for suggesting attention to the distinctive aspects that can sit between these two poles.

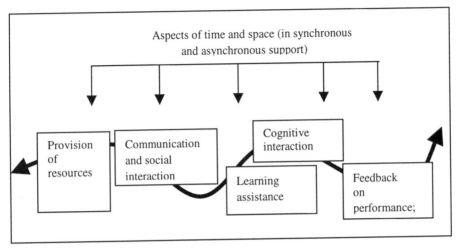

Figure 19.1 A continuum of design aspects for 'e-learning'

Provision of resources concerns giving access to web sites for example to learners to read articles, to find information, *etc.* Lecture notes on the web is an example of this kind of provision for learners to access at any time. A bulletin board with course notices could be another. It is concerned with provision of information to the learner. It does offer a form of provision that is easily accessible and can be useful to the learner who missed the lecture or as an additional resource to that lecture. But as Goodyear has commented (see Chapter 4, this volume) it concurs with learning as passive reception. A most crude and least effort interpretation of e-learning provision sees it as being wholly/largely about HE institutions giving access to resources on the web that an individual learner can access and use independently and then describing this as an online course. In certain circumstances, this may be exactly what is required, but there are many more situations and contexts in HE in which learning requires more than this kind of provision to be enabled. For example, in situations where a learner will benefit from the help and guidance of tutors or support of others, including other peers.

Another design aspect concerns the provision of opportunities for *communication and social interaction,* using networked technologies to connect learners and tutors, and learners and learners. These connections for communication are the basis for what we are calling in this chapter 'networked learning'. Elsewhere, we have defined networked learning as:

"... learning in which information and communications technology (ICT) is used to promote connections: between one learner and other learners, between learners and tutors; between a learning community and its learning resources" (Goodyear & NLinHE team, 2001).

Some of the richest examples of networked learning involve interaction with online materials *and* with other people. But we don't see the use of online materials (such as web resources) as a *sufficient* characteristic to define networked learning. The foreground needs to promote connections for interaction. The interactions between people in networked learning environments can be synchronous, asynchronous or both. The interactions can be mediated through text, voice, graphics, video, shared workspaces or combinations of these forms. This aspect also endorses the importance of the social dimension for learning, which we believe to be fundamental for good learning. Later in this chapter we explore connections for communication through multimedia and how these can offer rich and innovative ways to support distributed practitioner communities in their professional development.

We also want to add ways to help support the learner or to give the learner *learning assistance* e.g., through computer-based tools that are integrated into the online environment to assist the learner. We mean for example devices like intelligent agents or 'bots' that can conduct refined searches for the learner, advance organizers that help the learner plan ahead, and tools to aid workflow or collaboration, such as in collaborative writing. Learning assistance can also operate at a meta-level, helping the learner to think about the learning process and to develop strategies for learning (see for example, Mayes *et al*, Chapter 12 this volume, on tertiary courseware that was found to promote meta-learning).

Cognitive interaction is to do with the design of the online environment such that the learner is encouraged to cognitively engage with the materials provided, e.g., through allowing high levels of learner control. It is about the learner doing something (albeit cognitively and therefore not necessarily visible to anyone else) rather than passively receiving information. High-level interactivity can be offered in learning resources and these will be intellectually challenging, according to Macdonald (2000). There can be interaction with online materials such as web pages when learners are required to actively engage with those materials, e.g., perhaps by asking learners to make contrasts between the material presented and their own perspective. To continue with this example, equally interaction can be encouraged through dialog online, when different learners say are presenting their viewpoints and the learner is required to contribute their own. So we can see that there can be a close coupling between the design aspects of communication and interactivity.

A much deeper provision for learning could be offered if *feedback on performance and opportunities for reflection* can be designed into the environment to support the learner. Of course in a communications-based online environment, a tutor and other learners can give feedback to the learner, e.g., on their contributions. More sophisticated computer-based technologies such as intelligent tutoring systems have attempted to adapt to the learner's actions and to emulate the role of the tutor. Such systems attempt to provide contextually sensitive feedback on the learner's performance such that the learner is assisted to make progress. Such systems will in a sense converse with the learner in an educational dialog.

Sadly, as Goodyear notes, we know of no such online environment currently, that can offer support to this level to the learner (Goodyear, draft).

Affecting all aspects of this continuum are the aspects of time and space. The timing of support in networked learning or e-learning is usually discussed in terms of synchronous versus asynchronous systems.

Synchronous support is provided for the learner through interactions which are closely interleaved in time. The logistical constraint of synchronization means that the participants have to be available to interact at the same time. This has the disadvantage of reducing the participants' control over their use of time but brings with it the possibility of rapid turn-taking in a discussion. This is of great benefit when (for example) the tutor needs to refine his or her understanding of the learner's problem and can embark on a series of questions and answers to focus in on the core of the problem. It gives correspondingly less time for the participants to reflect on the interaction, to clarify their understanding of an issue or consult reference material (McConnell, 2000).

Asynchronous support does not require (and does not permit) simultaneous interaction between participants. The most commonly used networked learning systems are essentially asynchronous, in that they neither require nor support interactions which are closely interleaved in time. The advantages and disadvantages mirror those of synchronous interaction: participants get time to reflect, think, consult resources, *etc.*, but the passage of time separating each exchange imposes a different discipline on communication/messages. There is a strong need for clarity, lack of ambiguity, coherence, *etc.* in messages.

However, the basis of the distinction between synchronous and asynchronous communication is in fact far from obvious as we see convergences between the two emerging in contemporary online environments. One could argue that they are not discrete categories, rather that there is a continuum along which the frequency of interchange of message decreases. But this would deny the experienced nature of synchronous and asynchronous communication, as well as ignore some important differences. Two key differences are the possibility of interruption and the cost of communication failures. One message cannot be interrupted by another in asynchronous communication, whereas interruption is often the norm in synchronous communication. This has implications for students' perception of the medium. Regarding communication failure, in synchronous communication, the consequences of a malformed message, or (conversely) of an interpretive failure by the message's receiver, can be repaired rapidly and with relatively little effort. Indeed, our tacit knowledge of the repairability of synchronous interactions often underpins the strategies we use in tutorial discourse (e.g., Goodyear & Stone, 1992). In asynchronous communication, such rapid interactive clarification is almost impossible. This can have benefits, in so far as it causes participants to think more deeply about what they want to 'say' and to attend to the clarity with which they say it. In turn, this influences the style of communicative exchanges in asynchronous systems, which tend to be more formal than one finds in transcripts of telephone or face-to-face conversations, yet less formal than one finds in academic writing in essays, for example (Hardy, Hodgson, & McConnell, 1994).

There are of course limitations to this depiction of design aspects in Figure 19.1, not least disguising complexity by its simplicity. It can be criticized as it suggests a left to right reading that might suggest a hard and fast rule that poor quality is on the left and optimized learning only ever on the right. This would be contentious and is not our intention. We say this because in certain circumstances provision of information is exactly what's needed and should not be viewed as a 'poor relation'. Also, the middle ground aspects e.g., of interaction and communication should not necessarily be seen as sequentially progressive towards the best form of e-learning we can achieve. For example an effective and successful online environment might be created that is used only for information sharing and for social, communication purposes. Neither are we suggesting such design can displace the critical need for tutorial support online (Goodyear *et al.*, 2001).

This chapter therefore looks next at the succeeding stage in our interpretation of networked learning design. We try to offer some guidance to practitioners on what we believe are the fundamental principles that need to be addressed if we are to take seriously a commitment to networked learning

19.3   A Pedagogical Framework for Networked Learning Design

As more and more teachers in higher education begin to experiment with networked learning, so we are beginning to hear tales about how time-consuming online tutoring can be. This may well be the case. But in our experience much of the problem of excessive calls on tutor time can be avoided through careful design. Design is typically a multi-team affair for networked learning environments. It is important for the team to be able to identify common values and beliefs e.g., about learning, in preparation for the design effort and we believe this will help in taking a principled approach to networked learning design. This attention to first principles we suggest encourages building good pedagogy into the design and development process e.g. by promoting close links between learning objectives and the design of learning activities (see also Ganesan, Chapter 6 this volume).

To start with, it may prove expedient for the designers to draw upon pedagogical models for academic discourse, traditionally utilized in face-to-face contexts (eg Paulsen discusses a set of online learning techniques (Paulsen, 1995)). While these provide easily recognized models for tutors and learners to work with and adapt for use in online environments, some argue we do need to think differently for online learning rather than using new technologies in traditional ways and repeating "past inadequacies ... with the new media" (Miller, 2000:8; but see also e.g. Koschmann, 1996; Darby, Chapter 2 this volume).

Design needs to attend to structure, but we also need to factor in scope for dynamic evolution. We suggest this is required because in our experience we, like others, have not been able to come up with adequate prescriptions thus far that can determine a routinely successful recipe for online programs (see also Jones &

Asensio, Chapter 15 this volume). While there is a developing set of fundamental principles about networked learning, it still seems to be true that what seems to work for one group of learners is not of itself necessarily guaranteed to translate to another course or another group of learners.

We have attempted to address some of these concerns through the JISC funded Networked Learning in Higher Education project and the guidelines document, especially its description of a pedagogical framework for networked learning we feel offers a way forward to teams to make first steps in networked learning design activity, and a means to avoid expensive failures (Goodyear & NLinHE team, 2001). Our goal is not so much to erect an ideal pedagogical framework. Rather, the point is to suggest the kind of *architecture* that such conceptual entities ought to have. This architecture has to reflect a balance between the needs of innovative practitioners and the complexities of the field within which we work. It has to speak to practice, but not trivialize what it represents.

Figure 19.2 is Goodyear and the NLinHE team's (2001) attempt to capture what we mean by a pedagogical framework. In using this framework in a number of workshops on online learning that we have run for UK HE staff, we have been impressed by how people find it compelling as a means to address first principles for networked learning design.

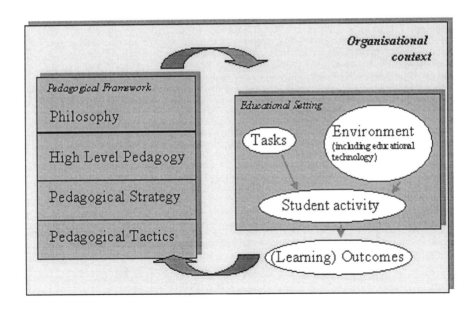

Figure 19.2 Pedagogical framework, educational setting, organizational context

A danger and a strength of representations like Figure 19.2 is that they overly simplify complex processes and relationships. Figure 19.2 falls into three main parts. The pedagogical framework itself is on the left hand side. It needs to be understood in relation to concrete educational activity in a real world setting. On the right hand side of the figure is what we have called the educational setting. This is a way of describing the real-world, concrete activities, processes, people and artefacts involved in a learning activity. Both the pedagogical framework and the educational setting exist within an organizational context, such as a university. Goodyear and NLinHE team (2001) usefully point out that the organizational context exerts its influence mainly by conditioning (a) the design and management of the educational setting and (b) the processes through which a pedagogical framework feeds into the design and management of an educational setting.

In the following sections we briefly sketch the components of the pedagogical framework (but see Goodyear & NLinHE team (2001) for greater detail).

19.3.1 The Educational Setting

The educational setting is a way of representing the coming together of tasks, activities and environment. The distinction between tasks and activities is necessitated by two factors: the strengthening influence of so-called constructivist approaches to learning (e.g. Wilson, 1996) and the high value placed on learner-managed learning.

Learning Tasks

A learning task is a specification for learner activity. Its design needs to draw on the best of what we know about how people learn, on a deep knowledge of academic subject matter and/or vocational competencies, and on knowledge of the learners. Essays, laboratory exercizes, a structured discussion session or debate, a diagnostic exercize, a topic to research, an artefact to build, a program to write – all these are examples of kinds of learning task. A task needs to be sufficiently well-specified that the chances of a learner engaging in unproductive activity are kept within tolerable limits. Its specification may also need a degree of openness in order to meet variable learner needs and initiate a creative response.

Learning Environment

The second kind of work required of teachers is the design and management of the learning environment. We use the term to mean the physical environment or physical setting (and all that learners call upon in that 'space' e.g. paper and pens, textbooks, computers, the Internet and all its online information resources) within which learners work. The important point here is that learning is severely constrained by the learning environment. Part of the point of networked learning is to ensure that more flexible access to learning opportunities is accompanied by appropriate redesign of the learning environment.

Learning Activity

Tasks are what managers set – they are the prescribed work. Activity is what people actually do. Teachers set tasks. Learners interpret the specifications of the task (Jones & Asensio, in press). Learners' subsequent activity is a more or less rational response to the task, shaped and constrained by all the other tasks they have to face, all the other calls on their time, and their experiential knowledge of what their teachers actually value. It is perfectly legitimate for activity to be different from the task which initiated it. If we want learners to take more responsibility for their own learning, we have to rely on them to make their own interpretations of learning tasks. We also have to recognize that learners are busy people and learning is only one of the things they have to fit into the day. Like all busy people, successful learners know how to cut corners – how to satisfy a learning task (Simon, 1969).

Task, Activity, Environment

A consequence of accepting the legitimate distinction between task and activity is that we should design the learning environment so that it is compatible with activity rather than task. This claim is crucial to user-centered educational technology (Preece, 2000). If it is possible to construct the environment so that it encourages real world activity which is close to the task as set, so much the better. But technology which enforces an unacceptably restricted interpretation of the task will be rejected by its intended users. Understanding what learners actually do is a cornerstone of good design when it comes to environments for networked learning.

Learning Outcomes

The consequence of learning activity is a set of learning outcomes. Achieving clarity and consensus about valued learning outcomes is a key step in designing good learning tasks. Different kinds of knowledge are acquired through different kinds of learning process. Being clear about the kinds of knowledge tied up in a particular learning outcome can be extremely useful in designing tasks which stand the best chance of stimulating the kinds of learning activity appropriate for that kind of knowledge.

19.3.2 The Pedagogical Framework

The left-hand part of Figure 19.2 is the pedagogical framework itself. Its four elements are ordered and loosely coupled. This internal structure can be described in a number of ways – to which we return after describing the individual elements.

Philosophy

The 'top' element is composed of a number of sets of beliefs: about the nature of knowledge and competence, about the purposes of learning in HE, about how learning occurs, about how people should and should not be treated, *etc.* In many innovative teaching projects, we suspect philosophy is left implicit or is only rarely discussed, or is held to be too remote from the hard day-to-day problems of making an educational innovation work to justify spending time on it. There can also be a sense that an innovative teaching project starts with some exciting concrete ideas and commitments, and that unravelling their philosophical assumptions will move the project backwards. Deep and unexplored philosophical differences within a team can lead to fatal divergence in the day-to-day operational work. The sooner such discrepancies are found, discussed and reconciled, the less likely is catastrophic failure. The underlying beliefs that the designers have about how learning can be, have to be articulated in order to be used to inform the design of the networked environment and to determine the types of activity that will take place within it. As a practical illustration, if it is held among the team that learning can be fostered by encouraging learners to articulate and share ideas and perspectives, then the online environment will need to support group-based communication e.g., around key substantive themes.

Why are we trying to encourage this sharing of underlying beliefs and principles? Few teachers in higher education are used to talking with each other about pedagogy and design (Dunkin, 2001). What passes for educational design is often driven by the language and taken-for-granted constructs of the teachers' discipline. It's rare to find people spending time making sure that they understand each other when using words like 'learning' or 'learning outcome' or 'skill'. It's rare to find teachers and technical support staff or managers making sure they have a shared model of how good learning occurs (and see also Hammond, Trapp & Bennett, Chapter 14 this volume). This is beginning to change. In-service teacher training or staff development programs are beginning to make a difference (see McNaught, also Foster *et al.*, Chapters 7 and 8 this volume). Discussion is also being prompted when groups of teachers have to collaborate in the production of documents about teaching and learning. But it's far from clear that participation in such rites necessitates a firm grounding in shared beliefs about learning, learners or teaching.

High Level Pedagogy

This element is concerned with the concrete instantiation of philosophical positions in the context of creating and managing an educational setting. At a philosophical level, someone might say 'I see great advantages in using a Problem-Based Learning approach'. When one makes a commitment to using PBL in a specific educational setting, then one is in the realm of high level pedagogy. There are many candidate forms of high level pedagogy and not all would have the same scale, scope, complexity or coherence. Claims might be made for such things as 'guided discovery learning', 'problem-based learning', 'cognitive apprenticeship', 'programed learning', or 'computer-supported collaborative learning'. From the point of view of their place in the framework, the important thing is that they are at a level of abstraction which is intermediate between philosophy and action. They are a way of turning a philosophical position into a space of commitments and possibilities. A high level pedagogy does not contain direct prescriptions for action, but it puts some forms of possible action into the foreground and others into the background.

Strategy

Strategy is directly concerned with action. A strategy is a broad-brush depiction of plans – of what should be done to achieve certain objectives. Strategy needs to account for uncertainties; a good strategy will plan for alternative ways of reaching the objectives. What we mean by strategy is something open, co-operative and egalitarian, since its main purpose is communicative – it supports a description of actions and intentions at a level that hides confusing details. This description of actions and intentions may be constructed for the benefit of members of a team of teachers. It may also be constructed for the mutual benefit of learners and their teachers. In both cases, the point is to promote a shared understanding of intentions and permit co-ordinated action.

Tactics

The only difference between pedagogical strategy and pedagogical tactics is one of grain size. Tactics are the detailed moves through which strategy is effected. Take an example from work on the use of asynchronous text-based computer conferencing. A team of tutors, acting as conference moderators, might agree to adopt a strategy which is intended to encourage all the learners to participate in a conference. This strategy might involve a number of tactics – including writing an encouraging, positive response whenever a learner makes a contribution to the conference; providing examples of valued kinds of contribution; posing stimulating and non-threatening questions to the group; writing private e-mails to 'lurkers' (people reading but not contributing), to encourage them to participate; rewarding contributions to the conference through the assessment system, *etc.*

The Internal Structure of the Pedagogical Framework

Figure 19.2 partitions the pedagogical framework in two different ways. First, the 'philosophical cap' is separated from the other three elements. It is a division between (a) a set of general philosophical positions which are independent of any one instance of a real world educational setting and (b) a set of commitments (high level pedagogy, strategy and tactics) specific to one instance of a real world educational setting.

Second, the two upper elements can be described as 'declarative' or 'conceptual' while the two lower elements can be described as 'procedural' or 'operational'. Philosophical positions and high level pedagogy can be described in ways which are not prescriptive of action. Prescriptions for action are to be found in descriptions of strategy and tactics. These need to contain well-formed specifications of the action that should be taken to achieve certain objectives given certain conditions.

A final point to be made about the internal structure of the pedagogical framework is that the four elements need not be tightly coupled. Indeed the real world practices of educational innovators are sufficiently undisciplined that we should say the elements are 'loosely coupled' (at best). Loose coupling is both real and advantageous. It reflects the need to work with under-specified conceptual entities, particularly in the early stages of a project. One can become clearer about the nature of what one is trying to do once one has made commitments in doing it. Thus, it is hard to make a case that the consequences of choices in one element or 'layer' of the pedagogical framework have clear, precise implications for activity in another layer. It is not a deductive process or one that we can see ways of automating. But neither are the elements/layers free floating. External forces cause us to account for our activity and intuitions in rational terms: high value is placed on coherence. Co-operation within a project team, and between learners and teachers, depends on mutual intelligibility – our intentions and actions have to be sufficiently coherent to be understood. The loose coupling of elements gives space within which we can be both disciplined and creative, listen to our instincts and make them accountable to others.

19.4   Advances in Using Multimedia Technologies for Networked Learning

We have thus far (in this chapter) stressed the future for e-learning or networked learning from the perspective of looking forward to more carefully designed, integrated environments that offer support to learners in e.g. accessing resources, communicating with tutors and other learners, participating in engaging cognitive interaction and receiving timely and relevant feedback.

In this section we look at one innovative use of multimedia in networked learning, drawing upon recent research we have conducted in a project funded by the UK Economic, Social and Research Council (ESRC) on Voice Annotations of Multimedia Artefacts (VAMA). This work has concentrated on looking at the ways in which we might use multimedia technologies in networked environments to sustain and build rich interactions around the working practices of practitioners in professional communities. So we have been attempting to make closer matches between the design of the online environment and the facilities provided *and* the needs of the learners using the environment to work in flexible but (close to) naturalistic ways on authentic tasks around professional concerns.

The underlying rationale to this work is that the learning of skills embedded in real world work practices is only poorly understood. Networked environments we believe can offer useful ways of supporting the acquisition of such skills. Studies into the nature of adult learning, alongside current interest in situated approaches to learning are revealing the importance of learners taking active roles in authentic tasks if learning is to be meaningful. Networked environments provide opportunities whereby we can connect members of distributed professional communities, for mutual exchange of information and exploration of working practices and the underlying or tacit knowledge. Others, looking at the use of online environments for problem-solving, have found benefits in the online environment over face-to-face problem-solving groups in terms of keeping groups focused on task and engaging in more purposive communication (e.g. Jonassen & Kwon, 2001).

In the VAMA project, multimedia elements were used within a distributed community of learning technologists for professional development purposes e.g. to allow members to interact collaboratively with rich resources: using them to define problems; to represent ideas in different media; and to augment the resources with personal commentary or alternative viewpoints. We were trying to uncover tacit knowledge and to render it shareable. What we tried was to have practitioners make a recording of carrying out some task, show them the recording and interview them about how and why they did what they did. Multimedia technologies proved to be very useful for this kind of work, using small video cameras to help capture a task quickly, which is then digitally stored and to which can be added annotations of the practitioner's explanations e.g. as text or voice messages. These multimedia artefacts *i.e.*, the clips and annotations were next made available to the community for discussion and reflection, by sharing them in the online, networked environment.

Some of the initial findings from this work indicate the value in using multimedia representations of practices in distributed practitioner communities for professional learning and development. For example, different *kinds of video clips*, used to capture representations of practice, were found to offer support for continuing professional development needs (Steeples & Goodyear, 1999). The purpose of the video clips needs to be considered in the creation process, in order to use an appropriate kind of clip. 'Fly on the wall' type of representations are vivid and were seen to evidence direct engagement in the practice but they do require time and effort thereafter in selecting incidents for sharing as clips. 'Talking head' kinds of representation were more abstract or discursive, and the subjects found they needed to introduce ways to inject interest into the clip e.g. by the use of an interviewer or a paired discussion, rather than a straight, to-camera individual presentation.

Using artefacts and group interaction in the clips helped 'ground' or anchor a video clip representation in realistic ways. Artefacts helped keep the representation from becoming more abstracted from the practice. Artefacts can be things used in the clips to act as memory aids, to help recall and to help the subject in articulating about a practice.

Video clips and voice annotations were rapidly created. Speed was seen as a significant benefit, and regarded as more important than a finished product, especially in fluid, evolving work such as the learning technology field.

The stored *voice annotations* attached to the video clips were found to be useful to these practitioners. For example, it was found in the studies of this project that stored voice annotations are:

- quickly created, much faster than typing a message;
- permanent rather than lacking persistence (as in face-to-face speech) – giving opportunities for participants to revisit, reuse, and to reflect upon the message;

- rapidly replayable and controllable – diminishing the serial limitations of real-time auditory information;
- a means to reduce the amount of visual information on screen (ie the amount of text and/or graphics);
- a means of capturing a more naturalistic communication with the richness and expressive nature of speech.

However there was less agreement that voice annotations offer a means to enable the learner to maintain attention, and avoid visual attention switching that can cause cognitive overload and so this remains an issue requiring further attention.

Voice annotations that were created to add to fly-on-the-wall kinds of representations were found to be both substantively rich, but also that the subjects used them to give highly critical reflective commentary on the group processes and their own personal performance.

We are well aware current technological constraints such as limited bandwidth make the sharing of multimedia resources like videoclips and voice annotations highly problematic just now. However, future improvements in bandwidth will eliminate these current technical limitations. We therefore believe this work can feed into specifications for improving distributed environments for collaborative learning: to enable us to be in a position to realize the pedagogical potential of these technologies in appropriate ways when such limitations are no longer at issue.

19.5 Conclusion

In this chapter we have contrasted current trends in e-learning with our own interpretation of networked learning, to offer a way to move forward. The way forward is contingent upon a commitment to design for networked learning. We see this as essential in a future for networked learning.

Attention to the planning and preparation of networked learning environments is paramount. It involves careful and meticulous effort in the initial stages of design work that will establish the basis for subsequent development. This effort will ensure agreement on an underlying philosophy in the project team, that can be translated through to pedagogical strategies and tactics. This effort will ensure we pay due respect to what is required of learners and tutors, and will help create a more 'constructive alignment' between the learning environment, the learner tasks and learner activities (Biggs, 1999). We assert this effort will not go unwasted, not least because this kind of attention to networked learning design is also causing a closer examination and reflection upon our teaching practices more generally. As we give efforts to design for networked learning, this has value for improving teaching performance generally as well as online. And that can't be a bad thing can it?

The role of the tutor remains critical in our conception of networked learning, and we envisage future online environments that offer a judicious mixing of technological support and human teaching. Our definition of networked learning foregrounds the human-human connectivity. The role of the tutor online seems essential too, in the view of learners. For example, Masie (2000) suggests strongest interest from learners for e-learning courses where tutorial support is offered. How the tutor or moderator affect the learning process is an important area for developing understanding, if online courses are to rise above the "negligible and trivial state that [they] currently occupy (Miller, 2000:18; but see also Goodyear *et al.*, 2001on developing competencies for online tutoring).

Equally, it would be naive and a serious neglect not to recognize the similarities between face-to-face and online teaching and assume there is no transfer between conventional teaching skills and online teaching skills. However it will be equally important that we better understand the specifics of different kinds of online learning environments in terms of ways in which good teaching may be expressed (Goodyear *et al*, 2001).

19.6 Acknowledgements

We are pleased to acknowledge the support of JISC/CALT for our Networked Learning in Higher Education (NL in HE) project, and the ESRC funding for the Voice Annotation of Multimedia Artefacts (VAMA) project. We also acknowledge the valued contributions of other members of the NL in HE team that have informed this chapter: Susan Armitage, Mireia Asensio, Mark Bryson, Vivien Hodgson and Mike O'Donoghue. Any errors or omissions however, remain our responsibility.

19.7 References

BBC (2000) Friday, 17 March 2000, 11:52 GMT
    http://news.bbc.co.uk/hi/english/education/newsid_681000/681072.stm
Berge, Z. (2001) (Ed) Sustaining distance training: integrating learning technologies into the fabric of the enterprize. San Francisco: Jossey Bass
Biggs, J (1999) *Teaching for quality learning at university.* Buckingham: Society for Research into Higher Education & Open University Press
Bonk, C.J. & King, K.S. (1998) (Eds) *Electronic collaborators: learner-centered technologies for literacy, apprenticeship and discourse.* Mahwah, New Jersey: Lawrence Erlbaum Associates
Carlson, S. (2000) Universities find wireless systems bring them convenience and savings. *Chronicle of Higher Education, Information Technology: daily news* October 11. www.chronicle.com/free/2000/10/2000101101t.htm
Chabot, A.A. (1999) *Student portable computing: network support for itinerant and mobile computers.* Birmingham: University of Birmingham, Information Services

Clark, R. (1994) Media will never influence learning. *Educational Technology Research and Development, 42*, pp21-29

Dunkin, M. (2001). Novice and award winning teachers' concepts and beliefs about teaching in higher education. In N. Hativa & P. Goodyear (Eds.), *Teacher thinking, knowledge and beliefs in higher education* Dordrecht: Kluwer.

Goodyear, P. (2000a) Environments for lifelong learning: ergonomics, architecture and educational design. In Spector, J.M. & Anderson, T. (Eds.) *Integrated and Holistic Perspectives on Learning, Instruction & Technology,* Dordrecht: Kluwer Academic Publishers, Chapter 1

Goodyear, P. (2000b) E-learning, knowledge work and working knowledge, *Proceedings of the IST Conference,* Nice, France, November 2000 (available at http://istevent.cec.eu.int/en/)

Goodyear, P. (draft) *Learning and digital environments: lessons from European research.* C SALT working paper. Lancaster

Goodyear & NLinHE team (2001) *Effective networked learning in higher education: notes and* guidelines. C SALT, Lancaster University http://csalt.lancs.ac.uk/jisc/advice.htm

Goodyear, P. & Stone, C. (1992) Domain knowledge, epistemology and intelligent tutoring in social science, in *Knowledge Negotiation,* Eds. Moyse, R. & Elsom-Cook, M., Academic Press, London, 69-96

Goodyear, P., Salmon, G., Spector, M., Steeples, C. & Tickner, T. (2001) Competences for online teaching. *Educational Technology Research & Development,* 49(1), pp65-72

Hardy, V., Hodgson, V. & McConnell, D. (1994) Computer conferencing: a new medium for investigating issues in gender and learning, *Higher Education* (28) 403-418

Jonassen, D.H. & Kwon, H. (2001) Communication patterns in computer mediated versus face-to-face group problem solving. *Educational Technology Research and Development 49* (1) pp35-51

Jones, C. & Asensio, M. (in press) *JCAL*

Jones, C., Asensio, M. & Goodyear, P. (2000) Networked learning in higher education: practitioners' perspectives. *Journal of the Association for Learning Technology,* 8(2), pp18-28

Koschmann, T. (Ed) (1996) *CSCL: Theory and Practice of an Emerging Paradigm.* Mahwah, NJ. Lawrence Erlbaum Associates

Laurillard, D. (1993) *Rethinking university teaching,* Routledge, London

Lave, J. & Wenger, E. (1991). *Situated learning: legitimate peripheral participation.* Cambridge: Cambridge University Press

McConnell, D. (2000) *Implementing computer supported cooperative learning* (2nd edition), Kogan Page, London

Macdonald, G. (2000) Universities and knowledge economies: a paradigmatic change? In Asensio, M., Foster, J., Hodgson, V. & McConnell, D. (Eds.) *Networked learning 2000: innovative approaches to lifelong learning and higher education through the internet.* Proceedings of the 2nd International Conference on Networked Learning, Lancaster University, April 2000

Mactaggart, M. (2000) Into the mobile millennium. *Computer Weekly,* August 17 http://www.findarticles.com/cf_0/m0COW/2000_August_17/64518903/print.jhtml

Masie, E. (2000) *Survey result: roles and expectations for e-trainers.* http://www.techlearn.com/trends/trends168.htm

Miller, I. (2000) Distance learning – a personal history. *The Internet and Higher Education,* *3* (1-2) pp7-21

Moore, M.G. (1993) Theory of transactional distance, (2nd edition). In Keegan, D. (Ed.) *Theoretical Principles of Distance Education.* Routledge, New York

National Committee of Inquiry into Higher Education (1997) *Higher Education in the Learning Society* (the Dearing Report). London: HMSO

Noble, D. (1998) Digital diploma mills: the automation of higher education. *Educom Review, 33* (3)

Oliver, R. (1999) Exploring strategies for online teaching and learning. *Distance Education,* *20*(2), pp240-254

Paulsen, M. (1995) *The online report on pedagogical techniques for computer-mediated communication* (http://www.nki.no/~morten)

Preece, J. (2000) *Online communities: designing usability, supporting sociability.* Chichester: Wiley

Romiszowski, A. & de Haas, J.A. (1989) Computer mediated communication for instruction: Using e-mail as a seminar. *Educational Technology,* (29,10) pp7–14

Scigliano, J.A. (2000) The internet and higher education: special issue on the history of online learning. *The Internet and Higher Education, 3* (1-2) pp1-6

Sharples, M. (2000) The design of personal mobile technologies for lifelong learning. *Computers & Education 34,* pp177-193

Simon, H. (1969). *The sciences of the artificial.* Cambridge Mass.: MIT Press

Slavin, R. (1990) *Co-operative learning: theory, research and practice,* Prentice Hall, Englewood Cliffs, New Jersey

Smith, M. & Kollock, P. (Eds.) (1999) *Communities in cyberspace.* London: Routledge

Steeples, C. (2001) *Voice annotation of multimedia artefacts.* ESRC End of Award Report (available from the author)

Steeples, C. (2000) Reflecting on group discussions for professional learning: annotating videoclips with voice annotations. *Proceedings of International Workshop on Advanced Learning Technologies (IWALT 2000)* Palmerston North, New Zealand: IEEE Computer Society

Steeples, C. & Goodyear, P. (1999) Enabling professional learning in distributed communities of practice: descriptors for multimedia objects. *Journal of Network and Computer Applications 22,* pp133-145

Webb, N. & Palincsar, A-M. (1996) Group processes in the classroom, In Berliner, D. & Calfee, R. (Eds.), *Handbook of Educational Psychology,* New York: Macmillan, pp841-873

Wenger, E. (1998) *Communities of practice.* Cambridge: Cambridge University Press

Wilson, B. (Ed.) (1996) *Constructivist Learning Environments.* Englewood Cliffs NJ: Educational Technology Press

Subject index

Academic
  ability, 249
  curriculum, 32, 146, 301, 332
  departments, 30, 147, 175, 188, 297
  discipline, 215
  institutions, 126, 289
  libraries, 139–64, 185, 189
  planning, 31
  practice, 111, 132, 138, 189–90
  skill, 236
  standards, 288
  support services, 143
  time, 42
  writing, 329
Academic Management System (AMS), 117
Academics, 18, 27, 28, 31–33, 69, 134–5,
    137, 138, 147, 149, 151, 152, 156, 159,
    162, 171, 175–76, 190, 275, 298, 321
Access, 27, 34, 71, 117, 133, 134, 188, 202,
    294, 303, 332
  to online conferences, 316
  cost-effective, 145
  to information, 31, 98, 144, 229, 320
  to learners' experiences, 213
  points, 302, 325
  to resources, 68, 69, 93, 102, 139, 146,
    149, 151, 157, 158, 180, 187, 221, 223,
    248, 295, 327
  restricting, 24
  technology, 154, 230
  Web, 261
Action research, 11, 196, 198, 199–209, 202
  and CMC, 199–201
  examples of, 204–8
  limits and problems of, 201–2
  and reflection, 203–4
  role of researcher in, 202
Actor Network Theory (ANT), 77–90
Active learning, 66, 153–4, 161, 247
  environments, 117

Assessment, 6, 9, 10, 68, 116, 131, 150, 155,
    258, 270, 273, 298, 318, 335
  academic, 279
  competitive, 306
  continuous, 316
  criteria for, 280
  critical, 223
  methods or forms of, 23, 57, 284
  online, 121, 249
  online collaborative, 279–292
  peer, 280, 282, 285
  procedures, 57, 80
  process, 282, 284, 288, 290
  self-, 207, 215, 217, 280
  traditional, 280, 284, 287
  tutor, 280
ASTER project, 243–52
Asynchronous, 33, 56, 145, 146, 207, 243,
    260, 327, 328, 329
  CMC, 195
  conferencing, 309
  dialog, 206
  discussion, 208
  learning networks, 295
  text messaging, 296
Asynchronous Learning Networks (ALN),
    22–3
Audio, 29, 30, 147, 220, 221, 222, 262,
    296
  conferencing, 309, 310, 313, 314, 315,
    319
Australian Department for Education,
    Training and Youth Affairs (DETYA),
    38–40, 46

Bandwidth, 3, 300, 338
Business, 25, 39, 197, 200, 324
  model, 216
Business Process Re-engineering (BPR)
  model, 43, 117

Campus, 12, 23, 149, 293–308, 325
  off-campus, 33, 243
  on-campus, 24, 29, 33, 131, 145, 216, 244,
    249, 296
  virtual, 27, 324
Campus Computing Survey, 7, 33
Cognition, 51, 259
  meta-, 95
  socially shared, 98
  situated, 257
Collaboration, 6, 22, 27, 93, 99–101, 104,
    139, 155–8, 161, 199, 204, 270, 287,
    302, 304, 311, 318
  across time and space, 106
  external, 125, 129, 133, 138
  forms of, 106
  in learning, 145, 243, 269, 326 *see also*
    Collaborative learning
  institutional, 27, 112, 129
  methods, 6, 284
  peer, 244
  in reflective process, 203
Collaborative activity, 6
Collaborative learning, 51, 56, 60–62, 126,
    132, 161, 200, 231, 244, 245, 258,
    260–1, 270, 334, 338 *see also*
    Collaboration, in learning
  cognitive mechanisms for, 56, 60–2
C&IT *see* Communications and
    Information Technology
Communications and Information
    Technology, 2, 6, 11, 18, 20, 30, 43, 56,
    127–9, 130, 136, 138, 144, 145, 149–55,
    157, 158, 159, 160, 162, 177, 179, 180,
    182, 184, 195, 196, 199, 200, 204,
    243–51, 309
Communities of practice, 8, 56, 63, 81–3,
    85, 86, 136, 225, 258, 259–60, 269
CBCGW *see* Computer Based
    Collaborative Group Work project
Computer Based Collaborative Group
    Work project, 125–6, 130–6
  methodology and methods, 130
Computer conferencing, 6, 29, 145, 151,
    159, 160, 195, 202, 205, 237, 260
CMC *see* Computer Mediated
    Communication
Computer Mediated Communication
    (CMC), 3, 6, 195, 196–7, *196*, 198–9,
    203–9, 217, 229–34, 240, 258

action research and, 199–201
democracy and social identity issues,
    229–42
research, 196
theoretical and practical assumptions
    about, 229–34
theory and models, 198–9
Computer Supported Collaborative
    Learning (CSCL), 6, 257
Computer Supported Cooperative Work
    (CSCW), 10, 94, 99–101, 103, 105, 106,
    263
Computers in Teaching Initiative (CTI),
    18–20, 181
Conceptions of learning, 52–6, 306
  academic, 52
  generic competence, 52–3
  critical being and reflexivity,
    53–4
Conferencing system(s), 145, 261, 262, 274,
    309, 316
Constructive alignment, 57, 338
Convergence, 3, 5, 257, 306, 329
Costing structures, 28
Costs of networked learning, 7, 10, 24,
    27–48, 97, 99, 138, 226, 325
  current studies, 35–44
  earlier work, 29–35
  hidden costs, 40–2
Costs of Networked Learning (CNL)
    project, 40–4

Dearing report, 7, 34, 126–9, 153
Design for networked learning, 10, 11, 12,
    24, 50, 59, 253–78, 256–261 *see also*
    Learning design
  collaborative, 10
  good design, 276
  implications, 65–71
  nature of, 254–5
  pedagogical framework, 330–6
  using multimedia, 336–8
Dialog in learning, 206, 214–16, 217, 224–6,
    230, 232, 237, 243, 244, 246, 247, 248,
    262, 269, 270, 282, 328
Digital
  information, 88, 101, 102, 119, 146
  democracy, 79
  technology, 3
Digital diploma mills, 324

Distance education, 5, 27, 29, 44, 114, 197, 257, *314,* 316

Distance learners, 95, 154, 216

Distance learning, 5, 21, 29, 33, 79, 81, 94, 128, 133, 145, 147, 151, 153, 154, 161, 198, 204, 207, 220, 230, 249, 257, *314* 324

Distributed
communication, 63, 98
design, 10, 101
education, 299
environment, 93, 96, 98, 101, 338
knowledge, 85
learners, 56
learning, 95, 97, 226, 294, 326, 328, 336, 337
working, 10

Distributed Learning System (DLS), 117–19

E-learning, 12, 27, 60, 67, 216, 294, 323–30, *327,* 334, 336, 338
definition of, 325–6

Electronic
campuses, 27
community, 149
delivery of courses, 30
format, 32
groups, 207, 208
journals, 146
learning, 33, 89, 113, 145, 292, 302
learning environments, 33, 117, 155
libraries, 143, 144, 148, 157
e-mail, 18, *94,* 144, 207, 208, 283, 296
materials or resources, 33, 68, 144, 145, 146, 147, 148, 149, 151, 156, 157, 190, 245, 247, 248, 305
performance support systems, 93, *94*
publishing, 146
seminar, 65
texts, 68, 141

E-moderators, 11, 191, 200–2

Epistemic tasks, 51, *62,* 62–3

Epistemic fluency, 54, 55, 57, 220

Equality, 9, 282, 287, 289, 290
and power, 9
social equality, 280

E-University, 20–21, 138, 215, 250

Evaluation, 43, 46, 97, 115, 118, 122, 125, 126, 128, 150, 169–92, 196, 197, 207,

246, 249, 280, 282, 285, 286, 290
course evaluation, 103
evaluating networked learning, 169–92
of institutional readiness, 130, 136–8
LTDI case study, 173–76
materials, 120
methods, 7
models, *42*
multi-disciplinary approach, 171–2
multi-disciplinary team, 172
multi-method design, 172–3
planning, 120
PUSHE case study, 187–90
strategies, 119
student evaluations, 249, 290
studies, 150, 196, 207
TLTP case study, 176–87
tool kits, 37
value of, 197

Experiential learning, 161

Face-to-face, 23, 79, 82–3, 96, 120, 133, 145, 151, 152, 160, 207, 208, 216, 220, 243, 244, 247, 248, 249, 300, 301, 305, 310, 311, 312, 316, 318, 323, 329, 330, 337, 339, 340

Facilitation, 23, 63, 112, 120, 136, 138, 145, 150, 152, 153, 155, 160, 189, 213, 225, 243, 245, 246, 249, 260, 285, 286,

Facilitator, 9, 152

Faculty *see* Academics

Flashlight, 33, 35, 37–8, 40, 45–6

Global alliance, 139

Global markets, 123

Global reach, 8

Global resources, 158

Globalisation, 7–8, 138, 139, 158, 294

Grounded guidelines, 320–1

Groupware, 100, 126, 145,

HEFCE (Higher Education Funding Council for England) 19, 34, 44, 127, 169, 176, 251

ICT (Information and Communications Technology) *see* Communications and Information Technology (C&IT)

Identity, 11, 158, 163, 225, 229–42, 289, 295, 307

Inequality, 289
Information literacy, 112, 148–9, 151,
    153–5, 157, 160, 161, 163
Information specialist, 9, 10, 11, 106,
    143–67
Institute for Learning and Teaching (ILT),
    7, 162, 250, 274
Instructional design, 93–109, 112, 160,
    188
    collaborative design, 103–6
    complexity of, 99–101
    and CSCW, 101–3
Intelligent Tutoring Systems (ITS), 214,
    257, 328

Just-In-Time Open Learning (JITOL)
    project, 5, *64*
Just-In-Time Teaching (JITT), 247

Knowledge, 3, 23, 41, 53–54, 58, 59, 61, 66,
    79, 81, 84–6, 95, 106, 132, 135, 144,
    149, 154, 160, 161, 162, 171, 190, 214,
    221, 231, 256, 260, 306, 320, 333
    academic, 64
    acquisition, 51
    -based economy, 3, 54
    construction of, 50, 55–6, 59, 63–5, 197,
        244, 260
    declarative, 52, 207
    deficit, 58
    development, 197, 245–6
    dissemination of, 324
    domains, 82, 190
    experiential, 333
    expert, 58
    as organizing device, 84
    pedagogical, 49, 250
    power of, 85
    prior, 203, 311, 312
    resource-based, 190
    sharing, 69
    Society, 2
    specialist, 190
    stolen knowledge, 259
    tacit, 64, 198, 255, 274–6, 329, 336–7
    technical, 52
    theoretical, 160
    transmission of, 17, 80, 295
    workers, 99
    working, 51, 54–5, 63–5

Knowledge management system, 94–6, 99,
    101–4

Learning, 2, 5, 7, 10, 12, 20, 23, *44*, 51, 56,
    62, 75, 82, 195, 197, 213, 229, 253, 281,
    294, 299, 306, 334 *see also*
    Collaborative learning; Conceptions
    of learning; Models of learning;
    Situated learning
    academic, 50,
    accounts of, 49, 50,
    activities, 57, 59, 69, 95, 98, 155, 247, 309,
        330
    approaches to, 6, 19, 24, 240, 262, 280,
        285, 326, 327
    learning community, 51, 56, 65, 66, 69,
        77–9, 226, 259
    cooperative, 195
    critical, 286
    cycle of, 63, *64*
    educationalised, 75–6, 77
    experience, 43, 69, 222
    failure, 259, 306, 325
    forms of, 29
    gains, 61
    good learning, 50, 59, 326, 330
    groups, 282, 289
    independent, 153–4
    life-long, 99, 116, 126, 145, 151, 250
    management of, 279
    materials, 33, 56, 120, 151, 160, 295
    natural, 50, 76
    objectives, 57
    objects, 24
    outcomes, 24, 35, 52, 57, 60, 65, 71, 98,
        117, 121, 196, 208, 244, 247–9, 333, 334
    paradigms27, 29, 98–9, 253
    placed-based, 3
    problem-based, 249, 334
    relationships, 66
    sciences, 49–50, 51
    sets, 283
    situations, 40, 61
    skills, 145, 151, 154, 334, 336
    small group, 244
    social theories of, 2, 8, 81–3
    students', 9, 171
    tasks, 57, 66, 96, 154, 244, 332
    wild learning, 89
Learning design, 256–7, 330–6

Learning environments, 24, 66, 97, 116, 244, 262, 332–3 see also Networked learning environments; MLEs; VLEs
Learning nests, 12, 293–4, 325
Learning Society, 126
Learning support, 11, 93, 104, 114, 158, 184, 226, 306, 323
Learning Technology Mentors (LTM), 118–19, 122
Learning Networked and Communication Skills (LNCS) project, 309–22
project methodology, 309–22
Learning and Teaching Support Network (LTSN), 7, 20
    Generic Centre, 7, 20
    Technology Centre, 20

Managed Learning Environments (MLEs), 27, 69
Mobile computing, 1, 8, 12, 325
Models of learning, 50, 57–60, 112, 286, 307
    Shuell's model, 58–60
Moderate, 65, 208, 217, 225, 249, 287, 335
Moderators, 70, 335, 339

Networked learner support, 143–67
    changing support roles, 147–52
    and collaboration, 155–8
    and professional development, 159–62
Networked learning
    characteristics of, 50, 56
    and communication skills, 309–22
    communities, 69–71
    conceptions of, 52–6
    and continuing professional development, 54, 63
    convergence, 3
    costs, see Costs of networked learning
    and critical pedagogy, 77–9
    definitions of, 2, 56, 93, 327
    designs for, 253–78, see also Design
    design implications, 65–71
    design preparation, 326–30
    and effective use of technology, 312–13
    educational context, 245–6
    expectations of practitioners, 269–70
    impact of, 248–50
    innovation and refinement, 270–2
    issues, 6–9

participation, 266–9
perspectives, 4–6
preparation time for, 33
psychology of, 49–75
second generation, 24
and socially situated learning, 79–81
special characteristics of, 56–7
students' experiences of, 2
and study patterns, 303–5
tasks, 66–8
teaching techniques, 67–8
tight and loose structures, 272–4
Networked learning environments, 11, 12, 21, 33, 43, 49, 68, 93, 95, 96, 98, 100, 101, 107, 108, 111, 117, 145–6, 148, 152, 157, 161, 163, 196, 197, 217, 220, 240, 258, 260, 276, 280, 281, 283, 289, 295, 297, 299, 321, 325, 326, 328, 330, 338, 339
students' uses of, 301–3
Networked Learning in Higher Education (NLinHE) project, 324, 331, 339
Networked learning practitioners, 253–78
Networked resources, students' perceptions of, 299–301

Online assessment
    collaborative, 279–92
    and critical learning, 279–92
    and critical perspectives, 281–2
    and power and authority, 284–6
    and tutor and student roles, 286–7
Online learning, see also Networked learning
    researching online learning, 195–212
Online teaching, see Online learning

Phenomenography, 9, 12, 253–4
    and design, 262–3
    phenomenographic research, 261–4
    criticisms of, 263–4

Reflection, 58, 59, 117, 122, 195, 198, 203–4, 205, 206, 207, 208, 209, 215, 222, 233, 240, 243, 246, 248, 249, 256, 261, 262, 265, 285, 318, 319, 328, 337, 338
Requirements, 9, 11, 31, 41, 44, 53, 66, 70, 80, 97, 99, 171, 199, 225, 248, 273

Situated learning, 10, 56, 65, 66, 68, 77–90, 99, 99, 258, 259, 260, 336 *see also* Learning
and networked learning, 81–3
Situated cognition, 257
Small group teaching, 243–52
discipline context, 246–8
Staff development, 9, 10, 31, 109–124 127, 133, 135, 137, 138, 145, 149, 152, 157, 159, 160, 162, 163, 189, 275, 321, 334
flexible methods for, 120–2
and training, 113–15
Student-centred, 5, 116, 120, 248, 249, 280, 282
Synchronous, 56, 145, 147, 150, 159, 207, 208, 222, 243, 296, 309, 327–9

Task Directed Discussions (TDD), 218–20
Teachers, *see* Academics
Technological convergence, 18, 149
Technology Costing Methodology (TCM), 35–7

Tele-tutors, 207–8
Tertiary courseware, 216–17
Tutor's role, 9, 12, 286, 290, 328, 339

Vicarious learning, 11, 213–27
Vicarious learning environment, 225
Vicarious Learning Project, 213–14
experiments, 217–24
Video, 29, 44, 98, 101, 146, 151, 220, 221, 222, 296, 301, 337, 338
conferencing, 17, 146, 150, 159, 309, 310, 313, *313*, 316, 319, 320
Virtual
learner, 294
learning, 294, 299, 300
Virtual Learning Community, 281
Virtual Learning Environments (VLEs), 23, 27, 69, 146, 247, 248, 249

Web, teaching use of, 297–9

Out of print titles

Dan Diaper and Colston Sanger
CSCW in Practice
3-540-19784-2

Steve Easterbrook (ed.)
CSCW: Cooperation or Conflict?
3-540-19755-9

John H. Connolly and Ernest A. Edmonds (eds)
CSCW and Artificial Intelligence
3-540-19816-4

Mike Sharples (ed.)
Computer Supported Collaborative Writing
3-540-19782-6

Duska Rosenberg and Chris Hutchison (eds)
Design Issues in CSCW
3-540-19810-5

Peter Thomas (ed.)
CSCW Requirements and Evaluation
3-540-19963-2

John H. Connolly and Lyn Pemberton (eds)
Linguistic Concepts and Methods in CSCW
3-540-19984-5

Alan Dix and Russell Beale (eds)
Remote Cooperation
3-540-76035-0

Stefan Kirn and Gregory O'Hare (eds)
Cooperative Knowledge Processing
3-540-19951-9